*For selectiv*

## ITALY

Barolo, Barb

Chianti Class

| | | | | | | | | | |
|---|---|---|---|---|---|---|---|---|---|
| Brunello, Vino Nobile | 8 | 9 | 8 | 8 | 5 | 7 | 10 | 6 | 9 |
| Veneto (Amarone) | 7 | 9 | 7 | 8 | 5 | 5 | 10 | 6 | 9 |
| **SPAIN** | | | | | | | | | |
| Ribera del Duero | 8 | 8 | 9 | 4 | 6 | 8 | 9 | 6 | 6 |
| Rioja (R) | 8 | 8 | 9 | 5 | 6 | 7 | 7 | 8 | 4 |
| **PORTUGAL** | | | | | | | | | |
| Alentejo | 6 | 7 | 7 | 5 | 6 | 7 | 9 | 8 | 6 |
| Dão | 7 | 8 | 7 | 4 | 7 | 7 | 6 | 6 | 6 |
| Port (vintage) | 8 | 8 | 10 | 2 | 9 | 8 | 6 | 6 | 5 |
| **USA** | | | | | | | | | |
| California Cabernet | 6 | 8 | 9 | 7 | 8 | 9 | 8 | 5 | 7 |
| California Chardonnay | 6 | 7 | 8 | 7 | 7 | 9 | 8 | 7 | 7 |
| Oregon Pinot Noir | 6 | 5 | 10 | 6 | 9 | 8 | 9 | 8 | 8 |
| Wash. State Cabernet | 9 | 7 | 9 | 7 | 9 | 8 | 7 | 9 | 7 |
| **AUSTRALIA** | | | | | | | | | |
| Coonawarra Cabernet | 8 | 5 | 8 | 7 | 7 | 9 | 10 | 5 | 9 |
| Hunter Chardonnay | 8 | 7 | 7 | 7 | 8 | 10 | 5 | 8 | 5 |
| Barossa Shiraz | 9 | 8 | 9 | 7 | 6 | 8 | 8 | 6 | 7 |
| Marg. River Cabernet | 8 | 8 | 8 | 9 | 6 | 9 | 8 | 8 | 6 |
| **NEW ZEALAND** | | | | | | | | | |
| M'lborough Sauvignon | 9 | 4 | 10 | 7 | 7 | 10 | 6 | 9 | 8 |
| Hawkes Bay Cabernet | 8 | 6 | 8 | 5 | 5 | 9 | 7 | 9 | 5 |
| **SOUTH AFRICA** | | | | | | | | | |
| Cape Cabernet | 5 | 9 | 8 | 8 | 8 | 9 | 7 | 8 | 6 |

*Numerals (1–10) represent an overall rating for each year.* ◐ *Not ready* ● *Just ready* ● *At peak* ◑ *Past best* ○ *Not generally declared*

# OZ CLARKE'S

# WINE
# ADVISOR
# 1998

Little, Brown and Company
Boston  New York  Toronto  London

Revised Edition

ISBN 0-316-14210-7
ISSN 1071-9733

Created and designed by Websters International Publishers Ltd,
Axe & Bottle Court, 70 Newcomen Street, London, SE1 1YT

10 9 8 7 6 5 4 3 2 1

Published simultaneously in Great Britain by Little, Brown and Company
(UK) and in Canada by Little, Brown & Company (Canada) Limited

Printed in China

Thanks are due to the following people for their invaluable help with
the 1998 edition and the generous spirit in which they have shared
their knowledge: Jim Budd, Bob Campbell MW, Huon Hooke, James
Lawther MW, Angela Lloyd, Richard Mayson, Jasper Morris MW,
Richard Neill, Stuart Pigott, Norm Roby, Victor de la Serna, Phillip
Williamson.

# CONTENTS

# INTRODUCTION

I love this modern world of wine. So many of the old certainties falling by the wayside. So many new and different certainties in their place. Grape varieties and winemakers tumbling into vogue and slithering out again. Vintages hyped and then derided, or dismissed then 'rediscovered' almost before the wines have settled in their bottles. But, amid all this hubbub, one truth shines through brighter than all the others: wine is getting better all the time. And that is what this book is about – the world of wine as it is NOW.

Every year more winemakers full of bright ideas get their hands on some grapes for the first time. Every year more old-timers pluck up courage to bottle their own wine and make a stand for individuality after decades of seeing their precious juice disappear into anonymous blending vats. Every year new vineyards are planted in every corner of the globe, bringing the thrill of the first crop from land where grapes had never grown before. And every year more ancient vines are saved from the bulldozer by our willingness to experiment and to pay more for character-filled wine whose roots stretch back tantalisingly to antiquity.

We wine drinkers should thank our lucky stars that we are living in such thrilling times. Cheap wine has never been better nor more plentiful. At the same time, the classic wine regions, especially France, Italy and Spain, are showing a new spirit of determination that is producing a flood of fine wine, frequently from estates and villages that had let complacency rule for generations. And then there's a buzzing pack of wannabes – Chile, Argentina, South Africa, Washington State – aping the classics as far as they can, yet in the meantime developing their own particular style – and often at a fraction of the price.

This guide is designed to help explain this frenzied, exciting world at every level. I've used an A–Z organization to make it as easy as possible to use. All you need to know is the name of the wine, producer, grape variety or region: just look it up and you'll find all you need to know about its taste, its styles, its history where relevant, and its importance. And if there's a producer without its own entry, the Index at the back will point you straight to the relevant A–Z features.

The great classics, new and old, are fully covered – and criticized where need be. But so are the basic wines. Regions and grape varieties are explained and explored in full-length Special Features. And you get up-to-the-minute vintage knowledge, too: what's hot, what's not, what's ready, what still needs time.

I try to cover every *interesting* aspect of wine and to allow enough space in each entry to give you a proper idea of what makes the wine, the producer etc. tick. If you find some wines enthusiastically described and some wines – often well known – talked about in less than flattering terms, that's because I'm an opinionated kind of guy. And so, although this is a pocket book and facts must be squeezed in to all the available space, you get opinions, too. Well, you wouldn't expect anything less from me, would you?

OZ CLARKE

# HOW TO USE THE A–Z

The A–Z section starts on page 33 and covers over 1400 entries on wines, producers, grapes and wine regions from all over the world. There are also entries on some of the more common wine-making terms, especially the ones often seen on labels.

Detailed Vintage Charts with information on which of the world's top wines are ready for drinking in 1998 can be found on the inside front and back covers; the front chart features vintages back to 1988; the back chart covers a selection of older vintages for premium wines.

---

**Glass Symbols**  These indicate the wines produced.

  Red wine            Rosé wine        White wine

The order of the glasses reflects the importance of the wines in terms of volume produced. For example:

  White followed by rosé wine

  Red followed by white wine

  Red followed by rosé, then white wine

---

**Grape Symbols**  These identify entries on grape varieties.

  Red grape          White grape

---

**Star Symbols**  These indicate wines and producers that are highly rated by the author.

★       A particularly good wine/producer in its category

★★      An excellent wine/producer in its category – one especially worth seeking out

★★★    An exceptional, world-class wine/producer

---

**Best Years**  Recommended vintages are listed for some producer and appellation entries. Those listed in bold, e.g. **1996**, **95**, indicate wines that are ready for drinking now, although they may not necessarily be at their best; those appearing in brackets, e.g. (1996) (95), are preliminary assessments of wines that are not yet ready for drinking.

---

**Cross References**  To help you find your way round the A–Z, wine names, producers and regions that have their own entries elsewhere in the A–Z are indicated by SMALL CAPITALS.

---

**Special Features**  The A–Z section includes special 2-page features on the world's most important wine styles and grape varieties. These features include recommended vintages and producers, as well as lists of related entries elsewhere in the A–Z.

---

**Index**  The Index on page 272 will help you find over 2500 recommended producers, including those that don't have their own entry in the A–Z.

# PICK OF THE YEAR

One of the marvellous things about the modern world of wine is that when I sit down to write about what wines I'll be drinking during the next 12 months, I can virtually guarantee not to get it all right. I can be almost sure that some of my favourites are missing a year hence, because each year there are so many thrilling new wines – and many haven't even been released yet.

In areas of rapid expansion, like New Zealand, Australia, South Africa, Argentina and Chile, every tasting I go to, every trip I make, is a revelation. It's the same in the old areas – the south of France, the north of Spain, the south of Italy and Portugal – where the message is at last getting through: quality matters, individuality will pay.

After years of the easy pleasures of Chardonnay and Sauvignon Blanc, Cabernet Sauvignon and Merlot, there is an increasing body of consumers who want something different. The joyous thing about our world of wine today is that those who want more of the same can have it, often better than ever before. But for those of us prepared to be a little more adventurous, forgotten grape varieties are re-emerging, moribund wine areas are waking up and unfashionable wines are confounding critics with their wild and off-beat flavours. For now, at least, we *can* have our cake and eat it. So what will I be drinking?

● **France**'s wines in the 1990s have been more of a disappointment than a thrill. Yet I sense a change. Now there are signs that at least some of France's winemakers are ready and willing to woo us back.

● **Bordeaux** has probably suffered more tricky vintages than anywhere recently. This is less of a problem at the top of the range, where ruthless selection of the best barrels and massive investment has meant that good wine could still be made in unpromising conditions. Here, 95 and 96 will be good to very good when they come on stream, and 93 and 94 aren't at all bad in a rather lean way, but I'd largely give a miss to 92 and 91 and start nibbling at the stunning 90s, the very good 89s and the restrained but fine 88s. The problem is that if I haven't bought them already, I'm unlikely to start now because prices for the Classed Growth band at the quality peak have gone barmy. And at the lower end of red wines, there are simply better wines from elsewhere at similar or lower prices. But I *will* be drinking Bordeaux rosé – increasingly some of the best in France – and Bordeaux white, one of France's most underrated styles. 1996s are delicious now, 97s won't take long either.

● The **Loire** had two excellent vintages in 95 and 96 – the 96 whites from Sancerre and reds from Chinon and Bourgueil are as good as I can remember.

● In **Burgundy** conditions during the 1990s have rarely been perfect, but good wines have been made here every year. From good producers in the Côte d'Or and Chablis the 90s are exceptional and the reds could take more aging. 1991 reds are dry but surprisingly good, 92 whites will be exquisite now and for quite a few years yet. 1993 reds are only good from the best people and are still rather closed, but 94 whites are already delightful and will age. 1995 should be excellent for both red and white. Further south, the **Mâconnais** revival seems to have petered out, although **Beaujolais** has produced good 95s and 96s.

● **Southern France** still gives me the most pleasure. The **Rhône** has had difficult vintages but has still produced a pile of decent reds and some very pleasant whites. 1995 looks to have produced classics in the northern zone, 94 is also good and, although 93 and 92 weren't great, there's lots of decent wine still to be had, especially from the southern vineyards. And the far south of France, now producing almost too much Vin de Pays Chardonnay and Cabernet, is also bringing out more exciting traditional reds every year.

● **Germany**'s 96 vintage isn't up to the same level as previous years, but consumer indifference means it is possible to find wonderful wines right back to the 88 vintage on the shelves.

● **Italy** has had a difficult time since the fabulous 1990 vintage, but the best producers have produced good wines from tricky vintages. It's still the re-birth of fine wine in the South that I find most exciting, so that's what I'll be drinking.

● **Spain and Portugal** are on a roll again. Serious drought has held both countries back recently but, starting with the 94 vintage, lots of thrilling reds are appearing.

● **California** has a shortage of wine now, so the cheaper end is uninspiring and pricy, but there's magic at the top. Now is the time to try wonderful Zinfandel, Syrah, Pinot Noir and Viognier. Otherwise it's back to top-flight 94 Pinot Noir and Chardonnay, and to the early 90s for the fine run of Cabernet. There's a wine shortage, too, in **Washington State** and **Oregon**, which is sad because Washington is producing some beautiful stuff. But Oregon Pinot Noir shines out like a beacon from the exceptional 94 vintage, and will get better.

● **Chile**'s reds seem to get better every year, though some of her whites don't quite justify recent price rises. **Argentina** isn't doing much with whites just yet, but has arrived on the red wine scene with a tremendous bang. Things can only get better.

● **South Africa**'s difficult 96 and 97 vintages, and a reluctance on the part of many producers to embrace change wholeheartedly, means I can't be as enthusiastic as I'd like. More good producers are appearing each year, but it's a trickle not a flood.

● **New Zealand** has had a tough time of it recently, but is now very much back on song. Because Marlborough Sauvignon was poor in 1995, the whole vintage was damned, when in fact Chardonnay was – and is – excellent. 1996 looks first rate across the board and 97 could be even better, so I'll be knocking back these tangy, intensely flavoured wines.

● And **Australia**? Well, there was a bit of a crisis last year. The 95 vintage wasn't very good and there was quite a severe shortage of wine. But it's 96 that's mostly on our shelves now. And as soon as I can get hold of them, they'll be going to where they belong – straight down my throat.

# MODERN WINE STYLES

Not so long ago, if I were to outline the basic wine styles, the list would have been strongly biased towards the classics – Bordeaux, Burgundy, Sancerre, Mosel Riesling, Champagne. These flavours were the models against which would-be imitators had to be judged and, in any case, there weren't many imitators.

This just isn't so any more. The great old classic names have, over time, become expensive and unreliable – thus opening the door to other, perhaps less established wine-producing regions, and giving them the chance to offer us wines that may or may not owe anything to the old originals. *These* are the flavours to which ambitious winemakers now aspire.

*WHITE WINES*

**Ripe, up-front, spicy Chardonnay** Fruit is the key here: round, ripe, apricot and peach fruit, sweetened and spiced up by some new oak – probably American oak – to make a delicious, approachable, easy-to-drink fruit cocktail of taste. Australia created this style and still effortlessly leads the field.

**Green tangy Sauvignon** New Zealand is the master of this style – all tangy, grassy, nettles and asparagus and then green apples and peach. Chile has the potential to produce something similar and there are hopeful signs in southern France. Bordeaux and the Loire are the original sources of dry Sauvignon wines, but only the most committed modern producers manage to match green tang with fruit.

**Bone-dry neutral whites** This doesn't sound very appetizing, but it is the limit of what most white wine aspires to. Many Italian whites fit this bill. Southern French wines, where no grape variety is specified, will be like this; so will many wines from Bordeaux, the South-West, Muscadet and Anjou. Modern young Spanish whites and Portuguese Vinho Verdes are good examples, as are Swiss Fendant and southern German Trocken wines. Most Eastern European whites could actually *use* more neutrality.

**White Burgundy** By this I mean the nutty, oatmealy-ripe but dry, subtly oaked styles of villages like Meursault at their best. It's a difficult style to emulate and few people do it well, even in Burgundy itself. California makes the most effort. Washington, Oregon and New York State each have occasional successes.

**Perfumy, off-dry whites** Gewürztraminer, Muscat and Pinot Gris from Alsace will give you this style and in southern Germany Gewürztraminer, Scheurebe, Kerner, Grauburgunder and occasionally Riesling may also do it. Riesling in Australia is often aromatic and mildly fruity. In New Zealand Riesling and Müller-Thurgau can produce excellent results.

**Mouthfuls of luscious gold** Good sweet wines are difficult to make. Sauternes is the world's most famous sweetie, but the Loire, too, and sometimes Alsace, is in the running. Germany made wonderful examples in 1990 and since then Australia and New Zealand have produced some beauts.

**Spicy warm-hearted reds** Australia is out in front at the moment through the ebullient resurgence of her Shiraz reds – ripe, almost sweet, sinfully easy to enjoy. France's Rhône Valley is also on the up and Syrahs from the far south of France are looking good. In Italy Piedmont is producing delicious beefy Barbera and juicy exotic Dolcetto. Spain's Ribera del Duero and Portugal's south also deliver the goods.

**Juicy fruity reds** This used to be the Beaujolais spot, but there hasn't been much exciting Beaujolais recently. Gamay Vins de Pays are better bets, as are grassy, sharp Loire reds. Modern Spanish reds from Navarra, Valdepeñas and La Mancha do the trick, while in Italy young Chianti and Teroldego hit home.

**Blackcurranty Cabernet** Australia leads the field here, but New Zealand also strikes the blackcurrant bell in a much greener, sharper way. California only sometimes hits the sweet spot, and often with Merlot rather than Cabernet. Chilean Cabernets get there less often than they used to. Eastern Europe, in particular Hungary, is doing well, as is southern France. And what about Bordeaux? Only a few of the top wines reach the target; for the price Tuscan Cabernet often does it better.

**Tough, tannic long-haul boys** Bordeaux does lead this field, and the best wines are really good after 10 years or so – but don't expect wines from minor properties to age in the same way. It's the same in Tuscany and Piedmont – only the top wines will get there – especially Chianti Classico, Barolo and Barbaresco. In Portugal there's plenty of tannin to be found and some increasingly good long-lasting reds from the Douro.

**Soft, strawberryish charmers** Good Burgundy definitely tops this group. Rioja in Spain can sometimes get there too, but Navarra and Valdepeñas do so more often. Pinot Noir in California is frequently delicious, as it is in New Zealand. Germany gets there with Spätburgunder now and then. Italy's Lago di Caldaro often smooches in; and over in Bordeaux, of all places, both St-Émilion and Pomerol can do the business.

## SPARKLING AND FORTIFIED WINES

**Fizz** This can be white or pink or red, dry or sweet, and I sometimes think it doesn't matter what it tastes like as long as it's cold enough and there's enough of it. Champagne can be best, but frequently isn't – and there are lots of new-wave winemakers who produce good-value lookalikes. Australia is tops for super-tasty bargain fizz, followed by California and New Zealand.

**Fortified wines** For once in my life I find myself saying that the old ways are definitely the best. Because there's still nothing to beat the top ports and sherries in the deep, rich old-fashioned stickies stakes – though for the glimmerings of a new angle look to Australia and South Africa.

# MATCHING FOOD AND WINE

Give me a rule, I'll break it – well, bend it anyway. So when I see a proliferation of publications laying down rules as to what wine to drink with what food, I get very uneasy and have to quell a burning desire to slosh back a Grand Cru Burgundy with my Chilli con Carne.

The pleasures of eating and drinking operate on so many levels that hard and fast rules simply make no sense. What about mood? If I'm in the mood for Champagne, Champagne it shall be, whatever I'm eating. What about place? If I'm sitting gazing out from the Amalfi cliffs across the glimmering waters of the bay, hand me anything, just anything local – it'll be perfect.

Even so, there are some things that simply don't go well with wine. Artichokes, asparagus, spinach, kippers and mackerel, chilli, salsas and vinegars, chocolate, all flatten the flavours of wines. The general rule here is avoid tannic red wines and go for juicy young reds, New World styles or whites with plenty of fruit and fresh acidity. And for chocolate, liqueur Muscats are just about the only thing. Tomatoes are both sweet and acidic, proving a challenging match that can ruin most red wines; and, contrary to expectation, salty cheeses go best with sweet white wines (Roquefort and Sauternes is classic). So, with these factors in mind, the following pairings are not quite rules – just my recommendations.

## FISH

**Plain grilled or baked white fish** White Burgundy, fine Chardonnay, Pessac-Léognan, Viognier, Australia and New Zealand Riesling.

**Plain grilled or baked more strongly flavoured fish** (e.g. salmon, salmon trout) Alsace aromatics, fruity New World Chardonnay or Sémillon, Chinon/Bourgueil (unoaked), New World Pinot Noir.

**Fried/battered fish** Simple, fresh whites, e.g. Soave, Mâcon Blanc, Pinot Gris, white Bordeaux.

**Shellfish** Soft dry whites, e.g. Pinot Blanc or unoaked Chardonnay; *clams and oysters*: Aligoté, Vinho Verde, Seyval Blanc.

**Smoked fish** Ice-cold basic fizz, Manzanilla or Fino sherry, Pinot Gris from Alsace or southern Germany, New World Riesling or Gewürztraminer.

## MEAT

**Beef/steak** *Plain roasted or grilled*: tannic reds, e.g. top Bordeaux, New World Cabernet or Merlot, South African Pinotage, Chianti Classico Riserva.

**Lamb** *Plain roasted or grilled*: top red Burgundy, soft top Bordeaux, e.g. St-Émilion, Rioja Reserva, fine New World Pinot Noir or Merlot.

**Pork** *Plain roasted or grilled*: full, soft dry whites, e.g. Alsace Pinot Gris, soft oaky Chardonnays, Rioja, Alentejo; *ham and bacon*: young, fruity reds, preferably unoaked, e.g. Beaujolais, Teroldego, unoaked Tempranillo or Malbec, Lambrusco Secco; *prepared pork products*: forthright, uncomplicated young reds, Beaujolais, Italian Merlot, Zinfandel, Pinotage.

**Veal** *Plain roasted or grilled*: (reds) old Rioja, mature Côte de Beaune or Pessac-Léognan/Margaux; (whites) Alsace/German/Austrian Pinot Gris, Vouvray, Châteauneuf-du-Pape; *with cream-based sauce*: full, ripe whites, e.g. Alsace Pinot Blanc or Pinot Gris, Vouvray, white Châteauneuf-du-Pape, oaked New World Chardonnay; *with rich* *red-wine sauce* (e.g. *osso buco*): young Italian reds, New World Zinfandel, Gamay or Grenache.

**Venison** *Plain roasted or grilled*: Barolo, St-Estèphe, Pomerol, Côte de Nuits, Hermitage, big Zin, Alsace or German Pinot Gris; *with red-wine-based sauce*: Piedmont reds, Pomerol, St-Émilion, New World Syrah/Shiraz or Pinotage, Portuguese Garrafeira.

**Chicken and Turkey** *Plain roasted or grilled*: fine red or white Burgundy, red Rioja Reserva, New World Chardonnay or Sémillon.

**Duck** *Plain roasted*: gutsy reds, e.g. Pomerol, St-Émilion, Côte de Nuits, Rhône reds, New World Syrah/Shiraz or Merlot; *also* full, soft whites; *with orange*: off-dry weighty whites, or Barsac.

**Game birds** *Plain roasted or grilled*: top reds, e.g. Rhône, Burgundy, Tuscan and Piedmont, Ribera del Duero, New World Cabernet; also whites, e.g. Pinot Gris or New World Sémillon.

**All meat casseroles, stews and mince dishes** Match the dominant ingredient, e.g. red wine for *boeuf à la bourguignonne*, robust reds for *coq au vin*, dry whites for a fricassee. The weight of the wine should match the richness of the sauce, e.g. not too heavy for *navarin* of lamb. For strong tomato flavours see under Pasta.

## EGGS

Light, fresh reds from Gamay or Grenache, full, dry unoaked whites, New World rosé or fizz.

## PASTA

*With tomato sauce*: Soave, Verdicchio, New World Sauvignon Blanc; *with meat-based sauce*: basic north/central Italian reds, French/New World Syrah/Shiraz, Zinfandel; *with cream- or cheese-based sauce*: soft, full, dry unoaked whites from northern Italy, light Austrian reds, New World Gamay; *with seafood/fish sauce*: basic dry, tangy whites, e.g. Verdicchio, Vermentino, Austrian Grüner Veltliner, Muscadet; *with pesto*: New World Sauvignon Blanc, Dolcetto, Minervois.

## SALADS

Sharp-edged whites, e.g. New World Sauvignon, dry Riesling, Vinho Verde.

## ETHNIC CUISINES

**Chinese** Riesling or Gewürztraminer, unoaked New World Chardonnay; mild German and Austrian reds.

**Indian/Tex-Mex** Spicy whites, e.g. Gewürztraminer, New World Sauvignon, Viognier; soft reds, e.g. Rioja, Valpolicella, New World Cinsaut, Grenache, Syrah/Shiraz.

**Thai** Riesling, Gewürztraminer, New World Sauvignon.

## CHEESES

**Hard (mild and mature)** Strong reds from southern Italy, southern France or northern Spain, New World Merlot or Zinfandel, Alsace Pinot Gris, dry oloroso sherry, tawny port.

**Soft (mild and mature)** LBV port, rich, fruity reds, e.g. Rhône, Shiraz, Zinfandel, Alsace Pinot Gris, Gewürztraminer.

**Blue** Botrytized sweet whites, e.g. Sauternes, vintage port, Malmsey Madeira, old oloroso sherry.

**Goats'** Sancerre, New World Sauvignon Blanc, cool-climate reds, e.g. Chinon, Saumur-Champigny, Teroldego.

## DESSERTS

**Chocolate** Liqueur Muscat, Asti Spumante.

**Fruit-based** Botrytized sweet whites, e.g. Sauternes.

11

# MAKING THE MOST OF WINE

Most wine is pretty hardy stuff and can put up with a fair amount of rough handling. Young red wines can knock about in the back of a car for a day or two and be lugged from garage to kitchen to dinner table without coming to too much harm. Serving young white wines when well chilled can cover up all kinds of ill-treatment – a couple of hours in the fridge should do the trick. Even so, there are some conditions that are better than others for storing your wine – especially if they are on the mature side. And there are certain ways of serving wines which will emphasize any flavours or perfumes they have.

*STORING*
Most wines are sold for drinking soon, and it will be hard to ruin them in the next few months before you pull the cork. Don't stand them next to the central heating or the cooker, though, or on a sunny windowsill.

Light and extremes of temperature are also the things to worry about if you are storing wine long-term. Some wines, Chardonnay for instance, are particularly sensitive to exposure to light over several months, and the damage will be worse if the bottle is made of pale-coloured glass. The warmer the wine, the quicker it will age, and really high temperatures can spoil wine quite quickly. Beware in the winter of garages and outhouses, too: a very cold snap – say -4°C (25°F) or below – will freeze your wine, push out the corks and crack the bottles. An underground cellar is ideal, with a fairly constant temperature of 10°–12°C (50°–53°F). And bottles really do need to lie on their sides, so that the cork stays damp and swollen, and keeps out the air.

*TEMPERATURE*
The person who thought up the rule that red wine should be served at room temperature certainly didn't live in an efficient, modern, centrally-heated flat. It's no great sin to serve a big beefy red at the temperature of your central heating, but I prefer most reds just a touch cooler. Over-heated wine tastes flabby, and may lose some of its more volatile aromas. In general, the lighter the red, the cooler it can be. Really light, refreshing reds, such as Beaujolais, are nice lightly chilled. Ideally, I'd serve Burgundy at larder temperature, Bordeaux a bit warmer, Australian Cabernet at the temperature of a draughty room.

Chilling white wines makes them taste fresher, emphasizing their acidity. White wines with low acidity especially benefit from chilling, and it's vital for sparkling wines if you want to avoid exploding corks and a tableful of froth. Drastic chilling also subdues flavours, however – a useful ruse if you're serving basic wine, but a shame if the wine is very good.

A good guide for whites is to give the cheapest and lightest a spell in the fridge, but serve bigger and better wines – Australian

12

Chardonnays or top white Burgundies – perhaps half-way between fridge and central-heating temperature. If you're undecided, err on the cooler side, for whites or reds.

## OPENING THE BOTTLE

There's no corkscrew to beat the Screwpull and the Spinhandle Screwpull is especially easy to use. Don't worry if bits of cork crumble into the wine – just fish them out of your glass. Tight corks that refuse to budge might be loosened if you run hot water over the bottle neck to expand the glass. If the cork is loose and falls in, push it right in and don't worry about it.

Opening sparkling wines is a serious business – point the cork away from people! Once you've started, never take your hand off the cork until it's safely out. Take off the foil, loosen the wire, hold the wire and cork firmly and twist the bottle. If the wine froths, hold the bottle at 45 degrees, and have a glass at hand.

## AIRING AND DECANTING

Scientists have proved that opening young to middle-aged red wines an hour before serving makes no difference whatsoever. The surface area of wine in contact with air in the bottle neck is too tiny to be significant. Decanting is a different matter, because sloshing the wine from bottle to jug or decanter mixes it up quite thoroughly with the air. The only wines that really need to be decanted are those that have a sediment which would cloud the wine if they were poured directly – mature red Bordeaux, Burgundy and vintage port are the commonest examples. Ideally, if you are able to plan that far in advance, you need to stand the bottle upright for a day or two to let the sediment settle in the bottom. Draw the cork extremely gently. As you tip the bottle, shine a bright light through from underneath, so that you can see the sediment as you pour, all in one, steady movement. Stop pouring when you see the sediment approaching the bottle neck.

Contrary to many wine buffs' practice, I would decant a mature wine only just before serving. Elderly wines often fade very rapidly once they meet with air, and an hour in the decanter could kill off what little fruit they had left.

## KEEPING LEFTOVERS

Leftover white wine keeps better than red, since the tannin and colouring matter in red wine is easily attacked by the air. Any wine, red or white, keeps better in the fridge than in a warm kitchen. And most wines, if well made in the first place, will be perfectly acceptable if not pristine after 2 or 3 days re-corked in the fridge. But for better results it's best to use one of the gadgets sold for this purpose. The ones that work by blanketing the wine with heavier-than-air inert gas are much better than those that create a vacuum in the air space in the bottle.

# FRANCE

I've visited most of the wine-producing countries of the world by now, but the one I come back to again and again, with my enthusiasm undimmed by time, is France. The sheer range of its wine flavours, the number of wine styles produced, and indeed the quality differences, from very best to very nearly worst, continue to enthral me, and as each year's vintage nears, I find myself itching to leap into the car and head for the vineyards of Champagne, of Burgundy, of Bordeaux and the Loire.

## CLIMATE AND SOIL

France lies between the 40th and 50th parallels north, and the climate runs from the distinctly chilly and almost too cool to ripen grapes in the far north near the English Channel, right through to the swelteringly hot and almost too torrid to avoid grapes overripening in the far south on the Mediterranean shores. In the far north the most refined and delicate sparkling wine is made in Champagne. In the far south rich, luscious dessert Muscats and fortified wines dominate. In between is just about every sort of wine you could wish for.

The factors that influence a wine's flavour are the grape variety, the soil and climate, and the winemaker's techniques. Most of the great wine grapes, like the red Cabernet Sauvignon, Merlot, Pinot Noir and Syrah, and the white Chardonnay, Sauvignon Blanc, Sémillon and Viognier find conditions in France where they can ripen slowly but reliably – and slow ripening always gives better flavours to a wine. Since grapes have been grown for over 2000 years in France, the most suitable varieties for the different soils and mesoclimates have naturally evolved. And since wine-making was brought to France by the Romans, generation upon generation of winemakers have refined their techniques to produce the best possible results from their different grape types. The great wines of areas like Bordeaux and Burgundy are the results of centuries of experience and of trial and error, which winemakers from other countries of the world now use and are the role models for their attempts to create good wine.

## WINE REGIONS

White grapes ripen more easily than red grapes and they dominate the northern regions. Even so, the chilly Champagne region barely manages to ripen its red or white grapes on its chalky soil. But the resultant acid wine is the ideal base for sparkling wine, and the acidity of the young still wine can, with good wine-making and a few years' maturing, transform into a golden honeyed sparkling wine of incomparable finesse.

Alsace, on the German border, is much warmer and drier than Champagne but still produces mainly white wines. The German influence is evident in the fragrant but dry wine styles from grapes like Riesling, Pinot Gris and Gewürztraminer.

Just south-east of Paris, Chablis marks the northernmost tip of the Burgundy region, and the Chardonnay grape here produces very dry

14

wines usually with a streak of green acidity, but nowadays with a fuller softer texture to subdue any harshness.

It's a good 2 hours' drive further south to the heart of Burgundy – the Côte d'Or which runs between Dijon and Chagny. World-famous villages such as Gevrey-Chambertin and Vosne-Romanée (where the red Pinot Noir dominates) and Meursault and Puligny-Montrachet (where Chardonnay reigns) here produce the great Burgundies that have given the region renown over the centuries. Lesser Burgundies – but they're still good – are produced further south in the Côte Chalonnaise, while between Mâcon and Lyon are the white Mâconnais wine villages and the villages of Beaujolais, famous for bright, easy-going red wine from the Gamay grape.

South of Lyon in the Rhône Valley red wines begin to dominate. The Syrah grape makes great wine at Hermitage and Côte-Rôtie in the north, while in the south the Grenache and a host of supporting grapes make full, satisfying reds of which Châteauneuf-du-Pape is the most famous. The white Viognier makes lovely wine at Condrieu and Château-Grillet in the north.

Main vineyard areas

0    50    100 km
0         50 miles

The whole of the south of France is now changing and improving at a bewildering rate. Provence and the scorched Midi vineyards are learning how to produce exciting wines from unpromising land and many of France's tastiest and most affordable wines now come under a Vin de Pays label from the south. In Roussillon the red wines are warm-spirited but good, but the sweet Muscats and Grenache-based fortifieds are better.

The south-west of France is dominated by wines of Bordeaux, but has many other gems benefiting from the cooling influence of the Atlantic. Dry whites from Gascony and Bergerac can be exciting. Jurançon down in the Basque country produces some remarkable dry and sweet wines, while Madiran, Cahors and Bergerac produce good to excellent reds.

But Bordeaux is the king here. The Cabernet Sauvignon and Merlot are the chief grapes, the Cabernet dominating the production of deep reds from the Médoc peninsula and its famous villages of Margaux, St-Julien, Pauillac and St-Estèphe. Round the city of Bordeaux are Pessac-Léognan and Graves, where Cabernet and Merlot blend to produce fragrant refined reds. On the right bank of the Gironde estuary, the Merlot is most important in the plump rich reds of St-Émilion and Pomerol. Sweet whites from Sémillon and Sauvignon Blanc are made in Sauternes, with increasingly good dry whites produced in the Entre-Deux-Mers, and especially in Graves and Pessac-Léognan.

The Loire Valley is the most northerly of France's Atlantic wine regions but, since the river rises in the heart of France not far from the Rhône, styles vary widely. Sancerre and Pouilly in the east produce tangy Sauvignon whites, the centre of the river produces fizzy wine at Vouvray and Saumur, sweet wine at Vouvray and the Layon Valley, red wines at Chinon and Bourgueil, and dry whites virtually everywhere, while down at the mouth of the river, as it slips past Nantes into the Atlantic swell, the vineyards of Muscadet produce one of the world's most famous but least memorable dry white wines.

## CLASSIFICATIONS

France has an intricate, but eminently logical system for controlling the quality and authenticity of its wines. The system is divided into 4 broad classifications (in ascending order): Vin de Table, Vin de Pays, VDQS (Vin Délimité de Qualité Supérieure) and AC (Appellation Contrôlée). Within the laws there are numerous variations, with certain vineyards or producers singled out for special mention. The 1855 classification in Bordeaux or the Grands Crus of Alsace or Burgundy are good examples. By and large this is a system which rewards quality. VDQS and Vin de Pays wines can be promoted to AC, for example, after a few years' good behaviour. The AC system is now under increasing attack from critics, both inside and outside France, who feel that it is outmoded and ineffectual and that too many poor wines are passed as of Appellation Contrôlée standard.

*1996 VINTAGE REPORT*

The variable weather meant that 1996 will be the year of the vigneron: those with the best-managed vineyards made the best wines. In Bordeaux, first reports suggest that 1996 may be better than 1995 and there will be many good bottles coming from Burgundy, Champagne and the Loire.

Weatherwise, France was turned upside down: the north was dry, the south very wet. But flowering was quick and very successful in June, meaning that the crop will be above average in quantity. Much of August was unseasonably cool and wet in the south.

In Bordeaux, the Médoc is probably the most successful area, as St-Émilion and Pomerol had very heavy rain at the end of September. Sauternes will be good as there was plenty of noble rot in October.

For the second year the Loire has had a fine harvest. Conditions in September and October were extremely good and some exceptional reds have been made, which should keep well. Dry and sweet whites will be good, but perhaps the top sweeties will be less extraordinarily concentrated than in 1995.

Champagne had a high-quality harvest and fair quantity – the second-largest since 1992. There will be vintages declared, which will be just about ready for those who maintain that the millennium commences on January 1st 2001.

In Burgundy, a dry, sunny September ensured a healthy harvest of good quality potential. The whites (except for hail-damaged Chablis) will have plenty of fruit flavours and good natural alcoholic degrees. There should be many excellent reds, especially from Pommard, Corton and Gevrey-Chambertin, although others may taste hollow later.

August was stormy in the Rhône and there was little sunshine. Fortunately the Mistral started blowing at the beginning of September, which stopped the rot and helped the grapes to ripen. Because of a very successful flowering, bunch thinning was necessary in July to ensure concentration. In the northern Rhône the grapes had good sugar levels but high acidity, although more rain in the southern Rhône puts a question mark over quality.

Modern wine-making techniques mean that reasonable wines were made in Provence, Languedoc-Roussillon and south-west France, although they won't be as good as in 1994 and 1995. However, the whites may well be crisper than usual because of higher acidity.

The Alsace harvest is of average size, excepting Gewürztraminer, which is very short. A long, dry autumn allowed growers to pick when the grapes were properly ripe. The three Pinots are purported to have been particularly successful in 1996. Both Vendange Tardive and Sélection de Grains Nobles were made.

See also ALSACE, BORDEAUX RED WINES, BORDEAUX WHITE WINES, BURGUNDY RED WINES, BURGUNDY WHITE WINES, CHAMPAGNE, CORSICA, JURA, LANGUEDOC-ROUSSILLON, LOIRE VALLEY, MIDI, PROVENCE, RHONE VALLEY, ROUSSILLON, SAVOIE, SOUTH-WEST FRANCE; AND INDIVIDUAL WINES AND PRODUCERS.

# ITALY

The cultivation of the vine was introduced to Italy over 3000 years ago, by the Greeks (to Sicily and the south) and by the Etruscans (to the north-east and central zones). Despite their great tradition, Italian wines as we know them today are relatively young. New attitudes have resulted, in the last 25 years or so, in a great change in Italian wine. The whole industry has been modernized, and areas like Tuscany are now among the most dynamic of any in the world.

*GRAPE VARIETIES AND WINE REGIONS*

Vines are grown all over Italy, from the Austrian border in the north to the island of Pantelleria in the far south, nearer to North Africa than to Sicily. The north-west, especially Piedmont, is the home of many of the best Italian red grapes, like Nebbiolo, Dolcetto and Barbera, while the north-east (Friuli-Venezia Giulia and Alto Adige) is more noted for the success of native white varieties like Garganega,

Tocai and Ribolla, as well as imports like Pinot Grigio, Chardonnay and Sauvignon. The central Po Valley is Lambrusco country. Moving south, Tuscany is best known for its red Chianti and Brunello wines from the native Sangiovese grape. South of Rome, where the Mediterranean climate holds sway, the traditional heavy whites and reds are gradually giving way here and there to some admirable wines.

## CLASSIFICATIONS

**Vino da Tavola**, or 'table wine', is used for a wine that is produced either outside the existing laws, or in an area where no delimited zone exists. Both cheap, basic wines and inspired innovative creations like Tignanello and other so-called Super-Tuscans may fall into this anonymous category, but the Italians are gradually coming into line with the rest of Europe. The fancy wines will become either DOC or IGT and the rest will be labelled simply as *bianco*, *rosso* or *rosato* without vintages or geographical indications.

**IGT** (Indicazioni Geografiche Tipiche) began taking effect with the 1995 vintage to identify wines from certain regions or areas as an equivalent of the French Vin de Pays.

**DOC** (Denominazione di Origine Controllata) is the fundamental classification for wines from designated zones made following traditions that were historically valid but too often outdated. Recently the laws have become more flexible, encouraging producers to lower yields and modernize techniques, while bringing quality wines under new appellations that allow for recognition of communes, estates and single vineyards. The trend to form new regionwide DOCs – Piedmont is a prime example – will permit classification of many quality table wines.

**DOCG** (Denominazione di Origine Controllata e Garantita) was conceived as a 'super-league' for DOCs with a guarantee of authenticity that promised high class but didn't always provide it. Still, despite some dubious promotions to this élite category, wines must be made under stricter standards that have favoured improvements. The best guarantee of quality, however, remains the producer's name.

## 1996 VINTAGE REPORT

Like 1995, another coolish year, although quantities this time round are improved. Rain in the early autumn, a feature that is becoming the norm in the 1990s, will lead to a somewhat uneven result, so specific location, the timing of picking and the rigour of grape selection are determining factors for quality. In Tuscany, where the rain was confined mostly to September, there is potential in red wines, which is certain to translate into fine Super-Tuscans and Riservas. Some excellent single-vineyard Barolo and Barbaresco are anticipated in Piedmont.

See also ABRUZZO, ALTO-ADIGE, CALABRIA, CAMPANIA, EMILIA-ROMAGNA, FRIULI-VENEZIA GIULIA, LAZIO, LIGURIA, LOMBARDY, MARCHE, PIEDMONT, PUGLIA, ROMAGNA, SARDINIA, SICILY, TRENTINO, TUSCANY, UMBRIA, VALLE D'AOSTA, VENETO; AND INDIVIDUAL WINES AND PRODUCERS.

# GERMANY

German wine has been in a state of flux for some years now. Exports are still dominated by semi-sweet Liebfraumilch-type wines, but the domestic market, only recently exposed to the drier, riper styles from warmer countries, now demands similar wines from German growers.

*GRAPE VARIETIES*

The best wines come from Riesling, Scheurebe, Ruländer (also called Grauburgunder or Pinot Gris), Pinot Blanc (Weissburgunder), Gewürztraminer and Silvaner, although the widely planted Müller-Thurgau produces much of the simpler wine. Good reds can be made in the south of the country from Pinot Noir (Spätburgunder), Lemberger and Dornfelder.

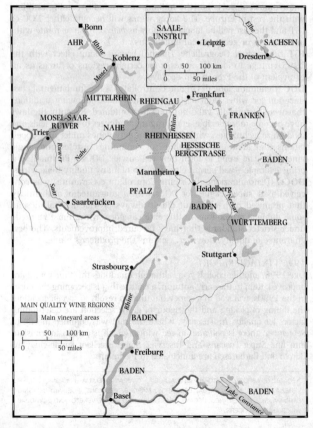

*WINE REGIONS*

Many of the most delectable Rieslings come from villages such as Bernkastel, Brauneberg, Graach and Ürzig on the Mosel, and Eltville, Johannisberg and Rüdesheim in the Rheingau. The Nahe also makes superb Rieslings in the communes of Schlossböckelheim and Traisen, and Niederhausen has the best vineyards in the entire region. Franken is the one place the Silvaner grape excels, often made in an earthy style. Rheinhessen is unfortunately better known for its sugary Niersteiner Gutes Domtal than it is for the excellent racy Rieslings produced on its steep Rhine slopes in the villages of Nackenheim, Nierstein and Oppenheim. The Pfalz is climatically similar to Alsace and has a similar potential for well-rounded, dry white (and some red) wines. Baden produces wine styles which appeal to an international market increasingly reared on fuller, drier wines. In Württemberg most of the red wines are dull, but there are a few producers who understand the need for weight and flavour in red wine-making. The other smaller wine regions make little wine and little is exported.

*CLASSIFICATIONS*

Germany's classification system is based on the ripeness of the grapes and therefore potential alcohol level.

**Tafelwein** (Table Wine) is the most basic term used for any low-grade blended wine.

**Landwein** (Country Wine) is a slightly more up-market version, linked to 17 large vineyard areas. These must be Trocken (dry) or Halbtrocken (medium-dry).

**QbA** (Qualitätswein bestimmter Anbaugebiete) is 'quality' wine from a designated region, but the grapes don't have to be very ripe, and sugar can be added to the juice to increase alcohol.

**QmP** (Qualitätswein mit Prädikat) or 'quality wine with distinction' is the top level. There are 6 levels of QmP (in ascending order of ripeness): Kabinett, Spätlese, Auslese, Beerenauslese, Eiswein and Trockenbeerenauslese.

*1996 VINTAGE REPORT*

Like 1995, the new vintage had two dramatically contrasting faces. The southerly regions of Baden and the Pfalz shone, with wines of plenty of body and excellent balance. Further north and east the very small crop was thin and acidic. Exceptions are Rüdesheim and Hochheim in the Rheingau, and the top estates of the Mosel-Saar-Ruwer, but fine 1996s will be in short supply. The price of top Riesling looks set to rise in order to finance low yield policies; the simplest wines of 1996 will perhaps be the weakest of the decade.

---

See also AHR, BADEN, FRANKEN, HESSISCHE BERGSTRASSE, MITTELRHEIN, MOSEL-SAAR-RUWER, NAHE, PFALZ, RHEINGAU, RHEINHESSEN, SAALE-UNSTRUT, SACHSEN, WURTTEMBERG; AND INDIVIDUAL WINE VILLAGES AND PRODUCERS.

# SPAIN

From the green, damp north to the arid south, Spain has more land under vine than any other country in the world, yet because of its harsh climate, and often outmoded viticultural methods, the average grape yield in Spain is tiny.

## WINE REGIONS

Galicia in the green, hilly north-west grows Spain's most aromatic whites. The heartland of the great Spanish reds, Rioja, Ribera del Duero and Navarra, is situated between the central plateau and the northern coast. Catalonia is principally white wine country (much of it sparkling Cava), though there are some good reds, too. The central plateau of La Mancha makes mainly cheap whites, but with some attractive reds. Valencia in the south-east can rival La Mancha for fresh, unmemorable but inexpensive reds and whites. Andalucía's specialities are the fortified wines, sherry, Montilla and Málaga.

## CLASSIFICATIONS

**Vino de Mesa**, the equivalent of France's Vin de Table, is the lowest level, but is also used for a growing number of non-DO 'Super-Spanish'.
**Vino de la Tierra** is Spain's equivalent of France's Vin de Pays, but is so far rarely used.
**DO** (Denominación de Origen) is the equivalent of France's AC, regulating grape varieties and region of origin.
**DOC** (Denominación de Origen Calificada) is a new super-category. In 1991 Rioja was the first region to be promoted to DOC.

*1996 VINTAGE REPORT*
A wet spring restored the drought-striken vineyards. The dry but rather cool summer resulted in an unusually long, slow grape maturation. Only Rioja had some rain problems at harvest, but overall quality and quantity are good to excellent in all regions.

# PORTUGAL

Things seem to be happening at last in this varied and attractive country, with climates that vary from the mild, damp Minho region in the north-west to the sub-tropical island of Madeira.

*WINE REGIONS*
The lush Vinho Verde country in the north-west gives very different wine from the parched valleys of the neighbouring Douro, with its drier, more continental climate. In Bairrada and Dão, soils are more important in determining the character of the wines. Estremadura and Ribatejo supply generous quantities of wine from regions either close enough to the coast to be influenced by the maritime climate, or softened by the river Tagus. South of Lisbon is the Terras do Sado, home of some exciting table wines. The other dynamic wine region is the Alentejo, with some top-class red wines. And Madeira is unique, a volcanic island 400km (250 miles) out in the Atlantic Ocean.

*CLASSIFICATIONS*
**DOC** (Denominação de Origem Controlada) The regions that were formerly classified as Região Demarcada ('demarcated region') are now known as DOC. There are 18 in all.
**IPR** (Indicação de Proveniência Regulamentada) is the intermediate step for 29 wine regions hoping to move up to DOC status in due course. Their wines are referred to as Vinhos de Qualidade Produzidos em Região Determinada (VQPRD).
**VR** (Vinho Regional) is equivalent to French Vins de Pays with laws and permitted varieties much freer than for DOC and IPR. There are 8 regions and a few sub-regions.

*1996 VINTAGE REPORT*
Heavy rain in the winter of 1995/6 resulted in a huge harvest. The unusually cool summer posed difficulties for crop ripening and some went on picking into November. Those who controlled yields made some excellent wines, but many are left wondering what to do with large quantities of wine that is rather light in character. In the Douro, those who picked late produced some fine ports.

---

See also (SPAIN) ANDALUCIA, ARAGON, CANARY ISLANDS, CASTILLA-LA MANCHA, CASTILLA Y LEON, CATALONIA, GALICIA; (PORTUGAL) ALENTEJO, ALGARVE, ESTREMADURA, RIBATEJO, TERRAS DO SADO, TRAS-OS-MONTES; AND INDIVIDUAL WINES AND PRODUCERS.

# USA

The United States has more varied growing conditions for grapes than any other country in the world, which isn't so surprising when you consider that the 50 states of the Union cover an area that is larger than Western Europe; and although Alaska doesn't grow grapes in the icy far north, Washington State does in the north-west, as does Texas in the south and New York State in the north-east, and even Hawaii, lost in the pounding surf of the Pacific Ocean, manages to grow grapes and make wine. Altogether there are over 40 states that make wine of some sort or another; it ranges from some pretty dire offerings which would have been far better distilled into brandy or used for marinating the sirloin, to some of the greatest and original wine flavours to be found in the world today.

California is far and away the most important state for wine production. In its determination to match the best red Bordeaux and white Burgundy, California proved that it was possible to take the classic European role models and successfully re-interpret them in an area thousands of miles away from their home. However, there is more to California than this. The Central Valley produces the majority of the simple beverage wines that still dominate the American market. Napa and Sonoma counties north of San Francisco Bay do produce great Cabernet and Chardonnay, but grapes like Zinfandel and Merlot are making their mark and Carneros is highly successful for Pinot Noir, Chardonnay and sparkling wines. In the north, Mendocino and Lake counties manage to produce good grapes, while south of San Francisco, in the cool, foggy valleys between Santa Cruz and Santa

Main vineyard areas

Seattle
WASHINGTON STATE
Portland
OREGON
MENDOCINO
NORTH COAST
LAKE
SONOMA NAPA
San Francisco
CALIFORNIA
CENTRAL VALLEY
CENTRAL COAST
San Luis Obispo
Santa Barbara
Los Angeles
SOUTH COAST

| 0 | 150 km |
| 0 | 100 miles |

Barbara, exciting cool-climate flavours are appearing, especially from Pinot Noir and Chardonnay.

There are those that say that much of California is too hot for the best table wines – and many of the critics are based in Oregon and Washington, both keen to wrest the quality crown from California. Oregon, with a cooler but capricious climate, perseveres with Pinot Noir, Chardonnay, Pinot Gris and Riesling with patchy success. Washington, so chilly and misty on the coast, becomes virtual desert east of the Cascade Mountains and it is here in irrigated vineyards that superb reds and whites are made with thrillingly focussed fruit. New Yorkers also believe that Long Island has all the makings of a classic region: this warm, temperate claw of land to the east of New York City is well suited to Merlot, Riesling and Chardonnay. Hudson Valley and Finger Lakes can produce good wine but the winters are too cold for many classic vines. Consequently much of New York State's wine comes from hybrid vines, or the native labrusca varieties which can give flavours few people associate with fine wines.

Of the other states, Texas has the most widespread plantings of classic vinifera wine varieties, but producers of excellence exist in Maryland, Virginia and Pennsylvania on the east coast, and Idaho and New Mexico in the west.

## CLASSIFICATIONS

The appellation concept is very new in the US and it was only during the 1970s that a rudimentary system was established. AVA (American Viticultural Area) merely defines a spread of land and decrees that at least 85% of the wine's volume must be derived from grapes grown within that AVA.

## 1996 VINTAGE REPORT

Following two light vintages, winemakers began 1996 with great expectations for a return to normality. But the 96 growing season was anything but normal. Washington State suffered a killer February freeze; Oregon endured an extended rainy season well into late May, resulting in a small crop. In California the weather turned ugly shortly after May rains interfered with the set, and the hottest August in over a decade sizzled the crop, bringing most winemakers to their knees. New York State survived its rainy summer season quite well, but quantity was disappointing, although quality ranges all over the board. Wines from California's North Coast, most of New York and part of Oregon are of average quality. California's Central Coast fared much better, as did Washington State, where low yields gave concentrated wines. California Cabernet will struggle to rise above average; Chardonnay quality ranges from average to very good.

See also CALIFORNIA, NEW YORK STATE, OREGON, WASHINGTON STATE; AND INDIVIDUAL WINE AREAS AND WINERIES.

# AUSTRALIA

Australian wine today enjoys a reputation well out of proportion to the quantity of wine produced (total output is barely one-twelfth of Italy's). The heavy, alcoholic wines of the past are long gone; sheer volume of fruit aroma and flavour is the hallmark of today's styles. Production of fortified wines has plunged while sparkling wines boom and fine white and red table wines are the bread and butter.

*GRAPE VARIETIES AND WINE REGIONS*
Most of Australia's wine regions are in the south-east, in South Australia, Victoria and New South Wales. In Western Australia are the other important wine zones, including Margaret River and Swan Valley. Riesling, Sémillon and Shiraz have long been key varietals but now Chardonnay and Cabernet Sauvignon are the most fashionable. The use of small oak barrels for aging is important in modern reds as well as Chardonnays. Pinot Noir is yielding occasional success.

*CLASSIFICATIONS*
Appellation control is unknown except in the tiny regions of Mudgee and Tasmania, and there it is more a guarantee of authenticity than a guide to quality. In a country so keen on inter-regional blending a system resembling France's Appellation Contrôlée could be problematic

although the Label Integrity Program (LIP) guarantees all claims made on labels. As part of LIP, and also the wine trade treaty between Australia and the EU, regional names must be legislated, but first there's the tricky problem of drawing boundaries and these are still under lively debate.

*1997 VINTAGE REPORT*
Quality appears adequate to very good, but seldom exciting, with yields (especially for reds) down on 1996 almost everywhere. In South Australia and Victoria a record February heatwave affected ripeness and yields, although a cooler autumn saw grapes picked in good conditions. Some attained high sugars without flavour ripeness. McLaren Vale and Barossa made good whites but reds are patchy, with Grenache and dryland old-vine Shiraz suffering in the heat. Coonawarra and Tasmania look reasonable. Hunter quality is below average: a very wet start to the vintage damaged whites more than reds.

# NEW ZEALAND

New Zealand's wines are characterized by intense fruit flavours, zesty acidity and pungent aromatics – the product of cool growing conditions and high-tech wine-making. Styles are diverse due to regional differences, vintage variation and wine-making philosophy.

*GRAPE VARIETIES AND WINE REGIONS*
Nearly 1600km (1000 miles) of latitude separate New Zealand's northern-most wine region from the country's (and the world's) most southerly region, Central Otago. Warmer northerly climates, especially Waiheke, Matakana and Hawkes Bay, produce New Zealand's best reds from Cabernet, Merlot and Cabernet Franc (or a blend of all three). Pinot Noir is good in Martinborough and in South Island. Chardonnay performs well in all regions, with riper, fleshier wines in the north and finer, zestier styles to the south. Expect a big difference between pungent, grassy Sauvignon Blanc grown in Marlborough and the more conventional riper stone-fruit flavours of North Island.

*1997 VINTAGE REPORT*
Quantities are down, but quality varies from good to excellent, particularly in South Island. Low yields helped achieve good, ripe flavours. Marlborough had mostly excellent results for early-ripening whites to late-picked reds. In Gisborne and Hawkes Bay early varieties, notably Müller-Thurgau and Sauvignon, were affected by warm, humid weather, although reds fared better, with many deep, ripe wines.

See also (AUSTRALIA) NEW SOUTH WALES, SOUTH AUSTRALIA, TASMANIA, VICTORIA, WESTERN AUSTRALIA; (NEW ZEALAND) AUCKLAND, CANTERBURY, CENTRAL OTAGO, GISBORNE, HAWKES BAY, KUMEU/HUAPAI, MARLBOROUGH, MARTINBOROUGH, NELSON, WAIHEKE ISLAND; AND INDIVIDUAL WINERIES.

# SOUTH AMERICA

Several countries in this vast continent have vines, but in only a few places does the climate favour the production of fine wines. In the north there is desert or tropical rainforest; in the south lies Antarctica.

## ARGENTINA

Such is foreign faith in this giant, relatively untouched country that even Chileans are investing in MENDOZA vineyards. Yet quality has still to arrive at the top end, although there are encouraging cheap commercial blends now appearing regularly on the shelves. Torrontés, Malbec, Tempranillo, Sangiovese and Syrah are the grape varieties to watch, with promising Chardonnay coming from Tupungato Valley. Poor communications continue to hinder export growth.

## BRAZIL

Wine-making is confined to the southern tip of this huge country, and winemakers have a hard time combating the rot that results from a generally damp sub-tropical climate. The fact that hardy labrusca and hybrid varieties still outnumber classic vinifera varieties by 7 to 1 reflects these climatic difficulties. PALOMAS and Vinicola Aurora are the only serious export producers. See also Rio Grande do Sul.

## CHILE

Chile is making full use of rejuvenated vineyards and a new self-belief among the indigenous wine-making talent. New projects are sprouting everywhere, helped by a predictable climate, an asset that France and California have been quick to invest in. The search for a second CASABLANCA continues, while for reds, the Rapel region is generating most excitement, particularly with Merlot. And, at last, greater risk-taking is delivering stunning results at the premium end of the market. However, Chile still stands first and foremost for good-value wines, and there are increasing numbers of newcomers to choose from. Drink the most recent vintage available. See also Central Valley.

## MEXICO

This is basically brandy country, but in the far north-west in Baja California, some excellent reds are being made by L A CETTO. It is the high-altitude areas in Mexico that have the most potential for producing quality wines, and these include the Parras Valley and Zacatecas. New investment from companies such as González Byass, Seagram and Suntory may be the spur for further improvements.

## URUGUAY

With its main wine region sitting on roughly the same latitude as the Barossa in Australia, Uruguay has greater climatic potential than Brazil for producing good wines. Peter Bright's work at Juanico and John Worontschak's wines from Castillo Viejo show that clean, international styles can be made, with best results coming from the tough, black-berried Tannat smoothed over with some Merlot.

# SOUTH AFRICA

South Africa's vineyards cover nearly 100,000ha (250,000 acres) running roughly 400km (250 miles) north and east of Cape Town, and are divided into districts under the WINE OF ORIGIN system, each with a great mix of soils, climates and topography. The major grape varieties are planted over the entire Cape and, although there is little typicity of origin, some areas are historically associated with specific varieties or styles. STELLENBOSCH produces some of the best red wines. CONSTANTIA, with its sea-facing slopes, is acknowledged as ideal for Sauvignon Blanc but, more recently, cooler spots have started to produce some of the best examples. Sémillon looks set to make for interesting variation here in this cooler climate, although its spiritual home is FRANSCHHOEK. Other cooler areas include Walker Bay in OVERBERG, where the focus is Pinot Noir. The sprawling district of PAARL produces excellent reds and some very good whites, mainly from mountain slopes. Inland, Worcester is noted for fortified Hanepoots and Colombard, although it is mainly bulk wine country. ROBERTSON makes good Chardonnay and fortified Muscadels; further east, in the hot, arid Klein Karoo, Calitzdorp is putting port-styles on the map.

The industry has been dominated by co-ops, which account for 85% of annual wine production. There are now around 170 estates and private producers, 100 of which have sprung up in the last 10 years, and these are focussing on premium varieties and high-quality wine.

# OTHER WINE COUNTRIES

**ALGERIA** The western coastal province of Oran provides three-quarters of Algeria's wine production, with Alger making up the rest. French traditions live on in the soft but muscular wines of the Coteaux du Tlemcen, near the Moroccan border, while the dark, beefy reds of the Coteaux du Mascara in central Oran recall old-style Rhônes.

**AUSTRIA** Much of Austria's viticulture falls either side of the Danube. The WACHAU, the best region for dry whites, produces great Riesling and excellent pepper-dry Grüner Veltliner. Next along the Danube are KAMPTAL and KREMSTAL, also fine dry white wine regions with a few good reds now being made. Austria's best reds come from BURGENLAND and CARNUNTUM, south of Vienna. Further south, on the Slovenian border in STEIERMARK, the use of oak-aging for Chardonnay and Sauvignon is becoming more widespread. In Burgenland, around the Neusiedler See, some magnificent dessert wines in both the Germanic and Sauternes styles are made. See also Donauland, Thermenregion, Wien.

**BULGARIA** Eastern Europe's biggest success story, built mainly on the success of soft, curranty red wine. Easy-drinking renderings of the classic grape varieties (Cabernet, Merlot, Pinot Noir, Chardonnay, Riesling, Sauvignon), which occupy 75% of the vineyards, are the main attraction. Local red varieties, such as the plummy Mavrud, the meaty and toothsome Gamza and the deep though less common Melnik, can be good. The Dimiat can produce gentle, creamy, summer-fruit-bowl whites, while Misket (despite its name and grapy flavour, not a Muscat cousin) combines, if well handled, lively fruit with a haunting muskiness. Whites and lighter reds are mainly from the north and east (the freshest whites are those from the Black Sea coast), while richer, fuller reds come from the mountainous south and south-west. Unrestricted competition has now arrived as the remaining state-owned wineries have been privatized during 1997. Best wineries include ASSENOVGRAD, KHAN KRUM, RUSSE, SLIVEN and SUHINDOL.

**CANADA** The Canada-US Free Trade Agreement, allowing free access for cheap California wine, forced Canadian growers to adopt a more quality-first approach, and the strict VQA (Vintners Quality Alliance) now maintains those standards. There has been enormous progress in the 2 most important regions of OKANAGAN VALLEY in British Columbia and in the NIAGARA PENINSULA in Ontario. Pinot Gris and Chardonnay lead the way in non-sweet wines (ICEWINE still being Canada's main white trump card) and Pinot Noir shows some potential in reds.

**CHINA** Despite some major Western and Japanese investment (most notably by Rémy-Martin), China's wine-producing potential remains unfulfilled. Viticulture is best suited to the non-tropical northern part of the country. So far, Tsingtao Riesling and Chardonnay are the only wines showing promise.

**CROATIA** Inland Croatia produces mainly bulk whites; the best vineyards are on the Dalmatian coast, turning out gutsy, mouthfilling Postup, Peljesac and Faros reds.

**CYPRUS** The island has not had a high reputation for wine since the Crusades – when COMMANDARIA was reputedly a rich, succulent nectar worth risking your neck for. Modern Cyprus has survived on mediocre sherry-style wines and bulk shipments to the old USSR but, with the highest per capita grape production in the world, Cyprus desperately needs to modernize to find new markets.

**THE CZECH REPUBLIC** After the division of the former Czechoslovakia, the Czech Republic has been left with only a third of the vineyards, divided between the provinces of Bohemia and Moravia. With mainly cool-climate vineyards, planted with white varieties like Pinot Blanc, Muscat, Grüner Veltliner, Gewürztraminer and the strangely grapy Irsay Oliver, as well as pockets of red, a lack of a sense of direction has been the chief problem. Western investment will help produce good dry, aromatic whites.

**ENGLAND** With under 1000ha (2470 acres) of vineyards, England remains a statistically insignificant wine-producing nation. Yet no other spot can manage to infuse white wines with such haunting mayflower aromas and slender, graceful, willowy fruit, particularly in vintages like 1995. The most popular wine-making counties are Kent (Biddenden, Chapel Down, English Vineyard, LAMBERHURST, STAPLE ST JAMES, Tenterden) and Sussex (BREAKY BOTTOM, CARR TAYLOR, Hidden Spring, Nutbourne Manor, Nyetimber, St George's), with other top producers in Berkshire (THAMES VALLEY), Dorset (The Partridge), Gloucestershire (THREE CHOIRS), Oxfordshire (Chiltern Valley), Somerset (Pilton Manor, Wootton) and Surrey (DENBIES). The main problem is an unpredictable weather pattern. The most successful grape varieties – the hybrid Seyval Blanc and German-developed crosses like Schönburger, Huxelrebe, Bacchus, Kerner and Ortega – are those that can hold off disease while waiting for the last rays of October sunshine.

**GREECE** Best known for RETSINA, Greece still offers a depressing winescape. A few modern companies like Boutari, Achaia Clauss and Kourtakis are trying to make wines that are at least clean and fresh, and estates like CHATEAU CARRAS, Gerovassiliou, CHATEAU LAZARIDI and Skouras do well. Pockets of quality are Naoussa and Nemea for reds and Patras and SAMOS for sweet Muscats.

**HUNGARY** Unfortunately the country's great wine traditions did not prosper under the Communists, but inspired wine-making by Englishman Hugh RYMAN and others, foreign investment in TOKAJI, and renewed interest in its native grape varieties has made Hungary an important player during the 1990s.

**ISRAEL** Wine production was initiated by Baron Edmond de Rothschild at the end of the 19th century. Nowadays much is sweet red wine for Jewish family use, but there are excellent dry wines from the GOLAN HEIGHTS WINERY and CARMEL (near Haifa and Tel Aviv). Askalon's Ben Ami (Cabernet-Carignan) also makes good Cabernet-based reds.

**JAPAN** Some quality wines have been produced in Japan from homegrown grapes, as those of Chateau Lumière show, but much purportedly Japanese wine contains imported grapes, grape juice and wine that is sometimes, but not always, mixed with the local product.

**LEBANON** CHATEAU MUSAR is Lebanon's talisman of courage and quality. In this war-torn land, Musar's excellent red sounds above the conflict a clear clarion call of hope. Watch out for Chateau Kefraya and the Ksara co-op.

**MOLDOVA** The most forward-thinking of the ex-USSR wine producers, and its Bordeaux-like, mature Rochu and Negru red wines from the Purkar winery are first class. Cabernet from the Krikova winery can also be good. Hugh RYMAN is producing good results with Chardonnay-Sauvignon and Merlot-Cabernet blends at Hincesti.

**MOROCCO** Traditionally known for big, rich sweet-fruited reds that found a ready blending market in France, Morocco still produces firm supple reds – Tarik, Toulal Guerrouane and Chante Bled – as well as refreshing but heady rosés.

**ROMANIA** An ancient wineland of enormous potential. It has great traditional vineyards on the Black Sea and the Moldovan border that can provide wonderful sweet wines. The Dealul Mare region produces good Pinot Noir, Merlot and Cabernet; blending Pinot Noir and Merlot has become popular. Impressive results have also been achieved with botrytized Chardonnay and Pinot Gris in the MURFATLAR region.

**SLOVAKIA** This eastern part of the old Czechoslovakia is now independent, with cool-climate vineyards making mostly white wines from Pinot Blanc, Rhine Riesling, Gewürztraminer, Irsay Oliver and others, plus some reds. Western investment, particularly at the Nitra winery, is rapidly improving the quality.

**SLOVENIA** Many of the old Yugoslav Federation's best vineyards are found here, either on the Italian or the Austrian borders. Lutomer Laski Rizling comes from north-east Slovenia.

**SWITZERLAND** Fendant (Chasselas) is the primary grape for the dry neutral whites produced in the VALAIS. Like the fruity Dôle reds, they are best drunk young. German-speaking cantons mainly produce light reds and rosés from Pinot Noir (Blauburgunder), and easy-drinking whites from Müller-Thurgau (Rivaner). Italian-speaking TICINO concentrates on Merlots, juicy at best but often lean and grassy. More serious wines use Cabernet, Chardonnay and traditional varieties such as Arvine and Amigne. See also Neuchâtel, Vaud.

**TURKEY** The world's fifth-largest grape producer – but 97% ends up as raisins and the few remaining grapes make pretty poor red and white wines.

**UKRAINE** Vineyards mostly line the southern coast of the peninsula. Sparkling wine production in Odessa can be dated back to 1896, when a member of the ROEDERER family established the 'Russian-French Company' to produce fizz from local grapes. See also Crimea.

**YUGOSLAVIA** What remains of Yugoslavia is predominantly the red wine-producing part of the old federation. The Vranac grape grows full-throated bulky reds in Montenegro.

**ZIMBABWE** Three companies (Afdis, Monis and Philips) produce wines from grape varieties common in South Africa (Colombard, Chenin Blanc, Pinotage and Cabernet Sauvignon, among others). The country's best-known wines are Philips' Marondera range.

# A–Z

## OF WINES,
## PRODUCERS, GRAPES
## & WINE REGIONS

In the following pages there are
over 1400 entries covering the world's top wines, as
well as leading producers, main wine regions, grape
varieties, wine terms and classifications.

*On page 5 you will find a full explanation of
How to Use the A–Z. On page 272 there is an index
of main recommended producers to help you find the
world's best wines.*

**ABBOCCATO** Italian term used to describe lightly sweet wine. Particularly used for off-dry ORVIETO wine.

**ABFÜLLUNG** German term for 'bottled by'. In general, the best wines are bottled by the grower rather than a merchant, in which case the label says Erzeugerabfüllung or Gutsabfüllung (estate-bottled).

**ABRUZZO** *Italy* East of Rome, this region stretches from the Adriatic coast to the mountainous Apennine interior. Main wines are the white Trebbiano d'Abruzzo DOC, usually dry and neutral, and the MONTEPULCIANO D'ABRUZZO DOC, sometimes rosé but generally a strapping, peppery red of real character. Overproduction is a problem, but there are a number of good producers.

**AC/AOC (APPELLATION D'ORIGINE CONTRÔLÉE)** The top category of French wines, defined by regulations covering vineyard yields, grape varieties, geographical boundaries and alcohol content. It guarantees the origin and, up to a point, the style of a wine, but not its quality, although it ought to!

**ACACIA** *Carneros AVA, California, USA* A leading producer of Chardonnay and Pinot Noir from the CARNEROS region for almost 2 decades. Chardonnay from Marina Vineyard★★ is consistently exciting and the regular Carneros bottling isn't exactly chopped liver, either. Pinot Noirs include the stunning Reserve★★★ as well as a Madonna Vineyards★ and a Carneros★ – except for the deep, velvety Reserve, they tend to be on the bright cherry fruit side. Acacia also makes an excellent Zinfandel★ from old vines and a Brut sparkling wine which is moving from an experimental programme into a commercial venture. Best years: (red) **1994** 93 92 91 90 87 86; (white) **1994** 93 92 91.

**TIM ADAMS** *Clare Valley, South Australia* Important maker of fine, old-fashioned wine from bought-in grapes. Classic dry Riesling★★, subtly wooded Sémillon★★, and rich, full-bodied Shiraz★★ and Cabernet★. The 1994 botrytis Sémillon★★ is super stuff, and minty, peppery Aberfeldy Shiraz★★★ is a remarkable, at times unnerving, mouthful of brilliance from 90-year-old vines growing near WENDOUREE.

**ADANTI** *Umbria, Italy* Adanti produces an astonishing range of characterful wines. The whites, based primarily on the Grechetto grape, are tight, ripe and nutty, but the reds – Montefalco Sagrantino★★ and Rosso d'Arquata★ – are the real stars, pulsating with dark, unexpected flavours. Best years: (Sagrantino) 1995 94 93 **91 90 88 86 85**.

**ADEGA** Portuguese for 'winery'.

**ADELAIDE HILLS** *South Australia* Small, new but exciting region 30 minutes' drive from Adelaide. High altitude affords a cool, moist climate ideal for fine table wines and superb sparkling wine base. Best producers: Ashton Hills, Chain of Ponds, HENSCHKE★★, Lenswood Vineyards★★, PETALUMA★★★, SHAW & SMITH★★, STAFFORD RIDGE★.

**GRAF ADELMANN** *Kleinbottwar, Württemberg, Germany* Small estate which manages to produce some oak-aged reds with real colour and taste, although the Trollingers are best avoided. Also makes Rieslings up to Auslese and Eiswein levels. Best years: 1996 **95 93 90 89**.

**ADELSHEIM VINEYARD** *Willamette Valley AVA, Oregon, USA* This vineyard first hit the headlines with wine labels depicting various local beauties, including the owner's wife. Adelsheim has established a reputation for fine Pinot Noir – especially a rich Reserve★★★ – and a lovely, bright, super-fresh Pinot Gris★★ with good depth of flavour. Best years: **1994 92 91 90 89 88 87**; (Reserve) **1994 92 90 89 87**.

**AGE** *Rioja DOC, Rioja, Spain*  A huge recent investment to build RIOJA's largest vinification plant may improve the whole range. The Siglo Saco★ red Crianza is its best-known wine, perhaps because it comes wrapped in a hessian sack – but, luckily, this does not affect the taste.

**AGLIANICO DEL VULTURE DOC** *Basili-cata, Italy*  Red wine from the Aglian-ico grape grown on the steep slopes of Mt Vulture. Despite being one of Italy's most southerly DOCs, the har-vest is later than in BAROLO, 750km (470 miles) to the north-west, because the Aglianico grape ripens very late. The best wines are structured, com-plex and long-lived. Best producers: D'Angelo★★, Carbone, Armando Martino★, Paternoster★★. Best years: 1995 **93 90 88**.

**AHR** *Germany*  The Ahr Valley is a largely red wine region, south of Bonn. The chief grape varieties are the Spätburgunder (Pinot Noir) and the (Blauer) Portugieser. Many Ahr reds are made sweet for the traditional market in Bonn, but this style does not find many supporters outside Germany. Only Meyer-Näkel has achieved anything like an international reputation, and that has been won by sticking to dry reds.

**AIGLE** *Vaud, Switzerland*  Village in the CHABLAIS sub-region of the Vaud, making white wines from the Dorin (as the locals call the Chasselas grape) and reds from the Pinot Noir. Best known are the whites, with their 'flinty' bouquet, light and refreshing from their slight prickle. Best producers: Badoux, Landolt, Urs Saladin, Testuz.

**AIRÉN** Spain's – and indeed the world's – most planted white grape can make gently fruity, fresh modern whites, or thick, yellow, old-fashioned brews, depending upon the skills of the winemakers. The Spanish used to prefer the latter, but now have joined the northern Europeans in favouring the modern version. It grows all over the centre and south of Spain, especially in La MANCHA, VALDEPEÑAS and ANDALUCIA (where it is called Lairén).

**AJACCIO AC** *Corsica, France*  Situated in the west of the island around the town of Ajaccio, this is one of the better Corsican ACs. The reds often need 2–3 years in bottle to show at their best. Best producers: Clos d'Alzeto★, Clos Capitoro, Comte Péraldi★, Martini.

**ALBANA DI ROMAGNA DOCG** *Romagna, Italy*  In the hills south of Bologna and Ravenna, Italy's first white DOCG was a 'political' appointment that caused outrage among wine enthusiasts because of the totally unmemorable flavours of most Albana wine. Though also made dry and sparkling, the sweet version is the best, memorable in the Albana Passito Scacco Matto★★ of Zerbina. Best producers: Celli, Conti★, Ferrucci★, Paradiso, Riva, Tre Monti, Zerbina★★.

**ALBARIÑO** Possibly Spain's most characterful white grape. It grows in GALICIA in Spain's rainy north-west and, as Alvarinho, in Portugal's VINHO VERDE region. When well made, Albariño wines have fascinating flavours of apricot, peach, grapefruit and Muscat grapes, refreshingly high acidity, highish alcohol – and very high prices.

**ALCAMO DOC** *Sicily, Italy*　One of SICILY's best dry whites. Made from the indigenous Catarratto grape of western Sicily, grown between Marsala and Palermo, it is dry, nutty and rounded. Drink young. Best producers: Rapitalà★, Rincione.

**ALEATICO** An ancient, native Italian grape that produces sweet after-dinner wines of quite notable alcoholic strength in PUGLIA, LAZIO, UMBRIA and in TUSCANY, where a small revival is underway. Best producers: AVIGNONESI (Tuscany), Candido (delicious Aleatico di Puglia★).

**ALELLA DO** *Catalonia, Spain*　The city of Barcelona is fast encroaching on this tiny hilly region. Alella wines, mainly white, were traditionally medium-dry, but are now increasingly bone dry. Those made from Chardonnay can be good, though the unexciting Xarel-lo grape (locally called Pansa Blanca) is still the main staple. There are now some quality Merlots, both reds and rosés. Drink young. Best producers: Parxet, Roura.

**ALENTEJO** *Portugal*　The 2 provinces, Alto and Baixo Alentejo, making up most of southern Portugal south and east of Lisbon, are Portugal's fastest improving red wine regions. There are 3 IPRs and 5 DOCs. Potential is far from realized but I believe many of Portugal's finest reds will come from here. Best producers: BORBA co-op, ESPORAO★★, CAVES ALIANCA★, José Maria da FONSECA SUCCESSORES (Portalegre★ and REGUENGOS★★), Herdade de Cartuxa★★, Herdade de Mouchão★★, Quinta do Carmo★★, Redondo co-op, Reguengos de Monsaraz co-op, Roqueval★, SOGRAPE★, J P VINHOS★. See also Borba, Reguengos.

**ALEXANDER VALLEY AVA** *California, USA*　Important AVA centred on the Russian River, fairly warm with only patchy summer fog. Cabernet is highly successful here with lovely, juicy fruit not marred by an excess of tannin. Chardonnay can also be good but doesn't give such ripe, round flavours. Zinfandel and Merlot can be outstanding on hillsides. Best producers: Alexander Valley Vineyards★, Chateau Souverain, CLOS DU BOIS★, GEYSER PEAK★, JORDAN★, Murphy-Goode★★, Seghesio★★, SILVER OAK★★, SIMI★.

**ALGARVE** *Portugal*　It is extraordinary that the predominantly red, feeble-flavoured wines from this holiday region should have not 1 but 4 DOCs – Lagoa, Lagos, Portimão and Tavira. However these seem likely to be demoted to IPRs. I'd stick to the beer.

**ALIGOTÉ** French grape, found almost exclusively in Burgundy, whose basic characteristic is a lemony tartness. It can make extremely nice wine, especially from old vines, but is generally rather dull and lean. Traditionally used with local crème de cassis to make the apéritif Kir.

In ripe years it can resemble Chardonnay, especially if a little new oak is used. The best traditionally comes from Bouzeron in the CÔTE CHALONNAISE. Occasionally found in Moldova, Bulgaria and California, and widely planted in Switzerland. Best producers: (Burgundy) Jean-Claude Bachelet, COCHE-DURY★, Cogny, Confuron, JAYER-GILLES★, Jobard, RION, de Villaine.

**ALL SAINTS** *Rutherglen, Victoria, Australia* Old winery revived with great flair since 1992 by new owner BROWN BROTHERS. Superb fortifieds: Old Liqueur Tokay★★★, Muscat★★, Tawny★★, Madeira★★ and Amontillado★ are rediscovering past glory. Classic Release fortifieds are good but younger, while table wines can surprise. Pink Aleatico is unusual.

**ALLEGRINI** *Valpolicella, Veneto, Italy* Now a medium-sized and high-profile producer in VALPOLICELLA Classico. Refusing to produce mass-market wines, Allegrini has concentrated increasingly on quality, and especially on the single-vineyard Valpolicellas La Grola★★ and Palazzo della Torre★★. Barrique-aged La Poja★★, made solely with the Corvina grape, has shown the great potential that exists in Valpolicella. Since 1990, Palazzo della Torre has been made by a new-style *ripasso*, using dried grapes from the vineyard. Makes fine AMARONE★★★ and RECIOTO★ (especially Giovanni Allegrini★★). Best years: 1995 **93 91 90 88**.

**ALOXE-CORTON AC** *Côte de Beaune, Burgundy, France* An important village at the northern end of the Côte de Beaune producing mostly red wines from Pinot Noir. Its reputation is based on the 2 Grands Crus, CORTON (red and very occasional white) and CORTON-CHARLEMAGNE (white only). The wines from the other vineyards in Aloxe-Corton used to be some of Burgundy's tastiest at a fair price, but nowadays the reds rarely exhibit their characteristically delicious blend of ripe fruit and appetizing savoury dryness. Almost all the white wine is sold as Grand Cru: straight Aloxe-Corton Blanc is very rare. Best producers: Bize, Chandon de Briailles★, Chapuis★, Delarche★, DROUHIN, Dubreuil-Fontaine★, C Gros★, Guyon★, Jacob★, JADOT, LATOUR, Rapet★, Senard, TOLLOT-BEAUT★★, Voarick★. Best years: 1995 93 **92 90 89 88 85**.

**ALSACE AC** See pages 38–9.

**ALSACE VENDANGE TARDIVE** *Alsace, France* Vendange Tardive means 'late-harvest'. The grapes (Riesling, Muscat, Pinot Gris or Gewürztraminer) are picked late and almost overripe, giving higher sugar levels and therefore much more intense, exciting flavours. The resulting wines are usually rich and mouthfilling and often need 5 years or more to show their personality. Best producers: Léon Beyer★, Dopff & Irion★, HUGEL★★, KUENTZ-BAS★★, Schlumberger★★, TRIMBACH★★, Turckheim co-op★, ZIND-HUMBRECHT★★★. Best years: (1996) 95 94 **93 92 90 89 88 85 83 76**. See also pages 38–9.

**ALTARE** *Barolo DOCG, Piedmont, Italy* Elio Altare crafts some of the most stunning of Alba's wines – 2 outstanding Dolcetto d'Alba★★ (La Pria and Bricco Cascina Nuova) and even finer BAROLO★★ and Barolo Cru Vigneto Arborina★★★. Though a professed modernist, his wines are intense and tannic while young, but with clearly discernible fruit flavours, thanks largely to tiny yields. He also makes 2 barrique-aged wines: a Nebbiolo (Vigna Arborina★) and a Barbera (Vigna Larigi★★). Best years: (Barolo) (1996) 95 94 93 **90 89**.

# ALSACE AC
*Alsace, France*

Tucked away on France's eastern border with Germany, Alsace produces some of the most individual white wines of all, rich in aroma and full of ripe, distinctive flavours. To the visitor, Alsace appears the most Germanic of France's wine regions – a legacy of intermittent German occupation over the last century and a quarter. The food tastes German, the buildings look German and, perhaps unsurprisingly, there's plenty of beer on offer. As the reputation of German wines has moved down-market this perception has almost certainly restricted the popularity of Alsace wines. In their tall green bottles they could easily be mistaken for something produced in the German Mosel-Saar-Ruwer. The irony of all this is that Alsace is proudly French. More to the point, its wines taste nothing like those from Germany. They're generally drier, richer, less acidic and more alcoholic.

Alsace is almost as far north as Champagne, but its climate is considerably warmer. The key factor is the presence of the Vosges mountains, which act as a natural barrier, protecting the vineyards from rain and westerly winds, and making Alsace one of the driest places in France. In the crucial early autumn months, when the grapes are brought to full ripeness, Alsace is frequently warmer than Burgundy.

## *GRANDS CRUS*

Since 1975 the best vineyard sites in Alsace can call themselves Grands Crus. There are currently 50 of these, but the list is expanding all the time. These vineyards are restricted to 1 of 4 grapes – Riesling, Muscat, Gewürztraminer or Pinot Gris (sometimes labelled Tokay-Pinot Gris) – generally considered the finest varieties in Alsace, though Sylvaner and Pinot Blanc can produce good wines. These 4 are also the only grapes permitted for Vendange Tardive and Sélection de Grains Nobles, the late-picked and sometimes sweet wines which are a regional speciality. Pinot Noir, the area's only red grape, is usually confined to less well-appointed vineyards. As a result, it frequently produces wines that are closer to a rosé than a red Burgundy, although in hot vintages Alsace Pinot Noir can be excellent.

Alsace was one of the first regions to label its wines by grape variety – a practice which is now common in Australia and California, but is still frowned upon in France. Apart from Edelzwicker, which is a blend, and Crémant d'Alsace, all Alsace wines are made from a single grape variety.

See also ALSACE VENDANGE TARDIVE, CREMANT D'ALSACE, SELECTION DE GRAINS NOBLES; AND INDIVIDUAL PRODUCERS.

BEST PRODUCERS

**Gewürztraminer** Léon Beyer, Bruno Hertz, Kreydenweiss, KUENTZ-BAS, JOS MEYER, Meyer-Fonne, Ostertag, Schlumberger, TRIMBACH, Turckheim co-op, Weinbach, Willm, ZIND-HUMBRECHT.

**Muscat** J Becker, Ernest Burn, Dirler, Dopff & Irion, Kreydenweiss, KUENTZ-BAS, Rolly Gassman, Bruno Sorg, TRIMBACH, ZIND-HUMBRECHT.

**Pinot Blanc** Caves J B Adam, Joseph Cattin, Charles Koehly, JOS MEYER, Turckheim co-op, ZIND-HUMBRECHT.

**Pinot Gris** Léon Beyer, Ernest Burn, Dopff & Irion, HUGEL, KUENTZ-BAS, Ostertag, Rolly Gassmann, Schleret, Schlumberger, TRIMBACH, ZIND-HUMBRECHT.

**Pinot Noir** Albert Hertz, Turckheim co-op.

**Riesling** Becker, Beyer, Deiss, Albert Hertz, HUGEL, Kreydenweiss, JOS MEYER, Ostertag, Edgar Schaller, Schlumberger, Jean Sipp, TRIMBACH, Weinbach, ZIND-HUMBRECHT.

**Sylvaner** Kientzler, Ostertag, Rolly Gassmann, Martin Schaetzel, Schoffit, ZIND-HUMBRECHT.

**ALTESINO** *Brunello di Montalcino DOCG, Tuscany, Italy* One of the first producers in Montalcino to make a more modern style of BRUNELLO. Its range includes a good Brunello★ and a more refined Cru from the great hill of Montosoli★★, and 2 Super-Tuscans: a barrique-aged Sangiovese (Palazzo Altesi★★) and a Sangiovese-Cabernet blend (Alte Altesi★). Best years: (Brunello) (1996) (95) 94 93 **90 88**.

**ALTO ADIGE** *Trentino-Alto Adige, Italy* A largely German-speaking province, originally called Südtirol. The region-wide DOC covers 24 types of wine. A large proportion of its production comes from well-run co-ops producing reliable and sometimes admirable wines. Reds are invariably varietal and range from light and perfumed, when made from the Schiava grape, fruity from Cabernets or Merlot, to dark and velvety if the Lagrein is used. Whites include Chardonnay, Pinot Grigio and Riesling, and are usually fresh and fragrant. Best producers: Abbazia di Novacella★, Colterenzio co-op★, Giorgio Grai★★, Franz Haas★, Hofstätter★, LAGEDER★★, San Michele Appiano co-op★, Schwanburg★, Tiefenbrunner★. See also Santa Maddalena, Terlano, Trentino.

**ALVARINHO** See Albariño.

**AMABILE** Italian for 'semi-sweet'. Generally sweeter than ABBOCCATO wines, but less so than some dolce or PASSITO styles.

**AMARONE DELLA VALPOLICELLA** *Valpolicella DOC, Veneto, Italy* A brilliantly individual, bitter-sweet style of VALPOLICELLA made from grapes shrivelled on mats for months after harvest. The wine, which can reach up to 16% of alcohol, may be drunk with game dishes or cheeses, though some prefer it for 'meditation' at the end of a meal. It differs from the sweet RECIOTO DELLA VALPOLICELLA in that it is fermented to dryness. As with all Valpolicella, Classico is generally the best, though an exception can be made for Dal Forno. It can age impressively for 10 years or longer. Best producers: ALLEGRINI★★★, Bertani★★★, BOLLA★, Dal Forno★★★, Guerrieri-Rizzardi★, MASI★, Mazzi★, QUINTARELLI★★★, Le Ragose★, Speri★, Tedeschi★. Best years: 1995 93 **91 90 88 86 85 83**.

**AMIGNE** Swiss grape variety that is virtually limited to the region of Vétroz in the VALAIS. The wine has an earthy, nutty intensity and benefits from a few years' aging. Best producers: Caves Imesch, Granges Frères (Escalier de la Dame), Jean-René Germanier.

**AMITY VINEYARDS** *Willamette Valley AVA, Oregon, USA* Myron Redford was one of the pioneers in OREGON, opening his winery in 1976. The Gewürztraminer★★ is outstanding and the Riesling★★ is almost as good. The showpiece, of course, is the Pinot Noir, with the Winemakers Reserve★★ showing great power and style.

**AMONTILLADO** See Jerez y Manzanilla DO.

**AMTLICHE PRÜFUNG** See Prüfungsnummer.

**ANBAUGEBIET** German for 'growing region' and these names will appear on labels of all QbA and QmP wines. In unified Germany there are 13: Ahr, Mosel-Saar-Ruwer, Mittelrhein, Rheingau, Nahe, Rheinhessen, Pfalz, Hessische Bergstrasse, Franken, Württemberg, Baden, Saale-Unstrut and Sachsen.

**ANDALUCÍA** *Spain* Fortified wines, or wines naturally so strong in alcohol that they don't need fortifying, are the speciality of this southern stretch of Spain. Apart from sherry (JEREZ Y MANZANILLA DO), there are the lesser, sherry-like wines of Condado de Huelva DO and MONTILLA-MORILES DO, and the rich, sometimes treacly-sweet wines of MALAGA DO. All these regions now also make some admittedly modern but extremely bland dry whites.

**ANDREW WILL WINERY** *Washington State, USA* Sourcing the finest grapes and striving for elegance in his wines, winemaker Chris Camarda is making what many critics believe to be the finest Washington Merlots – the Reserve★★ is unbeatable. His Cabernets are not far behind and a dry Chenin, Cuvée Lulu, has also earned rave reviews. Best years (reds) **1995 94 92**.

**CH. L'ANGÉLUS**★★★ *St-Émilion Grand Cru AC, 1er Grand Cru Classé, Bordeaux, France* One of the biggest and best-known ST-ÉMILION Grands Crus with an energetic owner and talented winemaker. Increasingly good wines throughout the 80s, recognized by promotion to Premier Grand Cru Classé in 1996. Best years: (1996) (95) 94 93 90 89 88 **86 85**.

**CH. D'ANGLUDET**★★ *Margaux AC, Cru Bourgeois, Haut-Médoc, Bordeaux, France* This English-owned château makes one of my favourite wines. Always of Classed Growth standard, it has one of the best price–quality ratios in Bordeaux and ages superbly for a decade or more. Best years: (1996) (95) 94 93 **90 89 88 86 85 83 82**.

**ANGOVES** *Riverland, South Australia* Family company delivering masses of decent varietals sourced mainly from its Nanya vineyard, one of Australia's largest plantings. The low prices are kept that way by rock-bottom production costs. Chardonnay and Colombard are cheerful cheapies to quaff young.

**ANJOU BLANC AC** *Loire Valley, France* A much-abused and ill-defined AC. Ranges from bone dry to sweet and, in quality, from excellent to dreadful. The best are dry and from individual producers. Although up to 20% Chardonnay or Sauvignon can be added, many of the leading producers prefer to use 100% Chenin. Best producers: Angeli★, Bidet, Cady, Cailleau, Daviau★, Haute Perche, V Lebreton, Ogereau★, J Renou, RICHOU★. Best years: **1996 95 93**.

**ANJOU MOUSSEUX AC** *Loire Valley, France* A rare AC for Anjou sparkling wines, with Chenin Blanc the principal grape. Most producers instead sell their wines as (more prestigious) CREMANT DE LOIRE.

**ANJOU ROUGE AC** *Loire Valley, France* Anjou is best known for ROSE D'ANJOU but the reds (from Cabernets Sauvignon and Franc or Pineau d'Aunis) are increasingly successful. Usually a fruity, easy-drinking wine, with less tannin than ANJOU-VILLAGES. Wines made from Gamay are sold as Anjou Gamay. Best producers: Angeli, Cailleau, Cochard, Daviau★, Musset-Roullier, RICHOU★, Touche Noire. Best years: **1996 95 93**.

**ANJOU-VILLAGES AC** *Loire Valley, France* As the Anjou AC is such a blanket term, taking in red, white, rosé and fizz of inconsistent quality, the better Anjou red producers asked for a separate AC. Since 1985, 46 villages have been entitled to the AC Anjou-Villages, only for red wine from Cabernet Franc and Cabernet Sauvignon. Some extremely attractive dry, fruity reds are emerging in the region, with better aging potential than ANJOU ROUGE. Best producers: Bidet, Closel,

Daviau★★, Haute Perche, J-Y H Lebreton★★, Ogereau★, Pierre-Bise, RICHOU (Vieilles Vignes★★), Touche Noire. Best years: 1996 **95 93 90 89**.

**ANSELMI** *Soave DOC, Veneto, Italy* Along with PIEROPAN, Roberto Anselmi has shown that SOAVE can have personality when carefully made. Using ultra-modern methods he has honed the fruit flavours of his Soave Classico and Cru Capitel Foscarino★★ and introduced small-barrel-aging for his single-vineyard Capitel Croce★★ and his luscious, Sauternes-like Recioto dei Capitelli★★.

**ANTINORI** *Tuscany, Italy* World-famous Flo-rentine family firm that has been involved in wine since 1385, but it is Piero Anti-nori, the current head, who has made the Antinori name synonymous with quality and innovation. The quality of its CHIANTI CLASSICO wines like Badia a Passignano, Pèppoli, Villa Antinori and Tenute March-ese Riserva is generally ★★, but it was its  development of the Super-Tuscan concept of superior wines outside the DOC that launched a quality revolution during the 1970s. Intro-ducing small-barrel-aging to Tuscany for the first time, TIGNANELLO★★ (Sangiovese-Cabernet) and SOLAIA★★★ (Cabernet) can be great wines. Antinori's Tuscan interests now extend to VINO NOBILE, La Braccesca and BOLGHERI's Tenute Belvedere. Ownership further afield includes PRUNOTTO in Piedmont and ATLAS PEAK in California. Best years: (1996) 95 **94 93 90** 88. See also Castello della Sala, Super-Tuscans.

**APPELLATION D'ORIGINE CONTRÔLÉE** See AC.

**ARAGÓN** *Spain* Most of Aragón, stretching from the Pyrenees south to Spain's central plateau, has traditionally been responsible for much of the country's cheap red wine. There have been improvements, however, espe-cially in the cooler, hilly, northern SOMONTANO DO, which is making some top-quality wines with international grapes. Further south, wine-making technology is improving in Campo de Borja DO and CARINENA DO.

**ARBOIS AC** *Jura, France* The largest of the specific ACs in the Jura region. The whites are made from Chardonnay or the local Savagnin, which can give the wines a sherry-like flavour that is most concen-trated in VIN JAUNE. There is also a rare, sweet VIN DE PAILLE. Good sparkling, now called CREMANT DE JURA, is made mainly from Chardon-nay. Some of the best reds and sparklers come from the commune of Pupillon. Best producers: Arbois co-op, d'Arlay★, Aubin co-op, Aviet, Bourdy★, Désiré, Maire★, Puffeney★, Pupillin co-op, Rolet★★, Tissot.

**ARGIANO** *Brunello di Montalcino DOCG, Tuscany, Italy* A mini-renaissance continues here: renewed investment and the hand of Giacomo Tachis can be seen in radically refashioned BRUNELLO★★ that combines richness and accessibility. Best years: (1996) (95) 94 93 90.

**LEONCIO ARIZU** *Mendoza, Argentina* Old winery with great potential in reds: solid Syrah★, a powerhouse Malbec★ and Pinot Noir that swings from elegant to dull, depending on the vintage. The tendency to keep the wines too long before release means that the 1994 Chardonnay is on the shelves only now.

**ARNEIS** White Italian grape grown in the Roero hills in Piedmont. Arneis is DOC in ROERO, producing dry white wines which, at best, have an attractively nutty, herbal perfume. They can be expensive. Best producers: Almondo★, Castello di Neive★ (Barbaresco), CERETTO, Correggia★, Deltetto★, Bruno GIACOSA★, Malvirà★, Negro★, PRUNOTTO★, Vietti★.

**CH. L'ARROSÉE★★** *St-Émilion Grand Cru AC, Grand Cru Classé, Bordeaux, France* This small property, just south-west of the small historic town of St-Émilion, makes really exciting wine: rich, chewy and wonderfully luscious, with a comparatively high proportion (40%) of Cabernet Sauvignon. Drink after 5 years but may be cellared for 10 or more. Best years: (1996) (95) 94 93 **90 89 88 86 85 83 82**.

**ARROWOOD VINEYARDS WINERY** *Sonoma Valley AVA, California, USA* Dick Arrowood was the winemaker at CHATEAU ST JEAN during its glory years of Chardonnay. In 1988 he left to start his own winery a few miles down the road. The wines have been simply sensational – beautifully balanced Cabernet★★★, superb Merlot★★, lovely, velvety Chardonnay★★ and the recent addition of a crisp, lively Viognier★. Whites should be drunk young, reds with a little age. Best years: (reds) **1994 93 92 91 90 88**; (whites) **1995 94 93 91**.

**ISMAEL ARROYO** *Ribera del Duero DO, Castilla y León, Spain* This family bodega has reached the pinnacle of RIBERO DEL DUERO producers in just 15 years, with long-lasting, dense, tannic wines, headed by Val Sotillo Reserva★★★, Gran Reserva★★★ and Crianza★★.

**ARRUDA IPR** *Estremadura, Portugal* A one-co-op region just north of Lisbon, but luckily, that co-op at Arruda dos Vinhos is one of the best in the ESTREMADURA and makes a decent, inexpensive red.

**ARVINE** Swiss variety from the VALAIS found between the communes of Vétroz and Martigny. The best grapes come from Fully and the Mont d'Or of Sion. Typical Arvine has a bouquet of peach and apricot, and develops a spicy, honeyed character with age. Of Switzerland's indigenous grapes, Arvine gives the wines with the best aging potential. Best producers: Caves Imesch★, Chanton, Chappaz★, Dom. du Mont d'Or★, Maye & Fils, Raymond, Roduit, Savioz (Ch. Ravire).

**ASCHERI** *Piedmont, Italy* Winemaker in PIEDMONT for at least 5 centuries, Ascheri's style is forward and appealingly drinkable, whether it be BAROLO★, Dolcetto★ (especially Vigna Nirane), or NEBBIOLO D'ALBA★ from the San Giacomo vineyard. A barrique-aged blend of Barbera and Nebbiolo called Bric Mileui★ is startlingly good, with supple fruit and dark, chocolaty flavours. Best years: (Barolo) (1996) (95) 94 **93 90 89 88**.

**ASSENOVGRAD** *Southern Region, Bulgaria* Lush, plummy Cabernet Sauvignon and earthy, mineral-dusted Mavrud are both good from this predominantly red wine winery. The best Assenovgrad Mavrud ages well, but doesn't gain in complexity.

**ASTI DOCG** *Piedmont, Italy* Asti Spumante, the world's best-selling sweet sparkling wine, was long derided as light and cheap, though promotion to DOCG signalled an upturn in quality. Made in the province of Asti south-east of Turin, under the new appellation (which includes the rarer MOSCATO D'ASTI) the wine may be called simply Asti to avoid confusion with other sparklers. Its light sweetness and refreshing sparkle make it ideal with fruit and at the end of a meal. Drink young. Best producers: (Spumante) Bera★, Cascina Fonda★, Cascina Pian d'Or★, Cinzano★, FONTANAFREDDA, Gancia★, Martini & Rossi★.

**ATA RANGI** *Martinborough, North Island, New Zealand* Small, high-quality winery run by 2 families. Produces concentrated wines with style and individuality, including big, rich Chardonnay★★, seductively soft cherry/plum Pinot Noir★★★ and a Cabernet Sauvignon-Merlot-Syrah blend called Célèbre★★. Best years: 1996 **94 91 90 89**.

**ATLAS PEAK** *Atlas Peak AVA, Napa, California, USA* The hillside vineyards, now owned by ANTINORI of Italy, are demonstrating a new sense of direction after several years of drift. A 100% Sangiovese shows promise, particularly the 1990 vintage, as does a tasty Sangiovese-Cabernet blend called Consenso. Each has a cellaring potential of 5–10 years. Chardonnay and Cabernet are recent additions.

**AU BON CLIMAT** *Santa Maria Valley AVA, California, USA* Pace-setting winery in the cool SANTA MARIA region, run by the highly talented Jim Clendenen, who spends much time in the best cellars in Burgundy and Italy's Piedmont. The result is lush Chardonnay★★, intense Pinot Noir★★, and Bordeaux styles under the Vita Nova label. Watch out for Parabla★, a Nebbiolo with 4 years in barrel, 2 Barberas and a Pinot Blanc. QUPE, a specialist in Rhône varieties, operates from the same winery. Best years: (reds) **1994 91 90 89 87 86**; (whites) **1995 92 90 89 87**.

**AUCKLAND** *North Island, New Zealand* Vineyards in the region of Auckland are centred around the small districts of Henderson, KUMEU/HUAPAI and Waimauku. Many of the better wines are made in the recently established districts of WAIHEKE ISLAND and Matakana. Best producers: COLLARDS★, Fenton★★, Goldwater★★, Heron's Flight★, KUMEU RIVER★, Peninsula★, Providence, STONYRIDGE, Te Motu★★.

**L'AUDE, VIN DE PAYS DE** *Languedoc, France* One of the largest VdPs in the region, mainly covering red wines. Quality varies accordingly: the best reds are soft, fruity, with a bit of southern spice. Best producers: Boyer, CLOS CENTEILLES, de Gourgazaud, de Lalande, Nicolas.

**AUSBRUCH** Both the Germans and Austrians rely on precise measurements of sugar content to place wines in their different quality categories. Ausbruch is the Austrian Prädikat category used for sweet wines with minimum residual sugar levels of 27 KMW (139 Oechsle), but top producers often sell wines picked at 32–35 KMW as Ausbruch. The wines are fermented to a higher alcoholic and lower sugar content than Beerenauslese or Trockenbeerenauslese. The result is closer to SAUTERNES than Germanic sweet styles, with less fruit flavour but richer texture. Best producers: FEILER-ARTINGER★★★, Opitz★★, Schandl★★, Ernst Triebaumer★★, Paul Triebaumer★★, Wenzel★★. See also KMW and Oechsle.

**AUSLESE** German and Austrian QmP category meaning that the grapes were 'selected' for their higher sugar levels. A Riesling Auslese from the Mosel can have as little as 83 Oechsle, while most Baden Ausleses are sweeter and start at 105. The Austrian Auslese level is 21 KMW or 105 Oechsle.

**CH. AUSONE★★** *St-Émilion Grand Cru AC, 1er Grand Cru Classé,
Bordeaux, France* This elegant property, situated on what are
perhaps the best slopes in ST-EMILION, made a dramatic return to form
in the 1980s, but I'm not yet convinced these new-breed Ausones will
develop and improve in bottle. Best years: (1996) (95) 94 93 90 89 88 **86
85 83 81 79 78**.

**AUXEY-DURESSES AC** *Côte de Beaune, Burgundy, France* Auxey-
Duresses is a backwater village up in the hills behind world-famous
MEURSAULT. The reds should be light and fresh but can often lack
ripeness. At its best, and at 3–5 years, the white is dry, soft, nutty and
hinting at the creaminess of a good Meursault, but without the loony
prices. Best producers: (reds) Diconne★, Duc de Magenta★, Jessiaume,
Maison LEROY; (whites) Ampeau★, Creusefond, Diconne★, Duc de
Magenta★, Fichet★, Maison LEROY, Prunier, Roulot. Best years: (reds)
1995 **93 90 89 88 85**; (whites) 1995 **94 92 90 89**.

**AVA (AMERICAN VITICULTURAL AREA)** System of appellations of origin
established for American wines in the 1970s.

**AVIGNONESI** *Vino Nobile di Montepulciano DOCG, Tuscany, Italy* The
Falvo brothers of Avignonesi led Montepulciano's revival as one of
Tuscany's best zones. Although VINO NOBILE★★ is often the best of the
dry wines, the varietals, which include Chardonnay (Il Marzocco★),
Sauvignon (Il Vignola★) and Merlot★★, have received more attention.
Also famous is the Vino da Tavola Grifi★★ (Sangiovese-Cabernet) and
sweet red Aleatico. The VIN SANTO★★★ is the most sought after in Tuscany, and a rare red version from Sangiovese, Occhio di Pernice★★★,
is beyond compare. Best years: (1995) 94 **93 90 88 85**.

**AYL** *Saar, Germany* A top Saar village. The best-known vineyard in Ayl
is Kupp, which produces classy, slaty wines on its steep slopes. Best
producers: Bischöflicher Konvikt, Peter Lauer, Heinz Wagner.

**AZIENDA AGRICOLA** Italian for 'estate' or 'farm'. It also indicates wine
made from grapes grown by the proprietor.

**BABICH** *Henderson, North Island, New Zealand* Family-run winery
specializing in quality wines. Irongate Chardonnay★★ is an intense,
steely wine that needs plenty of cellaring, while intense, strongly
varietal reds under the Mara Estate label, including Merlot★★,
Syrah★★ and Cabernet Sauvignon★, show even greater potential for
development. The newly released Patriarch label now offers the company's top-of-the-line Chardonnay★★ and Cabernet-Merlot★★, both
from HAWKES BAY. Best years: 1996 **94 91 90 89**.

**BACKSBERG ESTATE** *Paarl WO, South Africa* The late Sydney Back,
widely respected doyen of South African producers and a driving force
behind the Estate concept, pioneered Chardonnay★ in the Cape, and
Backsberg's remains consistently satisfying without being showy.
Wines to suit every taste sit comfortably beside specialist items like
pot-still brandy★★. Merlot, Bordeaux-style blend Klein Babylonstoren
and Pinotage reflect ever more characterful reds. Best years: (Chardonnay) **1995 94 93 92**.

**BAD DÜRKHEIM** *Pfalz, Germany* This spa town may not be as famous as
its neighbours but it has some good vineyards and is the headquarters
of the decent Vier Jahreszeiten Kloster Limburg co-op. Best producers:
Kurt DARTING★, Fitz-Ritter, Karl Schaefer★.

**BAD KREUZNACH** *Nahe, Germany* Spa town with 22 individual vine-
yard sites, the best wines coming from the steepest sites such as
Brückes, Kahlenberg and Krötenpfuhl. Not to be confused with the
NAHE district of Bereich Kreuznach. Best producers: Paul Anheuser,
Reichsgraf von Plettenberg.

**BADEN** *Germany* Very large wine region stretching from Baden-Baden to
the Bodensee. Recently took the lead in making dry whites and reds which
show off the fuller, softer flavours Germany is capable of producing in the
warmer climate of its southerly regions. Many of the best non-Riesling
German wines of the future will come from Baden, as well as many of the
best barrel-fermented and barrel-aged wines. Good co-operative cellars at
Breisach (the largest in Europe), Steinbach, DURBACH, Bickensohl, Bötzingen
and Königsschaffhausen.

**BAGA** Important red grape in BAIRRADA, which is one of the few regions in
Portugal to rely mainly on one variety. Also planted in much smaller
quantities in DÃO and the RIBATEJO.

**BAILEY'S** *North-East Victoria, Australia* Old, very traditional winery at
Glenrowan, where Australia's most famous bush bandit, Ned Kelly,
made his last stand. Bailey's make hearty, thickly textured reds from
Shiraz★★ and Cabernet★ as well as some of Australia's most luscious
fortified liqueur Muscat and Tokay (Winemakers Selection★★★) –
heavenly and irresistible stickies.

**BAIRRADA DOC** *Beira Litoral, Portugal* Bairrada
has for ages been the source of many of
Portugal's best red table wines even though
the region was only demarcated in 1979.
These can brim over with intense raspberry
and blackberry fruit, though the tannin levels
may take a few years to soften. The whites
are coming on fast with modern vinification
methods. Best producers: Casa de Saima★★,
CAVES ALIANCA★, CAVES SAO JOAO★, Gonçalves
Faria★★, Luis PATO★★, SOGRAPE★.

**CH. BALESTARD-LA-TONNELLE★** *St-Émilion Grand Cru AC, Grand Cru
Classé, Bordeaux, France* This is a popular ST-EMILION property,
making reliable wine, full of strong, chewy fruit. It is decently priced
too. Best years: 1994 **90 89 88 86 85**.

**BANDOL AC** *Provence, France* Bandol, a lovely fishing port with vineyards high above the Mediterranean, produces some of the most exciting reds and rosés in Provence. The Mourvèdre grape gives Bandol its
character – gentle raisin and honey softness with a slightly tannic,
herby fragrance. The reds happily age for 10 years but can be very
good at 3–4. The rosés, delicious and spicy but often too pricy, should
be drunk young. There is a small amount of white, most of it rather
neutral and sold at horrendous prices. Drink as young as possible. Best
producers: (reds) Bastide Blanche, Cagueloup, l'Hermitage,
Ray Jane★, Mas de la Rouvière★, Pibarnon★★, Ste-Anne★, TEMPIER★★,
Vannières★. Best years: (1996) 95 **93 90 89 88 86 85**.

**BANFI** *Brunello di Montalcino DOCG, Tuscany, Italy*   This American-owned firm, variously known as Castello Banfi, Villa Banfi and Banfi Vintners, has become a force in Italian production, and the wines, if initially dull, are now gradually being refined. In the late 1970s the Mariani brothers, New York wine importers, enlisted the services of Ezio Rivella – one of Italy's premier winemakers – to carve out an estate in the southern part of the BRUNELLO DI MONTALCINO zone. They built a high-tech winery, where premium wines like Brunello★, Chardonnay (Fontanelle★) and Cabernet (Tavanelle★) are proving to be successful. Brunello Riserva Poggio all'Oro★★ can be very good, Super-Tuscan Summus★ (Sangiovese-Cabernet-Syrah) and ROSSO DI MONTALCINO Certine★ can also impress. Banfi also has cellars in PIEDMONT for GAVI and fizz.

**BANNOCKBURN** *Geelong, Victoria, Australia*   The experience gleaned from regular vintage stints spent at Burgundy's Domaine DUJAC is reflected in Gary Farr's powerful, gamy Pinot Noir★★ and Meursault-like Chardonnay★★★, which are among Australia's best. Much-improved Shiraz★★ is influenced by Rhône's Alain GRAILLOT. Best years: **1994 91 90 88 86 85**.

**BANYULS AC** *Roussillon, France*   One of the best Vins Doux Naturels. Made mainly from Grenache Noir, the strong plum and raisin flavour tastes good in a young, sweet version and older tawny styles are even better. Best producers: Casa Blanca, Cellier des Templiers★, l'Étoile★, Mas Blanc, la RECTORIE★★, la Tour Vieille★.

**BARBADILLO** *Jerez y Manzanilla DO, Andalucía, Spain*   Antonio Barbadillo, the largest sherry company in the coastal town of Sanlúcar de Barrameda, makes a wide range of good to excellent wines, in particular salty, dry manzanilla styles, particularly the Solear★★★ and Principe★★★, and intense, nutty, but dry amontillados and olorosos, led by Oloroso del Río. It also makes a neutral-flavoured dry white, Castillo de San Diego.

**BARBARESCO DOCG** *Piedmont, Italy*   This prestigious red wine, grown near Alba in the Langhe hills south-east of Turin, is often twinned with its neighbour BAROLO as the noblest examples of the Nebbiolo grape. Barbaresco can be a shade softer and less powerful, due to the slightly warmer climate in its lower altitude position adjacent to the Tanaro river. The wine usually takes less time to mature (only 1 year of wood-aging is required as opposed to Barolo's 2) and is often considered the most approachable of the two, as exemplified by the internationally followed style of GAJA. But, as in Barolo, traditionalists also excel, led by Bruno GIACOSA. The zone covers 475ha (1174 acres) of vineyards in the communes of Barbaresco, Neive and Treiso. Even though the area is relatively compact, wine styles can differ significantly between vineyards and producers. Best vineyards: Asili, Bricco di Neive, Costa Russi, Crichet Pajè, Gallina, Marcorino, Martinenga, Messoirano, Moccagatta, Montestefano, Ovello, Pora, Rabajà, Rio Sordo, San Lorenzo, Santo Stefano, Serraboella, Sori Paitin, Sori Tildin. Best producers: Barbaresco co-op★★, Cantina del Glicine★★, Castello di Neive★★, CERETTO★★, Cigliuti★★, Cortese, GAJA★★★, Bruno GIACOSA★★★, I Paglieri★★, Marchesi di Gresy★★, Moccagatta, Paitin★★, Pio Cesare★, Bruno Rocca-Rabajà★★, Vietti★. Best years: (1996) (95) 93 **90 89 88 86 85 82**.

**BARBERA** A native of north-west Italy, Barbera vies with Sangiovese as the most widely planted red grape in the country. When grown for high yields its natural acidity shows through, producing vibrant quaffers. Low yields from the top Piedmont estates create intensely rich and complex wines. When small oak barrels are used the results can be stunning. Best producers: (Alba) ALTARE★★, CLERICO★★, Aldo CONTERNO★★, Conterno-Fantino★, GAJA★★, Elio Grasso★★, Giuseppe MASCARELLO★, Parusso★★, Prunotto★★, Albino Rocca★, Paolo Scavino★★, Vajra★★, Viberti★★, Vietti★; (Asti) Braida★★, Cascina La Barbatella★, Cascina Castlèt★, Chiarlo★, Coppo★, Gastaldi★★, Scarpa★, La Spinetta★.

**BARCA VELHA★★** *Douro DOC, Portugal* Portugal's most sought-after and expensive red table wine, made by FERREIRA, modelled on fine red Bordeaux, but using DOURO grape varieties (mainly Tinta Roriz). It is made only in the very finest years – just 12 vintages since 1953, the most recent being 1985.

**BARDOLINO DOC** *Veneto, Italy* Substantial zone centred on Lake Garda, giving, at best, light, scented red and rosé (Chiaretto) wines to be drunk very young, from the same grape mix as neighbouring VALPOLICELLA. Best producers: Corte Gardoni★, Gorgo, Guerrieri-Rizzardi★, Lamberti★, MASI★, Le Vigne di San Pietro★, Fratelli Zeni★.

**BAROLO DOCG** *Piedmont, Italy* Renowned red wine, named after a village south-west of Alba, from the Nebbiolo grape grown in 1175ha (2900 acres) of vineyards in the steep Langhe hills. Its status as 'king of wines and wine of kings' for a time proved to be more of a burden than a benefit among Italians, who considered its austere power too much for modern palates, with tough, chewy tannins which took years of cask-aging to soften. But many winemakers, aided by a series of fine vintages between 1985 and 90, have applied new methods to make fresher, cleaner wines of greater colour, richer fruit and softer tannins without sacrificing Barolo's noble character. Distinct styles of wine are made in the zone's villages. Barolo and La Morra make the most perfumed wines; Monforte and Serralunga the most structured; Castiglione Falletto strikes a balance between the two. Barolo is usually labelled by vineyards, though the producer's reputation often carries more weight. Best vineyards: Bricco Boschis, Bricco delle Viole, Brunate, Bussia Soprana, Cannubi, Cerequio, Fiasco, Ginestra, La Serra, Marcenasco, Monfalleto, Monprivato, Pianpolvere Soprano, Rocche di Castiglione, Rocche di La Morra, Santo Stefano di Perno, Villero, Vigna Rionda. Best producers: ALTARE★★, Anselma★, ASCHERI★, Azelia★★, Batasiolo★, Cavallotto, CERETTO★★, Chiarlo★, CLERICO★★, Aldo CONTERNO★★★, Giacomo CONTERNO★★, Conterno-Fantino★★, Riccardo Fenocchio★★, GAJA★★★, Bruno GIACOSA★★, Elio Grasso★★, Marcarini★, Bartolo MASCARELLO★★★, Giuseppe MASCARELLO★★★, Parusso★, Pio Cesare★★, PRUNOTTO★★, Ratti★★, Rocche dei Manzoni★★, Sandrone★★★, Paolo Scavino★★, Sebaste★, Vajra★, Vietti★★, VOERZIO★★. Best years: (1996) (95) 93 **90 89 88 86 85 82**.

**BARÓN DE LEY** *Rioja DOC, Navarra, Spain* Barón de Ley Reserva and El Mesón Crianza are red RIOJAS made only from grapes grown on the estate, including some 'experimental' Cabernet Sauvignon. Best years: 1994 **91 87**.

**BAROSSA VALLEY** *South Australia* Headquarters to such giants as PENFOLDS, SEPPELT, ORLANDO and YALUMBA, this region, noted for port-style wines, Shiraz and Riesling, has less than 10% of the nation's vineyards yet makes 60% of the wine, largely from grapes grown elsewhere in South Australia. A new lease of life for Barossa Valley grapes has come from producers such as Bethany, Grant BURGE★, Charles Melton, ROCKFORD★ and ST HALLETT★★.

**BARRIQUE** The *barrique bordelaise* is the traditional Bordeaux oak barrel of 225 litres capacity. Fermenting and aging in barrels adds to the overall texture, spice and richness of a wine. The term barrique is also used by the Italians and Germans.

**JIM BARRY** *Clare Valley, South Australia* Initially very much a white wine outfit, with the famous Florita vineyard as the source for perfumed, classy Rieslings★. Now creating bigger waves with reds, such as the much-improved Cabernet Sauvignon★ and the heady, palate-busting (wallet-busting, too) Armagh Shiraz★★★.

**BARSAC AC** *Bordeaux, France* Barsac, the largest of the 5 communes in the SAUTERNES AC, also has its own AC, which is used by most of the top properties. In general, the wines are a little less luscious than other Sauternes, but from good estates they can be marvellous. Best producers: (Classed Growths) BROUSTET★, CLIMENS★★★, COUTET★★, DOISY-DAENE★, Doisy-Dubroca★, DOISY-VEDRINES★★, NAIRAC★★; (others) Liot★, Ménota, Piada. Best years: (1996) (95) 90 89 88 86 83 81 80 76 75.

**BASSERMANN-JORDAN** *Deidesheim, Pfalz, Germany* An estate making good Riesling★ wines with the majority in dry styles. The vineyard sites are mostly in the excellent villages of Deidesheim and FORST and the wines manage to show a rich, full texture without being fat and soft. The early 90s vintages were a bit listless, but new winemaker Ulrich Mell has put things back on track. Best years: 1996 90 89 88 86.

**CH. BASTOR-LAMONTAGNE★★** *Sauternes AC, Cru Bourgeois, Bordeaux, France* Year after year this estate produces luscious, honeyed wine at a price which allows us to enjoy high-class SAUTERNES without taking out a second mortgage. Best years: (1996) 95 94 90 89 88 86 85 83 82.

**CH. BATAILLEY★** *Pauillac AC, 5ème Cru Classé, Haut-Médoc, Bordeaux, France* A byword for value-for-money and reliability among the PAUILLAC Classed Growth estates. Marked by a full, obvious blackcurrant fruit, not too much tannin and a luscious overlay of creamy vanilla. Lovely to drink at only 5 years old, the wine continues to age well for up to 15 years. Best years: (1996) (95) 94 90 89 88 86 85 83 82.

**BÂTARD-MONTRACHET AC** *Grand Cru, Côte de Beaune, Burgundy, France* This Grand Cru produces some of the world's greatest whites – they are full, rich and balanced, with a powerful, minerally intensity of fruit and fresh acidity. There are 2 associated Grands Crus: Bienvenues-Bâtard-Montrachet and the minuscule Criots-Bâtard-Montrachet. All can age for a decade. Best producers: J-N GAGNARD★, GAGNARD-DELAGRANGE★★, Louis JADOT★★, Dom. LEFLAIVE★★★, Olivier LEFLAIVE★★, Pierre Morey★★, RAMONET★★★, Sauzet★★★. Best years: 1995 92 90 89 88 86 85.

**DOM. DE LA BAUME** *Vin de Pays d'Oc, Languedoc, France* The French outpost of BRL HARDY, chiefly making varietal wines. The operation was set up in 1989, when the estate's wine-making equipment was completely renewed with stainless steel and a refrigeration unit replaced concrete. The wines are sold under various names: Domaine de la Baume (Merlot and a Chardonnay-Viognier blend) comes from the estate; Philippe de Baudin and Chai Baumière are a mix of estate and contract grapes and the range includes Merlot★, Cabernet Sauvignon and Syrah, Chardonnay★ and Sauvignon Blanc.

**LES BAUX-DE-PROVENCE AC** *Provence, France* This AC has proved that organic farming can produce spectacular results. Good fruit and inspirational wine-making produce some of the best reds and rosés in the south of France. There is very little white made so far. From 1994, TREVALLON is VdP des Bouches-du-Rhône. **Best producers:** Mas de la Dame★, Mas de Gourgonnier★, Terres Blanches★, TREVALLON★★★.

**BÉARN AC** *South-West France* While the rest of south-west France has been busy producing some unusual and original flavours in recent years, Béarn hasn't managed to cash in. The wines (90% red and rosé) just aren't special enough, despite some decent grape varieties. **Best producers:** Bellocq co-op, Lapeyre.

**BEAU-SÉJOUR-BÉCOT★★** *St-Émilion Grand Cru AC, 1er Grand Cru Classé, Bordeaux, France* Demoted from Premier Grand Cru Classé in 1986 and promoted again in 1996, this estate is now back on top form. Brothers Gérard and Dominique Bécot produce firm, ripe, richly textured wines that need at least 8–10 years to develop. **Best years:** (1996) (95) 94 **90 89 88 86 85 83**.

**CH. DE BEAUCASTEL** *Châteauneuf-du-Pape AC, Rhône Valley, France* François Perrin makes some of the richest, most tannic reds★★★ in CHATEAUNEUF-DU-PAPE, with an unusually high percentage of Mourvèdre and Syrah, which can take at least a decade to show at their best. The white★★★, made almost entirely from Roussanne, is exquisite, too. **Best years:** (reds) (1996) 95 94 93 **90 89 88 86 85 83 82 81**; (whites) 1996 95 **94 93 92 90 89 88**. See also la Vieille Ferme.

**BEAUJOLAIS AC** *Beaujolais, Burgundy, France* Famous red wine from a large area of rolling hills and valleys in southern Burgundy. Most Beaujolais nowadays appears as BEAUJOLAIS NOUVEAU or Beaujolais Primeur, but Beaujolais AC is the basic appellation. In the north, toward Mâcon, most of the reds qualify either as BEAUJOLAIS-VILLAGES or as a single Cru (10 villages which produce better but more expensive wine: BROUILLY, CHENAS, CHIROUBLES, COTE DE BROUILLY, FLEURIE, JULIENAS, MORGON, MOULIN-A-VENT, REGNIE, ST-AMOUR). In the south, toward Lyon, most of the wine is simple AC Beaujolais, a light red to be drunk within months of the vintage, which should be lovely and fresh but is now too often dilute. Beaujolais Supérieur means wine with a minimum strength of 1% more alcohol than simple Beaujolais. A tiny amount of white is made from Chardonnay. The EVENTAIL DE VIGNERONS PRODUCTEURS is the most high-profile of the Beaujolais co-ops. **Best producers:** (reds) Bernardin, Michel Carron, Charmet, Ch. de la Plume, DUBOEUF, Fessy, des Fortières, P Germain, Jambon, Labruyère, Texier; (whites) Charmet, Dalissieux, DUBOEUF. **Best years: 1996 95**.

**BEAUJOLAIS NOUVEAU** *Beaujolais AC, Burgundy, France* This is the first release of bouncy, fruity Beaujolais on the third Thursday of November after the harvest. Once a simple celebration of the new vintage, then a much-hyped beano, now increasingly *passé*. Quality is generally good since much of the best BEAUJOLAIS AC is used for Nouveau. The wine usually improves by Christmas and the New Year, and the best ones are perfect for summer picnics. Best producers: Boutinot, CELLIER DES SAMSONS, la Chevalière, DROUHIN, DUBOEUF, Ferraud, JAFFELIN, Loron, Sapin, Sarrau.

**BEAUJOLAIS-VILLAGES AC** *Beaujolais, Burgundy, France* Beaujolais-Villages can come from any one of 39 villages in the north of the region. Carefully made, it can represent all the gurgling excitement of the Gamay grape at its best. Best villages: Beaujeu, Lancié, Lantignié, Leynes, Quincié, St-Étienne-des-Ouillières, St-Jean-d'Ardières. Best producers: Aucoeur★, Bel-Air, Colombier, Descombes★, DUBOEUF, B Faure, Jaffre, Large, Loron, Dom. Perrier★, Pivot★, Tissier, Verger. Best years: **1996** 95.

**BEAULIEU VINEYARD** *Napa Valley AVA, California, USA* The late André Tchelistcheff had a major role in creating the icon for Napa Cabernet Sauvignon while winemaker in the late 1930s, 40s and 50s. After he left, Beaulieu missed a few beats and lived on its reputation for too long, even though Tchelistcheff continued to consult. However, recent bottlings of the Private Reserve Cabernet Sauvignon★★ show some flashes of the old style. A new Meritage red called Tapestry is also promising. Recent bottlings of Chardonnay★ from Carneros have been a pleasant surprise. Best years: (Private Reserve) 1992 91 90 **85 70 68**.

**BEAUMES-DE-VENISE** *Rhône Valley, France* Area famous for its sweet wine: MUSCAT DE BEAUMES-DE-VENISE, France's best-known Vin Doux Naturel. The local red wine is also very good, one of the meatier COTES DU RHONE-VILLAGES, with a ripe, plummy fruit in warm years. Best producers: (reds) les Goubert, Pascal, local co-op.

**BEAUNE AC** *Côte de Beaune, Burgundy, France* Beaune gives its name to the southern section of the Côte d'Or, the Côte de Beaune. Almost all the wines are red, with delicious, soft red-fruits ripeness. There are no Grands Crus but some excellent Premiers Crus (Boucherottes, Bressandes, Clos des Mouches, Fèves, Grèves, Marconnets,

Teurons, Vignes Franches). A small amount of white – DROUHIN make an outstandingly good creamy, nutty Clos des Mouches★★. Best producers: (growers) Besancenot-Mathouillet★★, Jacques GERMAIN★★, Lafarge★★, André Mussy★, TOLLOT-BEAUT★★; (merchants) Camille-Giroud★, Champy★, DROUHIN★★, JADOT★★, JAFFELIN★, LABOURE-ROI★, Moillard, Morot★★. Best years: (reds) 1995 93 **90 89 88 85**; (whites) 1995 **93 92 90 89**.

**BEAUX FRÈRES** *Willamette Valley AVA, Oregon, USA* A new venture that has already generated much interest due to the participation of wine critic Robert Parker. Grapes are sourced from his brother-in-law's vineyards (hence the name), while the wine-making philosophy is likely to be French. Inspired, perhaps, by Burgundian superstar Henri JAYER, the intention seems to be to make ripe, unfiltered Pinot Noir★★ that expresses the essence of the grape and vineyard. Its immediate success has attracted a cult following. Best years: **1994 93 92 91**.

**GRAHAM BECK** *Robertson WO, South Africa*   A highly professional team producing a small range full of personality. Winemaker Pieter Ferreira's passion is Cap Classique sparkling; his rich yet elegant delicate NV Brut, 50/50 Pinot Noir-Chardonnay, was the only non-Champagne gold medal winner in the 1996 International WINE Challenge; the barrel-fermented dry Blanc de Blancs★★ is rich and creamy. There is also a nicely paced Lone Hill Chardonnay.

**BEERENAUSLESE** German and Austrian Prädikat category applied to wines made from 'individually selected' grapes, which, since the grapes are always overripe and sugar-packed, give wines that have a rich, luscious dessert quality to them. The berries are often affected by noble rot (*Edelfäule* in German). Beerenauslese wines are only produced in the best years in Germany, but in Austria they are a pretty regular occurrence. They start at 110 Oechsle in the Mosel rising to 128 Oechsle in southern Baden. Austrian Beerenauslese wines start at 25 KMW or 127 Oechsle.

**CH. BELAIR★** *St-Émilion Grand Cru AC, 1er Grand Cru Classé, Bordeaux, France*   Next door to AUSONE. Belair has the same owner and winemaker and, like its neighbour, it has experienced a revival of fortunes since the 1970s. Belair is lighter than Ausone. Best years: (1996) (95) 94 93 **90 89 88 86 85 83 82**.

**BELLET AC** *Provence, France*   A tiny AC of usually overpriced wine, mostly white, in the hills behind Nice. Ch. de Crémat and Ch. de Bellet are the most important producers and their wines are worth seeking out if you're in the area, but don't search too hard if you aren't.

**BENDIGO DISTRICT** *Victoria, Australia*   Warm, dry, former gold-mining region, which produced some decent wines in the 19th century, then faded away completely. It was triumphantly resurrected by Stuart Anderson, who planted Balgownie in 1969, and other wineries followed (including Chateau Leamon, Water Wheel, Heathcote, Jasper Hill, Passing Clouds and YELLOWGLEN). The best wines are full-bodied Shiraz and Cabernet.

**BERBERANA** *Rioja DOC, Rioja, Spain*   A dynamic new boss has transformed one of RIOJA's largest companies. Berberana has bought Lagunilla and formed a partnership with MARQUES DE GRINON, and is making lightly oaked Dragon label Berberana red★ and respectable Reservas and Gran Reservas. Best years: 1994 **90 89 88**.

**BERCHER** *Burkheim, Baden, Germany*   The down-to-earth Bercher brothers run the top estate of the KAISERSTUHL. The high points are the powerful new oak-aged Spätburgunder reds★ and Weissburgunder★★ and Grauburgunder dry whites, which marry richness with perfect balance. Drink young or cellar for 3–5 years or more. Best years: 1996 **94 93 92 90 89**.

**BEREICH** German for region or district within a wine region or Anbaugebiet. Bereichs tend to be large, and the use of a Bereich name, such as Bereich Bingen, without qualification is seldom an indication of quality – in most cases, quite the reverse.

**BERGERAC AC** *South-West France*   Bergerac is the main town of the Dordogne and the overall AC for this underrated area on the eastern edge of Bordeaux. The grape varieties are mostly the same as those used in the BORDEAUX ACS. The red is generally like a light, fresh claret, a bit grassy but with a good, raw blackcurrant fruit and hint of earth.

In general drink young although a few estate reds can age for at least 3–5 years. The whites are generally lean and dry for quick drinking. Best producers: le Barradis, de Conti, Court-les-Mûts★, de Gouyat, la JAUBERTIE★, Lestignac, Miaudoux, Panisseau, du Priorat, la Raye, Tourmentine. Best years: (reds) 1996 **95 93 90 89 88**.

**BERGKELDER** *Stellenbosch, South Africa* Wholesaler buying in wine as well as grapes from contract growers. Best own labels are top-of-the-range Stellenryck, good-value Fleur-du-Cap, and well-crafted Cap Classique bubblies, including ripe, yeasty Pongracz NV★★. Also provides aging and marketing facilities for 12 estates, the best being La Motte, MEERLUST and Le Bonheur. Bergkelder's 'what's good for one is good for all' cellar regime tends to dampen the estates' singularity.

**BERINGER VINEYARDS** *Napa Valley AVA, California, USA* Beringer produces a full range of wine but, in particular, offers a spectacular range of top-class Cabernet Sauvignons. The Private Reserve Cabernet★★★ is one of NAPA VALLEY's finest yet most approachable; the Lemmon Ranch★★ and Chabot Vineyards★★, when released under their own label, are only slightly less impressive; the Knight's Valley Cabernet★ is a lighter but engagingly juicy style. The Reserve Chardonnay★★ is a powerful wine that should age well. HOWELL MOUNTAIN Merlot★★ from Bancroft Vineyard is also good. Best years: (Cabernet Sauvignon) 1994 93 **92 91 90 87 86 85 84 80**.

**BERNKASTEL** *Mosel, Germany* Both a town in the Middle MOSEL and the name of a large Bereich. Top wines, however, will come only from vineyard sites within the town – the most famous of these is the over-priced DOCTOR vineyard. Many wines from the Graben and Lay sites are as good or better and cost a fraction of the price. Best producers: Dr LOOSEN★★, J J PRUM★★, WEGELER-DEINHARD★★.

**BERRI RENMANO** *Riverland, South Australia* Twin RIVERLAND co-ops which can crush up to 15% of Australia's total grape harvest. Purchased the famous HARDY wine company in 1992. They produce largely bulk and bag-in-box wines, but top label Renmano Chairman's Selection is good for buxom Chardonnay★ and oaky Cabernet. Given the muscle this company has, I am glad to see that wine quality has improved considerably.

**BEST'S** *Grampians, Victoria, Australia* Small winery run by Viv Thomson, who makes attractive wines from estate vineyards first planted in 1868. Delicious, clear-fruited Shiraz★★ and Cabernet★ are good, and the Riesling is rapidly improving. Tropical-fruity but finely balanced Chardonnay★ is his new star wine. Best years: (reds) 1994 **92 91 90 88 87 84 80 76**.

**CH. BEYCHEVELLE**★★ *St-Julien AC, 4ème Cru Classé, Haut-Médoc, Bordeaux, France* Although ranked as a 4th Growth, this beautiful château usually makes wine of 2nd Growth quality. The wine has a charming softness even when young, but takes at least a decade to mature into the cedarwood and blackcurrant flavour for which ST-JULIEN is famous. Generally worth its high price despite occasional wobbles. Second wine: Réserve de l'Amiral. Best years: (1996) (95) 94 90 89 86 **85 83 82**.

**BIANCO DI CUSTOZA DOC** *Veneto, Italy* Dry white from an area over-lapping the southern part of BARDOLINO. Similar in style to neighbouring

53

## B | BIENVENUES-BÂTARD-MONTRACHET AC

SOAVE, but the addition of up to 30% Tocai Friulano can give extra breadth and richness. Drink young. **Best producers:** Arvedi d'Emilei, Cavalchina, Corte Gardoni, Gorgo★, Lamberti, Le Vigne di San Pietro★.

**BIENVENUES-BÂTARD-MONTRACHET AC** See Bâtard-Montrachet.

**BIERZO DO** *Castilla y León, Spain* Sandwiched between the rainy mountains of GALICIA and the arid plains of the rest of CASTILLA Y LEON, Bierzo makes mostly commonplace reds. But the best ones – fruity and grassy green – are a revelation and quite unlike any other Spanish efforts. Ideally the red wines are made entirely from the Mencía grape, but all must contain at least 70%. **Best producers:** Pérez Caramés, Prada a Tope.

**JOSEPH BIFFAR** *Deidesheim, Pfalz, Germany* Father and daughter team Gerhard and Lilli Biffar run this first-class estate, currently making the best dry and sweet Rieslings from top sites in Deidesheim, Ruppertsberg and WACHENHEIM. Consistent ★★ quality in recent vintages. Drink young or cellar for 5 years or more. **Best years:** 1996 **95 94 93 92 90**.

**BILLECART-SALMON** *Champagne AC, Champagne, France* Top-notch CHAMPAGNE house and one of the few still under family control. The wines are extremely elegant, fresh and delicate, but become simply irresistible with age. The non-vintage Brut★★, non-vintage Brut Rosé★★, Blanc de Blancs★★, vintage Cuvée N-F Billecart★★★ and Cuvée Elisabeth Salmon★★ are all excellent. **Best years:** 1990 **89 88 86 85 82**.

**BINGEN** *Rheinhessen, Germany* Small town and also a Bereich, the vineyards of which fall in both the NAHE and RHEIN-HESSEN. The best vineyard in the town is the Scharlachberg, which produces exciting wines, stinging with racy acidity and the whiff of coal smoke. **Best producer:** VILLA SACHSEN.

**BINISSALEM DO** *Mallorca, Balearic Islands, Spain* Alcoholic reds and rosés are the mainstay of this DO. A few growers make reasonable wines but they are in short supply, even on the island. **Best producers:** José Ferrer, Bodega Franja Roja, Herederos de Ribas, Jaume Mesquida.

**BIONDI SANTI** *Brunello di Montalcino DOCG, Tuscany, Italy* Estate that in less than a century created both a legend and an international standing for BRUNELLO DI MONTALCINO★. The modern dynamism of the zone owes more to other producers, however, since quality has slipped over the last 2 decades. Yet the very expensive Riserva★★, with formidable levels of extract, tannin and acidity, deserves a minimum 10 years' further aging after release before serious judgement is passed on it.

**BLAGNY AC** *Côte de Beaune, Burgundy, France* The red wine from this tiny hamlet above the communes of MEURSAULT and PULIGNY-MONTRACHET can be fair value, if you like a rustic Burgundy. The white is sold as Puligny-Montrachet, Meursault Premier Cru or Meursault-Blagny. **Best producer:** Jobard. **Best years:** 1995 93 **92 90 89 88**.

**BLANC DE BLANCS** French term used for white wine made from one or more white grape varieties. The term is used all over France, especially for sparkling wines, but is mostly seen in CHAMPAGNE, where it denotes wine made entirely from the Chardonnay grape.

54

**BLANC DE NOIRS** French term used for white wine made from black grapes only – the juice is separated from the skins to avoid extracting any colour. Most often seen in CHAMPAGNE, where it is used to describe wine made from Pinot Noir and/or Pinot Meunier grapes.

**BLANQUETTE DE LIMOUX AC** *Languedoc-Roussillon, France* Most southern whites are singularly flat and dull, but this fizz is sharp and refreshing. The secret lies in the Mauzac grape, which makes up over 80% of the wine and gives it its striking 'green apple skin' flavour. The Champagne method is used to create the sparkle, although the more rustic *méthode rurale*, finishing off the original fermentation inside the bottle, is also used. Best producers: Collin, Delmas★, Guinot, Laurens★, Martinolles★, SIEUR D'ARQUES CO-OP, les Terres Blanches. Best years: **1995 94 92 91 90**. See also Crémant de Limoux AC.

**WOLF BLASS** *Barossa Valley, South Australia* Wolf Blass stands as one of the most important men in the modern Australian wine world for mastering reds and whites of high quality and consistency which were nonetheless *easy* to enjoy. His reds, blended from many regions and aged mostly in American oak barrels, have a delicious mint and black-currant, easy-going charm. His Rieslings are soft and sweetish, while his other whites also possess juicy fruit and sweet oak. Gold Label Riesling★★ from the CLARE and Eden valleys is impressively intense, Black Label★★, the top label for red wines released at 5 years old, is expensive but good, the Yellow Label cheaper but immensely cheerful. Now owned by MILDARA. Best years: **1994 92 91 90 88 86 82**.

**BLAUBURGUNDER** See Pinot Noir.

**BLAUER LIMBERGER** See Blaufränkisch.

---

**BLAUFRÄNKISCH** Good, ripe Blaufränkisch has a taste similar to rasp-berries and white pepper or even beetroot. It does well in Austria, where it is the principal red wine grape of BURGENLAND. The Hungarian vineyards (where it is called Kékfrankos) are mostly just across the border on the other side of the Neusiedler See. Called Lemberger in Germany, almost all of it is grown in WÜRTTEMBERG.

---

**BODEGAS Y BEBIDAS** *Spain* The largest wine-producing company in Spain, with wineries including CAMPO VIEJO, AGE and Marqués del Puerto in RIOJA, Vinícola de Navarra, Casa de la Viña in VALDEPEÑAS, Bodegas Alanís in Ribeiro, and others in La MANCHA and JUMILLA.

**JEAN-CLAUDE BOISSET** *Burgundy, France* From humble origins Boisset has become a power in the land, with new acquisitions every year. He has now expanded into Beaujolais by taking control of CELLIER DES SAMSONS. Others controlled by Boisset include JAFFELIN, Bouchard Aîné and Ropiteau. Together, the Boisset group markets a vast quantity of Burgundy, but most of it is not much better than adequate.

**BOLGHERI DOC** *Tuscany, Italy* This zone near the coast south of Livorno recently extended its DOC beyond simple white and rosé to cover red wines based on Cabernet, Merlot and Sangiovese in various combinations, while creating a special category for SASSICAIA. The DOC Rosso Superiore, which covers wines from the prestigious estates of Grattamacco★★, Le Macchiole★★ and Michele Satta★★, could also apply to ORNELLAIA and ANTINORI's new red Guado al Tasso★★.

**BOLLA** *Soave DOC and Valpolicella DOC, Veneto, Italy* The largest
producer of SOAVE★ and VALPOLICELLA★. Founded in 1857, the firm
helped create the market for these 2 perennial favourites. The basic
wines are uninspired, but Soave Castellaro and Valpolicella Jago are
good single-vineyard wines, and there is an interesting Creso Rosso
made from Cabernet and the local Corvina grape. Also good
AMARONE★.

**BOLLINGER** *Champagne AC, Champagne, France* One of the great
CHAMPAGNE houses, with good non-vintage (Special Cuvée★★) and
vintage wines (Grande Année★★), made in a full, rich, rather old-
fashioned style. (Bollinger is one of the few houses to ferment its base
wine in barrels.) It also produces a range of rarer vintage Champagnes, including a Vintage RD★★★ (RD stands for *récemment dégorgé*,
or recently disgorged, showing that the wine has been lying in bottle
on its yeast for longer than usual, picking up loads of flavour on the
way) and Vieilles Vignes Françaises Blanc de Noirs★★ from ancient,
ungrafted Pinot Noir vines. Best years: 1990 **89** 88 **85** 82 **79**.

**CH. LE BON PASTEUR**★★ *Pomerol AC, Bordeaux, France* Small château
which has established an excellent reputation under the ownership of
Michel Rolland, one of Bordeaux's leading winemakers. Expensive in
recent years, but the wines are always deliciously soft and full of lush
fruit. Best years: (1996) (95) 94 93 **90 89 88 85 83 82**.

**BONNES-MARES AC** *Grand Cru, Côte de Nuits, Burgundy, France* A
large Grand Cru straddling the communes of CHAMBOLLE-MUSIGNY and
MOREY-ST-DENIS and one of the few great Burgundy vineyards to main-
tain consistency during the turmoil of the last few decades. Bonnes-
Mares generally has a deep, ripe, smoky plum fruit, which starts red
and chewy and matures over 10–20 years. Best producers: Clair-
Daü★, DROUHIN★★, DUJAC★★, Groffier★, Mugnier★★, Roumier★★, de
Vogüé★★. Best years: 1995 93 90 **89** 88 **85** 78.

**BONNEZEAUX AC** *Grand Cru, Loire Valley, France* One of France's great
sweet wines, Bonnezeaux is a Cru inside the larger COTEAUX DU LAYON
AC. It is made in the same way as SAUTERNES but the flavours are
different, as only Chenin Blanc is used. Extensive recent plantings
have made quality less reliable. It can age very well in vintages like
1990 and 89. Best producers: Angeli★★, de Fesles★★, Petite Croix★,
Petit Val★. Best years: (1996) 95 94 93 **90 89 88 85 83 76 71 64 59 47**.

**BONNY DOON** *Santa Cruz Mountains AVA, California, USA* Iconoclastic
operation under Randall Grahm, who revels in the unexpected. He has
a particular love for Rhône, Italian and Spanish varietals and for
fanciful brand names: Le Cigare Volant★★ is a blend of Grenache and
Syrah and is Grahm's homage to CHATEAUNEUF-DU-PAPE. Old
Telegram★★ is 100% Mourvèdre; Le Sophiste★ is a blend of Rhône
white grapes. Particularly delightful are his Ca' del Solo Italianate
wines, especially a bone-dry Malvasia Bianca★★ and a white blend,
Il Pescatore, his eccentric answer to Verdicchio. He also makes a
delicious if bewildering line of eaux de vie and an Icewine from grapes
frozen in a refrigeration plant.

**BORBA DOC** *Alto Alentejo, Portugal* Promising DOC in the Alto ALENTEJO,
specializing in rich, raspberry-fruited reds. Best producers: Borba co-
op, Quinta do Carmo★★.

**BORDEAUX AC** *Bordeaux, France*   One of the most important ACs in France. It can apply to the reds and rosés as well as the dry, medium and sweet white wines of the entire Gironde region. Most of the best wines are allowed more specific geographical ACs (such as MARGAUX or SAUTERNES) but a vast amount of unambitious, yet potentially enjoyable wine is sold as Bordeaux AC. Straight red Bordeaux is one of the most consistent of all generic wines, with bone-dry grassy fruit and an attractive earthy edge. Good examples will often benefit from a year or so of aging. Bordeaux Blanc, on the other hand, had until recently become a byword for flabby, fruitless, over-sulphured brews. There is now an increasing number of refreshing, pleasant, clean wines, frequently under a merchant's rather than a château label. Drink as young as possible. Best producers: (reds) Canteloup, Castéra, Coste, Ducla, Goélane, Haut Riot, du Moulin, de Roques, Terrefort, Thieuley, Tour de Mirambeau, le Trébuchet; (whites) Alpha★★, Cayla, Coste, DOISY-DAENE★, Dourthe, Grand Mouëys, du Juge, Lamothe, LYNCH-BAGES★★, MARGAUX (Pavillon Blanc), Reynon★, Roquefort, de Sours★, Thieuley★, Tour de Mirambeau. See also pages 58–61.

**BORDEAUX CLAIRET AC** *Bordeaux, France*   A very pale red wine, virtually rosé in fact, which isn't much seen around Bordeaux any more. The name 'claret', which in Britain is now applied to *any* red wine from the Bordeaux region, derives from *clairet*.

**BORDEAUX SUPÉRIEUR AC** *Bordeaux, France*   This AC covers the same area as the basic BORDEAUX AC but the wines must have an extra ½% of alcohol and a lower yield from the vines, resulting in a greater concentration of flavours. Many of the petits châteaux are labelled Bordeaux Supérieur. The whites under this AC are medium-sweet.

**BOSCARELLI** *Vino Nobile di Montepulciano DOCG, Tuscany, Italy*   Arguably Montepulciano's best producer, Paolo de Ferrari and sons Luca and Niccolò, with guidance from star oenologist Maurizio Castelli, craft rich, stylish reds. Most outstanding are VINO NOBILE Riserva del Nocio★★ and the barrique-aged Sangiovese Boscarelli★★★.

**BOSCHENDAL** *Paarl WO, South Africa*   A major vineyard and cellar extension in 1996 now accommodates some very promising reds. Unashamedly commercial wines mingle with classier numbers, including a soft, lingering Chardonnay★ and Cap Classique bubblies Le Grand Pavillon Blanc de Blancs NV★ and rich vintage Boschendal Brut.

**BOUCHARD FINLAYSON** *Walker Bay, Overberg WO, South Africa*   Paul Bouchard's Burgundian know-how and financial support produce this first joint Franco-South African venture. Naturally, winemaker Peter Finlayson focusses on Pinot Noir★, firm and dense, and Chardonnay★★ (3 labels, variously sourced grapes), but his steely Sauvignon Blanc★ lacks nothing in quality.

**BOUCHARD PÈRE ET FILS** *Beaune, Burgundy, France*   Important merchant and vineyard owner, with vines in some of Burgundy's most spectacular sites, including CORTON, CORTON-CHARLEMAGNE, Chevalier-Montrachet and le MONTRACHET. The firm went through a rough patch in the 1980s but was then bought by Champagne whizz-kid Joseph Henriot, who immediately declassified large chunks of bottled stocks – expect a dramatic upturn here. Wines from the company's own vineyards are sold under the Domaines du Château de Beaune label.

# BORDEAUX RED WINES

*Bordeaux, France*

 This large area of south-west France, centred on the historic city of Bordeaux, produces a larger volume of fine red wine than any other French region. Wonderful Bordeaux-style wines are produced in California, Australia and South America, but the home team's top performers are still unbeatable. Around 580 million bottles of red wine a year are produced here. The best wines, known as the Classed Growths, account for a tiny percentage of this figure, but some of their lustre rubs off on the lesser names, making this one of the most popular wine styles.

## GRAPE VARIETIES

Bordeaux's reds are commonly divided into 'right' and 'left' bank wines. On the left bank of the Gironde estuary, the red wines are dominated by the Cabernet Sauvignon grape, with varying proportions of Cabernet Franc, Merlot and Petit Verdot. At best they are austere but perfumed with blackcurrant and cedarwood. The most important left bank areas are the Haut-Médoc (especially the communes of Margaux, St-Julien, Pauillac and St-Estèphe) and, south of the city of Bordeaux, the ACs of Pessac-Léognan and Graves. On the right bank, Merlot is the predominant grape, which generally makes the resulting wines more supple and fleshy than those of the left bank. The key areas for Merlot-based wines are St-Émilion and Pomerol.

## CLASSIFICATIONS

Red Bordeaux is made all over the region, from the tip of the Gironde estuary to the southern end of the Entre-Deux-Mers. At its most basic, the wine is simply labelled Bordeaux or Bordeaux Supérieur. Above this are the more specific ACs covering sub-areas (such as the Haut-Médoc) and individual communes (such as Pomerol, St-Émilion or Margaux). Single-estate Crus Bourgeois are the next rung up on the quality ladder, followed by the Classed Growths of the Médoc, Graves and St-Émilion. Many of these châteaux also make 'second wines', which are cheaper versions of their Grands Vins. Curiously Pomerol, home of Château Pétrus, arguably the most famous red wine in the world, has no official pecking order.

See also BORDEAUX, BORDEAUX CLAIRET, BORDEAUX SUPERIEUR, CANON-FRONSAC, COTES DE BOURG, COTES DE CASTILLON, COTES DE FRANCS, FRONSAC, GRAVES, GRAVES SUPERIEURES, HAUT-MEDOC, LALANDE-DE-POMEROL, LISTRAC, LUSSAC-ST-EMILION, MARGAUX, MEDOC, MOULIS, MONTAGNE-ST-EMILION, PAUILLAC, PESSAC-LEOGNAN, POMEROL, PREMIERES COTES DE BLAYE, PREMIERES COTES DE BORDEAUX, PUISSEGUIN-ST-EMILION, ST-EMILION, ST-ESTEPHE, ST-GEORGES-ST-EMILION, ST-JULIEN; AND INDIVIDUAL CHATEAUX.

**Graves, Péssac-Léognan**
Dom. de CHEVALIER, de FIEUZAL,
HAUT-BAILLY, HAUT-BRION,
la LOUVIERE, la MISSION-HAUT-
BRION, PAPE-CLEMENT.

**Haut-Médoc** CANTEMERLE,
la LAGUNE, SOCIANDO-MALLET.

**Margaux** d'ANGLUDET, Ferrière,
LASCOMBES, Ch. MARGAUX,
PALMER, RAUZAN-SEGLA.

**Médoc** POTENSAC, la Tour-de-By.

**Pauillac** GRAND-PUY-LACOSTE,
HAUT-BAGES-LIBERAL, LAFITE-
ROTHSCHILD, LATOUR, LYNCH-BAGES,
MOUTON-ROTHSCHILD, PICHON-
LONGUEVILLE, PICHON-LONGUEVILLE-
LALANDE, PONTET-CANET.

**Pomerol** BON PASTEUR,
la Conseillante, l'Église-Clinet,
l'EVANGILE, GAZIN, LAFLEUR,
PETRUS, le PIN, TROTANOY, VIEUX-
CH.-CERTAN.

**St-Émilion** l'ANGELUS, AUSONE,
BEAU-SEJOUR-BECOT, CANON,
CHEVAL-BLANC, FIGEAC,
MAGDELAINE, PAVIE.

**St-Estèphe** COS D'ESTOURNEL,
LAFON-ROCHET, MONTROSE,
les Ormes-de-Pez.

**St-Julien** BEYCHEVELLE, DUCRU-
BEAUCAILLOU, GRUAUD-LAROSE,
LANGOA-BARTON, LEOVILLE-BARTON,
LEOVILLE-LAS-CASES, LEOVILLE-
POYFERRE.

# BORDEAUX WHITE WINES

*Bordeaux, France*

 This is France's largest fine wine region but except for the sweet wines of Sauternes and Barsac, Bordeaux's international reputation is based solely on its reds. No one gives much thought to the area's other whites, despite the fact that they account for nearly a fifth of the 113,154ha (279,600 acres) of vines. Given the size of the region, the diversity of Bordeaux's white wines should come as no surprise. There are dry, medium and sweet styles, ranging from dreary to some of the most sublime white wines of all. Bordeaux's temperate southern climate – moderated by the influence of the Atlantic and of 2 rivers, the Dordogne and the Garonne, is ideal for white wine production, particularly south of the city along the banks of the Garonne.

## GRAPE VARIETIES

Sauvignon Blanc and Sémillon, the most important white grapes, are 2 varieties of considerable character and are usually blended together. They are backed up by smaller quantities of Muscadelle, Ugni Blanc and Colombard.

## DRY WINES

The last decade has seen enormous improvements, and the introduction of new technology and new ideas, many of them influenced by the New World, have transformed Bordeaux into one of France's most exciting white wine areas. The white wines, not only of Pessac-Léognan, an AC created for the best areas of the northern Graves in 1987, but also of basic Bordeaux Blanc and Entre-Deux-Mers, the 2 largest white wine ACs in Bordeaux, have improved beyond recognition.

## SWEET WINES

Bordeaux's most famous whites are its sweet wines made from grapes affected by noble rot, particularly those from Sauternes and Barsac. Quality improved dramatically during the 1980s as a string of fine vintages brought the wines fame, and the considerable price hike enabled many properties to make long-overdue improvements. On the other side of the Garonne river, Cadillac, Loupiac and Ste-Croix-du-Mont also make sweet wines, but these rarely attain the richness or complexity of a top Sauternes. They are considerably cheaper, however.

See also BARSAC, BORDEAUX, BORDEAUX SUPERIEUR, CERONS, COTES DE BLAYE, COTES DE BOURG, COTES DE FRANCS, ENTRE-DEUX-MERS, GRAVES, NOBLE ROT, PESSAC-LEOGNAN, PREMIERES COTES DE BLAYE, PREMIERES COTES DE BORDEAUX, STE-CROIX-DU-MONT, SAUTERNES; AND INDIVIDUAL CHATEAUX.

## BEST YEARS

(dry) **1996 95 94 90 89 88 87 86 85 83**; (sweet) (1996) (95) **90 89 88 86 83 81**

## BEST PRODUCERS

### Dry wines

*(Pessac-Léognan)* Dom. de CHEVALIER, Couhins-Lurton, de FIEUZAL, HAUT-BRION, LAVILLE-HAUT-BRION, la LOUVIERE, SMITH-HAUT-LAFITTE, la TOUR-MARTILLAC; *(Graves)* de Chantegrive, Clos Floridène; *(Entre-Deux-Mers)* Bonnet, de Fontenille; *(Bordeaux AC)* Alpha, Carsin, DOISY-DAENE (Sec), LYNCH-BAGES, Ch. MARGAUX (Pavillon Blanc), Reynon, de Sours, Thieuley; *(Premières Côtes de Blaye)* Haut-Bertinerie.

### Sweet wines

*(Sauternes and Barsac)* BASTOR-LAMONTAGNE, BROUSTET, CLIMENS, COUTET, DOISY-DAENE, DOISY-VEDRINES, de FARGUES, GILETTE, GUIRAUD, LAFAURIE-PEYRAGUEY, NAIRAC, Rabaud-Promis, Raymond-Lafon, RIEUSSEC, SUDUIRAUT, la Tour-Blanche, d'YQUEM; *(Graves)* Clos St-Georges, la Grave; *(Cérons)* Enclos du Ch. de Cérons; *(Loupiac)* de Ricaud; *(Ste-Croix-du-Mont)* Lousteau-Vieil, la Rame.

**BOUCHES-DU-RHÔNE, VIN DE PAYS DES** *Provence, France* Encompasses wines from 3 distinct areas – the coastal area, the area around Aix-en-Provence and the Camargue. Full-bodied, spicy reds predominate, but the rosés can be good, too. Best producers: Château Bas, l'Île St-Pierre, Lunard, Mas de Rey, de Valdition.

**BOURGOGNE AC** *Burgundy, France* Bourgogne is the French name anglicized as 'Burgundy'. As a generic AC, it mops up all the Burgundian wine with no specific AC of its own, resulting in massive differences in style and quality. The best wines (red and white) will usually come from a single grower's vineyards just outside the main village ACs of the COTE D'OR. In today's world of overblown prices such wines may be the only way we can afford the joys of fine Burgundy. If the wine is from a grower, the flavours should follow some sort of regional style. However, if the address on the label is that of a négociant, the wine could be from anywhere in Burgundy. Pinot Noir is the main red grape, with Gamay being used in the Mâconnais and BEAUJOLAIS. Red Bourgogne is usually light, overtly fruity in an up-front strawberry and cherry way, and should be drunk young (within 2–3 years). The rosé (from Pinot Noir) can be very pleasant but little is produced. Usually Bourgogne Blanc is a bone-dry Chardonnay wine from vineyards not considered quite good enough for a classier AC. Most straight white Burgundy should be drunk within 2 years. Best producers: (reds/growers) COCHE-DURY★, GERMAIN, Henri JAYER★, Pierre Morey, Parent, RION, Rossignol★; (reds/merchants) DROUHIN, JADOT, LABOURE-ROI, VALLET; (reds/co-ops) BUXY★, les Caves des Hautes-Côtes★; (whites/growers) Château de Meursault, Boyer-Martenot, COCHE-DURY★★, Javillier★, Jobard★, René Manuel, de Villaine; (whites/merchants) DROUHIN, FAIVELEY, JADOT★, JAFFELIN, LABOURE-ROI, Olivier LEFLAIVE★; (whites/co-ops) BUXY, les Caves des Hautes-Côtes. Best years: (reds) **1995 93 92 90**; (whites) **1995 94 93 92 90**. See also pages 66–9.

**BOURGOGNE ALIGOTÉ AC** See Aligoté.

**BOURGOGNE-CÔTE CHALONNAISE AC** *Côte Chalonnaise, Burgundy, France* The Côte Chalonnaise vineyards have gained enormously in importance recently, mainly because of spiralling prices on the Côte d'Or just to the north. This recent AC (1990) covers vineyards in the Saône-et-Loire *département* around the villages of Bouzeron, RULLY, MERCUREY, GIVRY and MONTAGNY. Best producers: Besson, BUXY co-op★, de Villaine. Best years: **1994 93 92 90**.

**BOURGOGNE GRAND ORDINAIRE AC** *Burgundy, France* This is the bottom rung of the Burgundy AC ladder. You won't find the wine abroad and even in Burgundy it's mostly sold as quaffing wine.

**BOURGOGNE-HAUTES-CÔTES DE BEAUNE AC** *Burgundy, France* As the supply of affordable Burgundy dwindled in the 1970s this backwater in the hills behind the great Côte de Beaune came into the spotlight. The red wines are fairly good and there is some pleasant, slightly sharp Chardonnay. Best producers: Bruck, les Caves des Hautes-Côtes★, Cornu, Durand, Jacob, Joillot, Lafouge, de Mandelot, de Mercey, Morot-Gaudry. Best years: (reds) **1995 93 90 89 88**; (whites) **1995 94 93 92 90**.

**BOURGOGNE-HAUTES-CÔTES DE NUITS AC** *Burgundy, France* Attractive, lightweight wines from the hills immediately behind the Côte de Nuits. So far the best wines are the reds, with an attractive cherry and plum flavour. The whites tend to be rather dry and flinty. In general drink young. Best producers: (reds) les Caves des Hautes-Côtes★, Dufouleur, Michel Gros★, Hudelot★, Thévenot-le-Brun; (whites) les Caves des Hautes-Côtes★, Chaley, Cornu, Devevey, Dufouleur, Hudelot, JAYER-GILLES★★, Moillard, Thévenot-le-Brun, Verdet★. Best years: (reds) **1995 93 90 89 88**; (whites) **1995 94 92 90**.

**BOURGOGNE-IRANCY AC**  See Irancy AC

**BOURGOGNE PASSE-TOUT-GRAINS AC** *Burgundy, France*  Almost always red, this is a mixture of Gamay with a minimum of one-third Pinot Noir. When young the former dominates, when old the latter. Best producers: BUXY co-op, Chaley, Charles, Cornu, Maison LEROY, RION★, Taupenot-Merme, Thomas.

**BOURGUEIL AC** *Loire Valley, France*  One of the LOIRE's best red wines comes from north of the river between the cities of Tours and Angers. Cabernet Franc is the main grape, topped up with a little Cabernet Sauvignon, and in hot years the results can be superb. If given 5–10 years of aging the wines can develop a wonderful raspberry and black-currant fragrance. Best producers: (reds) Amirault, Audebert (estate wines), Breton★, Caslot-Galbrun★, Chasle, Demont★, DRUET★★, Gambier, Lamé-Delille-Boucard★, Morin, des Raguenières★. Best years: 1996 **95 93 90 89 88 86 85**. See also St-Nicolas-de-Bourgueil.

**BOUVET-LADUBAY** *Saumur AC, Loire Valley, France*  Owned by the Champagne house TAITTINGER, Bouvet-Ladubay is not shy of promoting its wines, nor of charging high prices. The quality of the basic range (Bouvet Brut, Bouvet Rosé) is good. Cuvée Saphir, the top-selling wine, is over-sweet, but Trésor (Blanc★★ and Rosé★), fermented in oak casks, is very good. Weird and wonderful Rubis★ sparkling red is worth trying. Also sells non-sparkling wine from VOUVRAY and SAUMUR.

---

**BOUVIER**  Austrian and Slovenian grape short on acidity and so mainly used for sweet to ultra-sweet wines, where it achieves the richness but rarely manages to offer any other complexity. Best producers: KRACHER★, Opitz★, Unger, Weinkellerei Burgenland.

---

**BOUZY** *Coteaux Champenois AC, Champagne, France*  A leading CHAMPAGNE village growing good Pinot Noir, which is used mainly for *white* Champagne. However, in outstanding years, a little still red wine is made. It is light and high in acidity. Best producers: Bara, Georges Vesselle, Jean Vesselle. Best years: (1996) 95 93 **90 89 85**.

**BOWEN ESTATE** *Coonawarra, South Australia*  Doug Bowen makes some of COONAWARRA's best reds from estate grapes: peppery yet profound Shiraz★★ and Cabernet★★ with beautifully balanced flavours, although alcohol levels have been climbing very high recently. Chardonnay is presentable but less distinguished. Best years: (reds) 1994 **91 90 88 86 84 80 79**.

---

**BRACHETTO**  Piedmontese grape revived in dry versions and, with grow-ing popularity, in sweet, frothy types with a Muscat-like perfume, as exemplified by Brachetto d'Acqui DOC. Best producers: (dry) Correggia★, Scarpa★; (Brachetto d'Acqui) BANFI★, Braida★, Contero★, Gatti, Marenco★.

**CH. BRANAIRE★** *St-Julien AC, 4ème Cru Classé, Haut-Médoc, Bordeaux, France* One of ST-JULIEN's lesser lights, overshadowed by its classier neighbour BEYCHEVELLE, but now beginning to regain its form. Branaire has one of the highest percentages of Cabernet Sauvignon in the Médoc, yet its wines have a supple, chocolaty character with lots of aromatic fruit. These can be enjoyed after 4–5 years but will keep for a decade. Second wine: Ch. Duluc. Best years: (1996) (95) 94 **90 89 88 86 85 83 82.**

**BRAND'S LAIRA** *Coonawarra, South Australia* Low-profile COONAWARRA firm, owned by MCWILLIAMS, that is making big investments in new vineyards. An unsubtle, peachy Chardonnay★ is the best wine. There is also tobaccoey Cabernet and Cabernet-Merlot, limy Riesling, and peppery Original Vineyard Shiraz★.

**CH. BRANE-CANTENAC** *Margaux AC, 2ème Cru Classé, Haut-Médoc, Bordeaux, France* Owned by the wealthy Lurton family, Brane-Cantenac has not lacked investment in recent years but it doesn't show in the wines, which generally lack the concentration one expects from a Second Growth. Recent vintages do look a bit more promising. Second wine: Ch. Notton. Best years: (1996) (95) **90 89 88 86.**

**BRAUNEBERG** *Mosel, Germany* Small village in the Middle Mosel. Its most famous vineyard sites are Juffer and Juffer Sonnenuhr, whose wines have a honeyed richness and creamy gentleness rare in the Mosel. Best producers: Fritz HAAG★, RICHTER★★.

**BREAKY BOTTOM** *Sussex, England* Small vineyard tucked in the South Downs near Lewes, towards England's southern coast. Peter Hall is a wonderfully quirky, passionate grower, who makes dry, chunky Seyval Blanc★ that becomes creamy and honeyed and Burgundy-like after 3–4 years. His crisp Müller-Thurgau★ is full of hedgerow pungency.

**BREGANZE DOC** *Veneto, Italy* Small DOC in the hills east of Verona and north of Vicenza. A red primarily from Merlot and a dry white based on Tocai Friulano are supplemented by a range of varietals, including intense Cabernet and dry Vespaiolo. Best producers: Bartolomeo da Breganze CO-OP, MACULAN★★, Novello Villa Magna, Zonta (Vigneto Due Santi).

**BODEGAS BRETÓN** *Rioja DOC, Rioja, Spain* Pedro Bretón and winemaker Miguel Angel de Gregorio have set this winery apart from the bevy of commercially minded new bodegas launched in the mid-1980s. The single-vineyard Dominio de Conté★★ has become the best expression of their aim to return to RIOJA traditions of the long barrel-aging of wines from low-yielding vineyards. Best years: **1991 90 89.**

**GEORG BREUER** *Rüdesheim, Rheingau, Germany* Medium-sized estate run by Bernhard Breuer, who produces high-quality dry Riesling from vineyards on the Rüdesheimer Berg Schlossberg★★ and Rauenthaler Nonnenberg★★. Wines like the Rivaner (Müller-Thurgau, fermented dry) and the Grauer Burgunder have a little oak. Best years: 1996 **95 94 93 90.**

**BRIDGEHAMPTON** *Long Island AVA, New York State, USA* Outstanding Chardonnay★★ and late-harvest Riesling★★; however, it is the Merlot★★ that has come on fast to become the showcase wine. Best years: **1995 93 92.**

**BRIGHT BROTHERS** *Ribatejo, Portugal* Australian Peter Bright (formerly of J P VINHOS) has turned flying winemaker with his own company, making wines as far afield as Spain, Sicily and Argentina. Portugal is still the crux of his business, with wines from ESTREMADURA, BAIRRADA, the DOURO and (mainly) the RIBATEJO. Bright combines his enthusiasm for native varieties, like the spicy red Baga, fragrant Arinto and creamy-spicy Fernão Pires, with foreign varietals like Chardonnay, Sauvignon Blanc, Cabernet Sauvignon and Merlot.

**BROUILLY AC** *Beaujolais, Burgundy, France* The largest of the 10 BEAUJOLAIS Crus and the wine is inconsistent as a result. At its best, it's soft and fruity and gorgeously gluggable. It can also make the best BEAUJOLAIS NOUVEAU of all. Best producers: la Chaize, DUBOEUF (Combillaty, Garanches), Fessy★, Fouilloux, Hospices de Beaujeu★ (especially Pissevieille Cuvée), Alain Michaud, Pierreux, Dom. Rolland, Ruet, Ch. des Tours★. Best years: **1995 94 93 91**.

**CH. BROUSTET★** *Barsac AC, 2ème Cru Classé, Bordeaux, France* Good, pretty rich, sweet wine made to a high standard. Not a lot is produced (much of the wine is sold off under the Ch. de Ségur label). Best years: (1996) (95) **90 89 88 86 85**.

**BROWN BROTHERS** *North-East Victoria, Australia* Conservative but highly successful family winery that has way outgrown its small producer 'dad, mum and the boys' tag. There is a big emphasis on varietal table wines – Italian varietals are a new speciality – while vintage fizz is a rapidly rising star. Focussing on cool King Valley and mountain-top Whitlands for its premium grapes.

**BRÜNDLMAYER** *Kamptal, Niederösterreich, Austria* The top estate in Langenlois, Austria's most productive wine town. Willi Bründlmayer makes wine in a variety of Austrian and international styles, but his dry Riesling★★ and Gruner Veltliner★★ are the best. Good Sekt. Best years: 1995 **94 93 92 91 90 86 83 79**.

**BRUNELLO DI MONTALCINO DOCG** *Tuscany, Italy* The dynamic southern Tuscan zone of Montalcino is famous for its powerful red wine produced from Sangiovese (known locally as Brunello). Traditionally these wines have needed over 10 years to soften, but modern practices result in some wines which are packed with fruit, covering the tannins in their youth. Capable of aging into a spectacularly complex wine. Best producers: ALTESINO (Montesoli★★), ARGIANO★★, BANFI★★, Barbi★, BIONDI SANTI★, Caparzo★★, Casanova di Neri★★, Case Basse★★, La Cerbaiola★★, Cerbaiona★★, Ciacci Piccolomini d'Aragona★★, Col d'Orcia★★, Costanti★★★, FRESCOBALDI (Castelgiocondo★★), Fuligni★★, La Gerla★, Maurizio Lambardi★★★, Lisini★★, Mastrojanni★★, Pieve Santa Restituta★★, Poggio Antico★★, Il Poggiolo★★, Il Poggione★, Talenti★★. Best years: (1996) (95) 94 93 **91 90 88 85 83 82**.

**BRUT** French term for dry sparkling wines, especially CHAMPAGNE. Thought of as the driest style of fizz, although Brut Champagne can have up to 15g per litre of sugar added before bottling. Brut Zéro is the driest of all but rare. Extra Dry, Sec and Demi-Sec are all sweeter than Brut.

**BUÇACO PALACE HOTEL** *Beira Litoral, Portugal* Flamboyant 19th-century hotel with its own wines★★, which it lists in a profusion of vintages. They're some of the most interesting in Portugal, subtle and flavoursome, made from grapes from neighbouring DAO and BAIRRADA.

# BURGUNDY RED WINES

*Burgundy, France*

 Rich in history and gastronomic tradition, the region of Burgundy (Bourgogne in French) covers a vast tract of eastern France, running from Auxerre, just south of Paris, to the city of Lyon. As with its white wines, Burgundy's red wines are extremely diverse, sometimes frustratingly so. The explanation for this lies partly in the fickle nature of Pinot Noir, the area's principal red grape, and partly in the historic imbalance of supply and demand between growers – who grow the grapes and make and bottle much of the best wine – and merchants, whose efforts have established the reputation of the wines internationally.

## GRAPE VARIETIES

Pinot Noir is one of the world's most ancient varieties, prone to mutation – there are several dozen variations in Burgundy alone – and the range of flavours you get from the grape vividly demonstrates this. A red Épineuil from near Auxerre in the north of the region will be light, chalky, strawberry-flavoured; a Pinot from the Mâconnais toward Lyon will be rough and rooty; and in between in the Côte d'Or – the heartland of red Burgundy – the flavours sweep through strawberry, raspberry, damson and cherry to a wild, magnificent maturity of Oriental spices, chocolate and truffles. Gamay, the grape of Beaujolais to the south, is best at producing juicy fruit flavours of strawberry and plum, demanding neither aging nor undue respect.

## WINE REGIONS

The top red Burgundies come from the Côte d'Or, home to world-famous Grand Cru vineyards like Clos de Vougeot, Chambertin, Musigny, Richebourg and la Tâche. Givry and Mercurey in the Côte Chalonnaise are up-and-coming, as are the Hautes-Côtes hills behind the Côte d'Or, and light but pleasant reds as well as good pink sparkling Crémant can be found near Chablis in the north. Mâconnais' reds are generally earthy and dull. Beaujolais really is best at producing bright, breezy wines full of fruit, for quaffing at a mere one year old.

See also ALOXE-CORTON, AUXEY-DURESSES, BEAUJOLAIS, BEAUNE, BLAGNY, BONNES-MARES, BOURGOGNE, CHAMBERTIN, CHAMBOLLE-MUSIGNY, CHASSAGNE-MONTRACHET, CHOREY-LES-BEAUNE, CLOS DE LA ROCHE, CLOS ST-DENIS, CLOS DE TART, CLOS DE VOUGEOT, CORTON, COTE DE BEAUNE, COTE DE NUITS, COTE D'OR, CREMANT DE BOURGOGNE, ECHEZEAUX, FIXIN, GEVREY-CHAMBERTIN, GIVRY, LADOIX, MACON, MARSANNAY, MERCUREY, MEURSAULT, MONTHELIE, MOREY-ST-DENIS, MOULIN-A-VENT, MUSIGNY, NUITS-ST-GEORGES, PERNAND-VERGELESSES, PULIGNY-MONTRACHET, RICHEBOURG, LA ROMANEE-CONTI, ROMANEE-ST-VIVANT, RULLY, ST-AUBIN, ST-ROMAIN, SAVIGNY-LES-BEAUNE, LA TÂCHE, VOLNAY, VOSNE-ROMANEE, VOUGEOT; AND INDIVIDUAL PRODUCERS.

PRODUCE OF FRANCE

RE

1993

## CLOS-VOUGEOT

### GRAND CRU

APPELLATION CLOS-VOUGEOT CONTROLÉE

MIS EN BOUTEILLES A LA PROPRIÉTÉ

DOMAINE RENÉ ENGEL
A VOSNE-ROMANÉE, CÔTE-D'OR, FRANCE

CETTE CUVÉE AYANT DONNÉ 4800 BOUTEILLES
CETTE BOUTEILLE PORTE LE          Nº  03607
75ML 13.5% Alc. by. vol.

# BURGUNDY WHITE WINES

*Burgundy, France*

White Burgundy has for generations been thought of as the world's leading dry white wine. The top wines have a remarkable succulent richness of honey and hazelnut, melted butter and sprinkled spice, yet are totally dry. Such wines are all from the Chardonnay grape and are generally grown in the communes of Aloxe-Corton, Meursault, Puligny-Montrachet and Chassagne-Montrachet, where limestone soils and aspect of the vineyard provide perfect conditions for the slow ripening of grapes.

*WINE STYLES*

However, Burgundy encompasses many more wine styles than this, even if none of them quite attain the peaks of quality of those 4 villages on the Côte de Beaune.

Chablis in the north traditionally produces very good steely wines, aggressive and tart when young, but nutty and rounded – though still very dry – after a few years. Modern Chablis is generally a softer, milder wine, easy to drink young, and sometimes nowadays enriched with aging in new oak barrels.

There is no doubt that Meursault and the other Côte d'Or villages can produce stupendous wine, but it is in such demand that unscrupulous producers are often tempted to maximize yields and cut corners on quality. Consequently white Burgundy from these famous villages must be approached with caution. Lesser-known villages like Pernand-Vergelesses and St-Aubin often provide good wine at lower prices.

The Côte Chalonnaise is becoming more interesting for quality white wine now that oak barrels are being used more often for aging. Rully and Montagny are the most important villages, though Givry and Mercurey can produce nice white, too.

The minor Aligoté grape makes some reasonable acidic wine, especially in Bouzeron. Further south the Mâconnais is a large region, two-thirds planted with Chardonnay. Most of the wine is dull and flat and not all that cheap, but there is some fair sparkling Crémant de Bourgogne, and some good vineyard sites, in particular in St-Véran and in Pouilly-Fuissé, where an occasional stunning wine can be found.

---

See also ALOXE-CORTON, AUXEY-DURESSES, BATARD-MONTRACHET, BEAUJOLAIS, BEAUNE, BOURGOGNE, CHABLIS, CHASSAGNE-MONTRACHET, CORTON, CORTON-CHARLEMAGNE, COTE DE BEAUNE, COTE DE NUITS, COTE D'OR, CREMANT DE BOURGOGNE, FIXIN, GIVRY, LADOIX, MACON, MARSANNAY, MERCUREY, MEURSAULT, MONTAGNY, MONTHELIE, MONTRACHET, MOREY-ST-DENIS, MUSIGNY, NUITS-ST-GEORGES, PERNAND-VERGELESSES, PETIT CHABLIS, POUILLY-FUISSE, POUILLY-LOCHE, POUILLY-VINZELLES, PULIGNY-MONTRACHET, RULLY, ST-AUBIN, ST-ROMAIN, ST-VERAN, SAVIGNY-LES-BEAUNE, VOUGEOT; AND INDIVIDUAL PRODUCERS.

## BEST YEARS

1996 **95 92 90 89**

## BEST PRODUCERS

**Chablis** DAUVISSAT, Defaix, DROIN, Fèvre, Grossot, Louis MICHEL, RAVENEAU, G Robin, Simmonet-Febvre, Vocoret.

**Côte d'Or** Ampeau, Blain-Gagnard, Bonneau du Martray, CARILLON, COCHE-DURY, Marc COLIN, Colin-Deléger, Fontaine Gagnard, J-N GAGNARD, GAGNARD-DELAGRANGE, Javillier, F Jobard, LAFON, Laguiche, Dom. LEFLAIVE, Matrot, Michelot, Albert Morey, Jean-Marc Morey, Pierre Morey, Niellon, RAMONET, Roulot, Sauzet, Thénard, TOLLOT-BEAUT.

**Côte Chalonnaise** Jacqueson, RODET, de Villaine.

**Mâconnais** Bonhomme, Corsin, Denogent, J-M Drouin, Ferret, Forest, Ch. FUISSE, Goyard, Guffens-Heynen, Lassarat, Léger-Plumet, Luquet, Merlin, Thévenet.

**Merchants** DROUHIN, DUBOEUF, FAIVELEY, JADOT, LABOURE-ROI, Louis LATOUR, Olivier LEFLAIVE, Maison LEROY, RODET, Verget.

**Co-ops** BUXY, la CHABLISIENNE, Lugny, Prissé, Viré.

**BUCELAS DOC** *Estremadura, Portugal* A tiny but historic DOC. The wines are white, have very high acidity and need long aging. The torch had been kept flickering by CAVES VELHAS, but now there are at least 4 others. The most recent arrival, Quinta da Romeira, achieves exciting results. Best producers: Quinta da Murta, Quinta da Romeira.

**BUENA VISTA** *Carneros AVA, California, USA* Clear, lucid, appealing wines, especially a delicious Pinot Noir and a fairly simple but tasty unoaked Sauvignon. In a Reserve line Chardonnay★ and Cabernet are capable of aging. Best years: (Cabernet Reserve) **1994** 91 90.

**BUGEY** See Vin du Bugey VDQS.

**VON BUHL** *Deidesheim, Pfalz, Germany* Large, mainly Riesling estate which is currently leased to the Japanese Sanyo group. The wines are rarely subtle, but usually have a strong, confident Riesling character. Best years: 1996 **94 90** 89.

**BUITENVERWACHTING** *Constantia WO, South Africa* Beautifully restored property which has set the quality tone for the area since 1985. Whites established its reputation: a graceful, intricate Chardonnay★★, invigorating, ripe Sauvignon★★ and light, racily dry Riesling★. Reds are now elevated to a similar standing by Christine★★, an aristocratic Bordeaux blend. Best years: (whites) **1996 95 94 93 92 91**; (reds) **1992** 91 90 89.

**BULL'S BLOOD** *Eger, Hungary* Bull's Blood is no longer the barrel-chested red it once was; as Kékfrankos (Blaufränkisch) grapes have replaced Kadarka in the blend, the blood has somewhat thinned. Its legendary ability to inspire Magyar warriors is but a faint stain in the glass.

**GRANT BURGE** *Barossa Valley, South Australia* Former Krondorf guiding light now controls a large area of Barossa vineyards from which he makes chocolaty Shiraz★★ and Cabernet★, opulent Chardonnay★ and oaky Sémillon. Top label is rich but somewhat over-oaked Meshach★.

**BURGENLAND** *Austria* State bordering Hungary, with 4 wine regions: Neusiedler See, including the Seewinkel with its sweet Prädikat wines; Neusiedler See-Hügelland, famous for sweet wines, but also making big reds and fruity, dry whites; Mittelburgenland, which produces robust Blaufränkisch reds; and Südburgenland with some good reds and dry whites. Best producers: FEILER-ARTINGER★★★, KRACHER★★★.

**BURGUNDY** See Bourgogne AC and pages 66–69.

**BÜRKLIN-WOLF** *Wachenheim, Pfalz, Germany* With nearly 100ha (250 acres) of vineyards, this is one of Germany's largest privately owned estates, which celebrated its 400th anniversary in 1997. Under new director Christian von Guradze it has shot back up to the first rank of the region's producers since the 94 vintage. Regular wines are now ★ to ★★, with the magnificent dessert wines ★★★. Best years: 1996 95 **94 93 90 89 86 85**.

**BURRWEILER** *Pfalz, Germany* An exception in the PFALZ, Burrweiler is the region's only wine village whose vineyards have a slate soil like that of the MOSEL, most notably in the excellent Schäwer site. Produces elegant dry Rieslings and some fine dessert wines. Best producer: Herbert Messmer★.

**BUXY, CAVE DES VIGNERONS DE** *Côte Chalonnaise, Burgundy, France* Based in the Côte Chalonnaise, this is among Burgundy's top co-ops, producing affordable, well-made Chardonnay and Pinot Noir. The light, oak-aged BOURGOGNE Pinot Noir★ and the red and white Clos de Chenôves★, as well as the nutty, white MONTAGNY★, are all good and, hallelujah, reasonably priced.

**BUZET AC** *South-West France* Good Bordeaux-style red wines from the same mix of grapes and at a lower price. There is very little rosé and the whites are rarely exciting. Best producers: Buzet-sur-Baïse co-op (especially Baron d'Ardeuil and Ch. de Gueyze), Tissot.

**CA' DEL BOSCO** *Franciacorta DOCG, Lombardy, Italy* Model estate, headed by Maurizio Zanella, making some of Italy's finest and most expensive wines: outstanding FRANCIACORTA Brut★★, Dosage Zero★★ and Satèn★★ sparklers, good Terre di Franciacorta Rosso★, remarkably good Chardonnay★★, Pinèro★★ (Pinot Nero) and a Bordeaux blend, Maurizio Zanella★.

**CABARDÈS VDQS** *Languedoc, France* This wine region neighbours MINERVOIS but, as well as the usual Mediterranean grape varieties, Cabernet Sauvignon and Merlot are allowed. At its best, full-bodied, chewy and rustically attractive. Best producers: Salitis, de Ventenac.

**CABERNET D'ANJOU AC** *Loire Valley, France* Higher in alcohol than ROSÉ D'ANJOU and generally slightly sweeter. Drink young and fresh as a rule but it is still possible to find remarkable old vintages. Best producers: Bertrand, Daviau, Ogereau, Verdier.

**CABERNET FRANC** Often unfairly dismissed as an inferior Cabernet Sauvignon, Cabernet Franc comes into its own in cooler areas or areas where the soil is damper and heavier. It can have a grassy freshness linked to a raw but tasty blackcurrant and raspberry fruit. In France it thrives in the LOIRE VALLEY and Bordeaux, especially in ST-EMILION and POMEROL where it accounts for 19% of the surface planted. Italy has used the variety with considerable success for generations in the north-east. Plantings of Cabernet Franc on California's North Coast are showing promise as both a blending wine and a single varietal bottling. There are also a few good examples from South Africa.

**CABERNET SAUVIGNON** See pages 72–3.

**CAHORS AC** *South-West France* The leading red wine region of the South-West after BORDEAUX. The dark, tannic wine is made from at least 70% Auxerrois (Bordeaux's Malbec) and has an unforgettable flavour of plum and raisin richness. With age it takes on a deep tobaccoey, spicy hue. Best producers: la Caminade, Cayrou★, de Cèdre, Côtes d'Olt co-op, la Coutale★, de Gamot★, Gaudou★, Haute-Serre★★, Quattre★, Triguedina★★. Best years: 1995 **92 90 89 88 86 85**.

**CAIN CELLARS** *Napa Valley AVA, California, USA* This Spring Mountain estate appears to be going solidly on track. The Cain Five★★ is a particularly pleasing Bordeaux blend, which can be a bit slow off the mark but is worth waiting for. Also a lower-priced Cain Cuvée and strongly flavoured Sauvignon Musque are regular items. Best years: (Cain Five) 1994 93 **92 91 90 87 86 85**.

**CALABRIA** *Italy* The 'toe' of Italy is one of its poorest regions. CIRO, Donnici and Savuto, reds from the native Gaglioppo grape, and whites from Greco, are much improved thanks to greater wine-making expertise.

# CABERNET SAUVIGNON

Wine made from Cabernet Sauvignon in places like Bulgaria, Chile, Australia, California, even in parts of southern France, has become so popular that many people may not realize where it all started – and how Cabernet has managed to become the great, all-purpose, omnipresent red wine grape of the world.

## WINE STYLES

**Bordeaux Cabernet** It all began in Bordeaux. With the exception of a clutch of Merlot-based beauties in St-Émilion and Pomerol, all the greatest red Bordeaux wines are based on Cabernet Sauvignon, with varying amounts of Merlot, Cabernet Franc, and possibly Petit Verdot and Malbec also blended in. The blending is necessary because by itself Cabernet makes such a strong, powerful, aggressive and assertive wine. Dark and tannic when young, the great Bordeaux wines need 10–20 years for the aggression to fade, the fruit becoming sweet and perfumed as fresh blackcurrants, with a fragrance of cedarwood, of cigar boxes mingling magically among the fruit. It is this character which has made red Bordeaux famous for at least 2 centuries.

**Cabernet Worldwide** When winemakers in other parts of the world sought role models to try to improve their wines, most of them automatically chose Cabernet Sauvignon. It was lucky that they did, because not only is this variety easy to grow in almost all conditions – cool or warm, dry or damp – but that unstoppable personality always powers through. The cheaper wines are generally made to accentuate the blackcurrant fruit and the slightly earthy tannins. They are drinkable young, but able to age surprisingly well. The more ambitious wines are aged in oak barrels, often new ones, to enhance the tannin yet also to add spice and richness capable of developing over a decade or more. Sometimes the Cabernet is blended – usually with Merlot, but occasionally, as in Australia, with Shiraz.

**European Cabernets** Many vineyards in southern France now produce excellent, affordable Cabernet. Some of the best wines from Spain have been Cabernet, and Portugal has also had success. Italy's red wine quality revolution was sparked off by the success of Cabernet in Tuscany; Austria is beginning to crack the grape's code and even southern Germany is having a go. Eastern Europe, in particular Bulgaria, provides us with some of the most affordable, decent quality reds in the world.

**New World Cabernets** California's reputation was created by its strong, weighty Cabernets, though in recent vintages winemakers are working with a lighter hand. Both Australia and New Zealand place more emphasis on easy fruit in their Cabernets. Chile has made the juicy, blackcurranty style very much her own, and Argentina and South Africa are showing they want to join in too.

72

## BEST PRODUCERS

### France

*Bordeaux* COS D'ESTOURNEL, Dom. de CHEVALIER, GRUAUD-LAROSE, LAFITE-ROTHSCHILD, LATOUR, LEOVILLE-LAS-CASES, LYNCH-BAGES, Ch. MARGAUX, MOUTON-ROTHSCHILD, PICHON-LONGUEVILLE, RAUZAN-SEGLA; *Midi* MAS DE DAUMAS GASSAC, RICHEAUME, TREVALLON.

### Other European Cabernets

*Italy* ANTINORI, GAJA, ISOLE E OLENA, MACULAN, ORNELLAIA, REGALEALI, Marchese Incisa della Rochetta (SASSICAIA).

*Spain* GUELBENZU (Evo), Jean LEON, MARQUES DE GRINON, TORRES (Mas La Plana).

### New World Cabernets

*Australia* CAPE MENTELLE, CHAPEL HILL, CULLENS, HENSCHKE, LECONFIELD, MOSS WOOD, PENFOLDS (Bin 707), PENLEY ESTATE, PETALUMA, WYNNS, YARRA YERING.

*New Zealand* MATUA VALLEY Ararimu, MONTANA (Church Road Reserve), STONYRIDGE Larose, TE MATA Coleraine, Te Motu, VAVASOUR, Vidal (Reserve).

*USA* (California) ARROWOOD, BERINGER (Reserve), CAYMUS (Special Selection), DIAMOND CREEK, DUNN, HESS COLLECTION, LAUREL GLEN, MONDAVI (Reserve), NEWTON, Joseph PHELPS, RIDGE, SHAFER, SILVER OAK, STAG'S LEAP; (Washington) LEONETTI.

*Chile* CARMEN, ERRAZURIZ, PORTA.

*South Africa* Neil ELLIS, Plaisir de Merle, THELEMA.

**CÁLEM** *Port DOC, Douro, Portugal*   The largest family-owned Portuguese port shipper. Best are aged tawnies★ and Colheitas★★, with endless layers of flavour. Best years: (Colheitas) **1962 57**; (vintage ports) **1975 70**.

**CALERA** *San Benito, California, USA*   A pace-setter for California Pinot Noir with 4 different estate wines: Reed Vineyard★★, Selleck Vineyard★★★, Jensen Vineyard★★★ and Mills★. They are complex, balanced wines with power and originality and are capable of aging. Mt Harlan Chardonnay★★ looks set to be excitingly original too. Small amounts of Viognier★★★ are succulent with sensuous fruit. Best years: (reds) 1994 **92 91 90 88 87 86 85**; (whites) **1995 94 92 91**.

**CALIFORNIA** *USA*   California's importance is not simply in being the leading wine producer in the USA – the state's influence on the world of wine is far wider than that. Most of the great revolutions in technology and style that have transformed the expectations and achievements of winemakers in every country of the world – including France – were born in the ambitions of a band of Californian winemakers during the 60s and 70s. They challenged the old order with its regulated, self-serving élitism, democratizing the world of fine wine, to the benefit of every wine drinker. This revolutionary fervour is less evident now. And there are times recently when Californians seem too intent on establishing their own particular New World old order. A few figures: there are 141,530ha (350,000 acres) of wine grapes, producing over 450 million gallons of wine annually, about 90% of all wine made in the USA. A large proportion comes from the hot, inland Central Valley. See also Central Coast, Central Valley, Mendocino County, Monterey County, Napa County, San Luis Obispo County, Santa Barbara County, Sonoma County.

**CALITERRA** *Curicó, Chile*   The new joint venture with MONDAVI designed to promote and sell Caliterra wines in the US. Winemaker Irene Poiva has built up an impressive portfolio of 1996 wines: sprightly citrus-edged Chardonnay★★ from CASABLANCA, silky Curicó Merlot★ and an intense, grassy Sauvigon Blanc★. Whites impress more than reds.

**CH. CALON-SÉGUR★** *St-Estèphe AC, 3ème Cru Classé, Haut-Médoc, Bordeaux, France*   For a long time this was considered one of ST-ESTEPHE's leading châteaux. However, in the mid-1980s the wines were not as good as they should have been, given their high price. Recent vintages have been more impressive, and the best wines may be cellared for 10 years. Second wine: Marquis de Ségur. Best years: (1996) (95) 94 93 **90 89 86 82**.

**CAMBRIA WINERY** *Santa Maria Valley AVA, California, USA*   With over 500ha (1200 acres) at his disposal, owner Jess Jackson developed the biggest (100,000-case) winery in SANTA BARBARA COUNTY. Most of the production is Chardonnay (Katherine's Vineyard and Reserve★), with the remainder devoted to Pinot Noir, Syrah and Sangiovese. Look for fine Julia's Vineyard Pinot Noir★.

**CAMPANIA** *Italy*   The region of Naples and Vesuvius has been a desert for the wine lover, but more through inertia than any intrinsic viticultural defects. Until recently, that is. Certain producers besides the venerable MASTROBERARDINO have finally begun to realize the eminent potential of its soil, climate and grape varieties. DOCs of note are FALERNO DEL MASSICO, Fiano di Avellino, Greco di Tufo, Ischia, LACRYMA CHRISTI DEL VESUVIO and TAURASI. But the revelation is a Vino da Tavola called Montevetrano★★, from Cabernet, Merlot and Aglianico made at the Montevetrano estate near Salerno.

**CAMPILLO** *Rioja DOC, País Vasco, Spain*   The relaunch of Campillo (an upmarket subsidiary of FAUSTINO MARTINEZ) has produced some of the most exciting new red RIOJAS★★ seen for several years. The wines are pure Tempranillo, with masses of ripe, velvety fruit. Best years: **1994 89 87 86 85 82 81**.

**CAMPO VIEJO** *Rioja DOC, Rioja, Spain*   The largest producer of RIOJA. The Reservas★ and Gran Reservas★ are reliably good, as are the elegant, all-Tempranillo Reserva Viña Alcorta★ and the barrel-fermented white Viña Alcorta★. Albor is one of the best modern young Riojas, packed with fresh, pastilley fruit. Best years: (reds) **1994 91 89 88 87 85 83 82 80 78**.

**CANARY ISLANDS** *Spain*   Four DOs for the Canaries? Yes indeed – Tacoronte-Acentejo, Lanzarote, La Palma and Ycoden-Daute-Isora. The Malvasia from Lanzarote is worth trying, otherwise stick with the young reds, which are made mostly from Listán Negro. Best producers: Bodegas Monje, Viña Norte.

**CANBERRA DISTRICT** *New South Wales, Australia*   Cool, high altitude (800m/2600 ft) may sound good but such conditions here present many difficulties. Lark Hill makes exciting Riesling, Doonkuna refined Chardonnay and Shiraz, and Clonakilla surprisingly good Shiraz (with a dollop of Viognier). Best producers: Brindabella Hills, Clonakilla, Doonkuna, Helm's, Lark Hill (whites).

**CANEPA** *Maipo, Chile*   Family feuds and the departure of talented wine-maker Andrés Ilabaca will mean that this MAIPO giant will have to be watched closely. Ilabeca's legacy is an impressive range of reds, including a spicy Zinfandel★, Merlot★ and a Private Reserve Cabernet Sauvignon★ with great aging potential.

**CANNONAU** Sardinian grape variety essentially the same as Spain's Garnacha and France's Grenache Noir. In SARDINIA it produces deep, tannic reds but the modern, dry red table wines are gaining in popularity. Traditional sweet and fortified styles can still be found. Best producers: (lighter, modern styles) Argiolas, SELLA & MOSCA★, and Dolianova, Dorgali, Jerzu, Ogliastra and Oliena co-ops.

**CH. CANON★★** *St-Émilion Grand Cru AC, 1er Grand Cru Classé, Bordeaux, France*   Canon makes some of the richest, most concentrated ST-EMILIONS. It was purchased in 1996 by French fashion and perfume company Chanel, owners of Ch. RAUZAN-SEGLA in Margaux, so expect even greater things here. In good vintages the wine is impressively tannic to start with and will keep well for a dozen years or more. Second wine: Clos J Kanon. Best years: (1996) (95) 93 90 89 88 **86 85 83 82 81 79 78**.

**CANON-FRONSAC AC** *Bordeaux, France*  This AC is the heart of the FRONSAC region. The wines are quite strong when young but can age for 10 years or more. Best producers: Barrabaque, Canon★, Canon-de-Brem★, Canon-Moueix, Cassagne-Haut-Canon, la Fleur-Cailleau, Haut-Mazeris, Moulin-Pey-Labrie, Vrai-Canon-Bouché, Vrai-Canon-Boyer. Best years: (1996) 95 **94 90 89 88 85 83 82 79 78**.

**CH. CANTEMERLE**★★ *Haut-Médoc AC, 5ème Cru Classé, Bordeaux, France*  Since the wine-making has been handled by the large merchant house of Cordier, Cantemerle has improved beyond recognition. In general the wine is relatively delicate, needing only 5–7 years' aging. Second wine: Villeneuve de Cantemerle. Best years: **1990 89 83 82**.

**CANTERBURY** *South Island, New Zealand*  The long, cool ripening season of the arid central coast of South Island favours white varieties, particularly Chardonnay, Pinot Gris, Sauvignon Blanc and Riesling, as well as Pinot Noir. The northerly Waipara district produces Canterbury's most exciting wines, especially from Riesling and Pinot Noir. Best producers: GIESEN★, Pegasus Bay, Mark Rattray, ST HELENA★, Sherwood Estate.

**CANTINA SOCIALE** Italian for co-op, an important force in Italian viniculture, controlling about 60% of the country's production.

**CAPE MENTELLE** *Margaret River, Western Australia*  This leading MARGARET RIVER winery, together with New Zealand offshoot CLOUDY BAY, is majority-owned by VEUVE CLICQUOT. Its visionary founder, David Hohnen, produces full-throttle Cabernet★★ and Shiraz★★, impressive Chardonnay★★, tangy Sémillon-Sauvignon Blanc★★ and wonderfully chewy Zinfandel★★ which effectively expresses Hohnen's California training. All wines benefit from cellaring – whites up to 5 years, reds 8–10. Best years: (reds) 1993 92 91 **90 88 86 83 82 78**.

**CAPEL VALE** *South-West Coastal Plain, Western Australia*  Radiologist Peter Pratten's winery makes fine Riesling★, Gewürztraminer, Chardonnay★★ and Sémillon-Sauvignon Blanc★. The reds are big and rather stolid but the 93 Shiraz★ stands out like a beacon. Best years: (whites) **1995 93 92 91**.

**CARBONIC MACERATION** See Macération carbonique.

**CH. CARBONNIEUX** *Pessac-Léognan AC, Cru Classé de Graves, Bordeaux, France*  Carbonnieux is the largest of the GRAVES Classed Growth properties, now part of the PESSAC-LEOGNAN AC. The white wine★ has improved considerably since 1988, profiting from the introduction of 50% new oak. The red★ sometimes seems to lack stuffing, but has also gained in complexity over the last few years. Second wine: la Tour-Léognan. Best years: (whites) 1996 95 **94 90 89 88 85**; (reds) (1996) (95) 93 **90 89 88 86**.

**CARCAVELOS DOC** *Estremadura, Portugal*  Carcavelos is a tiny, moribund DOC for an undistinguished brown fortified wine made from red and white grapes in the suburbs between Lisbon and Cascais. The wine from Quinta dos Pesos, the zone's only remaining estate, is ludicrously expensive.

**CAREMA DOC** *Piedmont, Italy* Tiny quantities of wine trickle from the Nebbiolo vines grown on the steep, rocky slopes of this small zone in northern PIEDMONT. Lighter than most other Nebbiolos, these wines can nevertheless have great elegance and perfume. Production is confined to 2 producers: the local co-op, and Luigi Ferrando, who makes a good White label★ and, in the best vintages, a superior Black label★★, which has the potential to age for up to 25 years. Best years: 1995 **93 90 89 88 85**.

**CARIGNAN** The dominant red grape in the south of France is responsible for much boring, cheap, harsh wine. But when made by carbonic maceration, the wine can have delicious spicy fruit. Old vines are capable of thick, rich, impressive reds. Although initially a Spanish grape (as Cariñena or Mazuelo), it is not that widespread there, but is useful for adding colour and acidity in RIOJA and CATALONIA. Also common in CALIFORNIA for everyday reds.

**CARIGNANO DEL SULCIS DOC** *Sardinia, Italy* In the south-west of the island, Carignano is DOC, and now starting to produce wines of quite startling quality. Rocca Rubia★★, a barrique-aged Riserva from the co-op at Santadi with rich, fleshy and chocolaty fruit, is one of SARDINIA's best reds. In a similar vein, but more structured and concentrated, is Terre Brune★★. Best producer: Santadi co-op. Best years: (Riservas) (1996) 95 **94 93 91 90 89 88**.

**LOUIS CARILLON & FILS** *Puligny-Montrachet AC, Côte de Beaune, Burgundy, France* An excellent, but formerly underrated family-owned estate in PULIGNY-MONTRACHET. The emphasis here is on traditional, slightly savage white wines of great concentration, rather than new oak. Look out for the 3 Premiers Crus – les Referts★★★, Champ Canet★★★ and les Perrières★★★ – and the tiny but exquisite production of Bienvenues-Bâtard-Montrachet★★★. The red wines – from CHASSAGNE-MONTRACHET★, ST-AUBIN★ and MERCUREY★ – are extremely good, too. Best years: (whites) 1995 94 93 **92 90 89 88**.

**CARIÑENA DO** *Aragón, Spain* The largest DO of ARAGON, baking under the mercilessly hot sun in inland eastern Spain, Cariñena has traditionally been a land of cheap, deep red, alcoholic wines from the Garnacha grape. However, a switch to Tempranillo grapes has begun, and some growers now pick early. Even so most Cariñena, red, white or rosé, is still cheap and cheerless. Best producer: Bodegas San Valero (Monte Ducay, Don Mendo).

**CARMEL** *Israel* Israel's biggest wine-producing company sources grapes from 200 different farmers to make crisp, citrus Sauvignon Blanc from the Golan Heights, jammy Cabernet Sauvignon and highly aromatic dry Muscat. Other varieties include Sémillon, Chardonnay, Shiraz and Petite Sirah.

**CARMEN** *Maipo, Chile* Sister winery to SANTA RITA, but worlds apart in terms of quality, Carmen's high-tech winery and innovative young winemaker Alvaro Espinoza are leading the MAIPO VALLEY pack. Best wines include complex, well-structured Cabernet Sauvignon Reserve★★, juicy, fruit-driven Merlot★★ and the new Grande Vidure Cabernet★. Whites are less successful but the Gewürztraminer-

77

Sauvignon blend shows intelligent innovation and the unoaked Sauvignon Blanc big improvement. Experimental plots of organic viticulture and Italian varietals make this a name to watch. Best year: 1996.

**CARMENET VINEYARD** *Sonoma Valley AVA, California, USA* Carmenet sets out to make Bordeaux-style reds and whites and is probably one of California's most successful exponents of both, producing deep, complex reds★★ and long-lived, barrel-fermented whites★★. Best years: (reds) 1994 **92 91 90 88 87 86**.

**CARMIGNANO DOCG** *Tuscany, Italy* Red wine from the west of Florence, renowned since the 16th century and revived in the 1960s by Ugo Contini Bonacossi, the dominant producer at the estates of Capezzana and Villa di Trefiano. Arguing that Cabernet had been planted in the zone in the 18th century, he brought back cuttings from LAFITE in Bordeaux for his own vineyards. The blend (85% Sangiovese-15% Cabernet) is one of Tuscany's more refined wines and can be very long-lived. Although Carmignano is DOCG for its red wine, notable as Riserva★★, DOC applies to a lighter red Barco Reale, a rosé called Vin Ruspo and fine VIN SANTO★. Best producers: Ambra, Artimino★, Bacchereto, Capezzana★, Le Farnete, Il Poggiolo, Villa di Trefiano★. Best years: (1996) 95 **94 93 90 88 85**.

**CARNEROS AVA** *California, USA* Hugging the northern edge of San Francisco Bay, Carneros includes parts of both NAPA and SONOMA counties. The area is windswept and chilly with heavy morning fog off the Bay and is one of California's top cool-climate areas, making it highly suitable for Chardonnay and Pinot Noir as both table wine and a base for sparkling wine. Merlot has been coming on strong here recently. Best producers: ACACIA★, Bouchaine★★, Carneros Creek★★, DOMAINE CARNEROS★★, MUMM NAPA (Winery Lake), RASMUSSEN★★, SAINTSBURY★★.

**CARNUNTUM** *Niederösterreich, Austria* Wine region south of the Danube and east of Vienna, with a strong red wine tradition. Best producer: Pittnauer.

**CARR TAYLOR** *Sussex, England* David Carr Taylor's long-established vineyard and winery north of Hastings has consistently produced good whites from Reichensteiner, Gutenborner and Schönburger, and he now has plans to turn even more attention to his trail-blazing sparkling wines, made from vines on south-facing chalk slopes.

**CASA LAPOSTOLLE** *Rapel, Chile* New joint venture between Marnier-Lapostolle and Chile's Rabat family, with Michel Rolland at the wine-making helm. The Cuvée Alexandre Merlot★★ and Chardonnay★ both have the intensity for several years' aging. All the wines highlight the quality of Rapel fruit. A new Cabernet Rosé★ is one of Chile's best. Best years: **1996 95**.

**CASABLANCA** *Chile* A coastal valley that is Chile's strongest (and some say only) proof of regional style. Whites dominate, with best results from the lesser-planted Sauvignon Blanc and Gewürztraminer. Best producers: CONCHA Y TORO★★, VIÑA CASABLANCA★★.

**CASSIS AC** *Provence, France* Cassis is a picturesque fishing port near Marseille and, because of its situation, its white wine is the most over-priced on the French Riviera. Based on Ugni Blanc and Clairette, the wine isn't that special, but can be good if fresh. The red wine is dull at best but the rosé can be pleasant (especially from a single estate).

Best producers: de Boudard, Clos Ste-Magdelaine, Ferme Blanche, Fontblanche, Fontcreuse.

**CASTEL DEL MONTE DOC** *Puglia, Italy* An arid, hilly zone, this is the ideal habitat for the Uva di Troia grape, which can be transformed into long-lived red wine of astonishing character. The rosé is good, and whites from international varieties are improving. Best producers: RIVERA★, Santa Lucia, Torrevento.

**CASTELLBLANCH** *Cava DO, Catalonia, Spain* One of the world's largest Champagne-method sparkling wine companies, owned by another giant CAVA company, FREIXENET. Brut Zero★ and Cristal are fresh and simple fizzes.

**CASTELL'IN VILLA** *Chianti Classico DOCG, Tuscany, Italy* This is one of Chianti's finest estates, producing notable CHIANTI CLASSICO★★ and Sangiovese-based Santacroce★★, which combine power, elegance and longevity in a way that few Tuscan wines ever manage. Some variation in quality in recent vintages. Best years: (1996) 95 **94** 93 **90 88 85**.

**CASTELLO DELLA SALA** *Orvieto DOC, Umbria, Italy* Belonging to the ANTINORI family, producing good ORVIETO★ and oak-aged Cervaro della Sala★★ (80% Chardonnay-20% Grechetto) that gets better with each vintage. Also Pinot Nero that is one of Italy's most impressive. The sweet wines, particularly Muffato della Sala★★, are good. Best years: (white) (1996) 95 **94 93 92 90 88 86**.

**CASTELLO DI AMA** *Chianti Classico DOCG, Tuscany, Italy* Model estate of CHIANTI CLASSICO, with outstanding single-vineyard bottlings of Riserva★★ (Bellavista and La Casuccia). Vigna L'Apparita★★ is one of Italy's best Merlots; less impressive Vigna Il Chiuso is made from Pinot Nero. Also good VIN SANTO★. Best years: (1996) (95) (94) **90 88 85**.

**CASTELL'SCHES DOMÄNENAMT** *Castell, Franken, Germany* Summerfresh Müller-Thurgau wines come from the Casteller Herrenberg and a classic Franconian Silvaner from the Casteller Hohnart. Dornfelders from here age well. Best known for its rich Ausleses★ from Rieslaner and Scheurebe grapes. Best years: **1993 92 90**.

**CASTILLA-LA MANCHA** *Spain* The biggest wine region in Spain – the biggest, indeed, in the world at over 700,000ha (1.73 million acres). It is hot, dry country with poor soil. The DOs of the central plateau, LA MANCHA and VALDEPEÑAS, make mostly white wines from the Airén grape, and some good reds from the Cencibel (Tempranillo). Méntrida DO and Almansa DO make rustic, sometimes pleasant reds. Interestingly, the most ambitious wines made in this region fall outside the various DOs, particularly those from MARQUES DE GRIÑON's Dominio de Valdepusa estate in Toledo and Manuel Manzaneque's Sierra de Alcaraz vineyards in Albacete province. See also Jumilla DO.

**CASTILLA Y LEÓN** *Spain* This is Spain's harsh, high plateau, with long cold winters and hot summers (but always cool nights). A few rivers, notably the Duero, temper this climate and afford fine conditions for viticulture. After many decades of wine-making ignorance, with a few exceptions like VEGA SICILIA, the situation has changed radically for the better in 2 of the region's DOs, RIBERO DEL DUERO and RUEDA, and is fast improving in the other 3, BIERZO, Cigales and TORO.

**VIGNERONS CATALANS** *Roussillon, France*  This Perpignan-based association of growers and co-ops sells a wide range of wines. Founded in 1964, it has encouraged members to invest in modern technology and to experiment with new grape varieties. Its COTES DU ROUSSILLON★ and COTES DU ROUSSILLON-VILLAGES★ blends are relentlessly consistent. There are now more exciting wines in Roussillon but none more reliable.

**CATALONIA** *Spain*  Standards vary among the region's 8 DOs. PENEDES, between Barcelona and Tarragona, has the greatest number of technically equipped wineries in Spain. ALELLA, up the coast, makes attractive whites, and inland COSTERS DEL SEGRE makes potentially excellent reds and whites at the RAIMAT estate. In the south, mountainous PRIORATO and the hills of Tarragona and Terra Alta, most producers are still behind the times. Ampurdán-Costa Brava, by the French border, has been sadly left in the quality trough of an easy local tourist market lapping up whatever is made. Catalonia also makes most of Spain's CAVA sparkling wines. See also Conca de Barberá.

**CATENA** *Mendoza, Argentina*  Argentina's most progressive and export-orientated wine producer. The Esmeralda winery produces top-quality international-style Chardonnay★★, oak-aged Cabernet Sauvignon★ and powerful Agrelo vineyard Malbec★, with second label Alamos Ridge providing excellent value for money. Catena's takeover of La Rural has delivered an intense new Malbec★ and soft, jammy Merlot★. Best years: **1996 95**.

**DOMAINE CAUHAPÉ** *Jurançon AC, South-West France*  Henri Ramonteu has been a major influence in JURANCON, proving that the area can make complex whites as well as more traditional sweet wines. Ramonteu is the leading producer of both, but his top wines are sweet Noblesse du Petit Manseng★★ and barrel-fermented Quintessence★★.

**CAVA DO** *Spain*  Cava, the Catalan and hence Spanish name for Champagne-method fizz, is made in 159 towns and villages in northern Spain, but more than 95% are in CATALONIA. Grapes used are the local trio of Parellada, Macabeo and Xarel-lo. The best-value, fruitiest Cavas are generally the youngest, with no more than the minimum 9 months' aging. Some good Catalan Cavas are made with Chardonnay. A number of top-quality wines are now produced but are seldom seen abroad, since their prices are too close to those of CHAMPAGNE to attract international customers. Best producers: Can Feixes, Castell de Villarnau, CASTELLBLANCH, CODORNIU (Anna de Codorníu★, Première Cuvée Brut Chardonnay★), FREIXENET, JUVE Y CAMPS★, MARQUES DE MONISTROL★, Parxet, RAIMAT, Raventós i Blanc, Rovellats★, Agustí Torelló, Jané Ventura.

**CAVE CO-OPÉRATIVE** French for a co-operative cellar, where members bring their grapes for vinification and bottling under a collective label. In terms of quantity, the French wine industry is dominated by co-ops. The best are excellent, but many lack both investment and a director of sufficient vision to persuade the members that the effort is worthwhile. Nevertheless, the quality of co-op wines has improved enormously in the last decade. Often use less workaday titles, such as Caves des Vignerons, Producteurs Réunies, Union des Producteurs or Cellier des Vignerons. See Buxy, Catalans, Cellier des Samsons, la Chablisienne, Mont Tauch, Oisly-et-Thésée, Plaimont, Sieur d'Arques.

**CAVES ALIANÇA** *Beira Litoral, Portugal*   Based in BAIRRADA, this is one of Portugal's largest wine companies. Definitely among Bairrada's modernists, Aliança makes crisp, fresh, whites and soft, approachable red Bairradas★, as well as buying in wine to blend good red DAO★ and DOURO★. Also has vineyards in the ALENTEJO. Best years: (reds) **1995 94 92**.

**CAVES SÃO JOÃO** *Beira Litoral, Portugal*   A traditional-seeming but discreetly modernist company. It was a pioneer of cool-fermented, white BAIRRADA, and has made some tremendous Cabernet Sauvignons from its own vines. It is best known for its rich, complex reds, including Frei João★ from Bairrada and Porta dos Cavalheiros★★ from DAO – they demand at least a decade of aging to show their quality. Look out for Reservas. Best years: (reds) **1992 91 88 85 83**.

**CAVES VELHAS** *Estremadura, Portugal*   Caves Velhas buys, blends, matures and sells wines from all over Portugal. Its non-DOC brands (Romeira, Caves Velhas Clarete and Caves Velhas Garrafeira) are largely made from wines bought in from the RIBATEJO or Palmela regions. For many years, it was the only commercial producer of the historic BUCELAS DOC, though the wine was hardly memorable.

**CAYMUS VINEYARDS** *Napa Valley AVA, California, USA*   Caymus Cabernet Sauvignon is a ripe, intense and generally tannic style, that is good in its regular bottling★ and can be outstanding as a Special Selection★★★. There is also excellent Zinfandel★. Mer & Soleil, a new label for MONTEREY Chardonnay, was an instant success. Best years: (Special Selection) (1995) (94) 92 91 **90 88 87 86 85 84 80**.

**DOMAINE CAZES** *Rivesaltes, Roussillon, France*   The Cazes brothers make outstanding MUSCAT DE RIVESALTES★★, RIVESALTES Vieux★★ and the superb Aimé Cazes★★★, but also produce a wide range of red and white table wines, mainly as COTES DU ROUSSILLON and Vin de Pays des Côtes Catalanes. Look out for the soft, fruity le Canon du Maréchal★ and the small production of barrel-fermented Chardonnay. In 1996 they launched the Cabernet-based le Credo, a Vin de Pays grown on AC land. Best years: (reds) **1995 94 93 92 91 90 89 88**.

**CELLIER DES SAMSONS** *Beaujolais, Burgundy, France*   A group of 10 quality-minded co-ops, producing consistently decent wines from the Beaujolais and Mâconnais regions. Bought in 1996 by Jean-Claude BOISSET. The best are sold under the Cuvée Authentique label. Look out for MOULIN-A-VENT, BEAUJOLAIS-VILLAGES, ST-VERAN and MACON-VILLAGES.

**CELLIER LE BRUN** *Marlborough, South Island, New Zealand*   Champagne-method specialist. Vintage Blanc de Blancs is ★★, although blended vintage and non-vintage bubblies are consistently good.

**CENCIBEL** See Tempranillo.

**CENTRAL COAST AVA** *California, USA*   Huge AVA covering virtually every vineyard between San Francisco and Los Angeles, with a number of sub-AVAs, such as Santa Cruz, Santa Ynez, SANTA MARIA and Monterey, which include some excellent cooler areas for Pinot Noir and Chardonnay. See also Monterey County, San Luis Obispo County, Santa Barbara County.

**CENTRAL OTAGO** *South Island, New Zealand* The only wine region in New Zealand with a continental rather than maritime climate. The long, cool ripening season may prove to be ideal for flavour development in early-ripening varieties such as Pinot Noir, Gewürztraminer and Chardonnay, even if it's risky for later varieties such as Riesling. Ten wineries now, another 3 within a year or two, and many more planning vineyards in New Zealand's newest and fastest-growing wine region. Best producers: Black Ridge, Chard Farm, Gibbston Valley, Rippon Vineyards.

**CENTRAL VALLEY** *Chile* The heart of Chile's wine industry, encompassing the valleys of MAIPO, Rapel, Curicó and Maule. Almost all the major producers are located here and the key factor determining mesoclimate differences is distance relative to the coastal and Andean Cordilleras. Best producers: CANEPA★, CARMEN★★, CONO SUR★, LA ROSA★, VALDIVIESO★★.

**CENTRAL VALLEY** *California, USA* This vast area grows nearly 90% of California's grapes, used mostly for cheap wines. The quality has improved over the past few years, but it is still an overheated area where irrigated vineyards produce excess tonnage, often siphoned off into production of brandies and grape concentrate. It is said that you cannot produce exciting wine in the Central Valley, but the conditions are not that different to Australia's Riverland or many parts of Spain and southern France. In the 90s, growers in the Lodi AVA quickly expanded vineyards to 22,000ha (55,000 acres), making Lodi the volume leader for Chardonnay, Merlot, Zinfandel and Cabernet. Other sub-regions there with a claim to quality are the Sacramento Valley and the Delta area. Best producers: MONDAVI Woodbridge, Sutter Home.

**CERETTO** *Piedmont, Italy* This merchant house, run by brothers Bruno and Marcello Ceretto, has gained a reputation as one of the chief modern producers in BAROLO. The style is soft and fragrant, with low tannins, but wines failed for a time to live up to their hype. With the help of oenologist Donato Lanati, Barolo (from Bricco Rocche★★), BARBARESCO (Bricco Asili★★) and white Arneis Blangè have regained the quality they claimed. At La Bernardina, a model estate, Ceretto also produces Chardonnay★, Viognier★, Cabernet★, Pinot Nero and Syrah★.

**CÉRONS AC** *Bordeaux, France* An AC for sweet wine in the GRAVES region of Bordeaux. The rather soft, mildly honeyed wine is not quite so sweet as SAUTERNES (except in years like 1990), and for that reason not so well known, nor so highly priced. Most producers now make dry wine under the Graves label. Best producers: de Cérons★, Grand Enclos du Château de Cérons★★, Mayne-Binet, du Seuil. Best years: **1996 95 90 89 86 83**.

**L A CETTO** *Baja California, Mexico* Mexico's most successful winery relies on mists and cooling Pacific breezes to temper the heat of the Valle de Guadaloupe. Italian winemaker Carmelo Magoni is making ripe, fleshy Petite Sirah★, oak-aged Cabernet Sauvignon, Zinfandel and Nebbiolo. Chardonnay lacks acidity and varietal character but, paradoxically, Cetto makes a decent stab at fizz.

**CHABLAIS** *Vaud, Switzerland* A sub-region of the VAUD, south-east of Lake Geneva. Most of the vineyards lie on the alluvial plains but 2 villages, Yvorne and AIGLE, benefit from much steeper slopes and produce tangy whites and good reds. Most of the thirst-quenchingly dry whites are made from the Chasselas, or Dorin, as it is called locally. The reds are made from Pinot Noir, as is a rosé speciality Oeil de Perdrix, an enjoyable summer wine. Drink the whites and rosés young. Best producers: Badoux, Delarze, Grognuz, Undermühle.

**CHABLIS AC** *Burgundy, France*   Chablis, in the Serein Valley, halfway between Paris and Dijon, is Burgundy's northernmost outpost. Chardonnay ripens here with difficulty and there is a dreadful record of frost, which makes pricing volatile. Chablis' other problem is that its name has become synonymous with cheap, dry-to-medium, white-to-off-white wine from any available grape. Real Chablis is always white and dry, but with a light, unassertive fruit which can make for delicious drinking. An increasing number of producers are experimenting with oak barrel-aging, resulting in some full, toasty, positively rich dry whites. In general straight Chablis AC should be drunk young, but the better ones can improve for 3–5 years. Best producers: Bessin, Brocard★, la CHABLISIENNE co-op★★, Defaix★★, DROIN★, DROUHIN★★, DURUP, Grossot★★, LABOURE-ROI★, Laroche★, Long-Depaquit★, MICHEL★★, Picq, Pinson★, RAVENEAU★★★, Régnard★, Servin, Simonnet-Febvre★, Vocoret★. Best years: **1996 95 90 89**.

**CHABLIS GRAND CRU AC** *Burgundy, France*   The 7 Grands Crus (Bougros, les Preuses, Vaudésir, Grenouilles, Valmur, les Clos and les Blanchots) that face south-west across the town of Chablis are the heart of the AC. Grand Cru producers made some exceptional wines in the 1980s, especially those who used oak-aging, adding a rich warmth to the otherwise taut flavours. DROIN and Fèvre are the most enthusiastic users of new oak. Never drink young: 5–10 years is needed before you begin to see why you spent your money. Best producers: la CHABLISIENNE co-op★★, DAUVISSAT★★★, Defaix★★, DROIN★★, Fèvre★★, Laroche★, Long-Depaquit★, MICHEL★★, RAVENEAU★★★, Régnard★, Guy Robin★★, Servin★, Simonnet-Febvre★★, Vocoret★★. Best years: (1996) 95 93 92 **90 89 88 85 83**.

**CHABLIS PREMIER CRU AC** *Burgundy, France*   Just over a quarter of CHABLIS' vineyards are designated Premier Cru. Some are on splendid slopes (the best are Montée de Tonnerre, Vaillons, Mont de Milieu and Fourchaumes) but many of the newer ones are on slopes of questionable quality. As such Premiers Crus vary widely in quality, but the good ones are excellent value, at only about 20% above the price of basic Chablis. The wines should taste bigger and more intense than basic Chablis and may take as long as 5 years to show full potential. Best producers: Bessin, la CHABLISIENNE co-op★, DAUVISSAT★★, Defaix★★, DROIN★★, Fèvre★, Louis MICHEL★★, RAVENEAU★★, Régnard★, Simonnet-Febvre★, Testut★, Tremblay★, Vocoret★. Best years: (1996) 95 93 **92 90 89 88**.

**LA CHABLISIENNE** *Chablis, Burgundy, France*   A substantial co-op producing nearly one-third of all CHABLIS. The wines are always reliable and can sometimes aspire to greatness. The best are the oaky Grands Crus – especially les Preuses★★ and Grenouilles (sold as Ch. Grenouille★★) – but the basic unoaked Chablis★, the Cuvée Vieilles Vignes★★ and the numerous Premiers Crus★ are excellent, as is the red BOURGOGNE Épineuil from Pinot Noir. Best years: (whites) **1996 95 94 93 90**; (reds) **1995 93 90**.

# CHAMPAGNE AC

*Champagne, France*

The Champagne region produces the most celebrated sparkling wines in the world. East of Paris, it is the most northerly AC in France – a place where grapes struggle to ripen fully. Champagne is divided into 5 distinct areas – the best are the Montagne de Reims, where Pinot Noir grape performs brilliantly, and the Chardonnay-dominated Côte des Blancs south of Épernay. If you buy a bottle of Coteaux Champenois, a still wine from the area, you can see why they decided to make bubbly instead; it tastes mean and tart, but is transformed by the Champagne method into some of the most complex wines of all.

That's the theory anyway, and for 150 years or so the Champenois have suavely persuaded us that their product is second to none. It can be, too, except when it is released too young or sweetened to make up for a lack of richness. A combination of high prices and competition from other sparkling wines has produced a glut of Champagne. But as Champagne expertise begins to turn out exciting sparklers in California, Australia and New Zealand, the Champagne producers must re-focus on quality or lose much of their market for good.

The Champagne trade is dominated by large companies or houses, called négociants-manipulants, recognized by the letters NM on the label. The récoltants-manipulants (recognized by the letters RM) are growers who make their own wine.

## STYLES OF CHAMPAGNE

**Non-vintage** Most Champagne is a blend of 2 or more vintages. Quality varies enormously, depending on who has made the wine and how long it has been aged. Most Champagne is sold as Brut, which is a dry, but not bone-dry style. Interestingly, Extra Dry denotes a style less dry than Brut.

**Vintage** Denotes Champagne made with grapes from a single vintage. As a rule, it is made only in the best years.

**Blanc de Blancs** A lighter style of Champagne made solely from the Chardonnay grape.

**Blanc de Noirs** A white Champagne, but made entirely from black grapes, either Pinor Noir, Pinot Meunier, or a combination of the two. Generally rather solid.

**Rosé** Pink Champagne, made either from black grapes or (more usually) by mixing a little still red wine into white Champagne.

**De luxe cuvée** In theory the finest Champagne and certainly always the most expensive, residing in the fanciest bottles.

See also BRUT, CHAMPAGNE METHOD, CHAMPAGNE ROSE, GRANDE MARQUE; AND INDIVIDUAL PRODUCERS.

84

BEST PRODUCERS

**Houses** BILLECART-SALMON, BOLLINGER, Charbaut, DEUTZ, Gardet, Gosset, Alfred GRATIEN, Charles HEIDSIECK, Henriot, Jacquesson, KRUG, LANSON, LAURENT-PERRIER, Bruno Paillard, Joseph PERRIER, PERRIER-JOUET, POL ROGER, Louis ROEDERER, Pommery, RUINART, Salon, TAITTINGER, VEUVE CLICQUOT.

**Growers** Arnould, Bauser, Beerens, Billiot, Cattier, André Clouet, Dufour, Gimmonet, Goutorbe, Gremillet, Launois, Mandois, Vilmart.

**Co-ops** Beaumont les Crayères, Nicolas Feuillatte, Palmer.

**De luxe cuvées** Belle Époque (PERRIER-JOUET), Clos de Mesnil (KRUG), Comtes de Champagne (TAITTINGER), Cristal (Louis ROEDERER), Cuvée Josephine (Joseph PERRIER), Cuvée Sir Winston Churchill (POL ROGER), Dom Pérignon (MOET & CHANDON), Dom Ruinart (RUINART), Grand Siècle (LAURENT-PERRIER), Grande Dame (VEUVE CLICQUOT), Noble Cuvée (LANSON), Vintage RD (BOLLINGER).

**CHALONE** *Monterey County, California, USA*    Producers of full-blown but slow-developing Chardonnay★★ and concentrated Pinot Noir★★★ from vineyards on the arid eastern slope of the Coastal Range in mid-MONTEREY COUNTY. Also makes very good Pinot Blanc★ and Chenin Blanc★ – as well as Reserve bottlings of Pinot Noir★★★ and Chardonnay★★. These are strongly individualistic wines. Wines of less intensity are bottled under the Gavilan label. Best years: (Chardonnay) **1994 93 92 91 90 89 85**; (Pinot Noir) 1994 **92 91 90 88 86 83**.

**CHAMBERS** *Rutherglen, Victoria, Australia*    Family winery making sheer nectar in the form of liqueur Muscat and Tokay. The secret is Bill Chambers' ability to draw on ancient stocks put down in wood by earlier generations. His 'Special'★★ and 'Old'★★★ blends are national treasures. The Cabernet is inexpensive and good, the whites pedestrian.

**CHAMBERTIN AC** *Grand Cru, Côte de Nuits, Burgundy, France*    The village of GEVREY-CHAMBERTIN, the largest Côte de Nuits commune, has no fewer than 8 Grands Crus (Chambertin, Chambertin-Clos-de-Bèze, Chapelle-Chambertin, Charmes-Chambertin, Griotte-Chambertin, Latricières-Chambertin, Mazis-Chambertin and Ruchottes-Chambertin) which can produce some of Burgundy's greatest and most intense red wine. Its rough-hewn fruit, seeming to war with fragrant perfumes for its first few years, creates remarkable flavours as the wine ages. Chambertin and Chambertin-Clos-de-Bèze are the greatest vineyard sites, but overproduction is a recurrent problem. Even so, the best examples are wonderful and they can age for decades. Best producers: Denis Bachelet★★, CLAIR★★, Damoy★, DROUHIN, Dugat★★, FAIVELEY★★★, Mugneret★, Pernot-Fourrier★★, Perrot-Minot★★, Denis Mortet★★, Ponsot★, Dom. Remy★, Rossignol-Trapet★★, Roty★, Roumier★, ROUSSEAU★★★. Best years: 1995 93 91 90 **89 88 85 78**.

**CHAMBERTIN-CLOS-DE-BÈZE AC**    See Chambertin AC.

**CHAMBOLLE-MUSIGNY AC** *Côte de Nuits, Burgundy, France*    AC with the potential to produce the most fragrant, perfumed red Burgundy, when not over-cropped and over-sugared. Encouragingly, more young producers are now bottling their own wines. The 1995s will be outstanding. Best producers: Barthod-Noëllat★★, Bertheau, DROUHIN, DUJAC, JADOT, Dom. LEROY, Marchand★, Mugnier★★, RION, Roumier★★, Serveau★, de Vogüé★★. Best years: 1995 93 **92 90 89 88**.

**CHAMPAGNE**    See pages 84–5.

**CHAMPAGNE METHOD**    The Champagne method is now used for all of the world's finest sparkling wines. The key to the process is that a second fermentation takes place in bottle, producing carbon dioxide which, kept in solution under pressure, gives the wine its fizz. Following a fierce campaign by CHAMPAGNE makers, the term can now only be used on Champagne labels. Other sparkling wine producers now use terms like: Traditional method (*Méthode traditionelle* or *Metodo classico*), Crémant, bottle-fermented and Cap Classique. See also Cuve Close.

**CHAMPAGNE ROSÉ** *Champagne, France*    Good pink CHAMPAGNE has a delicious fragrance of cherries and raspberries. The top wines can age well, but most should be drunk on release. Best producers: BILLECART-SALMON★★, Charbaut, KRUG★, LANSON★, LAURENT-PERRIER★★, MOET & CHANDON★, Pommery, ROEDERER★, TAITTINGER (Comtes de Champagne★★). Best years: (1996) (95) **91 90 89 88 86 85 83 82**. See also pages 84–5.

**CHAPEL HILL** *Southern Vales, South Australia*  Pam Dunsford has wide wine-making experience, with big and small outfits (she worked at WYNNS and SEAVIEW for many years). Chapel Hill is a leading boutique where Pam blends McLaren Vale and COONAWARRA in her Cabernet Sauvignon★★ and Cabernet-Shiraz★. Oaky Reserve Shiraz★★ is all McLaren Vale. Smart Eden Valley Riesling★ and Chardonnay★ (look for the Reserve★★) too.

**CHAPELLE-CHAMBERTIN AC**  See Chambertin AC.

**M CHAPOUTIER** *Rhône Valley, France*  There have been huge improvements at this company since Michel Chapoutier took over the wine-making in 1988 but inconsistency is still worrying. It makes wines from all over the Rhône Valley, but specializes in the north. The HERMITAGE la Sizeranne★★ and le Pavillon★, CROZES-HERMITAGE★ and COTE-ROTIE are all good (these days). Best years: (1996) 95 **91 90 89 88**.

**CHARDONNAY**  See pages 88–9.

**CHARENTAIS, VIN DE PAYS** *France*  Wines from the Cognac area in western France. Ugni Blanc-based whites predominate and can be good if consumed young. There are also increasing amounts of Chardonnay and Sauvignon Blanc. The reds (from Bordeaux varieties) are good value, too, if you like a grassy tang to your wine. Best producers: Aubineau, Blanchard, Didonne, Mallinger.

**CHARMES-CHAMBERTIN AC**  See Chambertin AC.

**CHARTA**  A German organization with a distinctive symbol (representing a twin light Romanesque window), founded in 1984 in order to protect the image of the best Rheingau Rieslings. The accent is on dry wines which are thought to go well with food but the problem is that the wine often lacks enough flavour.

**CHASSAGNE-MONTRACHET AC** *Côte de Beaune, Burgundy, France*  Until recently Chassagne-Montrachet produced more red wine than white – although the whites are better. Some of Burgundy's greatest white wine vineyards (part of le MONTRACHET and BATARD-MONTRACHET and all of Criots-Bâtard-Montrachet) are within the village boundary. The white Chassagne Premiers Crus are not as well-known, but can offer nutty, toasty wines. Ordinary white Chassagne-Montrachet is usually an enjoyable high-quality Burgundy. Red Chassagne is always a little earthy, peppery and plummy and can be a bit of an acquired taste, even though the price is not too frightening. The top wines can age for up to a decade. Look out for the following Premiers Crus: Clos de la Boudriotte, Clos St-Jean and Clos de la Chapelle. Best producers: (whites) Amiot, Blain-Gagnard★★, COLIN★, Duc de Magenta★, Fontaine-Gagnard★★, J-N GAGNARD★★, GAGNARD-DELAGRANGE★★, Lamy★, Albert Morey★★, RAMONET★★; (reds) Jean-Claude Bachelet, CARILLON★, Clerget★, Albert Morey★, RAMONET★. Best years: (whites) 1995 93 **92 90 89 88 86 85**; (reds) 1995 93 **92 90 89 88**.

**CH. CHASSE-SPLEEN**★★ *Moulis AC, Cru Bourgeois, Haut-Médoc, Bordeaux, France*  Chasse-Spleen is not a Classed Growth – but you'd never know it, either from the marvellously concentrated wines, or from the tremendous reputation built during the 1980s by the late proprietor, Bernadette Villars. The château is now run by Villars' daughter Claire. Second wine: l'Ermitage de Chasse-Spleen. Best years: (1996) (95) 94 93 **90 89 88 86 83 82 81**.

# CHARDONNAY

I'm always getting asked, 'When will the world tire of Chardonnay?' And I reply 'Not in my lifetime.' The wine critics may pine for something else to write about, and the wine experts may decide that they want to explore the flavours available from other grape varieties, but for the vast majority of wine drinkers the Chardonnay revolution has only just begun, and to many people good dry white wine simply equals Chardonnay. And that's that. The amount of Chardonnay grown has increased dramatically over the last 10 years or so: it is now claimed to be the fourth-most planted white grape variety in the world.

*WINE STYLES*

**France** Although a relatively neutral variety if left alone (this is what makes it so suitable as a base wine for top-quality Champagne-method sparkling wine), the grape can ripen in almost any conditions, developing a subtle gradation of flavours going from the sharp apple core greenness of Chardonnay grown in Champagne or the Loire, through the exciting, bone-dry yet succulent flavours of white Burgundy, to a round, perfumed flavour in Languedoc-Roussillon.

**Other regions** Italy produces Chardonnay that is bone dry and lean as well as fat, spicy and lush. Spain does much the same. A few South African examples are beginning to show what the variety is really capable of there, but California and Australia have virtually created their reputations on great viscous, almost syrupy, tropical fruits and spice-flavoured Chardonnays. They've both toned down the flavours now, though New Zealand is currently producing some wonderfully exotic wine, and Chile and Argentina have found it easy to grow and are rapidly learning how to make fine wine from it too. Add Germany, Canada and New York State and you'll see it can perform almost anywhere.

**Using oak** The reason for all these different flavours lies in Chardonnay's wonderful susceptibility to the winemaker's aspirations and skills. And the most important manipulation is the use of the oak barrel for fermenting and aging the wine. Chardonnay is the grape of the great white Burgundies and these are fermented and matured in oak (not necessarily new oak) but the effect is to give a marvellous round, nutty richness to a wine that is yet savoury and dry.

The New World winemakers sought to emulate the great Burgundies, thus planting Chardonnay and employing thousands of oak barrels (mostly new) and their success – and the enthusiasm with which wine drinkers embraced the wine – has caused winemakers everywhere else to see Chardonnay as the perfect variety – easy to grow, easy to turn into wine and easy to sell to an adoring public.

## BEST PRODUCERS

### France

*Chablis* la CHABLISIENNE, DAUVISSAT, Defaix, DROIN, Louis MICHEL, RAVENEAU; *Côte d'Or* CARILLON, COCHE-DURY, Marc COLIN, DROUHIN, J-N GAGNARD, GAGNARD-DELAGRANGE, LAFON, Laguiche, Dom. LEFLAIVE, Pierre Morey, RAMONET, Roulot, Sauzet; *Midi* l'Aigle; *Pouilly-Fuissé* Ch. FUISSE, Guffens-Heynen, Merlin, Thévenet.

### Other European Chardonnays

*Italy* Bertelli, CA'DEL BOSCO, GAJA, GRAVNER, JERMANN, LAGEDER, Manzano, REGALEALI, RUFFINO.

*Spain* CHIVITE (Colección 125), Puig y Roca, TORRES (Milmanda), Viñas del Vero.

### New World Chardonnays

*Australia* BANNOCKBURN, COLDSTREAM HILLS, CULLENS, HARDY (Eileen), LEEUWIN, MOUNTADAM, PETALUMA, PIERRO, PIPERS BROOK, ROSEMOUNT, TYRRELL'S.

*New Zealand* COLLARDS, COOPER'S CREEK, CORBANS (Private Bin), DELEGAT'S (Proprietor's Reserve), HUNTER'S, KUMEU RIVER, MONTANA (Church Road Reserve), MORTON ESTATE (Black Label), NEUDORF, TE MATA (Elston), VAVASOUR.

*USA* (California) ARROWOOD, AU BON CLIMAT, BERINGER (Reserve), CALERA, CHALONE, FLORA SPRINGS, FRANCISCAN (Cuvée Sauvage), KISTLER, MATANZAS CREEK, MONDAVI (Reserve), NEWTON, QUPE.

*South Africa* BOUCHARD FINLAYSON, BUITENVERWACHTING, GLEN CARLOU, HAMILTON RUSSELL (Ashbourne), KLEIN CONSTANTIA, MEERLUST, MULDERBOSCH, THELEMA.

**CHASSELAS** Chasselas is considered a table grape world-wide. Only in BADEN (where it is called Gutedel) and Switzerland (called Dorin, Perlan or Fendant) is it thought to make decent light, dry wines with a slight prickle for everyday drinking. A few Swiss examples rise above this.

**CHÂTEAU** French for 'castle', used to describe a wide variety of wine estates. Some, such as MARGAUX, are truly palatial. Here, all French châteaux are listed under their individual names.

**CHATEAU CARRAS** *Macedonia, Greece* The reds from this no-expense-spared winery are better than the whites, but even so the Greek sun makes itself felt in dryish flavours of coffee and prunes. After a bright start quality became erratic, but is on the up again.

**CHÂTEAU-CHALON AC** *Jura, France* The most prized – and pricy – VIN JAUNE, Jura's great speciality. It is difficult to find, even in the region itself. Best producers: Bourdy★, Courbet★★, Macle, Maire, Perron.

**CHÂTEAU-GRILLET AC★★** *Rhône Valley, France* This rare and *very* expensive Rhône white, made from Viognier, has a magic reek of orchard fruit and harvest bloom when young and it can age well. However, the late 1980s and early 90s were poor, but fortunately this AC has much improved since 1993. Best years: **1996 95 93**.

**CHATEAU LAZARIDI** *Macedonia, Greece* A pioneering family operation with a long-term plan to repatriate vines planted by ancient Greeks in southern Italy. Production is based on noble French varieties with relatively long cask- and bottle-aging. The Lazaridi red★ is very dense and concentrated but still fresh and young, and both white and red Maghiko Vouno★ show great potential. Best years: (reds) 1995 94 **93 91**.

**CHATEAU MONTELENA** *Napa Valley AVA, California, USA* NAPA winery producing well-balanced Chardonnay and Cabernet★★ that is impressive, if slow to develop. There is also a Zinfandel★. Best years: (Cabernet Sauvignon) 1993 92 91 **90** 89 86 85 84 82; (Chardonnay) **1994 93 92** 91 90.

**CHATEAU MUSAR** *Ghazir, Lebanon* Founded by Gaston Hochar in the 1930s and now run by his Bordeaux-trained son Serge, Musar is famous for having made wine every year bar 2 (1976 and 84) throughout Lebanon's civil war. From an unlikely blend of Cabernet Sauvignon, Cinsaut and Syrah comes a wine of real, if wildly exotic, class – full, with lush, sweet, spicy fruit and deceptively good aging potential. Hochar himself says that red Musar★★ 'should be drunk at 15 years'. From the stunning 94 vintage Hochar also made a new rosé and a white, blending Chardonnay and Sémillon. Best years: (reds) (1994) 90 89 **87 85 83 81 77 72 70 69 64**; (whites) **1995 94**.

**CHATEAU REYNELLA** *Southern Vales, South Australia* Part of the proud BRL HARDY empire, this is more than a brand, as some fruit is still sourced from original Chateau Reynella vineyards, although vinified at Hardys. Cabernet★★, Cabernet-Merlot★★ and Shiraz★★ are classy open-fermented, basket-pressed reds to keep as well as drink young. They consistently give value well above their price. The Chardonnay★ is not to be ignored either. Best years: (reds) 1994 **92 91 90 88 86**.

**CHATEAU ST JEAN** *Sonoma Valley AVA, California, USA* Once known almost entirely for its rich Chardonnay★, St Jean has virtually reinvented itself in the past 5 years and has emerged as a producer of delicious Cabernet Sauvignon★ and a Meritage-style red called Cinq Cépage★★, which is a champion wine. A Reserve Merlot★★, released for the first time in 1995, is also worth seeking out. Best years: (white) **1994 92 91 90**; (reds) 1994 93 **92 91 90 89**.

**CHATEAU STE MICHELLE** *Washington State, USA* A pioneering winery with an enormous range of wines, including several vineyard-designated Chardonnays★★ and Cabernet Sauvignons★ of smashing quality, especially the Cold Creek Vineyard★ wines. Makes good Riesling, both dry and sweet, and increasingly interesting Sémillon, Sauvignon and Fumé★ (a blend of both). Columbia Crest, which began as a budget second label producing good-value wines, has blossomed into a stand-alone winery with an excellent range, especially a Reserve Chardonnay★, a juicy Cabernet Sauvignon and a Merlot★.

**CHATEAU TAHBILK** *Goulburn Valley, Victoria, Australia* Wonderfully old-fashioned family company making traditionally big, gumleafy/minty reds, matured only in old wood. Regional speciality white Marsanne★★ is perfumed and attractive. Other whites tend to lack finesse, but Shiraz★ and Cabernet★ are full of character, even if they need years of cellaring. Best years: (reds) 1994 91 90 88 **86 84 81 79 78 76 71 64 62**.

**CHÂTEAUNEUF-DU-PAPE AC** *Rhône Valley, France* A large vineyard area between Orange and Avignon that used to be one of the most abused of all wine names. Now, much Châteauneuf comes from single estates and deservedly ranks as one of France's top reds. Always get an estate wine, and these are distinguished by the papal coat of arms embossed on the neck of the bottle. Only 5% of Châteauneuf is white. Made mainly from Grenache Blanc, Bourboulenc and Clairette, these wines can be surprisingly good. The top reds will age for 8 years or more, while the whites are best drunk young. Best producers: (reds) BEAUCASTEL★★★, Bonneau★★, Bosquet des Papes★, Brunel★, Caboche, Chante-Cigale★, Chante-Perdrix★, Clos du Mont Olivet★, CLOS DES PAPES★★★, Font du Loup★★, FONT DE MICHELLE★★, Fortia★, GRAND TINEL★★, Marcoux★★, Nalys★, Pégau★★, RAYAS★★, Sabon, VIEUX TELEGRAPHE★★; (whites) BEAUCASTEL★★★, CLOS DES PAPES★★, FONT DE MICHELLE★★, Mont Redon, la Nerthe★, RAYAS★★, VIEUX TELEGRAPHE★. Best years (reds): 1995 94 93 **91 90 89 88 86 85 83 81 78**.

**CHAVE** *Rhône Valley, France* Jean-Louis Chave, son of founder Gérard, has deservedly achieved superstar status in recent years. His red HERMITAGE★★★ is one of the world's great wines, a thick, complex expression of the Syrah grape at its best, requiring 10 years in bottle to open out. His wonderful white Hermitage★★★ sometimes even out-lasts the reds as it quietly moves towards its honeyed, nutty zenith. Also a small amount of excellent red ST-JOSEPH★★. Very expensive, but worth the money. Best years: (reds) (1996) 95 94 92 91 90 89 88 **86 85 83 82 81 79 78**; (whites) (1996) 95 94 93 **92 91 90 89 88 82**.

**CHÉNAS AC** *Beaujolais, Burgundy, France* This is the smallest of the Beaujolais Crus and its wines, usually quite tough when young, benefit enormously from 2 or more years' aging and can often last a decade. Best producers: des Boccards, Braillon★, Champagnon★, de Chénas, Lapierre★★, Perrachon, Daniel Robin★, de Tremont. Best years: **1996 95 94 91 90 89 85**.

**CHENIN BLANC**  One of the most underrated white wine grapes in the world. Found mainly in the LOIRE VALLEY, where it is also called Pineau de la Loire, it is responsible for the great sweet wines of QUARTS DE CHAUME and BONNEZEAUX, as well as being the variety for VOUVRAY, sweet or dry, and much other Anjou white. It is also the main grape for the Loire sparkling wines. In South Africa, Chenin (also known as Steen) accounts for one-third of the vineyard area, used for everything from easy-drinking, dryish whites through botrytized desserts to modern barrel-fermented versions. California, with a few exceptions like Chappellet, only employs it as a useful blender, while New Zealand and Australia have produced the best varietal examples.

**CH. CHEVAL BLANC★★★** *St-Émilion Grand Cru AC, 1er Grand Cru Classé,*
*Bordeaux, France*  The leading ST-EMILION estate and likely to remain so for the foreseeable future. Right on the border with POMEROL, it seems to share some of its sturdy richness, but with an extra spice and fruit that is impressively, recognizably unique. An unusually high percentage (60%) of Cabernet Franc is used in the blend. Best years: (1996) (95) 94 93 90 89 88 **86 85 83 82 81**.

**CHEVALIER-MONTRACHET AC**  See Montrachet AC.

**DOM. DE CHEVALIER** *Pessac-Léognan AC, Cru Classé de Graves,*
*Bordeaux, France*  This estate mainly for red can produce some of Bordeaux's finest wines. The red★★★ always starts out dry and tannic but over 10–20 years gains that cedar, tobacco and blackcurrant flavour. The brilliant white★★★ is both fermented and aged in oak barrels and in the best vintages will still be improving at 15–20 years. Best

years: (reds) (1996) (95) 93 90 89 88 **85 83 81 78**; (whites) (1996) 95 **94 90 89 88 86 85 83 82 81 76**.

**CHEVERNY AC** *Loire Valley, France*  A little-known area south of Blois, producing mainly fairly acidic wines. The local speciality is the white Romorantin grape, which is used to make a harsh, bone-dry wine with the AC Cour Cheverny, but the best whites are from Chardonnay. Also pleasant Sauvignon, Pinot Noir and Gamay wines, too, and a bracing Champagne-method fizz. Best producers: Cazin, Cheverny co-op, Courtioux★, Gendrier, Gueritte, Salvard, Sauger, Tessier.

**CHIANTI DOCG** *Tuscany, Italy*  The most famous of all Italian wines, but there are many styles, depending on what grapes are used, where they are grown, and by which producer. It can be a light, fresh, easy-drinking red wine, but with a characteristic hint of bitterness, like a slightly aggressive Beaujolais, or it can be an intense, structured yet sleek wine in the same league as the best Bordeaux. The vineyards are scattered over central Tuscany. In 1932, a law defined 7 zones for Chianti – Classico, Colli Aretini, Colli Fiorentini, Colli Senesi, Colline Pisane, Montalbano and Rufina – and these have been reinforced by modern DOC and DOCG regulations. Sangiovese is the main grape, though it was traditionally blended with the red Canaiolo and the white Malvasia and Trebbiano. Modern winemakers often ignored the others, especially the white, and made Chianti from Sangiovese alone or blended with 10–15% of Cabernet, Merlot or Syrah. The DOCG for Chianti Classico sanctions this, and other zones are now expected to follow suit. See also Chianti Classico, Chianti Colli Fiorentini, Chianti Colli Senesi, Chianti Rufina, Super-Tuscans.

**CHIANTI CLASSICO DOCG** *Tuscany, Italy* The original (if slightly enlarged) CHIANTI zone from the hills between Florence and Siena. Much of the best Chianti originates here: there are 200-odd named producers and Classico has led the trend in making richer, more structured and better-balanced wines, but many producers use their best grapes for Super-Tuscans. From the 95 vintage Classico can be made from 100% Sangiovese; the Riserva (which many Super-Tuscans may become) may now be aged for 2 instead of 3 years but must only use red grapes. The finest Riserva can be aged for a decade or more. Most estates also offer regular bottlings, round and fruity for drinking 2–5 years after the harvest. Best producers: ANTINORI★★, Badia a Coltibuono★★, Brolio★, Cacchiano★, Capaccia★★, Carobbio★, Casa Emma★★, Casa Sola★, Castellare★★, CASTELL'IN VILLA★★, CASTELLO DI AMA★★, Cecchi (Villa Cerna★), Cennatoio★, Le Cinciole★, Dievole★, FELSINA BERARDENGA★★★, Le Filigare★, Fonterutoli★★, Fontodi★★★, ISOLE E OLENA★★, Lilliano★★, La Massa★, Melini, Monsanto★★, Monte Bernardi★★, Il Palazzino★★, Paneretta★, Poggerino★, Querceto★, Querciabella★, RAMPOLLA★★, RIECINE★★★, Rocca di Castagnoli★, Rocca di Montegrossi★, RUFFINO★★, San Felice★, San Giusto a Rentennano★★, San Polo in Rosso★, Terrabianca★, Valtellina★★, Vecchie Terre di Montefili★★, Verrazzano★, Vicchiomaggio★, Vignamaggio★, Villa Cafaggio★★, VOLPAIA★★. Best years: (1996) 95 **94 93 91 90 88 86 85**. See also Super-Tuscans.

**CHIANTI COLLI FIORENTINI** *Chianti DOCG, Tuscany, Italy* Colli Fiorentini covers the hills around Florence. The wines traditionally are made to drink young, though some estates make Riservas★ of real interest. Best producers: Baggiolino, Le Calvane★, Il Corno, Corzano e Paterno★, Dell'Ugo, Lanciola II, Pasolini dall'Onda★, Petriolo, Poppiano, La Querce, Sammontana, San Vito in Fior di Selva, Sonnino, Torre a Decima.

**CHIANTI COLLI SENESI** *Chianti DOCG, Tuscany, Italy* This CHIANTI subzone is a vast area of Siena province (including the wine towns of Montalcino, Montepulciano and San Gimignano), with wines ranging from everyday quaffers to some fairly elegant Riservas★. Best producers: Buracchi, Campriano★, Casale-Falchini★, Il Colle, Farnetella★, Montemorli, Pacina★, Pietraserena, Il Poggiolo★, Signano.

**CHIANTI RUFINA** *Chianti DOCG, Tuscany, Italy* This is the smallest of the CHIANTI sub-zones, situated in an enclave of the Apennine mountains to the east of Florence, where wines were noted for exceptional strength, structure and longevity long before they joined the ranks of Chianti. Today the wines, particularly the long-lived Riserva from both SELVAPIANA and the ancient FRESCOBALDI estate of Castello di Nipozzano, match the best of CHIANTI CLASSICO. Best producers: Basciano, Bossi★, Il Cavaliere, Colognole, FRESCOBALDI★★, SELVAPIANA★★★, Travignoli, Villa di Vetrice. Best years: (1996) 95 **94 93 90 88 86 85**.

**CHIARETTO** Italian for a rosé or rosato wine of medium pink colour. Used mainly in BARDOLINO and Riviera del Garda Bresciano.

**CHIMNEY ROCK** *Stags Leap AVA, California, USA* After a shaky start, winemaker Doug Fletcher stepped in to put Chimney Rock on the right track, with powerful yet elegantly-shaped Cabernet Sauvignon★★ and a Reserve-style Meritage called Elevage★★. The wines are superb, with deep elements of fruit, opening into a long, layered finish. Best years: 1994 **92 91 90 87 86**.

**CHINON AC** *Loire Valley, France* The best red wine of the LOIRE VALLEY, made mainly from Cabernet Franc. Full of raspberry fruit and fresh summer earth when young, yet can improve for 20 years and more. It's always worth buying a single-estate wine. Best producers: B Baudry★★, J & C Baudry★, COULY-DUTHEIL★★, JOGUET★★, Noblaie★, Jean-Maurice Raffault★★, Olga Raffault★, Raifault★. Best years: (reds) 1996 **95 93 90 89 88 85 83 82 78 76**.

**CHIROUBLES AC** *Beaujolais, Burgundy, France* The lightest, most delicately fragrant of the BEAUJOLAIS Crus but expensive for what is often only a marginally superior BEAUJOLAIS-VILLAGES. Best producers: Brunet, Charvet, de la Grosse Pierre, DUBOEUF, Javernand, Passot, Thulon. Best years: **1996 95**.

**CHIVITE** *Navarra DO, Navarra, Spain* The longtime leader in wine exports from NAVARRA, owned and run by the Chivite family. The wine is reliable to very good. The red 125 Aniversario★ and Colección 125 Chardonnay★★ are its top wines.

**CHOREY-LÈS-BEAUNE AC** *Côte de Beaune, Burgundy, France* One of those tiny, forgotten villages that make good, if not great, Burgundy at prices most of us can still afford, with some committed producers too. Can age for 5–8 years. Best producers: Arnoux, DROUHIN, GERMAIN★, Goud de Beaupuis, R & J Rémy, TOLLOT-BEAUT★. Best years: 1995 **93 90 89 88**.

**CHURCHILL** *Port DOC, Douro, Portugal* When Johnny and Caroline Graham started Churchill (her maiden name) in 1981, it was the first new port shipper for 50 years. The wines are good, particularly LBV★★, Crusted★★, single quinta★★ and well-aged dry white★★ ports. Best years: 1994 **91**.

**CINQUETERRE DOC** *Liguria, Italy* From beautiful hills that rise steeply above the sea west of La Spezia, this white wine sells to the tourists, no matter what the quality. At its best, it is dry and crisp, and provides a decent glass to go with local fish. The sweet white, called Sciacchetrà and made from PASSITO grapes, can be excellent. Best producers: De Battè, Forlini e Cappellini★, Gasparini, Riomaggiore co-op★.

---

**CINSAUT** Found mainly in France's southern Rhône, Provence and the Midi. It gives a light-coloured wine even at the best of times, with a fresh, but rather fleeting, neutral fruit. It is popular as a blender in South Africa and in Lebanon's CHATEAU MUSAR.

---

**CIRÒ DOC** *Calabria, Italy* The fact that this was the wine offered to champions in the ancient Olympics seemed a more potent reason to buy it than for quality. Yet Cirò Rosso, a full-bodied red from the Gaglioppo grape, has improved remarkably of late. New wines, such as Librandi's Gravello★★ (an oak-aged blend with Cabernet), are even better. The DOC also covers a dry white from Greco and a rare dry rosé. Best producers: Caparra & Siciliani, Librandi★, San Francesco★.

**CH. CISSAC★** *Haut-Médoc AC, Cru Bourgeois, Bordeaux, France* High-quality wines made by proudly traditional methods: old vines, lots of wood and meticulous selection for the final blend. The wines are deeply coloured, with a high proportion of Cabernet, and are very slow to mature. Best years: (1996) (95) 94 90 89 **88 86 85 83 82 81 78**.

**BRUNO CLAIR** *Marsannay, Côte de Nuits, Burgundy, France* A more than competent winemaker based in the comparatively unfashionable village of MARSANNAY, Bruno Clair produces a large range of excellent wines from a broad span of vineyards there, as well as in FIXIN, GEVREY-CHAMBERTIN, GIVRY, SAVIGNY and VOSNE-ROMANÉE. Most of his wine is red, but there is a small amount of white★ and a delicious Marsannay rosé★. Top wines are CHAMBERTIN Clos de Bèze★★ and vineyard-designated Marsannay reds★. Best years: 1995 93 **92 90 89 88**.

**CLAIRETTE DE DIE AC** *Rhône Valley, France* One of the undeservedly forgotten sparkling wines of France, made from a minimum of 75% Muscat, off-dry with a creamy bubble and an orchard-fresh fragrance. The *méthode Dioise* is used, which preserves the Muscat scent. By this method the bottle re-fermentation is stopped before all the sugar is converted to carbon dioxide and alcohol and the wine is filtered and re-bottled under pressure. Drink young. Best producers: Achard-Vincent★, Andrieux, Clairette de Die co-op★, Jacques Faure, Magord, Raspail★.

**A CLAPE** *Cornas, Rhône Valley, France* The leading estate in CORNAS. Clape's wines★★★ are consistently among the best in the Rhône – dense, tannic and full of rich, roasted fruit. Clape also makes fine COTES DU RHONE, both red★★ and white★. Best years: (1996) (95) 94 91 90 89 **88 86 85 82**.

**LA CLAPE** *Coteaux du Languedoc AC, Languedoc, France* The mountain of La Clape rears unexpectedly from the flat coastal fields south-east of Narbonne. The vineyards here are a Cru within the COTEAUX DU LANGUEDOC AC and produce some of the best Aude wines. There are excellent whites from Bourboulenc and Clairette, plus some good reds and rosés, mainly from Carignan. The whites and reds can age. Best producers: Boscary, Hue, Mire l'Étang, Pech-Redon★, de St-Exupéry, Ségura, de Vires.

**CLARE VALLEY** *South Australia* Upland valley north of Adelaide with a deceptively moderate climate, able to grow fine, aromatic Riesling, marvellously textured Sémillon, and rich, robust Shiraz and Cabernet-based reds. More recently several voluptuous Grenaches. Best producers: (whites) ADAMS★★, BARRY★, BLASS★★ (Gold Label), GROSSET★★, KNAPPSTEIN★, LEASINGHAM★, MITCHELL★, PETALUMA★★★, Pike; (reds) ADAMS★★, BARRY★, LEASINGHAM★★, MITCHELL★★, WENDOUREE★★★.

**CLARET** English for red Bordeaux wines, from the French *clairet*, which was traditionally used to describe a lighter style of red Bordeaux.

**CH. CLARKE** *Listrac-Médoc AC, Bordeaux, France* Part of the Rothschild empire, this property had millions spent on it during the late 1970s and the wines are now reaping the benefit. They have an attractive blackcurrant fruit and an oaky richness. And with a name like Clarke, how could they fail to be seductive? Best years: (1996) (95) **90 89 88 86 85 83**.

**CLERICO** *Barolo DOCG, Piedmont, Italy* Domenico Clerico is one of the best of the younger generation of BAROLO producers. He produces an impressive Barolo★★ and one of the best Barberas★★, both wonderfully balanced. His range also includes Arte★★, a barrique-aged blend of Nebbiolo and Barbera. Best years: (Barolo) (1996) (95) 94 93 90 89 **88**.

**CH. CLIMENS**★★★ *Barsac AC, 1er Cru Classé, Bordeaux, France* The leading estate in BARSAC, with a deserved reputation for rich, elegant wines with a light, lemony acidity that keeps them fresh. Easy to drink at 5 years, a good vintage will be richer and more satisfying after 10–15 years. Second wine: les Cypres (and delicious too). Best years: (1996) **91 90 89 88 86 83 76 75**.

**CLOS** French for a walled vineyard – as in Burgundy's CLOS DE VOUGEOT. Also commonly incorporated into the names of estates (CLOS DES PAPES), regardless of whether they are walled or not.

**CLOS DU BOIS** *Alexander Valley AVA, California, USA* Winery that generally shows off the gentle, fruit-dominated flavours of SONOMA Chardonnay, Merlot and Cabernet Sauvignon. Top vineyard selections can be exciting, especially Calcaire Chardonnay★, rich, strong Briarcrest Cabernet Sauvignon★, and Marlstone★, a red Bordeaux blend. Best years: (reds) **1994 91 90 88 87 86**.

**CLOS CENTEILLES** *Minervois AC, Languedoc, France* Although labels still feature the name Domergue, this estate has been retitled. From vineyards close to Caunes-Minervois, Daniel Domergue and his wife Patricia Boyer are producing both excellent MINERVOIS and innovative Vin de Pays. The impressive Clos de Centeilles★★ is their top wine; Cuvée Capitelle★ and Carignanissime★ are 100% Cinsaut and Carignan respectively. Best years: **1995 94 93**.

**CLOS DES PAPES** *Châteauneuf-du-Pape AC, Rhône Valley, France* Paul Avril is one of the outstanding CHATEAUNEUF-DU-PAPE producers. His reds★★★ have an unusually high proportion of Mourvèdre, which explains their longevity, but enough Grenache to be approachable in their youth and provide the initial blast of fruit. The whites★★ take on the nutty character of aged Burgundy after a decade. Best years: 1995 94 **93 90 89 88 86 85 83 82 79**.

**CLOS RENÉ**★ *Pomerol AC, Bordeaux, France* This is wonderfully plummy, juicy, fleshy wine from the less fashionable western side of the POMEROL AC. You can drink Clos René young, but it also ages well for at least 10 years. Sometimes sold under the label Moulinet-Lasserre. Best years: (1996) (95) 94 **90 89 88 85 83 82 81**.

**CLOS DE LA ROCHE AC** *Grand Cru, Côte de Nuits, Burgundy, France* The best and biggest of the 5 MOREY-ST-DENIS Grands Crus. It has a lovely, bright, red-fruits flavour when young, which should get richly chocolaty or gamy as it ages. Best producers: Castagnier-Vadey★★, DUJAC★★, Perrot-Minot★★, Ponsot★★★, ROUSSEAU★★. Best years: 1995 93 90 **89 88 85 78**.

**CLOS ST-DENIS AC** *Grand Cru, Côte de Nuits, Burgundy, France* This small (6.5ha/16 acres) Grand Cru, which gave its name to the village of Morey-St-Denis, produces wines which are often on the light side, but should be wonderfully silky, with the texture that only great Burgundy, so far, can give. Best with 10 years or more. Best producers: DUJAC★★, Dom. Georges Lignier★★★. Best years: 1995 93 90 **89 88 85 78**.

**CLOS DE TART AC**★★ *Grand Cru, Côte de Nuits, Burgundy, France*
Grand Cru in the village of MOREY-ST-DENIS, and entirely owned by one
firm – the Burgundy merchant Mommessin. The wine, light and dry
at first, can develop a delicious savoury richness as it ages. Best years:
1995 93 90 **89** 88 **85**.

**CLOS DU VAL** *Napa Valley AVA, California, USA* A sometimes overlooked
producer of elegant Cabernet Sauvignon★, Chardonnay★, Merlot,
Pinot Noir and Zinfandel★. The wines are nicely balanced and can age
with the best. Best years: (Cabernet) 1994 **92 91 90 87 86 85 84**.

**CLOS DE VOUGEOT AC** *Grand Cru, Côte de Nuits, Burgundy, France*
Enclosed by Cistercian monks in the 14th century, this large vineyard
is now divided among 80 owners. This has turned Clos de Vougeot
into one of the most unreliable Grand Cru Burgundies, but the best
wine tends to come from the upper and middle parts of the Clos. When
it is good it is wonderfully fleshy, turning dark and exotic with 10
years' age or more. Best producers: Arnoux★, Confuron★, DROUHIN,
Engel★★, GRIVOT★★, A & F Gros★★, J Gros★, JAFFELIN★★, Dom.
LEROY★★, MEO-CAMUZET★★★. Best years: 1995 93 **92** 90 **89 88 85** 78.

**CLOUDY BAY** *Marlborough, South Island, New Zealand* New Zealand's
most successful winery, Cloudy Bay achieved cult status with the first
release of the zesty, herbaceous Sauvignon Blanc★★★ in 1985. Now
controlled by the Champagne house VEUVE CLICQUOT, Cloudy Bay also
makes Chardonnay★★, Cabernet-Merlot★, a late-harvest Riesling★★,
Pinor Noir★★ and Pelorus★★, a high-quality old-style Champagne-
method fizz. Best years: **1996 94 91 89**.

**J F COCHE-DURY** *Meursault, Côte de Beaune, Burgundy, France* Jean-
François Coche-Dury is a modest superstar, quietly turning out some
of the finest wines on the Côte de Beaune. His best wines are his
CORTON-CHARLEMAGNE★★★ and MEURSAULT Perrières★★★, but everything he makes is excellent, even his BOURGOGNE Blanc★★. His red
wines, from VOLNAY★★ and MONTHELIE★★, tend to be significantly
cheaper than the whites and should be drunk younger, too. Best
years: (white) 1995 94 93 **92 90** 89 88 86 85.

**COCKBURN** *Port DOC, Douro, Portugal* Best known for its Special
Reserve Ruby, Cockburns has much more than that to offer. Cockburns Vintage★★ is stylishly cedary and now very much back on
form, and the aged tawnies★★ are creamy and nutty. Best years:
(vintage ports) 1994 91 **70 63**.

**CODORNÍU** *Cava DO, Catalonia, Spain* The biggest Champagne-method
sparkling wine company in the world. Anna de Codorníu★ and Première
Cuvée Brut★, both with 85% Chardonnay, are especially good but all
the sparklers are better than the CAVA average. The spectacular Art
Nouveau winery and 30km (19 miles) of underground cellars in San
Sadurní de Noya are really worth a visit. Codorníu also owns the top-
quality RAIMAT estate in Costers del Segre and the still wine company of
Masía Bach in the PENEDÉS, in addition to the quality-conscious
California winery Codorníu Napa. Drink young for freshness.

**COLARES DOC** *Estremadura, Portugal* The vineyards of this archaic
DOC are phylloxera-free and ungrafted with the Ramisco vines planted
on sand-dunes. The wines are tooth-curdlingly tannic and are *said* to
soften with age, but in fact generally just wither away.

**COLDSTREAM HILLS** *Yarra Valley, Victoria, Australia* Although South-corp purchased this formerly public company in 1996, James Halliday still holds the reins. Only YARRA VALLEY grapes are used, with the exception of the James Halliday export range. Pinot Noir★★ is one of Australia's best: sappy and smoky with cherry fruit and clever use of oak. Chardonnay★★ has subtlety and delicacy but real depth as well. Reserve★★★ labels of both can be outstanding. Cabernet Sauvignon★ and Cabernet-Merlot★ blend are increasingly good. Best years: (reds) 1994 **92 91 90 88**.

**COLHEITA** Aged tawny port from a single vintage. See Port.

**MARC COLIN** *St-Aubin, Côte de Beaune, Burgundy, France* An excellent, but often underrated domaine specializing in reds and whites from CHASSAGNE-MONTRACHET★ and ST-AUBIN★. The St-Aubin Premiers Crus★★ are fine value, but Colin's most exquisite wine is his tiny production of le MONTRACHET★★★. All the wines are ageworthy. Best years: 1995 93 **92 90 89 88 86 85**.

**COLLARDS** *Henderson, Auckland, New Zealand* A small family winery that produces some of the country's finest white wines, including Rothesay Chardonnay★★ and Sauvignon Blanc★, HAWKES BAY Chardonnay★★, and MARLBOROUGH Chardonnay★, Sauvignon★★, Pinot Noir★★ and Riesling★. The dry Chenin Blanc is one of New Zealand's few premium examples of this grape variety. Best years: **1996 94 91 90 89**.

**COLLI BOLOGNESI DOC** *Emilia, Italy* Wine zone in the Apennine foothills near Bologna. Traditionally slightly sweet and frothing, today some concessions have been made to international taste, notably in a fine Cabernet★★ from Terre Rosse. Other good reds are produced from Merlot, and increasing amounts of dry white are made from Sauvignon, Pignoletto and Pinot Bianco. Best producers: Bonzara★, Gaggioli (Vigneto Bagazzana), Terre Rosse★★, Vallona★.

**COLLI EUGANEI DOC** *Veneto, Italy* The sheer hills south of Padova produce an array of DOC wines, still and sparkling, that are mainly taken lightly. A serious exception is the Vignalta estate, whose Cabernet Riserva★★ and Merlot-Cabernet blend Gemola★★ have become rivals in their categories to Italy's best. Best producers: Ca' Lustra★, Vignalta★★. Best years: **1995 94 93 91 90**.

**COLLI ORIENTALI DEL FRIULI DOC** *Friuli-Venezia Giulia, Italy* North-east Italian DOC, covering 20 different types of wine. Best known for its sweet whites from the Ramandolo sub-zone and the overrated Picolit, but it is the reds, from the indigenous Refosco and Schioppettino, as well as imports like Cabernet and dry whites, from Tocai, Ribolla, Pinot Bianco and Malvasia Istriana, that show how exciting the wines can be. Prices are high. Best producers: Abbazia di Rosazzo★★, Bosco Romagno★, Ca' Ronesca★, Dario Coos★, Dorigo★, Dri★, Livio Felluga★, Rodaro★★, Ronco di Cialla★★, Ronco del Gnemiz★, Specogna★, Torre Rosazza★, La Viarte★, Vigne dal Leon★, Zamò e Zamò★.

**COLLI PIACENTINI DOC** *Emilia, Italy* Home to some of Emilia's best wines, this DOC covers 11 different types, the best of which are the red Gutturnio (an appealing blend of Barbera and Bonarda) and the medium-sweet white and bubbly Malvasia. Best producers: Campominosi, Fugazza★, Montesissa★, Mossi★, Romagnoli, La Stoppa★, La Tosa★.

**COLLINES RHODANIENNES, VIN DE PAYS DES** *Rhône Valley, France*
From between Vienne and Valence the best wines are varietal Gamay and Syrah, although there are some good juicy Merlots, too. Best producers: ST-DESIRAT CO-OP★, Tain-Hermitage co-op, les Vignerons Ardéchois.

**COLLIO DOC** *Friuli-Venezia Giulia, Italy* 80% of the Collio Goriziano DOC is situated in Slovenia, but the best wines, so far, come from the 20% that remains in Italy. These hills are the home of some of the country's best and most expensive dry white wines. The zone produces 19 types of wine, including 17 varietals, which range from the local Tocai and Malvasia Istriana to the international standards of Chardonnay, Sauvignon, Pinots Bianco and Grigio, Cabernet, Merlot and Pinot Nero. Among Collio's many small estates, the highly touted GRAVNER★★ and JERMANN★★ make wines that purposely remain outside the DOC. The best whites and reds are ageworthy. Best producers: Borgo Conventi★, Borgo del Tiglio★★, La Castellada★, Livio Felluga★★, Gradnik, Renato Keber★, Princic★, PUIATTI★, Ronco dei Tassi★, Russiz Superiore★, SCHIOPPETTO★, Venica★, Villa Russiz★.

**COLLIOURE AC** *Roussillon, France* This tiny fishing port tucked away in the Pyrenean foothills only a few miles from the Spanish border is also an AC, and makes a throat-warming red wine that is capable of aging for a decade but marvellously aggressive when young. Best producers: (reds) Dom. de Baillaury★, Casa Blanca, Cellier des Templiers, Mas Blanc, la RECTORIE★★, la Tour Vieille★. Best years: **1995 94 93 90 89 88 86 85**.

**COLOMBARD** In France, Colombard traditionally has been distilled to make Armagnac and Cognac, but is now emerging as a table wine grape in its own right, notably as a Vin de Pays des COTES DE GASCOGNE. At its best, it has a lovely, crisp acidity and fresh, aromatic fruit. The largest plantings of the grape are in California, where it generally produces rather less distinguished wines. Australia has some fair examples, and South Africa can produce very attractive basic whites, although it is used primarily for distilling or as a blender.

**COLUMBIA CREST** *Washington State, USA* Columbia Crest started life as a second label for CHATEAU STE MICHELLE but has evolved into a full-scale producer of good-value wines of very good quality. The Chardonnay★ and Estate Merlot★ are the strong suits. For fruit intensity, drink both with 2–3 years' age.

**COMMANDARIA** *Cyprus* The Crusaders went batty about this dark brown, challengingly treacly wine made from red Mavro and white Xynisteri grapes, sun-dried for 2 weeks before vinification and solera aging. Still pretty decent stuff but only potentially one of the world's great rich wines.

**COMTÉ TOLOSAN, VIN DE PAYS DU** *South-West France* A Vin de Pays covering most of the area to the south and east of Bordeaux. The reds, using local varieties such as Duras, Tannat and Fer Servadou blended with Cabernet Sauvignon, Cabernet Franc and Merlot, are your best bet, but don't overlook the rosés. Best producers: Labastide-de-Levis co-op, de Ribonnet★.

**COMTÉS RHODANIENS, VIN DE PAYS DES** *Rhône Valley and Savoie, France* Most of the wines are red, from Syrah, Gamay, Cinsaut and Grenache, but the whites, particularly those from Viognier, Sauvignon Blanc and Chardonnay, are good too. Best producers: Rouoms co-op, ST-DESIRAT co-op★, Tain-Hermitage co-op, les Vignerons Ardèchois.

**CONCA DE BARBERÁ DO** *Catalonia, Spain* A tip-top quality wine area, but most of it is sold to CAVA producers in the PENEDES. The cool climate here is ideal and TORRES and CODORNIU grow excellent Chardonnay, Cabernet Sauvignon, Pinot Noir, Merlot and Tempranillo here. Best producers: Concavins-RYMAN★, Sanstrave, TORRES (Milmanda★★).

**CONCHA Y TORO** *Maipo, Chile* Chile's biggest winery has over 1500ha (3700 acres) of vineyard resources but has lost winemaker Pablo Morandé to his own project in the Rapel Valley. Top whites include Amelia Chardonnay★★, CASABLANCA Sauvignon Blanc★★ and Trio Chardonnay. Don Melchor Cabernet Sauvignon★ leads the reds, along with vibrant Merlots★ under the Casillero del Diablo and Trio labels.

**CONDRIEU AC** *Rhône Valley, France* Because of the demand for this wonderfully fragrant wine made entirely from Viognier, Condrieu is decidedly expensive. Unfortunately, quality is alarmingly variable. Condrieu is a sensation everyone should try at least once, but make sure you choose a good producer. Best drunk young. Best producers: Cuilleron★★★, DELAS★, Dezormeaux★, Dumazet★, GUIGAL★★, Perret★, Pinchon★★★, du Rozay★, Vernay★★★. Best years: **1996 95 94 91**.

**CONO SUR** *Rapel, Chile* Dynamic sister winery to CONCHA Y TORO, whose Chimbarongo Pinot Noir put both grape and region on the Chilean map. New CASABLANCA Pinot★★ is more austere than the sweet, fleshy Rapel versions. Second labels Tocornal and Isla Negra offer easy-drinking blends. Best years: **1996 95**.

**CONSTANTIA WO** *South Africa* The historic heart of South African wine, now flying the flag of New World quality. The land originally granted to Simon van der Stel in 1685 was divided into 3 on his death; 2 estates, Groot Constantia and KLEIN CONSTANTIA, still exist, while BUITENVERWACHTING is partly carved from the third portion. Further along the same slopes are historic Steenberg and Uitsig. While the 2 'Constantia' estates continue tradition with wines based on the famed 18th-century sweet Constantias, white varieties, especially Sauvignon, are thrusting this cool-climate area into the modern limelight. Best producers: BUITENVERWACHTING★★, KLEIN CONSTANTIA★★, Steenberg★.

**ALDO CONTERNO** *Barolo DOCG, Piedmont, Italy* Since parting company from his brother in 1969, Aldo Conterno has forged a reputation as one of the finest producers in BAROLO. Good Freisa★, Grignolino and Dolcetto, excellent Barbera d'Alba Conca Tre Pile★★, a barrique-aged Nebbiolo Il Favot★★ and 2 Chardonnays, a young, non-oaked version called Printaniè★ and Bussia d'Or★★, fermented and aged in new wood. Pride of the range, though, are his Barolos from the finest vineyards on the hill of Bussia. In top vintages he produces Barolos Vigna Colonello★★★, Vigna Cicala★★★ and excellent Granbussia★★★, as well as a blended Barolo called Bussia Soprana★★. All his Barolos, though accessible when young, need several years to show their true majesty, but retain a remarkable freshness of fruit. Aldo's elder brother, Giovanni, has always taken a more traditional approach to wine-making at the Giacomo Conterno estate. His flagship wine is Barolo Monfortino★★. Best years: (Barolo) (1996) (95) 94 93 91 90 89 **88 85** 82.

**CONTINO** *Rioja DOC, Rioja, Spain* An estate on some of the finest RIOJA land, half-owned by CVNE. The wine is made by CVNE and always sold as a Reserva★★. Best years: **1991 86 85 82**.

**COONAWARRA** *South Australia* On a limestone belt thinly veneered with terra rossa soil, this flat patch of land can produce sublime Cabernet with blackcurrant leafy flavours and spicy Shiraz that age for many years. Chardonnay and Riesling can be good. An export-led boom has seen hundreds of acres of new vineyard go in and, in view of some disappointing light reds, I wonder if Coonawarra's great reputation is not at risk. Best producers: BOWEN★★, HOLLICK★, KATNOOK★★, LECONFIELD★★ (reds), LINDEMANS★, MILDARA★, ORLANDO★, PARKER★, PENFOLDS★★, PENLEY★★, PETALUMA★★★, ROSEMOUNT★★, ROUGE HOMME★, WYNNS★★.

**COOPERS CREEK** *Auckland, New Zealand* A small winery specializing in wines from HAWKES BAY and MARLBOROUGH grapes. Successful producer of Chardonnay★, especially Swamp Road Chardonnay★★ and luscious Marlborough Sauvignon Blanc★★. Dry Riesling★ and Late Harvest Riesling★★ styles are also very good. WAIHEKE red will soon be added to the range since the purchase of a vineyard on that island. Best years: **1996 94 91**.

**COPERTINO DOC** *Puglia, Italy* Based primarily on the Negroamaro grape, with a small percentage of Malvasia Nera. Copertino produces elegant wines. Best producers: Copertino co-op★, Leone de Castris, Monaci.

**CORBANS** *Auckland, Gisborne and Marlborough, New Zealand* New Zealand's second-largest wine company behind MONTANA and whose brand names include Cooks, Stoneleigh and Robard & Butler. Stoneleigh Sauvignon Blanc★ and Rhine Riesling★★, both made with MARLBOROUGH fruit, capture the best of each variety and display their regional styles well. Private Bin Chardonnay★★ and Noble Rhine Riesling★★★ and Merlot★★ are fine small production wines. Flagship wines from top varieties and all major wine regions are now produced under the Cottage Block label. Best years: **1996 94 91 90**.

**CORBIÈRES AC** *Languedoc, France* This AC now produces some of the best reds in the Languedoc, with juicy fruit and more than a hint of wild hillside herbs. Excellent young, they age for years when from the best estates. White Corbières is adequate – drink as young as possible. Best producers: (reds) Baillat, Caraguilhes★, Castex, Étang des Colombes★, Fontsainte★, Grand Moulin★, de LASTOURS★★, MONT TAUCH co-op★, Ollieux, du Parc, St-Auriol★, VOULTE-GASPARETS★★. Best years: (reds) **1995** 94 93 91 90 89.

**CORNAS AC** *Rhône Valley, France* Northern Rhône's up-and-coming star, whose wines are especially attractive since those of neighbouring HERMITAGE and COTE-ROTIE have spiralled upwards in price in recent years. When young, the wine is a thick, impenetrable red, almost black in the ripest years. Most need 10 years' aging. Best producers: de Barjac★, CLAPE★★★, Colombo★, DELAS, JABOULET, Juge★, LIONNET★★, R Michel★, VERSET★★. Best years: (1996) 95 94 **91 90 89 88 85 83 80** 78.

101

**CORSICA** *France*   This Mediterranean island has made some pretty dull and undistinguished wines in the past. The last decade has seen a welcome trend towards quality, with co-ops and local growers investing in better equipment and planting noble grape varieties – such as Syrah, Merlot, Cabernet Sauvignon and Mourvèdre for reds, and Chardonnay and Sauvignon Blanc for whites – to complement the local Nielluccio, Sciacarello and Vermentino. Whites and rosés are pleasant for drinking young; reds are more exciting and can age for 3–4 years. See also Ajaccio, l'Île de Beauté, Muscat de Cap Corse, Patrimonio, Vin de Corse.

**CORTESE**   White grape variety planted primarily in south-eastern PIEDMONT in Italy. It is also used in the Colli Tortonesi and Alto Monferrato DOCs as well as for GAVI, and can be labelled simply as Cortese del Piemonte. The grape can produce good, fairly acidic, dry whites.

**CORTON AC** *Grand Cru, Côte de Beaune, Burgundy, France*   The Corton AC covers both red and white wine. It is the only red Grand Cru in the Côte de Beaune and ideally the wines should have the burliness and savoury power of the top Côte de Nuits wines, combined with the more seductively perfumed fruit of Côte de Beaune. Red Corton should take 10 years to mature, but too many modern examples never make it. Very little white Corton is made. Best producers: Bonneau du Martray★★, Chandon de Briailles★★, Chevalier★, Dubreuil-Fontaine★★, MEO-CAMUZET★★★, Rapet★, Senard★, TOLLOT-BEAUT★★, Voarick★. Best years: (red) 1995 93 90 **89** 88 **85 83 78**.

**CORTON-CHARLEMAGNE AC** *Grand Cru, Côte de Beaune, Burgundy, France*   Corton-Charlemagne, at the top of the famous Corton hill, is the largest of Burgundy's white Grands Crus. It can produce some of the most impressive white Burgundies – rich, buttery and nutty with a fine mineral quality. The best wines show their real worth only at 10 years or more. Best producers: Bonneau du Martray★★, COCHE-DURY★★★, Dubreuil-Fontaine★, JADOT★★, LATOUR★★, Marey★, Rapet★, TOLLOT-BEAUT★★. Best years: 1995 94 **92** 90 **89 88 86 85**.

**CORVO** *Sicily, Italy*   The brand name for Sicilian wines made by the Duca di Salaparuta firm. Basic red and white Corvo are pretty basic, but there are superior whites, called Colomba Platino and Bianca di Valguarnera★, and 2 fine reds, Dagala del Corvo★ and Duca Enrico★.

**CH. COS D'ESTOURNEL★★★** *St-Estèphe AC, 2ème Cru Classé, Haut-Médoc, Bordeaux, France*   Now the top name in ST-ESTEPHE, and one of the leading châteaux in all Bordeaux. Despite a high proportion of Merlot (just under 40%) the wine is classically made for aging and usually needs 10 years to show really well. Recent vintages have been dark, brooding and packed with long-term potential. Second wine: les Pagodes de Cos (from 1994). Best years: (1996) (95) 94 93 92 90 89 88 86 **85 83 82 81 79 78 76**.

**COSECHA**   Spanish for 'vintage'.

**COSTERS DEL SEGRE DO** *Catalonia, Spain*   Originally created to cope with the huge RAIMAT estate near Lérida in western CATALONIA. A great array of grape varieties is grown, with the accent on French varieties. Quality is generally good and prices moderate. Best producers: Castell de Remei, RAIMAT★.

**COSTIÈRES DE NÎMES AC** *Languedoc, France*  A large improving AC between Nîmes and Arles in the Gard. The reds are often soft and make attractively easy drinking, and the rosés are at their best when really young. Only a little white is produced, which can be light and appley. Best producers: l'Amarine, Beaubois, de Belle-Coste, Blanc★, Campuget★, Durand, Roubaud, de la Tuilerie★.

**CÔTE**  French word for a slope or hillside, which is where many, but not all, of the country's best vineyards are to be found. The names of specific slopes have been adopted as ACs (CÔTE-RÔTIE, CÔTE DE BROUILLY) and even whole regions (CÔTE D'OR).

**CÔTE DE BEAUNE** *Côte d'Or, Burgundy, France*  The southern part of the CÔTE D'OR. Beginning at the hill of Corton, north of the town of Beaune, the Côte de Beaune progresses south as far as les Maranges, with white wines gradually taking over from red. A separate Côte de Beaune AC, on the hill above the town, makes relatively inexpensive red and white wine. Best producers: Allexant, Chantal Lescure, Joliette, LABOURE-ROI.

**CÔTE DE BEAUNE-VILLAGES AC** *Côte de Beaune, Burgundy, France*  The general AC covering 16 villages for Pinot Noir reds. Most producers use their own village name nowadays but if the wine is a blend from several villages it is sold as Côte de Beaune-Villages and most merchants produce a relatively undistinguished version.

**CÔTE DE BROUILLY AC** *Beaujolais, Burgundy, France*  A steep hill in the middle of the BROUILLY AC, producing extra-ripe grapes. The wine, a 'Super-Brouilly', is good young but can age well for several years. Best producers: Cellier des Samsons, Conroy★, DUBOEUF, Henry Fessy, Geoffray★, Ravier★, Thivin★★, Verger. Best years: 1996 **95 94 93 91**.

**CÔTE CHALONNAISE**  See Bourgogne-Côte Chalonnaise.

**CÔTE DE NUITS** *Côte d'Or, Burgundy, France*  This is the northern part of the great CÔTE D'OR and is *not* an AC. Almost entirely red wine country, the vineyards start in the southern suburbs of Dijon and continue south in a narrow swath to below the town of Nuits-St-Georges. The villages are some of the greatest wine names in the world – GEVREY-CHAMBERTIN, VOUGEOT and VOSNE-ROMANEE etc.

**CÔTE DE NUITS-VILLAGES AC** *Côte de Nuits, Burgundy, France*  An AC specific to the villages of Corgoloin, Comblanchien and Prémeaux in the south of the Côte de Nuits and Brochon and FIXIN in the north. Although not much seen, the wines are often good, not very deep in colour but with a nice cherry fruit. There is also a tiny amount of white. Best producers: (reds) René Durand, Julien★, RION, Rossignol, Tollot-Voarick.

**CÔTE D'OR** *Burgundy, France*  Europe's most northern great red wine area and also the home of some of the world's best dry white wines. The name, meaning 'golden slope', refers to a 48-km (30-mile) stretch between Dijon and Chagny which divides into the CÔTE DE NUITS in the north and the CÔTE DE BEAUNE in the south.

**CÔTE ROANNAISE AC** *Loire Valley, France*  In the upper LOIRE the nearest large town is Lyon, the capital of BEAUJOLAIS, and so it is quite logical that the chief grape variety here is Gamay. Most of the wine produced is red and should generally be drunk young. Best producers: Chaucesse, Lapandéry, Lutz, Montroussier, Plasse★, Serol, Vial★.

103

**CÔTE-RÔTIE AC** *Rhône Valley, France* The Côte-Rôtie, or 'roasted slope', produces one of France's greatest red wines. The Syrah grape bakes to super-ripeness on these steep slopes and the small amount of white Viognier sometimes included in the blend gives an unexpected exotic fragrance in a red wine. Lovely young, it is better aged for 10 years. Best producers: Gilles Barge★, Pierre Barge★★, Burgaud★★, Champet★★, Clusel-Roch★★, DELAS★★, GUIGAL★★★, JAMET★★, JASMIN★★, Rostaing★★, Vernay★. Best years: (1996) 95 94 91 **90 89 88 85 83 78**.

**COTEAUX D'AIX-EN-PROVENCE AC** *Provence, France* This AC was the first in the south to acknowledge that Cabernet Sauvignon can enormously enhance the local grape varieties of Grenache, Cinsaut, Mourvèdre, Syrah and Carignan. The red wines can age, but it is best to catch them young. Some quite good fresh rosé is made while the white wines, mostly still traditionally made, are pleasant but hardly riveting. Best producers: (reds) Château Bas, de Beaupré, Fonscolombe, Ste-Berthe, Salen, Ch. du Seuil, la Vallongue, Vignelaure; (whites) de Beaupré, de Calissanne, de Camaissette, Fonscolombe, Ch. du Seuil.

**COTEAUX DE L'ARDÈCHE, VIN DE PAYS DES** *Rhône Valley, France* Wines from the southern part of the Ardèche. Look out for the increasingly good varietal red wines made from Cabernet Sauvignon, Syrah, Merlot or Gamay and dry, fresh white wines from Chardonnay, Viognier or Sauvignon Blanc. Best producers: du Colombier, Louis LATOUR, Pradel, ST-DESIRAT CO-OP★, les Vignerons Ardèchois.

**COTEAUX DE L'AUBANCE AC** *Loire Valley, France* Smallish AC located parallel to the COTEAUX DU LAYON AC. It is now enjoying a renaissance for its sweet or semi-sweet whites made from Chenin Blanc. Most producers also make red, rosé or dry white ANJOU AC, which is easier to sell. Sweet styles can improve for 10–25 years. Best producers: Bablut★★, Haute Perche★, Montgilet★★, RICHOU★★. Best years: (1996) 95 **94 93 90 89 88 86 85 83**.

**COTEAUX CHAMPENOIS AC** *Champagne, France* The AC for still wines from Champagne. Fairly acid with a few exceptions, notably from BOUZY and Ay. The best age for 5 years or more. Best producers: Bara, BOLLINGER, Ch. de Saran★ (MOET & CHANDON), LAURENT-PERRIER, Joseph PERRIER, G Vesselle. Best years: (1996) 95 **90 89 88 85 82**.

**COTEAUX DU LANGUEDOC AC** *Languedoc, France* A large and increasingly successful AC situated between Montpellier and Narbonne in the Languedoc, producing over 40 million bottles of beefy red and tasty rosé wines. Eleven of the best villages (crus) can now add their own names to the AC name, including Cabrières, la CLAPE, Montpeyroux, PIC ST-LOUP, St-Drézery and St-Georges-d'Orques. Best producers: Abbaye de Valmagne, d'Auphilhac★, Bruguière, Calage★, Carignano co-op★, la Coste★, Hortus★, MAS JULLIEN★★. Best years: **1995 94 93 91**.

**COTEAUX DU LAYON AC** *Loire Valley, France* Sweet wine from the Layon Valley south of Angers. The wine is made from Chenin Blanc grapes that, ideally, are attacked by noble rot. In great years like 1990 and 89 and from a talented grower, this can be one of the world's great sweet wines. Seven villages can use the Coteaux du Layon-Villages AC (one of the best is Chaume) and put their own name on the label, and these wines, in particular, are definitely underpriced for the quality. Two small sub-areas, BONNEZEAUX and QUARTS DE CHAUME, have their own ACs. Can be aged for 5, 10 or 15 years or more. Best producers: Baudouin★★, Baumard★, Bidet★, de Breuil★★, Cady★★, Delesvaux★★, Ogereau★★, Pierre-Bise★★, Pithon★★, Joseph Renou★★, Robineau★, Sauveroy★, Soucherie★, Soulez★★, Touche Noire★★.

Best years: (1996) 95 **94 93 90 89 88 85 83 82 76 75**.

**COTEAUX DU LYONNAIS AC** *Burgundy, France* Good, light, Beaujolais-style reds and a few whites and rosés from scattered vineyards between Villefranche and Lyon. Drink young. Best producers: Cave des Vignerons de Sain Bel, Descotes, Fayolle.

**COTEAUX DU TRICASTIN AC** *Rhône Valley, France* From the southern Drôme these are light, fresh reds and rosés with attractive juicy fruit. Only a little white is made but is worth looking out for as a fairly good, nutty drink to consume within the year. Best producers: de Grangeneuve, Lônes, Tour d'Elyssas, Vieux Micocoulier.

**COTEAUX VAROIS AC** *Provence, France* An area to watch with new plantings of classic grapes. Best producers: Bremond, Clos de la Truffière, Deffends, Garbelle, Ch. St-Estève, St-Jean-le-Vieux.

**CÔTES DE BERGERAC AC** *South-West France* The AC covers good-quality reds made from the same grapes as BERGERAC AC but with a higher minimum alcohol level. Côtes de Bergerac Moelleux AC is the name for sweet wines. Best producers: Belingard-Chayne, Combrillac, le Mayne, Tour des Gendres.

**CÔTES DE BLAYE AC** *Bordeaux, France* The main AC for white wines from the right bank of the Gironde estuary. Almost all the best whites of the area are now dry. Drink young. Best producer: Cave de Marcillac.

**CÔTES DE BOURG AC** *Bordeaux, France* Mainly a red wine area to the south of the COTES DE BLAYE, where the best producers and the local co-op at Tauriac make great efforts. The reds are full and blackcurranty and can age for 6–10 years, though most are drunk at 3–5. Very little white is made, most of which is dry and dull. Best producers: de Barbe, Brulesécaille, Falfas★, Guerry, Haut-Guiraud, Macay, Nodoz, Roc-de-Cambes★, Rousset, Tauriac co-op, Tayac. Best years: 1996 **95 94 90 89 88**.

**CÔTES DE CASTILLON AC** *Bordeaux, France* As the price of decent red Bordeaux climbs ever upward, Côtes de Castillon wines have remained an excellent, reasonably priced alternative – a little earthy but full and round. Depending on the vintage the wine is enjoyable between 3 and 10 years. Best producers: d'Aiguilhe, de Belcier★, Cap-de-Faugères, Côte-Montpezat★, Lapeyrouie, de Parenchère, de Pitray, Poupille, Robin, Vieux-Ch.-Champs-de-Mars. Best years: 1996 95 **94 90 89 88 86 85**.

**CÔTES DE DURAS AC** *South-West France* AC between ENTRE-DEUX-MERS and BERGERAC in the Lot-et-Garonne, with 2 very active co-ops which offer extremely good, fresh, grassy reds and whites from traditional Bordeaux grapes but at distinctly lower prices. Drink the wines young. Best producers: Amblard, Conti, Cours★, Duras co-op, Ferrant, Lander-rouat co-op, Lapiarre★, Laulan.

**CÔTES DE FRANCS AC** *Bordeaux, France*   Mainly red wine from a tiny but up-and-coming area east of ST-EMILION. Quality is helped by investment in the area by several leading POMEROL and St-Émilion producers. Already impressive, you can expect more great wines from here in the future. Best producers: les Charmes-Godard, la Claverie★, de Francs★, la Prade, Puygueraud★★. Best years: 1996 95 **94 90 89 88 86 85 83**.

**CÔTES DU FRONTONNAIS AC** *South-West France*   From north of Toulouse some of the most distinctive reds in South-West France. Négrette is the chief grape and the wine can be superb and positively silky in texture. It can age well but I prefer it young. There is also a little fairly good rosé. Best producers: de Baudare, Bellevue-la-Forêt, la Colombière, Ferran★, Flotis★, Laurou, Montauriol★, la Palme★, le Roc.

**CÔTES DE GASCOGNE, VIN DE PAYS DES** *South-West France*   Mainly white wines from the Gers *département*. This is Armagnac country, but the tangy-fresh, fruity table wines are tremendously good – especially when you consider that they were condemned as unfit for anything but distillation a decade ago. Best producers: Aurin, GRASSA★, Union des Producteurs PLAIMONT★, Hugh RYMAN★, Dom. de Joy, Dom. St-Lannes.

**CÔTES DU JURA AC** *Jura, France*   The regional AC for Jura covers a wide variety of wines, including local specialities VIN JAUNE and VIN DE PAILLE. The Savagnin makes strong-tasting whites and Chardonnay is used for some good dry whites and Champagne-method fizz. The reds and rosés can be good when made from Pinot Noir, but when the local varieties Poulsard and Trousseau are used, the wines can be a bit weird. Drink young. Best producers: d'Arlay★, Bourdy, Grand, Gréa, Joly★, Pupillin co-op, Rolet, Tissot.

**CÔTES DU LUBÉRON AC** *Rhône Valley, France*   Wine production is dominated by the co-ops east of Avignon. The light, easy wines are for drinking young, when they are refreshing and enjoyable. Best producers: Ch. la Canorgue, Ch. de l'Isolette★, Val Joanis★, Ch. de Mille, la Sable, la Tour-d'Aigues co-op, Vendran.

**CÔTES DU MARMANDAIS AC** *South-West France*   The Marmandais producers have always set out to make Bordeaux look-alikes and the red wines achieve a fair amount of success. Syrah is also permitted. Best producers: Boissonneau, Cave de Beaupuy, Cocumont co-op.

**CÔTES DE MONTRAVEL AC** *South-West France*   Small area within the BERGERAC AC for sweet and medium-sweet whites from Sémillon, Sauvignon Blanc and Muscadelle. Drink young. Best producers: Gourgueil, de Perreau, Pique-Sègue.

**CÔTES DE PROVENCE AC** *Provence, France*   Large AC for mainly reds and rosés, showing signs of improvement in recent years. Now generally much fruitier but should still be drunk young. The whites are forgettable. Best producers: Barbeyrolles, de Berne, Commanderie de Peyrassol, l'Estandon, Féraud★, Gavoty★, Hauts de St-Jean, les Maîtres Vignerons de St-Tropez, Mentone, Minuty, Ott, Pampelonne, RICHEAUME★, Rimauresq, St-Baillon★, St-Maur.

**CÔTES DU RHÔNE AC** *Rhône Valley, France*   The general AC for the whole Rhône Valley. Over 90% is red and rosé mainly from Grenache with some Cinsaut, Syrah, Carignan and Mourvèdre to add lots of warm, spicy southern personality. Modern wine-making has revolutionized the style and today's wines are generally juicy, spicy and easy to drink, ideally within 2 years. Most wine is made by the co-ops and sold under merchants' labels. Drink as young as possible. Best producers: (reds) Aussellons, BEAUCASTEL, Cantharide, CLAPE★★, de Fonsalette★★, les Goubert, du GRAND MOULAS★, GUIGAL★★, JABOULET, Mont Redon, Mousset, Pascal, Richaud★, de Ruth, St-Estève d'Uchaux, STE-ANNE★; (whites) Chusclan co-op, CLAPE★, Laudun co-op, Pélaquié★, Rabasse-Charavin, STE-ANNE★. Best years: (reds) 1995 94 93 91 90.

**CÔTES DU RHÔNE-VILLAGES AC** *Rhône Valley, France* AC for wines with a higher minimum alcohol content than COTES DU RHONE, covering 16 villages in the southern Rhône that have traditionally made superior wine (especially Cairanne, Séguret, Valréas, Sablet, Visan, Chusclan, Laudun). Almost all the best Villages wines are red – they have a marvellous spicy flavour and can age for up to 10 years. Best producers: Alary★, Ameillaud★, BEAUMES-DE-VENISE co-op, Boisson, Brusset★, Cairanne co-op, Chamfort, Combe★, les Goubert, du GRAND MOULAS★, Roger Meffre, l'Oratoire St-Martin, Pélaquié★, Rabasse Charavin★★, Richaud★★, St-Antoine, STE-ANNE★★, Trignon★, Vacqueyras co-op, Verquière. Best years: 1995 94 93 90 89 88.

**CÔTES DU ROUSSILLON AC** *Roussillon, France* Large AC, with reds dominant, covering much of ROUSSILLON. The reds and rosés provide some of southern France's best-value drinking. The small amount of white is mainly unmemorable. Production is dominated by the co-ops, some with enlightened winemakers but estates are starting to make their presence felt. Best producers: (reds) Vignerons CATALANS★, Casenove★, CAZES★, Charmettes★, Forca Real★, GAUBY★, de Jau★, Joliette, Laporte, Mas Crémat★, Mas Rous, Piquemal, Rey, Rivesaltes co-op★, Rombeau, Salvat, Sarda-Malet★. Best years: 1995 94 93.

**CÔTES DU ROUSSILLON-VILLAGES AC** *Roussillon, France* AC covering reds from the best sites in the northern part of COTES DU ROUSSILLON. The wine from villages like Caramany and Latour-de-France is wonderfully juicy when young but can age. Best producers: Agly co-op, Cap de Fouste, Vignerons CATALANS★, CAZES★, des Chênes★, Forca Real★, GAUBY★★, de Jau★, Joliette, Mas Crémat★, Maury co-op, Ch. Montner, Rivesaltes co-op★, Sabazin★, St-Martin, Vingrau. Best years: 1995 94 93.

**CÔTES DE ST-MONT VDQS** *South-West France* A good VDQS for firm but fruity reds and some fair rosés and dry whites. Best producer: Union des Producteurs PLAIMONT★ (especially Château de Sabazan).

**CÔTES DU TARN, VIN DE PAYS DES** *South-West France* Wines from around Toulouse-Lautrec's home town of Albi. The whites should be sharp but fruity and the young reds are enjoyable too. Best producers: Chaumet-Lagrange, Gayrel, Labastide-de-Levis co-op.

**CÔTES DE THAU, VIN DE PAYS DES** *Languedoc, France* Red, white and rosé from the shores of Lake Thau, west of the Mediterranean town of Sète. The whites are often surprisingly good for the Midi. Best producers: de Gaujal, Genson, UCA Vignerons Garrigues, Pinet co-op, Pomérols co-op.

**CÔTES DE THONGUE, VIN DE PAYS DES** *Languedoc, France* Mainly red wines from north-east of Béziers. Most are dull quaffers made from Carignan, but recent plantings of classic grapes by dynamic estates can be excellent. Best producers: de l'Arjolle★, de Bellevue★, Condamine l'Evêque★, Croix Belle★.

**CÔTES DU VENTOUX AC** *Rhône Valley, France*   An increasingly successful AC, with vineyards on the slopes of Mt Ventoux on the eastern side of the RHONE VALLEY near Carpentras, especially when the wine is well-made from a single estate or blended by a serious merchant. The reds can have a lovely juicy fruit, or in the case of JABOULET and VIEILLE FERME, some real stuffing. There is only a little white. Best producers: Anges, Champ-Long, JABOULET★, Pascal, Pesquié, Union des Caves du Ventoux, VIEILLE FERME★.

**CÔTES DU VIVARAIS VDQS** *Rhône Valley, France*   In the Ardèche and northern Gard typical southern Rhône grapes produce light, fresh reds and rosés, for drinking young, but plantings of classic varieties (Cabernet Sauvignon and Syrah) are producing deep-flavoured wines of surprising quality and irresistible price. Best producers: Chais du Vivarais, les Vignerons Ardèchois, de Vigier.

**COTNARI** *Romania*   A hilly region close to the border with Moldova, whose warm mesoclimate is well suited to the development of noble rot. Romania's finest sweet wines are made here using a blend of Grasa, Tamiîoasă, Francusa and Fetească Albă grapes.

**EL COTO** *Rioja DOC, Rioja, Spain*   El Coto Crianza★ is one of the few utterly reliable, widely available reds in restaurants right across Spain. Coto de Imaz★ is the name for the savoury fragrant Reservas and Gran Reservas. Best years: (reds) **1994 92 91 89 88 87 86 85 82 81**.

**COULY-DUTHEIL** *Chinon, Loire Valley, France*   Large merchant house responsible for 10% of the CHINON AC. Uses its own vineyards for the best wines, particularly Clos de l'Écho★★ and Clos de l'Olive★. Top blend is la Baronnie Madeleine★, which combines delicious raspberry fruit with a considerable capacity to age. Also sells a range of other Touraine wines. Best years: (1996) 95 **93 90 89 88 86 85**.

**PIERRE COURSODON** *St-Joseph AC, Rhône Valley, France*   A good family-owned domaine producing rich ST-JOSEPH from very old vines. The red wines★★ need up to 5 years to show all the magnificent cassis and truffle and violety richness of the best Rhône reds, especially the top wine, called le Paradis St-Pierre★★. Pierre Coursodon also produces tiny quantities of white St-Joseph★, which should be drunk young. Best years: (reds) (1996) **95 94 90 89 88 86 85 83**.

**CH. COUTET★★** *Barsac AC, 1er Cru Classé, Bordeaux, France*   BARSAC'S largest Classed Growth property is not usually as rich as the AC's other First Growth, CLIMENS. The wines are aromatic, with a lively fruit character, and age well. Since 1981 a special Cuvée Madame★★★ is made in exceptional years, which ranks with the greatest sweet wines. Best years: (1996) 95 **90 89 88 86 83 81 76 75**.

**COWRA** *New South Wales, Australia*   New and very promising district with a reliable warm climate and good water supplies for irrigation. It produces soft, peachy Chardonnay and spicy, cool-tasting Shiraz. Best producers: Arrowfield, MCWILLIAMS (Barwang vineyard★), ROTHBURY, Charles Sturt University.

**CRÉMANT** French term for up-market sparkling wine from Alsace, Bordeaux, Burgundy, Die, Jura, Limoux, Loire and Luxembourg, imposing stricter regulations than those for ordinary fizz. The term was used for Champagnes with less pressure (3 atmospheres instead of 6) but it was banned in 1994.

**CRÉMANT D'ALSACE AC** *Alsace, France* Good Champagne-method sparkling wine from Alsace, usually made from Pinot Blanc, Chardonnay, Auxerrois, Pinot Gris and Pinot Noir are also permitted. Reasonable quality, if not great value for money. Best producers: Joseph Cattin, Dopff au Moulin, Dopff & Irion, Ginglinger, Willy Gisselbrecht, KUENTZ-BAS, Muré, Ostertag, Willm, Wolfberger.

**CRÉMANT DE BOURGOGNE AC** *Burgundy, France* Most Burgundian Crémant is white and is made either from Chardonnay alone or blended with Pinot Noir. The result, especially in ripe years, can be full, soft, almost honey-flavoured – if you give the wine the 2–3 years' aging needed for

mellowness to develop. The best rosé comes from the Chablis and Auxerre regions in northern Burgundy. Best producers: Delorme, Lucius-Grégoire, Parigot-Richard, Simonnet-Febvre; and the co-ops at Bailly (the best for rosé), Lugny★, St-Gengoux-de-Scissé and Viré.

**CRÉMANT DE DIE AC** *Rhône Valley, France* AC for fizz made entirely from the Clairette Blanche grape. Less aromatic than CLAIRETTE DE DIE.

**CRÉMANT DE JURA AC** *Jura, France* AC created in 1995 for fizz from Jura. Annual production is expected to be around 2 million bottles, largely Chardonnay-based, with Poulsard for the pinks.

**CRÉMANT DE LIMOUX AC** *South-West France* Sparkling wine AC introduced in Limoux in 1990. The wines must have a minimum of 30% Chardonnay, Chenin Blanc, or a combination of the 2; the rest of the blend is made from the local Mauzac grape. The wines are aged on lees for a year and generally have more complexity than straight BLANQUETTE DE LIMOUX, but should be drunk young. Best producers: Antech, Delmas, Guinot, Laurens★, Martinolles★, SIEUR D'ARQUES CO-OP★, Vadent.

**CRÉMANT DE LOIRE AC** *Loire Valley, France* The AC for Champagne-method sparkling wine in Anjou and Touraine, created in 1975 in an effort to improve Loire fizzes. With stricter regulations than VOUVRAY and SAUMUR, the result is an attractive wine, with more fruit and yeast character. Good to drink as soon as it is released and can be excellent value. Best producers: Berger★, Gabillière, Girault, GRATIEN & MEYER★, Lambert★★, Langlois-Château, Michaud★, OISLY-ET-THESEE CO-OP★, Passavant★.

**CRÉPY AC** *Savoie, France* Light, relatively acidic white wines made with Chasselas from vineyards south of Lake Geneva. Drink as young as possible. Best producers: Goy, Mercier.

**CRIANZA** Spanish term for the youngest official category of matured wine. A red Crianza wine must have had at least 2 years' aging (1 in oak, 1 in bottle) before sale; a white or rosé, 1 year.

**CRIMEA** *Ukraine* This Black Sea peninsula has been an important centre of wine production since the early 19th century. Its greatest wines are the historical treasures of the Massandra winery: superb dessert and fortified wines, originally destined for the Tsar's summer palace at Livadia. Present-day wine-making seems understandably but regrettably aimless.

**CRIOTS-BÂTARD-MONTRACHET AC** See Bâtard-Montrachet AC.

**CROFT** *Port DOC, Douro, Portugal* Croft's vintage ports★★ can be deceptively light in their youth, but they develop into subtle, elegant wines. The 10-year-old tawny★ is the best of the rest. Best years: (vintage ports) 1994 91 **77 70 66 63**.

**CROZES-HERMITAGE AC** *Rhône Valley, France* The largest of the northern Rhône ACs. Ideally the reds should have a full colour with a strong, meaty but rich flavour. You can drink it young but in ripe years from a hillside site it improves greatly for 2–5 years. The quality has improved dramatically since the late 1980s. The best whites are extremely fresh, clean and racy. In general drink white Crozes young before the floral perfume disappears. Best producers: (reds) Belle★★, Caves des Clairmonts, CHAPOUTIER★, DELAS★, Fayolle★, GRAILLOT★★★, JABOULET (Thalabert★★), Pochon★★, Tardy & Ange★★ (also sold as Domaine Barret); (whites) Entrefaux, Fayolle★, JABOULET, Pochon★★, Pradelle★. Best years: (reds) 1996 **95 94 91 90 89 88 85**; (whites) 1996 **95 94 91 90 89**.

**CRU** French for a specific plot of land or particular estate. Bordeaux, Burgundy and Champagne use the term for individual vineyard sites, or the estates which own them. In Burgundy, growths are divided into Grands (great) and Premiers (first) Crus, and apply solely to the actual land. In Champagne the same terms are used for whole villages. In Bordeaux there are various hierarchical levels of Cru referring to estates rather than their vineyards.

**CRU BOURGEOIS** French term for wines from the MEDOC and SAUTERNES that are ranked immediately below Crus Classés. The best of these, such as d'ANGLUDET in MARGAUX and CHASSE-SPLEEN in MOULIS, make very fine wines and are a match for many a Classed Growth.

**CRU CLASSÉ** The Classed Growths are the aristocracy of Bordeaux, ennobled by the classifications of 1855 (for the MEDOC, BARSAC and SAUTERNES), 1955, 1969, 1986 and 1996 (for ST-EMILION) and 1947, 1953 and 1959 (for GRAVES). Curiously, POMEROL has never been classified. The modern classifications are more reliable than the 1855 version, which was based solely on the price of the wines at the time of the Great Exhibition in Paris, but in terms of prestige, the 1855 classification remains the most important. With the exception of a single alteration in 1973, when Ch. MOUTON-ROTHSCHILD was elevated to First Growth status, the list has not changed since 1855. It is certainly in need of revision.

**HANS CRUSIUS** *Traisen, Nahe, Germany* Hans and Peter Crusius, father and son, produce historically good but no longer thrilling wines on their Traiser Bastei★ vineyard. Also good wines from the Schlossböckelheimer Felsenberg★, which manage to be both rich and flinty. Best years: 1996 95 94 **93 89 88 86 85 83**.

**CULLENS** *Margaret River, Western Australia* One of the original and best MARGARET RIVER vineyards, run by the Cullen women (winemakers are Vanya and her mother Diana). The Chardonnay★★★ is one of the region's richest and most complex; Sémillon★ and Sauvignon Blanc★ are made deliberately non-herbaceous; Cabernet-Merlot★★★ is gloriously soft, deep and scented, and Reserve Cabernet Sauvignon★★ can be particularly good. Best years: (reds) 1994 93 **92 91 90 86 84 82**.

110

**CUVAISON** *Napa Valley AVA, California, USA* Cuvaison built a reputation for brooding red wines in the 1970s but has taken a while to modernize styles. Now it produces delicious, focussed Merlot★★, and good but not thrilling Chardonnay. Most should be drunk young. A budget label, Calistope Cellars, was launched in 1993. Best years: (Merlot) **1994 92 91 90 88**.

**CUVE CLOSE** A bulk process used to produce inexpensive sparkling wines. The second fermentation, which produces the bubbles, takes place in tank rather than in the bottle (as in the superior, but more costly Champagne method). If the grapes are good, the results can be excellent, and often, as with ASTI Spumante, it is the best method for preserving freshness.

**CUVÉE** French for the contents of a single vat or tank, but more commonly used to describe a wine selected by an individual producer for reasons of style or quality.

**CVNE** *Rioja DOC, Rioja, Spain* Compañía Vinícola del Norte de España is the full name of this firm, but it's usually known as 'coonay'. Monopole★ is one of RIOJA'S only remaining well-oaked whites; the reds have had sulphide problems recently, but the Viña Real can be rich and meaty, and the top Imperial Gran Reserva★, long-lived and impressive. Best years: (reds) **1993 92 91 90 89 88 87 86 85 81**.

**DIDIER DAGUENEAU** *Pouilly-Fumé AC, Loire Valley, France* The wild man of POUILLY-FUME, a much-needed innovator and quality fanatic in a complacent region. Best-known for his barrel-fermented Sauvignon Blanc called Silex★★. Drink young or with short aging from better vintages. Best years: 1996 **95 94 93 90 89 88**.

**DÃO DOC** *Beira Alta, Portugal* Dão has steep slopes ideal for vineyards, and a great climate for growing the local grape varieties. Yet most wines are fruitless, flat and mean. At last things are changing, led by SOGRAPE and a few single quintas. Whites are being freshened up, and reds are beginning to realize their long-promised potential. Best producers: (reds) CAVES ALIANCA★, CAVES SAO JOAO★★, Conde de Santar, Fonte do Ouro★, SOGRAPE★; (single quinta) Quinta da Maias★★, Quinta de Pellada★, Quinta dos Roques★★, Quinta de Sães★.

**KURT DARTING** *Bad Dürkheim, Pfalz, Germany* Darting makes full, four-square wines in BAD DÜRKHEIM (Spielberg), Ungstein (Herrenberg) and WACHENHEIM (Mandelgarten), including rich and peachy Kabinett★ from Dürkheim, and a superb Ungsteiner Herrenberg 1992 Riesling Spätlese★★.

**VINCENT DAUVISSAT** *Chablis AC, Burgundy, France* One of the top 3 domaines in CHABLIS, specializing in concentrated, oak-aged wines from 2 Grand Cru and 3 Premier Cru sites. This is Chablis at its most complex – refreshing, seductive and beautifully structured with the fruit balancing the subtle influence of oak. Look out in particular for la Forêt★★ and the more aromatic Vaillons★★. Best years: 1995 94 93 **92 90 89 88**.

**DE BORTOLI** *Riverina, New South Wales, Australia* Large family-owned winery producing a truly sublime botrytized Sémillon★★★ that is head and shoulders above the rest of its vast range of inexpensive RIVERINA quaffers. De Bortoli is also crafting some of the YARRA VALLEY's best Chardonnay★★, Shiraz★★ and Pinot Noir★.

**DE WETSHOF** *Robertson WO, South Africa* Danie and Lesca de Wet are a formidable team who have made Chardonnay their speciality: the elegant Bateleur★ and spicy d'Honneur★, both barrel-fermented, are the pick of the range. Riesling, particularly dessert-style, can also tantalize. A much-needed new bottling line should improve quality further.

**DEHLINGER** *Russian River AVA, California, USA* Outstanding Pinot Noir★★★ from estate vineyards in the cool Russian River region a few miles from the Pacific, best at 5–10 years old. Also makes solid Chardonnay★ and bold, peppery Syrah★★. Best years: (reds) 1994 93 **92 91 90 87 86**.

**DEINHARD** See Wegeler-Deinhard.

**DELAS FRÈRES** *Rhône Valley, France* An underrated merchant based near Tournon, now part of DEUTZ, selling wines from the entire Rhône Valley. The wines from its own northern Rhône vineyards have improved enormously in recent vintages. Look out for the beguilingly aromatic CONDRIEU★, best drunk young, as well as its single-vineyard, dense, powerful HERMITAGE★★, which needs as much as a decade to reach its peak, and the perfumed single-vineyard COTE-ROTIE★★. In a lighter style, the CROZES-HERMITAGE★ is a good bet. Best years: (premium reds) (1996) 95 94 91 90 89 **88 86 85 83 78**; (whites) **1996 95 94 93 90 89**.

**DELATITE** *Mansfield, Victoria, Australia* The Ritchies were graziers who got involved in wine when diversifying their farm. Their high-altitude vineyard in sight of VICTORIA's snowfields grows delicate, aromatic Riesling★★ and Traminer★★; there is also subtle Chardonnay★ and extravagantly fruity reds. The Pinot Noir★ is perfumed, and Devil's River★★ is a very smart, minty Bordeaux blend. Best years: (reds) **1994 93 92 91 90 88 87 86 82**.

**DELEGAT'S** *Henderson, Auckland, North Island, New Zealand* Family winery specializing in Chardonnay, Cabernet-Merlot, and Sauvignon Blanc from the HAWKES BAY and MARLBOROUGH (under Oyster Bay★ label) regions. Until recently it was a reliable producer rather than a memorable one, but prices are keen and quality is improving rapidly, which is reflected in very good Proprietor's Reserve Chardonnay★★ and Merlot★★. Best years: **1996 94 92 91**.

**DEMI-SEC** French for medium-dry.

**DENBIES** *Surrey, England* This is the giant among English vineyards with 102ha (253 acres) planted since 1986 on the chalky soils outsides Dorking. Twenty different varieties have produced, so far, a range of wines from the adequate to the truly exciting. The Dornfelder red★ is memorable for an English effort, the Pinot Noir, sparklers and botrytized whites★ are good, and the dry white wines show a perfume that almost makes you forgive them their rather exalted prices.

**DEUTZ** *Champagne AC, Champagne, France* A Champagne house that is probably better known for its California and New Zealand fizz than for its Champagne. Unfairly so, perhaps, because this small company, now owned by ROEDERER, produces excellent, medium-priced Champagne. The non-vintage★ is always reliable, but the top wine is the weightier Cuvée William Deutz★★. Best years: **1990 89 88 85 82**.

**DÉZALEY** *Vaud, Switzerland* One of the top wine communes in the VAUD, making surprisingly powerful wines from the white Chasselas grape. Best producers: J D Fonjallaz (l'Arbalète)★, Conne, Pinget★, Testuz.

**DIAMOND CREEK VINEYARDS** *Napa Valley AVA,*
*California, USA* This small NAPA VALLEY estate
specializes in Cabernet; from 3 vineyards it
produces Volcanic Hill★★★, Red Rock Terrace★★
and Gravelly Meadow★. These are such huge,
tannic wines that when I taste them young I
swear they won't ever come round. Yet there's
usually a sweet, perfumed inner core of fruit that
gradually spreads out to envelop the tannin over

5–10 years, producing one of California's great Cabernet experiences.
Best years: 1994 92 91 90 **87 86 85 84 80 75**.

**DO (DENOMINACIÓN DE ORIGEN)** Spain's equivalent of the French
quality wine category AC, regulating origin and production methods.
Some Spanish DOs frankly don't deserve the title.

**DOC (DENOMINAÇÃO DE ORIGEM CONTROLADA)** The top regional
classification for Portuguese wines since 1990. Formerly called *Região
Demarcada* or RD.

**DOC (DENOMINACIÓN DE ORIGEN CALIFICADA)** Recent Spanish quality wine category, intended to be one step up from DO. So far only
RIOJA qualifies.

**DOC (DENOMINAZIONE DI ORIGINE CONTROLLATA)** Italian quality
wine category, regulating origin, grape varieties, yield and production
methods. Covers more than 250 zones, which seems excessive since
many wines are obscure. But a commitment to raise the proportion of
DOC wines in Italy's total from 15% to 50% in the near future (while
bringing many of the Super-Tuscan Vino da Tavolas under new
regional appellations) may help to give the system much-needed
credibility.

**DOCG (DENOMINAZIONE DI ORIGINE CONTROLLATA E GARANTITA)**
The highest tier of the Italian classification system has so far been
reached by 14 wines. It is a guarantee of authenticity, and supposedly
quality, since wines are made under strict regulations and are
approved by tasting panels. For such established wines as BAROLO,
BARBARESCO and BRUNELLO DI MONTALCINO the DOCG label serves mainly
as a further mark of prestige. But for others its main purpose seems to
be to stimulate improvement, as witnessed in CHIANTI, VINO NOBILE DI
MONTEPULCIANO, ALBANA DI ROMAGNA, ASTI and VERNACCIA DI SAN GIMIGNANO.

**DOCTOR** *Bernkastel, Mosel, Germany* Famous vineyard at Bernkastel
(not to be confused with the Doktor vineyard in the RHEINHESSEN).
Rather overrated and overpriced. Best producer: WEGELER-DEINHARD★★.

**CH. DOISY-DAËNE**★★ *Barsac AC, 2ème Cru Classé, Bordeaux, France* A
consistently good BARSAC property and unusual in that the sweet wine
is made exclusively from Sémillon, giving it extra richness. It ages well
for 10 years or more. Doisy-Daëne Sec★ is a good, perfumed, dry
white Bordeaux. Drink young. Best years: (sweet) (1996) (95) 94 **90 89
88 86 83 82 79**; (dry) (1996) **95 94 90 89 88 87**.

**CH. DOISY-VÉDRINES**★★ *Barsac AC, 2ème Cru Classé, Bordeaux, France*
Next door to DOISY-DAENE, Doisy-Védrines's sweet wine is quite different
in style as it is fermented and aged in barrel. This makes it fatter and
more syrupy than most BARSAC wines. Best years: (sweet) (1996) (95) 94
**90 89 88 86 85 83 82 76 75**.

**DOLCETTO** One of Italy's most charming native grapes, producing purple wines bursting at the seams with fruit. Virtually exclusive to PIEDMONT, it is DOC in 7 zones, with styles ranging from the intense and rich in Alba, Ovada and Dogliani, to the lighter, more perfumed versions in Acqui and ASTI. Usually best drunk within a year or two, top wines can age up to 4 years. Best producers: (Alba) ALTARE★★, Bartolo MASCARELLO★★, Giuseppe MASCARELLO★, Renato Ratti★, Vietti★★, VOERZIO★★.

**DÔLE** *Valais, Switzerland* Red wine from the Swiss VALAIS that must be made from at least 51% Pinot Noir, the rest being Gamay. Dôle is generally a light wine – the deeper, richer (100% Pinot Noir) styles have the right to call themselves Pinot Noir. Best producers: Caves Imesch, M Clavien★, J Germanier★, Mathier★, Orsat.

**DOMAINE CARNEROS** *Carneros AVA, California, USA* From its founding in 1987, this TAITTINGER-owned sparkling wine house has shown great promise. The pay-off to that promise came with the release in late 1995 of a 91 Brut★ and a remarkable 90 Blanc de Blancs★★, a vivid and powerful wine with a creamy, silky mouthfeel. Also just released is a very tasty Pinot Noir★★ still wine.

**DOMAINE CHANDON** *Napa Valley AVA, California, USA* The first of what turned out to be many French-owned (in this case, by MOET & CHANDON) sparkling wine producers in California. Has shown remarkable consistency and good quality over the years with non-vintage bubblies that stay reasonably priced. The Reserve★ bottlings, rich and creamy, are especially worth seeking out. Blanc de Blancs★ made entirely from CARNEROS Chardonnay is a welcome addition to the line. The super Reserve Étoile★ has reached ★★ on occasion. Shadow Creek is a quaffable budget line of sparklers.

**DOMAINE DROUHIN** *Willamette Valley AVA, Oregon, USA* Burgundy wine merchants Joseph DROUHIN bought 40ha (100 acres) in Oregon in 1987 with plans to make great Pinot Noir★★★, and has done it. The first vintage, 1988, made from bought-in grapes, was more than adequate. The 91, made from estate-grown grapes, is one of the best yet from Oregon. Best years: **1994 93 92 91 90**.

**DOMAINE PAUL BRUNO** *Maipo, Chile* Pontallier and Prats are the surnames behind this small premium project close to Santiago. After a disappointing start, the new vintages of the Cabernet blend show more promise (but still at a price). Given their experience, 'could do better' should still be pinned to the winery wall. Best years: **1996**.

**DOMECQ** *Jerez y Manzanilla DO, Andalucía and Rioja DOC, País Vasco, Spain* The largest of the sherry companies, best known for its reliable fino, La Ina★. However, the top-of-the-range wines, dry Amontillado 51-1A★★★, Sibarita Palo Cortado★★★ and Venerable Pedro Ximénez★★, are spectacular. Domecq is also the world's biggest brandy producer, and make light, elegant red RIOJA★ from its own vineyards.

**DOMINUS** *Napa Valley AVA, California, USA* Red wine only from this property owned by Christian Moueix, director of Bordeaux's PETRUS. Wines are based on Cabernet with leavenings of Merlot and Cabernet Franc. The dense, rich 1990★★ is the finest yet. Early vintages were mercilessly tannic, but recent ones are improved. Exciting winemaker David Ramey (ex-Chalk Hill and MATANZAS CREEK) took over in 1996.

**DONAULAND** *Niederösterreich, Austria*    Amorphous wine region on both banks of the Danube stretching from just north of Vienna west to St Polten.

**HERMANN DÖNNHOFF** *Oberhausen, Nahe, Germany*    Number one NAHE estate with sites in Oberhausen, Niederhausen and BAD KREUZNACH. There is some fine Kabinett★★ and Spätlese★★ and sensational Auslese★★★ and EISWEIN★★★ in top years. Best years: 1995 94 **93 92 90 89 88 86 83**.

**LA DORDOGNE, VIN DE PAYS DE** *South-West France*    Sémillon-based whites best drunk young, some Chardonnay (Ch. la JAUBERTIE), and fruity BERGERAC-style reds that can age for 1–2 years.

**DOURO DOC** *Douro, Portugal*    As well as a flood of port and basic table wine, some of Portugal's top, soft-textured reds come from here. There are good whites, made from the more aromatic white port varieties, such as SOGRAPE's Planalto★ and oak-aged Reserva. Whites are best young but reds may improve for 10 years or more. Best producers: CAVES ALIANCA★, FERREIRA (for BARCA VELHA★★), QUINTA DO COTTO (Grande Escolha★★), QUINTA DO CRASTO★★, Quinta da Gaivosa★★, QUINTA DE LA ROSA★★, SOGRAPE (★ for reds), Quinto do Vale de Raposa★.

**DOW** *Port DOC, Douro, Portugal*    The grapes for Dow's vintage ports★★★ come mostly from the Quinta do Bomfim★, near Pinhão. Quinta do Bomfim also makes single-quinta vintage ports in 'off-vintages'. Dow ports are all relatively dry, and there is some excellent 20-year-old tawny★★. Best years: (vintage ports) 1994 91 **85 83 80 77 70 66 63**.

**JEAN-PAUL DROIN** *Chablis AC, Burgundy, France*    Jean-Paul Droin sells some of his production to the Nuits-St-Georges merchant LABOURE-ROI, but manages to bottle no fewer than 14 different wines under his own label. Apart from his CHABLIS★ and PETIT CHABLIS, all of Droin's wines are fermented and/or aged in oak barrels. The best wines are the big, buttery Chablis Premiers Crus – Montmains★★ and Vosgros★★ – and Grands Crus – Vaudésir★★ and Grenouille★★. Best years: 1995 **93 92 90 89 88**.

**DROMANA ESTATE** *Mornington Peninsula, Victoria, Australia*    Garry Crittenden started the peninsula's model vineyard in 1982, using the latest techniques for Pinot Noir★, Chardonnay★★ and Cabernet-Merlot★★ wines, which are squeaky clean and well focussed. Italian varietals under the Garry Crittenden 'I' label are of special interest. Schinus is a popular second label.

**JOSEPH DROUHIN** *Beaune, Burgundy, France*    One of the best Burgundian merchants, now Japanese-owned, with substantial vineyard holdings in CHABLIS and the COTE D'OR, and DOMAINE DROUHIN in Oregon, USA. Drouhin makes a consistently good, if expensive, range of wines from all over Burgundy. Look for BONNE-MARES★★, ROMANEE-ST-VIVANT★★, BEAUNE Clos des Mouches (red★ and white★★), le Musigny★★ and le MONTRACHET★★★ from the Domaine du Marquis de Laguiche. Drouhin offers better value in Chablis★★ and less glamorous Burgundian ACs, such as RULLY★ and ST-AUBIN★. The BEAUJOLAIS is always good, but overall Drouhin's whites are (just) better than the reds. Quality reds and whites should be aged for at least 5 years, often better nearer 10. Best years: (reds) 1995 93 **92 90 89 88 85**; (whites) **1995 93 92 90 89 88**.

**PIERRE-JACQUES DRUET** *Bourgueil, Loire Valley, France*   A passionate producer of top-notch BOURGUEIL and small quantities of CHINON. Druet makes 5 Bourgueils, les Cent Boisselées★, Cuvée Beauvais★, Cuvée Reservée★★, Cuvée Grand Mont★★ and Vaumoreau (★★ in good years only), each a complex expression of the Cabernet Franc, but lacking obvious, up-front fruit. Best aged for 3–5 years. Best years: (1996) 95 **93 91 90 89 88 85 83**.

**DRY CREEK VALLEY AVA** *Sonoma, California, USA*   Best known for Sauvignon Blanc, Zinfandel and Cabernet Sauvignon, this valley runs west of ALEXANDER VALLEY

*Stefani Vineyard*
**CHARDONNAY**
DRY CREEK VALLEY
1995

AVA, and similarly becomes hotter moving northwards. Best producers: Dry Creek Vineyards★, DUXOUP★★, FERRARI-CARANO★★, GALLO (Chardonnay★), NALLE★★, PRESTON★★, QUIVIRA★★, Rafanelli (Zinfandel★★★), Michel Schlumberger★★.

**GEORGES DUBOEUF** *Beaujolais, Burgundy, France*   Known, with some justification, as the King of BEAUJOLAIS, Duboeuf is responsible for more than 10% of the wine produced in the region. Given the size of this operation, the quality of the wines is high. Duboeuf also makes and blends wine from the Mâconnais and the Rhône Valley. His BEAUJOLAIS NOUVEAU is usually one of the best, but his top wines are those he bottles for small producers, particularly Jean Descombes★★ in MORGON, Domaine des Quatre Vents★, la Madone★ in FLEURIE and Domaine de la Tour du Bief★★ in MOULIN-A-VENT. His ST-VERAN★ is also worth a try.

**DUCKHORN** *Napa Valley AVA, California, USA*   This Californian winery has earned a well-deserved reputation for its Merlot★, if you like a chunky, tannic style; however, the Cabernet Sauvignon★ and Sauvignon Blanc★ may provide easier drinking. A budget line of Decoy wines has been introduced. Best years: (Merlot) 1993 **92 91 90**; (Cabernet Sauvignon) **1993 92 91 90 87 86**.

**CH. DUCRU-BEAUCAILLOU**★★ *St-Julien AC, 2ème Cru Classé, Haut-Médoc, Bordeaux, France*   Traditionally the epitome of ST-JULIEN, mixing charm and austerity, fruit and firm tannins. In the 1970s it was effortlessly ahead of other Second Growths, but vintages in the mid-80s and early 90s were flawed. Recent tastings show improvement. Second wine: la Croix-Beaucaillou. Best years: (1996) (95) 94 93 **86 85 83 82 81 79 78**.

**DUJAC** *Morey-St-Denis AC, Côte de Nuits, Burgundy, France*   One of Burgundy's leading winemakers, based in MOREY-ST-DENIS, but also with some choice vineyards in VOSNE-ROMANEE, CHAMBOLLE-MUSIGNY and GEVREY-CHAMBERTIN. The wines are all good, including the small quantity of Morey-St-Denis white, but the outstanding Dujac bottlings are the 3 Grands Crus – CLOS DE LA ROCHE★★, BONNES-MARES★★ and CLOS ST-DENIS★★ – all of which will age for a decade or more. Owner Jacques Seysses has also had a very positive influence on many young Burgundian winemakers. Best years: 1995 93 **92** 90 89 88 **85 78**.

**DUNN VINEYARDS** *Howell Mountain AVA, California, USA*   Massive, concentrated, hauntingly perfumed, long-lived Cabernet Sauvignon★★★ is the trademark of Randy Dunn's wines from HOWELL MOUNTAIN. His NAPA VALLEY Cabernets★★ are more elegant but less memorable. Best years: 1994 93 92 91 **90 88 87 86 85 84 82**.

**DURBACH** *Baden, Germany* Unusually for BADEN, Riesling (here called Klingelberger) is something of a speciality in Durbach. Another speciality is Traminer, here called Klevner (normally a synonym for Pinot Blanc!). Best producers: Durbach co-op, Andreas Laible★, Heinrich Männle, Wolff-Metternich.

**DURIF** See Petite Sirah.

**JEAN DURUP** *Chablis, Burgundy, France* The largest vineyard owner in CHABLIS, Jean Durup is a great believer in unoaked Chablis, and his wines tend to be clean and well-made without any great complexity. His top Chablis is the Premier Cru Fourchaume★. Wines appear under a variety of labels, including l'Eglantière, Ch. de Maligny and Valéry.

**DUXOUP WINE WORKS** *Dry Creek Valley AVA, California, USA* Andy and Deborah Cutter are far too busy going to the opera or baseball games to make more than 2000 cases of wine a year, all red, at their spectacular hand-hewn hillside winery. Their lively fresh Napa Gamay★★ is easily the best in California and the Charbono★★ is a magnificent off-the-wall monster. The 1991 is particularly memorable, the 93 Syrah★★ is a real blast of flavour. Drink young for full fruit intensity.

**ÉCHÉZEAUX AC** *Grand Cru, Côte de Nuits, Burgundy, France* The village of Flagey-Échézeaux, hidden down in the plain away from the vineyards, is best known for its 2 Grands Crus, Échézeaux and the smaller and more prestigious Grands-Échézeaux, which are sandwiched between the world-famous CLOS DE VOUGEOT and VOSNE-ROMANÉE. Few of the growers here have really made a name for themselves but there are some fine wines with a lovely, smoky, plum richness, and a soft texture that age well over 10–15 years to a gamy, chocolaty depth. Best producers: DROUHIN, Engel★★, GRIVOT, Henri JAYER★★★, JAYER-GILLES★★, Lamarche★★, Mongeard-Mugneret★, Dom. de la ROMANÉE-CONTI★★, Sirugue★. Best years: 1995 93 **92** 90 **89** 88 **85** 78.

**EDELZWICKER** See Alsace AC.

**EINZELLAGE** German for an individual vineyard site or slope which is generally farmed by several growers. The name is preceded on the label by that of the village; for example, the Wehlener Sonnenuhr is the Sonnenuhr vineyard in Wehlen. The mention of a particular site should signify a superior wine. There will soon be a rule to oblige the bottlers from Einzellages to guarantee a higher must weight, but there has been a reluctance in Germany to tackle the high yields produced by some winemakers even on the best sites.

**EISWEIN** Rare, chiefly German and Austrian late-harvested wine made by waiting for winter frosts, picking the grapes and pressing them while frozen. This concentrates the sweetness of the grape as most of the liquid is removed as ice. Any grape variety may be used, but healthy grapes unaffected by rot are the ones that give the best results. Canadian examples, called ICEWINE, are showing some potential too.

**NEIL ELLIS** *Stellenbosch, South Africa* This leading winemaker/négociant quietly continues to extend the barriers of quality and site specificity in his wines. Grape sources are carefully selected and handled to retain precise origin. Elgin's cool, high-altitude vineyards produce a bracing, intense Sauvignon Blanc★★. A packed, minty Cabernet Sauvignon★★ and supple, fruity Cabernet-Merlot★★ come from warmer STELLENBOSCH vineyards.

117

**ELTVILLE** *Rheingau, Germany* This large wine town makes some of the Rheingau's most racy Riesling wines. Best producers: J B Becker, Fischer, Hans Hulbert.

**EMILIA-ROMAGNA** *Italy* Central-eastern region in Italy, divided into the provinces of Emilia (in the west) and ROMAGNA (in the east). It is chiefly infamous for LAMBRUSCO in Emilia. See also Colli Bolognesi, Colli Piacentini.

**ENTRE-DEUX-MERS AC** *Bordeaux, France* This AC increasingly represents some of the freshest, brightest, snappiest dry white wine in France. Behind the revival lie the techniques of cold fermentation and of leaving skins in contact with juice for a few hours before fermentation. In general, drink the wine of the latest vintage, though the better wines will last a year or two. The sweet wines are sold as PREMIERES COTES DE BORDEAUX, St-Macaire, LOUPIAC and STE-CROIX-DU-MONT. Best producers: Bonnet★, Canet, Castelneau, les Gauthiers, Ch. Launay, Laurétan, Moulin-de-Launay, Nardique-la-Gravière, la Rose-du-Pin, Ste-Marie, Tour-de-Mirambeau, Toutigeac, Turcaud.

**ERATH VINEYARDS** *Willamette Valley AVA, Oregon, USA* OREGON's third-largest producer, formerly known as Knudsen Erath before the partnership dissolved in 1996. Makes stylish Pinot Noirs, a Vintage Select★★ and a Willamette Valley★, that have been gaining greater concentration of fruit in recent vintages. Erath's Chardonnay can be good, and the new Pinot Gris is very attractive. Best years: (Pinot Noir Vintage Select) 1994 93 **92 91 86**; (Willamette Valley) **1994 93 92 90**.

**ERBACH** *Rheingau, Germany* Erbach's famous Marcobrunn vineyard is one of the top spots for Riesling on the Rhine. The village wines are elegant, off-dry, with those from the Marcobrunn being more powerful. Best producers: Jacob Jung, von Knyphausen, SCHLOSS REINHARTSHAUSEN, Schloss Schönborn.

**ERBALUCE DI CALUSO DOC** *Piedmont, Italy* Usually a pleasant, dry white, occasionally sparkling, made from the Erbaluce grape. However, as Caluso Passito, when the grapes are semi-dried before fermenting, this can be one of Italy's great sweet wines. Best producers: Giuseppe Bianchi★, Ferrando★, Orsolani★; (Caluso Passito) Boratto★★, Ferrando★★, Orsolani.

**ERDEN** *Mosel, Germany* Village in the Middle MOSEL, whose most famous vineyards are Prälat and Treppchen. The wines are rich and succulent with a strong mineral character and are among the region's finest. Best producers: J J Christoffel★, LOOSEN★★★.

**ERMITAGE** Swiss name for the Marsanne grape of the northern Rhône Valley. Mostly found in the central Valais where the wines stop short of fermenting out dry, producing a range of wines from slightly sweet to lovely honeyed dessert wines. Best producers: Chappaz★, Domaine du Mont d'Or★, Orsat (Marsanne Blanche★).

**ERRÁZURIZ** *Aconcagua, Chile* Suffering a lack of continuity on the wine-making front, but the signing of ex-CONO SUR wonderkid Ed Flaherty should bring results. Out on its own to the north of Santiago, it produces the reliably concentrated Don Maximiano Cabernet Sauvignon★★ and Merlot★. Slick-textured, citrussy Chardonnay★★ from CASABLANCA heads the whites.

**ESPORÃO** *Reguengos DOC, Alentejo, Portugal* Huge estate in the heart of the ALENTEJO, with Australian David Baverstock making a broad range of wines. The principal labels are Esporão★★, Monte Velho★ and Alandra and there are some excellent varietals, Trincadeira★★, Aragonez★★ and Cabernet Sauvignon★. Best years: **1995 94 92**.

**EST! EST!! EST!!! DI MONTEFIASCONE DOC** *Lazio, Italy* Modest white from the shores of Lake Bolsena accorded its undeserved reputation because of an apocryphal story of a bishop's servant sent ahead to scout out good wines. Getting so excited about this one, he re-iterated the thumbs-up code 3 times. Perhaps it had been a long day. The most credible exceptions are Falesco's Poggio dei Gelsi and barrique-aged Merlot Montiano★★. Best producers: Bigi (Graffiti), Falesco★, Mazziotti.

**CH. DES ESTANILLES** *Faugères AC, Languedoc, France* Don't be deceived by Michel Louison's *enfant terrible* appearance: he and his wife are completely serious about making the best wine they can. The Louisons know that quality begins in the vineyard. Their best site is the Clos de Fou, with its very steep schistous slope planted with Syrah; the grape 'dominates' his top red cuvée★★ (i.e. a 100% – but the AC regulations do not allow him to say so). They also make a wood-fermented and aged rosé plus a fine Coteaux du Languedoc white★★. Best years: **1995 94 91**.

**ESTREMADURA** *Portugal* The regional designation for the IPRs of Alcobaca, Alenquer, ARRUDA, Encostas d'Aire, Obidas and Torres Vedras near the north coast of Lisbon. More wine is produced here than in any other Portuguese region, but only Alenquer is producing anything of real quality. Most wine is instantly forgettable white, although there are some pleasantly sappy young reds being produced by a number of co-ops, especially at Arruda and São Mamede de Ventosa. Wine from the latter can be found bottled under the Alta Mesa, Ramada and Orla Maritima labels. Best producers: ARRUDA co-op, José Neiva, Quinta de Abrigada, Quinta de Pancas★, São Mamede de Ventosa co-op. See also Bucelas, Carcavelos, Colares.

**ETNA DOC** *Sicily, Italy* This wine zone around the famous volcano manages to produce some good wine. The red is based on varieties of Nerello, and the white is a blend using the local Carricante. Best producers: Tenuta di Castiglione★, Barone Sammacca del Murgo★, Barone di Villagrande.

**L'ÉTOILE AC** *Jura, France* A tiny area within the COTES DU JURA which has its own AC for whites, mainly from Chardonnay and Savagnin, and for VIN JAUNE. There is some good Champagne-method fizz too. Best producers: Ch. de l'Étoile★, l'Étoile co-op, Dom. de Montbourgeau.

**CH. L'ÉVANGILE★★** *Pomerol AC, Bordeaux, France* Made by one of Bordeaux's most talented winemakers, Michel Rolland, the wine can be rich and exciting. But I still remain unconvinced it's worth the high asking price. Now owned by the Rothschilds of LAFITE-ROTHSCHILD. Best years: (1996) (95) 94 93 **90 89 88 85 83 82 79 75**.

**EVANS FAMILY** *Hunter Valley, New South Wales, Australia* Len Evans' tiny HUNTER vineyard grows majestic Chardonnay★★, highly regarded sparkling wine (PETALUMA-made), as well as Gamay and Pinot Noir. Nearly all the wine is sold privately or ex-winery – or drunk by Len with his friends. From 1997, following the sale of ROTHBURY, Evans Family will be built into a 10,000-case brand with grapes from other vineyards.

**EVANS & TATE** *Margaret River, Western Australia* Important Western Australian winery and producer of complex MARGARET RIVER Chardonnay★★, 2-vineyards Chardonnay★, curranty Cabernet★ and structured Shiraz★★. Barrel-fermented Sémillon is ★★ and Gnangara is a leading SWAN VALLEY blended red. Brian Fletcher (ex-St Huberts and Seppelt) is the dynamic winemaker.

**ÉVENTAIL DE VIGNERONS PRODUCTEURS** *Beaujolais, Burgundy, France* The most successful and powerful of the BEAUJOLAIS growers' associations, formed to improve quality and marketing of their wines. The standard is generally high. Look out for Louis Desvignes★ in MORGON, Georges Passot★ in CHIROUBLES and Domaine M Pelletier★ in JULIENAS.

**EYRIE VINEYARDS** *Willamette Valley AVA, Oregon, USA* One of the leading Pinot Noir★ producers in Oregon, especially the Reserve★★, but in poor years the wines can be withdrawn and thin. Chardonnay★ shows nice varietal fruit, while the popular Pinot Gris flies off the shelves. Best years: (Pinot Noir) **1994 92 90 89 88**.

**FAIRVIEW** *Paarl WO, South Africa* Nothing stands still at this winery; Charles Back pushes innovation to the limit but value for money is a non-negotiable. His Shiraz-Merlot★ and Zinfandel-Cinsaut★★ represent wacky but hugely successful blends; Merlot★★, Shiraz★★, Pinotage★, Cabernet Sauvignon★ and Chardonnay★ carry the varietal flag.

**JOSEPH FAIVELEY** *Nuits-St-Georges, Côtes de Nuits, Burgundy, France* This Burgundian merchant makes excellent red wines (especially CHAMBERTIN-Clos-de-Bèze★★★ and Mazis-Chambertin★★), principally from its own substantial vineyard holdings. Indeed, Faiveley is more like an outsize grower than a négociant. The much cheaper MERCUREY reds★ are also very attractive. The Côte Chalonnaise whites from RULLY★★ and MERCUREY★★, and the oak-aged BOURGOGNE Blanc represent good value. Best years: (premium reds) 1995 93 **92 90 88 85 78**; (whites) 1995 **93 92 90 89 88**.

**FALERNO DEL MASSICO DOC** *Campania, Italy* Falernian, from north of Naples, was one of the ancient Romans' superstar wines. The revived DOC, with a white Falanghina and reds from Aglianico and Piedirosso, or Primitivo, looks promising. Best producers: Michele Moio, Villa Matilde★.

**CH. DE FARGUES★★** *Sauternes AC, Cru Bourgeois, Bordeaux, France* Property run by the Lur-Saluces family, who also own Ch. d'YQUEM. The quality of this fine, rich wine is more a tribute to their commitment than to the inherent quality of the vineyard. Best years: (1996) (95) 90 89 88 86 83.

**FAUGÈRES AC** *Languedoc, France*  Faugères, with its hilly vineyards stretching up into the mountains north of Béziers in the Hérault, was the first of the LANGUEDOC communes to make a reputation of its own. What marks it out from other Languedoc reds is its ripe, soft, rather plummy flavour, and though it is a little more expensive than neighbouring wines, the extra money is generally worth it. Best producers: Alquier★, ESTANILLES★★, Faugères co-op, du Fraisse★, Grézan★, Haut-Fabrègues★, la Liquière★, Ollier-Taillefer★, Raymond Roque★, St-Aimé. Best years: **1995 94 93 91 90 89**.

**FAUSTINO MARTÍNEZ** *Rioja DOC, País Vasco and Rioja, and Cava DO, Spain*  Family-owned and technically very well equipped, this RIOJA company makes good Reserva★ and Gran Reserva★ red Riojas in distinctive dark, frosted bottles, as well as a fruity, Beaujolais-style Vino Joven or Viña Faustina★, and pleasant whites and rosés. Best years: (reds) **1994 92 91 90 89 87 85 82 81**.

**FEILER-ARTINGER** *Rust, Neusiedlersee, Burgenland, Austria*  Father and son team Hans and Kurt Feiler make Ausbruch-style dessert wines★★★ of great elegance at this medium-sized estate housed in a fine Baroque building. Their dry whites★ and reds★ from a range of traditional Austrian and French grapes are also worthy of attention. Best years: **1995 93 92 91 90**.

**FELSINA BERARDENGA** *Chianti Classico DOCG, Tuscany, Italy*  Leading CHIANTI CLASSICO estate making full, chunky wines usually in need of several years' aging in bottle, but quality is generally outstanding. Most notable are the single-vineyard Riservas Rancia★★★ and Sangiovese Fontalloro★★★ (previously Vino da Tavola). Also good VIN SANTO★★. Best years: (reds) (1996) 95 **94 93 91 90 88 85**.

**FENDANT** *Valais, Switzerland*  Chasselas wine from the steep slopes of the Swiss VALAIS. Good Fendant should be ever so slightly *spritzig* with a spicy character. However, the average Fendant is thin and virtually characterless. It is best drunk *very* young, but a good example can age for years. The best is said to come from the slopes above Molignon and Montibeux, or from around Sion or Uvrier. Best producers: Caves Imesch, Chappaz, Gilliard, Jacques Germanier, Maye & Fils, Orsat.

**FERRARI-CARANO VINEYARDS** *Dry Creek Valley AVA, California, USA*  Really lovely Chardonnay★★, with balanced, elegant fruit made in a regular and a Reserve style. The Reserve is deeply flavoured with more than a touch of oak, while the regular bottling has delicious apple-spice fruit. A new red wine, Siena★★ (a blend of Cabernet Sauvignon and Sangiovese), shows great promise and could – in the end – outshine the Chardonnay. Merlot★★ and Fumé Blanc★ are also delicious. Reds can improve for 5–10 years. Best years: (reds) 1994 **92 91 88 87**.

**FERREIRA** *Port DOC, Douro DOC, Douro, Portugal*  This old port house has now been bought by SOGRAPE, producers of Mateus Rosé. However, Sogrape have shown great talent in modernizing and improving much of Portugal's table wine industry, so the new arrangement should prove good for quality. Ferreira already produces the famous BARCA VELHA★★ table wine, but is best known for excellent tawny ports, either the creamy, nutty Quinta do Porto 10-year-old★ or the Duque de Braganza 20-year-old★★. The vintage port★ is improving too. Best years: (vintage ports) 1994 91 **87 85 83 78 77 70 66 63**.

**FETZER VINEYARDS** *Mendocino County, California, USA* Winery making drinkable, fair-priced wines. The Reserve wines, Barrel Select Cabernet Sauvignon and Chardonnay, are a step up. The Zinfandel Special Reserves★ are concentrated, fruity wines with staying power. Chardonnay, Cabernet, Sangiovese, Syrah and Viognier from organically grown grapes have been released under the Bonterra label and more moves in this direction are expected soon.

**FIANO** Distinctive, low-yielding southern Italian white grape variety. Best producers: (Molise) Di Majo Norante; (Fiano di Avellino DOC in Campania) MASTROBERARDINO★, Struzziero, Vadiaperti, Vignadora★.

**CH. DE FIEUZAL** *Pessac-Léognan AC, Cru Classé de Graves, Bordeaux, France* One of the most up-to-date properties in the region and the delicious, oaky wine sells at a high price. The rich, complex red★★ is drinkable almost immediately because of its succulent fruit but it will age for a decade or more. Less than 10% of the wine is white★★★ but it is stupendous stuff. Second wine: l'Abeille de Fieuzal. Best years: (reds) (1996) (95) **94 93 90 89 88 87 86 85 83 82 78**; (whites) (1996) **95 94 93 90 89 88 87 86 85.**

**CH. FIGEAC★★** *St-Émilion Grand Cru AC, 1er Grand Cru Classé, Bordeaux, France* Leading property whose wine has a delightful fragrance and gentleness of texture. There is an unusually high percentage of Cabernets Franc and Sauvignon (70%) in the wine. Lovely young yet, ideally, should age for at least 10–12 years. Second wine: la Grange-neuve de Figeac. Best years: (1996) (95) 94 90 89 **88 86 85 83 82 78.**

**FILLIATREAU** *Saumur-Champigny, Loire Valley, France* The leading grower in SAUMUR-CHAMPIGNY, producing 4 different, richly flavoured Cabernet Francs – Jeunes Vignes★, Lena Filliatreau★★, la Grande Vignolle★★ and Vieilles Vignes★★ – as well as SAUMUR Rouge, called Château Fouquet★. In a good vintage, Filliatreau's top reds can age for up to 15 years. Best years: (1996) 95 **94 93 90 89 88 85.**

**FINGER LAKES AVA** *New York State, USA* Cool region in central NEW YORK STATE. Riesling and Chardonnay are the trump cards here, but a few growers are having success with Pinot Noir. Best producers: FOX RUN VINEYARDS, Heron Hill, LAMOUREAUX LANDING, Lucas, Wagner.

**FINO** See Jerez y Manzanilla DO.

**FITOU AC** *Languedoc-Roussillon, France* Dark red Fitou was one of the success stories of the 1980s – its burly flavour comes from Carignan and the wine will age well for at least 5–6 years. Best producers: Colomer, les Fenals★, MONT TAUCH CO-OP★★, des Nouvelles, Dom. de Rolland, Roudene★. Best years: **1995 94 93 91 90 89 88.**

**FIXIN AC** *Côte de Nuits, Burgundy, France* Despite being next door to GEVREY-CHAMBERTIN, Fixin never produces anything really magical. The wines are worthy enough to last, but rarely taste exciting and are often sold off under CÔTE DE NUITS-VILLAGES label. Recent vintages, though, have shown distinct improvements. Best producers: Berthaut, Durand-Roblot★, Gelin, Guyard★, Joliet, Molin, P Rossignol★. Best years: (reds) 1995 **93 92 90 89 88 85.**

**FLEURIE AC** *Beaujolais, Burgundy, France* The third-largest, but best-known BEAUJOLAIS Cru. Good Fleurie reveals the happy, carefree flavours of the Gamay grape at its best, plus heady perfumes and a juicy sweetness that can leave you gasping with delight. Not surprisingly, demand has meant that many wines are overpriced and ordinary. Best producers: Aujoux, Bernard, Chaintreuil, Chignard, DUBOEUF★ (named vineyards), Fessy★, Fleurie co-op★, la Grand Cour, Montgénas, Paul. Best years: **1996 95 94 93 91**.

**CH. LA FLEUR-PÉTRUS★★** *Pomerol AC, Bordeaux, France* Like the better-known PETRUS and TROTANOY, this is owned by the dynamic MOUEIX family. But, unlike its stablemates, la Fleur-Pétrus is situated entirely on gravel soil and tends to produce tighter wines with less immediate fruit flavours but considerable elegance and cellar potential. Among POMEROL's top dozen properties. Best years: (1996) (95) 94 93 90 89 **88 85 82**.

**FLORA SPRINGS** *Napa Valley AVA, California, USA* This NAPA VALLEY winery started life as a Chardonnay specialist, with the barrel-fermented Reserves★★ being particular treats. After some early stumbles, it is now beginning to come through with a Bordeaux blend called Trilogy★★, which seems to improve with every release. Best years: (Chardonnay) **1995 94 92 91 90**; (Trilogy) 1994 93 **92 91**.

**ÉMILE FLORENTIN** *St-Joseph AC, Rhône Valley, France* Traditional, organically produced ST-JOSEPH, both red★ and white★, from very old vines. The wines are rather rustic, and can seem to lack fruit when young, but they age well. Best years: (reds) (1996) (95) 94 **91 90 89 88 85 83**; (whites) (1996) 95 **94 91 90 89 85**.

**FONSECA** *Port DOC, Douro, Portugal* Owned by the same group as TAYLOR FLADGATE & YEATMAN, Fonseca makes ports in a rich, densely plummy style. Fonseca vintage★★★ is magnificent, the aged tawnies★★ uniformly superb – even its Late Bottled Vintage★ is way better than most. Fonseca Guimaraens★★ is the name of the 'off-vintage vintage'. Best years: (vintage ports) 1994 92 **85 83 77 70 66 63**.

**JOSÉ MARIA DA FONSECA SUCCESSORES** *Arrábida IPR, Terras do Sado, Portugal* One of Portugal's most go-ahead wineries, with so many projects it's difficult to keep up – the latest has been the take-over of the Lancers brand, the slightly sparkling pink (and white) wines bottled in crocks and massively popular in the USA. Its most exciting reds are from the ALENTEJO, in particular the J S Rosado Fernandes Tinto Velho★★ from REGUENGOS and the fleshy, oaky d'Avillez★ from Portalegre. In DAO the figgy, minty Casa da Insua★ red is much better than most. From the Setúbal Peninsula, south of Lisbon, it produces the tough, long-lived Periquita★, the blackcurranty Quinta da Camarate★ and the famous sweet, fortified SETUBAL★.

**FONT DE MICHELLE** *Châteauneuf-du-Pape AC, Rhône Valley, France* This much-improved estate is currently among the top performers in CHATEAUNEUF-DU-PAPE. The reds★★ and whites★★ are stylish but still heady, with richness and southern herb fragrance – and not too expensive. Best years: 1995 94 **93 90 89 88**.

**FONTANAFREDDA** *Barolo DOCG, Piedmont, Italy* One of the most important PIEDMONT estates, based in the old BAROLO hunting lodge of the King of Italy. In addition to a commercial Barolo, it also produces a range of Piedmontese varietals, several single-vineyard Barolos and a good dry ASTI, Contessa Rosa. Best years: (Barolo) (1996) (95) 94 93 90 89 **88 85**.

**FORST** *Pfalz, Germany* Small village with 6 individual vineyard sites, including the Ungeheuer or 'Monster'; wines from the Monster can indeed be quite savage, with a mineral intensity and richness in the best years. Other famous vineyards are the Kirchenstück, Jesuitengarten, Freundstück and Pechstein. Best producers: von BUHL, BÜRKLIN-WOLF★★, Georg Masbacher★★, WEGELER-DEINHARD★, Werlé★.

**FOX RUN VINEYARDS** *Finger Lakes AVA, New York State, USA* The Reserve Chardonnay★ is remarkable, with well-integrated oak and fruit in an elegant style. The just off-dry Riesling is also a treat, as is the vintage-dated Brut bubbly. Merlot and Pinot Noir both show great promise.

**FRANCIACORTA DOCG** *Lombardy, Italy* The 14th wine to achieve 'guaranteed' status is the Champagne-method sparkler Franciacorta, made from Pinot and Chardonnay grapes. The former DOC applied to still as well as sparkling wines: Bianco from Pinot Bianco and Chardonnay; Rosso from Cabernet, Barbera, Nebbiolo and Merlot. These remain DOC under the appellation Terre di Franciacorta. Best producers: Bellavista★★, CA' DEL BOSCO★★, Castellino★, Cavalleri★, La Ferghettina★, Enrico Gatti★, Monte Rossa★, Ricci Curbastro, Uberti★. Best years: (reds) (1996) (95) **94 93 90 88**.

**FRANCISCAN VINEYARD** *Napa Valley AVA, California, USA* Consistently good wines at fair prices from the heart of the NAPA VALLEY. The Cuvée Sauvage Chardonnay★★★ is an absolutely blockbusting, courageous mouthful, but the Cabernet Sauvignon-based Meritage Red★ is developing a very attractive style. Estancia is a second label, with remarkably good-value Chardonnay from CENTRAL COAST and Cabernet Sauvignon★ from ALEXANDER VALLEY,

as well as its own Meritage★. Franciscan also owns Mt Veeder Winery, where lean but intense Cabernet Sauvignon★ of great minerally depth and complexity is made. Best years: (Chardonnay) **1994 92 91 90**; (Cabernet Sauvignon) 1993 **91 88 87**.

**FRANKEN** *Germany* Wine region incorporated into the kingdom of Bavaria at the beginning of the 19th century and specializing in dry wines. Easily recognizable by their squat, green Bocksbeutel bottles (now more familiar because of the Portuguese wine Mateus Rosé). Silvaner is the traditional grape variety, although Müller-Thurgau now predominates. The most famous vineyards are on the hillsides around WÜRZBURG and IPHOFEN.

**FRANSCHHOEK WO** *South Africa* A picturesque valley encircled by breathtaking mountain peaks. The Huguenot refugees settled here in the 17th century and many of the 22 wineries still bear French names. Sémillon is a local speciality (a few vines are close to 100 years old) and Shiraz shows promise. Best producers: Bellingham, Clos Cabrière★, La Motte★, L'Ormarins.

**FRASCATI DOC** *Lazio, Italy* One of Italy's most famous whites, frequently referred to as Rome's quaffing wine. The wine is a blend of Trebbiano and Malvasia; the better examples have a higher proportion of Malvasia. Good Frascati is worth seeking out, most notably from the revelationary Castel de Paolis. Best producers: Casale Marchese★, Castel de Paolis★★, Colli di Catone★, Villa Simone★, Zandotti★.

**FREIE WEINGÄRTNER WACHAU** *Wachau, Niederösterreich, Austria* Co-op long producing fine WACHAU white wines. Since directors Fritz Miesbauer and Willi Klinger took over with the 95 vintage, regular wines★ and vineyard-designated Rieslings★★ have reached new heights. Best years: **1995 93 92 91 90 88 86 83 79 77**.

**FREISA** Italian Piedmont grape making sweet, foaming, 'happy juice' reds, now sadly rather out of fashion. Some producers are now making a dry style which is very tasty after 3 or 4 years. Best producers: (sweet) Aldo CONTERNO★, GAJA; (dry) Giacomo CONTERNO, Bartolo MASCARELLO★, Aldo Vajra★★.

**FREIXENET** *Cava DO, Catalonia, Spain* The second-biggest Spanish sparkling wine company (after CODORNIU) makes fresh, young Cordon Negro Brut CAVA (world famous for its black bottle) in a vast network of cellars in San Sadurní de Noya. However, most of its other Cavas are unexciting.

**FRESCOBALDI** *Tuscany, Italy* Florentine company selling large quantities of inexpensive blended CHIANTIS, but from its own vineyards it produces good to very good wines at Nipozzano (especially CHIANTI RUFINA Castello di Nipozzano Riserva★★ and Montesodi★★), Tenuta di Pomino★ in POMINO and from Castelgiocondo★★ in BRUNELLO DI MONTALCINO. Best years: (premium reds) (1996) 95 **94** 93 **91 90** 88 **85**.

**FRIULI GRAVE DOC** *Friuli-Venezia Giulia, Italy* DOC covering 19 wine types in western Friuli. Good affordable Merlot, Refosco, Chardonnay, Pinot Grigio, Traminer and Tocai. Best producers: Borgo Magredo★, La Delizia co-op, Le Fredis★, Pighin★, Pittaro★, Plozner★, Pradio★, Russolo★, Vigneti Le Monde★.

**FRIULI-VENEZIA GIULIA** *Italy* Located in north-east Italy, this region borders Slovenia and Austria. The hilly DOC zones of COLLIO and COLLI ORIENTALI produce some of Italy's finest whites from Chardonnay, Pinot Bianco, Pinot Grigio, Sauvignon and Tocai, and the reds can also be excellent mainly from Cabernet, Merlot and Refosco. The DOCs of Friuli Aquileia, ISONZO, Friuli Latisana and FRIULI GRAVE, in the rolling hills and plains, produce good-value wines.

**FRIZZANTE** Italian for semi-sparkling wine, usually made dry, but sometimes sweet.

**FROG'S LEAP** *Napa Valley AVA, California, USA* The winery motto is: Time's fun when you're having flies. But the wine's no joke. In fact, they take Sauvignon Blanc★★ very seriously here. Frog's Leap also produces better-than-average Merlot★ and Chardonnay★, plus Cabernet Sauvignon★ with more grassy, blackcurrant flavour than usual, and Zinfandel★★ with a delicious black cherry fruit. Whites should be drunk within 2–3 years, reds up to 6 or 7.

**FRONSAC AC** *Bordeaux, France* A small area west of POMEROL making wines of reasonable quality and value. With a bit more effort by

125

producers to upgrade the wine-making, they would be more widely known. Often better with at least 5 years' age. Best producers: de Carles, Clos du Roy, Dalem, la Dauphine★, Fontenil★, la Grave, Haut-Lariveau, Mayne-Vieil, Moulin-Haut-Laroque, la Rivière★, la Vieille-Cure, Villars★. Best years: (1996) 95 **94 90** 89 88 86 85 83 82.

**CH. FUISSÉ** *Pouilly-Fuissé, Mâconnais, Burgundy, France*  Owner Jean-Jacques Vincent is the leading grower in POUILLY-FUISSÉ, producing rich, ripe, concentrated Chardonnays. Top wines are the 3 Pouilly-Fuissés – Jeunes Vignes Cuvée Première★, the oak-fermented Ch. Fuissé★★ and the memorable, richly textured Ch. Fuissé Vieilles Vignes★★★. He also makes a fine ST-VERAN★, a BEAUJOLAIS and has a substantial négociant business specializing in wines of the Mâconnais. The best whites can be drunk for up to 5 years. Best years: 1995 **94 93 92 90 89 88**.

**FUMÉ BLANC**  See Sauvignon Blanc.

**RUDOLF FÜRST** *Bürgstadt, Franken, Germany*  Paul Fürst's dry Rieslings★★ are unusually elegant for a region renowned for its earthy white wines, and his Spätburgunder reds★ are some of the best in Germany. Wines as intellectual and sensual as their maker, with excellent aging potential. Best years: 1995 94 **93 92 90** 89 88.

**JEAN-NOËL GAGNARD** *Chassagne-Montrachet AC, Côte de Beaune, Burgundy, France*  One of a bewildering number of Gagnards in CHASSAGNE-MONTRACHET, Jean-Noël consistently makes some of the best wines. His top wine is rich, toasty BATARD-MONTRACHET★★, but his other whites are first rate, too, particularly Morgeot Premier Cru★★. Gagnard's reds★ are not quite as good as his whites, but are still among the most enjoyable in Chassagne. All whites are capable of extended cellaring. Best years: (whites) 1995 93 **92 90** 89 88.

**GAGNARD-DELAGRANGE** *Chassagne-Montrachet AC, Côte de Beaune, Burgundy, France*  Jacques Gagnard-Delagrange heads a distinguished family of interrelated winemakers – Jacques' brother is Jean-Noël GAGNARD, and the source of many of his vineyards was Jacques' father-in-law, Edmond Delagrange-Bachelet. Jacques makes excellent BATARD-MONTRACHET★★ and CHASSAGNE-MONTRACHET Premiers Crus Boudriottes★★ and Morgeot★★. His 2 daughters and their husbands are responsible for Domaines Blain-Gagnard (look out for Criots-Bâtard-Montrachet★★) and Fontaine Gagnard (also Criots-Bâtard-Montrachet★★ and several Chassagne-Montrachet Premiers Crus★★). Best years: 1995 94 93 **92** 90 **89 86**.

**GAILLAC AC** *South-West France*  The whites, mainly from Mauzac with its sharp but attractive green apple bite, are rather stern but, from a decent grower or the revitalized co-ops, can be extremely refreshing. Some more serious reds are now being made, which require some aging. The star of Gaillac at the moment is the outstanding fizz, made by either the Champagne method or the *méthode rurale*, and ideally not quite dry and packed with fruit. Tecou co-op makes oak-aged Cuvée Passion and Cuvée Séduction, but the labels don't say in which order they should be consumed. Drink as young as possible. Best producers: Albert, Boissel-Rhodes, Bosc-Long, Brun, Causse Marines, Clement Termes, Cros, Gayrel, Labarthe, Labastide-de-Lévis co-op★, Larroze, Mas Dignon, Plageoles★★, Tecou co-op★.

**GAJA** *Barbaresco DOCG, Piedmont, Italy*   Angelo Gaja brought about the transformation of PIEDMONT from a sleepy, old-fashioned region that Italians swore made the finest red wine in the world yet the rest of the world disdained, to an area buzzing with excitement. He introduced international standards into what was a parochial, backward area and charged staggeringly high prices, thus giving other Piedmont growers the chance at last to get a decent return for their labours. Into this fiercely conservative area, full of fascinating grape varieties but proudest of the native Nebbiolo, he also introduced French grapes like Cabernet Sauvignon (Darmagi★★), Sauvignon Blanc (Atteni di Brassica★) and Chardonnay (Gaia & Rey★★). Gaja's traditional strength has been in single-vineyard BARBARESCO (his Sorì San Lorenzo★★★, Sorì Tildìn★★★ and Costa Russi★★ are often cited as Barbaresco's best). His BAROLO Sperss★★★, introduced from the 88 vintage, made with grapes from his estate at Serralunga d'Alba, is outstanding. Gaja has also invested in BRUNELLO DI MONTALCINO and BOLGHERI. Best years: (Barolo/Barbaresco) (1996) (95) 94 93 91 90 89 88 **85 82 79 78 71 61**.

**GALESTRO** *Tuscany, Italy*   Bone-dry, neutral white from Trebbiano, Malvasia and other varieties grown in CHIANTI and designed for the mass market. Best producers: ANTINORI, FRESCOBALDI, RUFFINO, Teruzzi & Puthod.

**GALICIA** *Spain*   Up in Spain's hilly, verdant north-west, Galicia is renowned for its fine but expensive Albariño whites. There are 5 DOs: RIAS BAIXAS can make excellent, fragrant Albariño whites, with modern equipment and serious wine-making; Ribeiro has also invested heavily in new equipment, and better local white grapes are now being used, as is the case in the mountainous Valdeorras DO. Some young reds from the Mencía grape are also made there and in the new Ribeira Sacra DO. Monterrei DO, also new, is technically backward but shows some potential with its native white grape variety, Doña Blanca. Most wines are best consumed young.

**E&J GALLO** *Central Valley, California, USA*   With its second release of estate-bottled 1991 Sonoma Cabernet and its estate-bottled 92 Sonoma Chardonnay★, Gallo, the world's biggest winery, hoped to convince doubters that it can make good wine. Both come from grapes grown on 800ha (2000 acres) of premium vineyards in SONOMA COUNTY. These Reserves and the new Gallo Sonoma line of Zinfandel, Merlot, Chardonnay and Cabernet represent a big step up in quality, but the lower-priced varietals still lag way behind. After launching Turning Leaf in the mid-90s, it has added several other new brands: Gossamer Bay (mostly Chardonnay), Anapamu (mostly Central Coast Chardonnay) and Zabaco (Sonoma Country Zinfandel and other varietals).

**GAMAY**   The only grape allowed for red BEAUJOLAIS. In general Gamay wine is rather rough-edged and quite high in raspy acidity, but in Beaujolais, so long as the yield is not too high, it can achieve a wonderful, juicy-fruit gluggability, almost unmatched in the world of wine. Elsewhere in France, it is successful in the Ardèche and the Loire and less so in the Mâconnais. Of the rest of the world, California has produced good examples, but South Africa's very limited production has yielded mixed results.

127

**GARD, VIN DE PAYS DU** *Languedoc, France* Mainly reds and rosés from the western side of the Rhône delta. Most Gard red is light and spicy and increasingly attractive. Rosés can be fresh when young. With modern wine-making the whites can be good. Best producers: Christin, Coste, Maillac, St-Gilles co-op.

**GARGANEGA** An Italian white grape from the VENETO in north-east Italy, the main component of SOAVE. When grown in the hills, it shows it can have class, but its reputation has been tainted by the excessive yields produced on the Veronese plain.

**GARNACHA BLANCA** See Grenache Blanc.
**GARNACHA TINTA** See Grenache Noir.
**GARRAFEIRA** Portuguese term for wine from an outstanding vintage, with ½% more alcohol than the minimum required, and 2 years' aging in vat or barrel, followed by 1 in bottle for reds, and 6 months of each for whites. Also used by merchants for their best blended and aged wines.

**GATTINARA DOCG** *Piedmont, Italy* One of the most capricious of Italy's top red wine areas, capable of both great things and dross. Situated in northern PIEDMONT and recently elevated to DOCG, the Nebbiolo wines should be softer and lighter than BAROLO but possessing a delicious, black plums, tar and roses flavour – if you're lucky, but few producers have shown much consistency yet. Vintages follow those for Barolo, but the wines should be drunk within 10 years. Best producers: Antoniolo★, Le Colline★, Nervi, Travaglini★. Best years: 1995 90 88 85.

**DOMAINE GAUBY** *Côtes du Roussillon-Villages AC, Roussillon, France* Gérard Gauby used to make wines as burly as himself. The fruit was there but it was hidden by very hard tannins. In the last 2 vintages the wines have been softer while still retaining concentration, and Gauby is now a hot property in Roussillon. Highlights include a powerful COTES DU ROUSSILLON-VILLAGES★★ and a Vin de Pays Viognier★★. Best years: **1995 94 93**.

**GAVI DOC** *Piedmont, Italy* Fashionable, expensive PIEDMONT white wine. This Cortese-based, steely lemony white can age up to 5 years or more, providing it starts life with sufficient fruit. La Scolca's Spumante Brut Soldati★ is an admirable sparkling wine. Best producers: BANFI, Nicola Bergaglio★, Broglia★, Chiarlo★, FONTANAFREDDA, La Giustiniana, San Pietro★, Santa Seraffa★, La Scolca★, Tassarolo★, Villa Sparina★.

**CH. GAZIN★★** *Pomerol AC, Bordeaux, France* One of the largest châteaux in POMEROL, next to the legendary PETRUS. The wine, traditionally a succulent, sweet-textured Pomerol, wonderful to drink young but capable of long aging, has been a disappointing performer over the years, but has achieved top form since 1988, as Christian Moueix of Pétrus has taken an interest in the estate. Now one of the most improved Pomerol properties. Best years: (1996) (95) 94 93 **90 89 88**.

**GEELONG** *Victoria, Australia* Another wine region revived in the 1960s after being completely destroyed by phylloxera in the 19th century, but expansion has been erratic so far. The climate and wine potential match up to those of the YARRA VALLEY. Pinot Noir is exciting, but Chardonnay, Riesling, Sauvignon Blanc and Shiraz are also impressive. Best producers: BANNOCKBURN★★, Idyll, Scotchmans Hill★.

**GEISENHEIM** *Rheingau, Germany*   Village famous for its wine school, founded in 1872. It was here that the Müller-Thurgau grape, now one of Germany's most widely planted grapes, was bred in 1882. Geisenheim's most famous vineyard is the Rothenberg, the name indicating the vineyard's red soils, which produce strong, earthy wines. Best producers: Johannishof, RESS, WEGELER-DEINHARD.

**JACQUES GERMAIN** *Chorey-lès-Beaune, Côte de Beaune, Burgundy, France*   The sleepy village of CHOREY-LES-BEAUNE is the source of some of the Côte d'Or's best-value reds and, along with TOLLOT-BEAUT, François Germain is the AC's best-known producer. As well as an elegant red, called Ch. de Chorey★, he makes a series of richer BEAUNE Premiers Crus (Teurons★★ and Vignes Franches★★ are both superb) and reasonably priced ST-AUBIN and PERNAND-VERGELESSES Blanc★. The reds are best drunk after 2–6 years in bottle. Best years: 1995 **93 92 90 89**.

**GEVREY-CHAMBERTIN**   AC *Côte de Nuits, Burgundy, France*   In boom times the wines of Gevrey-Chambertin too often disappoint as growers cash in on the fame of the AC. However, a new generation of growers has restored the reputation of Gevrey as a source of well-coloured, firmly structured, powerful, perfumed wines

that become rich and gamy with age. Village wines should be kept for at least 5 years, Premiers Crus and the 8 Grands Crus for a decade or more, especially Chambertin and Clos-de-Bèze. Look out for the Premier Cru Clos St-Jacques, which is worthy of promotion to Grand Cru. Best producers: Denis Bachelet★★, Dom. L Boillot, Burguet★★, CLAIR, Damoy★, DROUHIN, Dugat★★, DUJAC, Michel Esmonin★★, FAIVELEY★★, JADOT, LABOURE-ROI★, Leclerc★, Denis Mortet★★, Rossignol★★, Roty★, ROUSSEAU★★, Trapet★, Varoilles★. Best years: 1995 93 **92** 90 **89** 88 **85** 78.

**GEWÜRZTRAMINER**   A popular grape all over the world, but reaching its peak in France's Alsace. It is also grown, with mixed results, in Australia, New Zealand, Oregon, California, the Czech Republic, Austria, Germany, South Africa and Italy's Alto Adige (where it is called Traminer or Aromatico) and Romania. As Heida it is grown in Switzerland. *Gewürz* means spice and the wine certainly can be spicy and exotically perfumed but remarkably, in Alsace, while they exude sensuality, the wines generally show delightful balance. Styles vary enormously, from the fresh, light, florally perfumed wines produced in Italy to the rich, luscious, late-harvest ALSACE VENDANGE TARDIVE.

**GEYSER PEAK** *Alexander Valley AVA, California, USA*   The arrival of Australian winemaker Daryl Groom raised Geyser Peak from the dead. The winery had been limping along for years, producing mediocre (at best) wines. Groom's wines tend to be accessible, fruity and fun to drink. Best is the Cabernet★ in a light, fruity style. The Reserve★★, a blend of Cabernet Sauvignon, Merlot, Cabernet Franc and Malbec, is made for aging. The Sémillon-Chardonnay blend, called Semchard, is quite pleasant. The Chardonnay shows steady improvement.

**GHEMME DOC** *Piedmont, Italy* A red, Nebbiolo-based wine, produced from vineyards on the opposite bank of the Sesia river to GATTINARA (and sometimes surpassing its neighbour in style) in Cantalupo's Collis Breclemae and Collis Carellae. Best producers: Antichi Vigneti di Cantalupo★★, Giuseppe Bianchi★, Le Colline.

**BRUNO GIACOSA** *Barbaresco DOCG, Piedmont, Italy* One of the great intuitive winemakers of the Langhe hills south of Alba. He is an unashamed traditionalist, leaving his BARBARESCOS and BAROLOS in cask for up to 6 years. His Barbaresco Santo Stefano★★★ and Barolo Vigna Rionda★★ are particularly good. Cellar for at least 5 years after release. Best years: (1996) (95) 94 93 90 89 **88 85**.

**GIESEN** *Canterbury, South Island, New Zealand* CANTERBURY's largest winery makes outstanding botrytized Riesling★★★ and botrytized Müller-Thurgau★, as well as fine dry Riesling★, complex, oaky Chardonnay★, and an attractive Sauvignon Blanc★. Best years: **1996 95 94 91**.

**GIGONDAS AC** *Rhône Valley, France* Gigondas gained its own AC in 1971. The wines, mostly red with a little rosé and made mainly from the Grenache grape, have fists full of chunky personality. Most drink well with 5 years' age, some a little more. Best producers: Beaumet-Bonfils, Chastan, DELAS, Faraud, les Goubert, GUIGAL★★, JABOULET, Longue-Toque, Christian Meffre, du Grand Montmirail, les Pallières★★, Pascal, de Piaugier, Raspail, St-Gayan★, Trignon. Best years: 1995 94 **93 90 89 88 86 85**.

**CH. GILETTE★★** *Sauternes AC, Bordeaux, France* These astonishing wines are stored in concrete vats as opposed to the more normal wooden barrels. This virtually precludes any oxygen contact, and it is oxygen that ages a wine. Consequently, when released at up to 30 years old, they are bursting with life and lusciousness. Best years: **1983 76 75 70 67 62 59 55 53 49**.

**GIPPSLAND** *Victoria, Australia* Diverse wineries along the southern Victoria coast, all tiny but with massive potential, are led by Nicholson River with its brooding Burgundy-style Chardonnay★★. Pinot Noir from Nicholson River★ is very good and McAlister★, a Bordeaux blend, has also produced some tasty flavours. Bass Phillip Reserve★★★ and Premium★★★ Pinots among the very best in Australia with a cult following – in years like 1991 and 94 they approach the silky charm of the COTE DE NUITS.

**GISBORNE** *North Island, New Zealand* Gisborne, with its hot, humid climate and fertile soils, has shown that it is capable of producing quality as well as quantity. Local growers have christened their region 'The Chardonnay Capital of New Zealand' and Gewürztraminer is also a success. Good reds, however, are hard to find. Best producers: CORBANS, MILLTON★★, MONTANA, Revington.

**CH. GISCOURS★★** *Margaux AC, 3ème Cru Classé, Haut-Médoc, Bordeaux, France* Large MARGAUX property with enormous potential that is not always realized. Giscours' magic is that it can produce wines of delectable scent yet pretty solid structure. After a dull patch recent vintages are picking up. Best years: (1996) (95) 90 86 83 **82 81 80 79**.

**GIVRY AC** *Côte Chalonnaise, Burgundy, France* An important CÔTE CHALONNAISE village. The reds have an intensity of fruit and ability to age that is unusual in the region. In recent years the whites have improved considerably and there are now some attractive fairly full, nutty examples. Best producers: Chofflet, Derain, Joblot, F Lumpp, Ragot, Sarrazin, Thénard★. Best years: (reds) 1995 **93 90 89 88**; (whites) **1995 93 92 90**.

**GLEN CARLOU** *Paarl WO, South Africa* Acknowledged red wine and Chardonnay supremo Walter Finlayson has handed over the wine-making to well-travelled son David and has attracted Donald Hess, owner of the California winery The HESS COLLECTION, as a partner. The Chardonnay★★ (Reserve★★★) develops red wine amplitude with toasty, smoky-limy intensity. Grande Classique★, a tightly packed Bordeaux blend designed for the long haul and more tender-textured Merlot★, show the Finlayson empathy with red wines.

**GLEN ELLEN** *Sonoma Valley AVA, California, USA* The Benziger family (owners of Glen Ellen) sold their Glen Ellen and M G Vallejo brands to Heublein. The popularly priced wines continue to be made in a style that appeals to the American sweet tooth and the Benzigers now concentrate on their Benziger Estate and Imagery series limited-release red and white wines.

**CH. GLORIA★★** *St-Julien AC, Cru Bourgeois, Haut-Médoc, Bordeaux, France* A fascinating property, created by one of Bordeaux's grand old men, the late Henri Martin, out of tiny plots of Classed Growth land scattered all round ST-JULIEN. His obsession raised Gloria's wine during the 1960s and 70s to both Classed Growth quality and price. Generally very soft and sweet-centred, the wine nonetheless ages well. But he desperately wanted to own a Classed Growth and he finally succeeded when he bought ST-PIERRE in 1982. Second wine: Peymartin. Best years: (1996) (95) 94 **93 90 89 88 86 85 83 82 81**.

**GOLAN HEIGHTS WINERY** *Golan Heights, Israel* Israel's leading quality wine producer. Cool summers, well-drained high-altitude vineyards and wine-making that combines the latest Californian techniques with kosher strictures have all resulted in good Sauvignon Blanc★ and Cabernet Sauvignon★, excellent, oaky Chardonnay★★ and, recently, good bottle-fermented fizz★. Yarden is the label used for top-of-the-range wines, while Golan and Gamla are mid-range labels.

---

**GOLDENMUSKATELLER** The Moscato Giallo grape is known as Golden-muskateller in Italy's ALTO ADIGE. Here and elsewhere in Italy's north-east it is made in both highly scented and dry, and slightly sweet versions. Best producer: Tiefenbrunner★, Villanova★.

---

**GONZÁLEZ BYASS** *Jerez y Manzanilla DO, Andalucía, Spain* Tio Pepe★, the high-quality fino brand of this huge top sherry firm, is the world's biggest-selling sherry. The top range of old sherries is superb: intense, dry Amontillado del Duque★★★, and 2 rich, complex olorosos, sweet Matusalem★★★ and medium Apostoles★★. One step down is the Alfonso Dry Oloroso★. The firm has pioneered the rediscovery of single-vintage (non-SOLERA) dry olorosos★★★, reviving what was a common practice in Jerez until the late 19th century.

131

**GOULBURN VALLEY** *Victoria, Australia*   The Goulburn river is a serene, beautiful thread of contentment running through VICTORIA's parched grazing lands. Surprisingly few vineyards have been established here but these do produce some very individual wines. The region's speciality is Marsanne white. Best producers: CHATEAU TAHBILK★, MITCHELTON★★, Tisdall (Mount Helen).

**GRAACH** *Mosel, Germany*   Important Middle MOSEL wine village with 4 vineyard sites, the most famous being Domprobst (also the best) and Himmelreich. A third, the Josephshöfer, is wholly owned by the von KESSELSTATT estate in Trier. The wines have an attractive roundness to balance their steely acidity. Best producers: VON KESSELSTATT★★, LOOSEN★★, J J PRUM★★, W Schaefer★★, SELBACH-OSTER★★.

**GRACIANO**   A rare but excellent Spanish grape, traditional in RIOJA and NAVARRA, but low-yielding. It makes lovely, plummy, fragrant reds and its high acidity adds life when blended with the good-quality, but low-acid Tempranillo.

**GRAHAM** *Port DOC, Douro, Portugal*   Another port shipper in the Symington empire, making rich, florally scented Vintage Port★★★, sweeter than DOW's and WARRE's, the 2 other main Symington brands, but with enough backbone to age. When a vintage is not declared, it makes a wine called Malvedos★. Best years: (vintage ports) 1994 91 **85** 83 **80 77 70 66 63**.

**ALAIN GRAILLOT** *Crozes-Hermitage AC, Rhône Valley, France*   This excellent estate, established only in 1985, stands out as a producer of powerfully concentrated rich, fruity reds. The top wine is called la Guiraude★★★, but his basic Crozes★★ is wonderful, too. Keep both for 5 years, though the best will become even finer with longer aging. Best years: (1996) **95 94 91 90 89 88**.

**GRAMPIANS** *Victoria, Australia*   This newly renamed area centres on Great Western, a distinguished old wine region in central-western Victoria, known mainly for sparkling wine. It is now much reduced in importance but still produces some of Australia's greatest Shiraz – as table wine, sparkling red and even port-style. Best producers: BEST'S★, Montara★, MOUNT LANGI GHIRAN★★, SEPPELT★.

**GRAN RESERVA**   Top category of Spanish wines from a top vintage, with at least 5 years' aging (2 of them in cask) for reds and 4 for whites.

**GRAND CRU**   French for 'great growth', or a vineyard. These are supposedly the best sites in Alsace, Burgundy, Champagne and parts of Bordeaux and should produce the most exciting wines. However, the term applies only to the vineyard site. What the grower decides to do, and what the winemaker then does with the grapes, is another matter.

**CH. DU GRAND MOULAS** *Côtes du Rhône, Rhône Valley, France*   Marc Ryckwaert makes first-rate COTES DU RHONE★ from Grenache and a lick of Syrah that is delicious young but will age for 2–4 years. He also makes very good COTES DU RHONE-VILLAGES★ (red and white) and a rich, Syrah-based Grande Reserve called Cuvée de l'Écu★★. Best years: **1995 94 93 91 90 89 88**.

**CH. GRAND-PUY-DUCASSE★** *Pauillac AC, 5ème Cru Classé, Haut-Médoc, Bordeaux, France* This used to be one of the duller PAUILLAC Classed Growths, but the wines have improved enormously since the mid-80s. Recent vintages have been consistently quite impressive, with lots of supple, blackcurrant fruit, which makes them approachable after 5 years, but allows the wines to improve for considerably longer. Second wine: Artigues-Arnaud. Best years: (1996) (95) 94 93 **92 90 89 88 86 85**.

**CH. GRAND-PUY-LACOSTE★★** *Pauillac AC, 5ème Cru Classé, Haut-Médoc, Bordeaux, France* This wine is classic PAUILLAC, with lots of blackcurrant and cigar-box perfume. As the wine develops, the flavours mingle with the sweetness of new oak into one of Pauillac's most memorable taste sensations. Second wine: Lacoste-Borie. Best years: (1996) (95) 94 93 90 89 88 **86 85 83 82 81 79 78**.

**GRAND TINEL** *Châteauneuf-du-Pape AC, Rhône Valley, France* One of the Rhône's most undervalued producers, Elie Jeune makes big, Grenache-dominated reds★★★ with a piercing aroma of cassis that age superbly. The vines are very old and it shows in the concentration of the wine. Best years: 1995 94 93 **91 90 89 88 86 85 83 81 79 78**.

**GRANDE MARQUE** Champagne's self-appointed élite – a grouping of the larger, better-known houses – is known as the Syndicat des Grandes Marques. Their products were known as Grandes Marques, or 'great brands'. Its rules were supposed to have been tightened up in 1993, but depressingly little has happened yet – reform is now increasingly unlikely.

**GRANDS-ÉCHÉZEAUX AC** See Échézeaux AC.

**GRANGEHUST** *Stellenbosch WO, South Africa* A boutique winery which has leapt to the top in only 4 years. Dramatic, bright-fruited reds are fermented in an old squash court and treated with a natural, hand-crafted approach by owner/winemaker Jeremy Walker. Pinotage★ is a passion: his are thoroughly modern with sweet juicy aromas and ripe tannins. Reserve Cabernet-Merlot★★ is firmer and more compact.

**YVES GRASSA** *Vin de Pays des Côtes de Gascogne, South-West France* The most innovative producer of COTES DE GASCOGNE, who transformed Gascony's thin raw whites into some of the snappiest, fruitiest, almost-dry wines in France. Grassa has also been experimenting with oak-aged★ and late-harvest★ styles.

**ALFRED GRATIEN** *Champagne AC, Champagne, France* This small company makes some of my favourite Champagne. In the modern world of Champagne, where many companies are obsessed with brand image, Gratien declares that its image is the quality of the wine and nothing else. Its wines are made in wooden casks, which is very rare nowadays. The non-vintage★★ blend is usually 4 years old when sold, rather than the normal 3 years. The vintage★★ wine is deliciously ripe and toasty when released but can age for another 10 years. Best years: 1988 **87 85 83 82**.

**GRATIEN & MEYER** *Loire Valley, France* Owners of the quality-minded Champagne house Alfred GRATIEN, Gratien & Meyer is an important Loire producer too. Its reputation rests on its SAUMUR MOUSSEUX, particularly its rich, biscuity Cuvée Flamme★ and Cuvée Flamme Rosé. It makes a little CREMANT DE LOIRE★ – and the sparkling red Cuvée Cardinal★ is unusual and fun.

**GRAVES AC** *Bordeaux, France* The Graves region covers the area south of Bordeaux to Langon, but the generally superior villages in the northern half broke away in 1987 to form the PESSAC-LEOGNAN AC. However, all is not lost, as a new wave of wine-making is sweeping through the southern Graves. Nowadays, there are plenty of clean, bone-dry white wines, with lots of snappy freshness, as well as more complex soft, nutty barrel-aged white wines, and some juicy, quick-drinking red wines. Best producers: Archambeau, le Bonnat, Brondelle★, de Chantegrive, Clos Floridène★, Domaine la Grave★, Landiras, Magence, du Seuil, Vieux-Ch.-Gaubert. Best years: (reds) (1996) 95 **94 90 89 88 86 85 83 82**; (whites) **1996** 95 94 90 89 88 87.

**GRAVES SUPÉRIEURES AC** *Bordeaux, France* White Graves, dry, medium or sweet, with a minimum alcohol level of 12% as opposed to 11% for Graves. The AC has never really caught on because of the confusion between dry and sweet wines, but the sweet wines can, in good years, make decent substitutes for the more expensive SAUTERNES. Best producers: (sweet) Clos St-Georges★, Lehoul. Best years: (sweet) 1996 **95 90 89 88 86**.

**GRAVINA DOC** *Puglia, Italy* This small DOC produces a rarity in PUGLIA, a dry white wine of real character. A blend of the native grape varieties Greco and Malvasia, grown in the hills of central Puglia, the wine has an intense peachy perfume combined with a hint of apricot. Botromagno, the only producer, has salvaged the region's potential.

**GRAVNER** *Friuli-Venezia Giulia, Italy* Josko Gravner, Friuli's most zealous winemaker, sets styles with wood-aged wines of uncommon stature, though all remain strictly outside the COLLIO DOC. Along with prized and high-priced Chardonnay★★, Sauvignon★★ and Ribolla Gialla★★, he combines 6 white varieties in Breg★★ and blends Merlot and Cabernet in Rosso Gravner★ and Rujno★★.

---

**GRECHETTO** An attractive Italian white grape variety centred on UMBRIA, making tasty, anise-tinged dry whites. It also contributes to VIN SANTO in Tuscany. Best producers: ADANTI, Antonelli, Caprai, Rocca di Fabbri.

---

**GREEN POINT VINEYARDS** *Yarra Valley, Victoria, Australia* MOET & CHANDON's Aussie offshoot makes leading Pinot Noir-Chardonnay Champagne-method fizz★★ and occasional Blanc de Blancs and Blanc de Noirs. The latest adventure is still wines from Chardonnay★★ and Pinot Noir, in a somewhat un-Aussie style. The Domaine Chandon label is used in the Australian market.

---

**GRENACHE BLANC** A common white grape in the south of France, but without many admirers. Except me, that is, because I love the pear-scented wine flecked with anise that a good producer can achieve. Best at 6–12 months old. Also grown as Garnacha Blanca in Spain.

---

**GRENACHE NOIR** Among the world's most widely planted red grapes – the bulk of it in Spain, where it is called Garnacha Tinta. It is a hot-climate grape and in France it reaches its peak in the southern Rhône, especially in CHATEAUNEUF-DU-PAPE, where it combines great alcoholic strength with rich raspberry fruit and a perfume hot from the herb-strewn hills. It is generally given more tannin and acid by blending with Syrah, Cinsaut or other southern French grapes. It can make wonderful rosé in TAVEL, LIRAC and COTES DE PROVENCE, as well as in NAVARRA in Spain. It is also the basis for the VINS DOUX NATURELS of BANYULS and MAURY. In RIOJA it adds weight to the Tempranillo. Also widely grown in California and Australia, but not respected except by original-thinkers like Randall Grahm of BONNY DOON in California, who makes lovely rosés and reds from old vines, and Charles Melton in Australia, who makes gutsy Nine Popes Red★. See also Cannonau.

**GRGICH HILLS CELLAR** *Napa Valley AVA, California, USA* Mike Grgich was the winemaker at CHATEAU MONTELENA when its Chardonnay shocked the Paris judges by finishing ahead of French versions in the famous 1976 tasting. At his own winery he makes ripe, tannic Cabernet and a huge, old-style Zinfandel★, but his reputation has been made by big, ripe, oaky Chardonnay★★ that proves to be one of Napa's best-selling, high-priced wines. Best years: (Chardonnay) **1994 92 91 90 88 87**.

**GRIGNOLINO** An Italian red grape native to PIEDMONT that can produce light-coloured but intensely flavoured wines. It is DOC in the Monferrato Casalese and Asti hills, and is also made in Alba. HEITZ makes a rare version in California. Best producers: Braida, Bricco Mondalino, Aldo CONTERNO, Pavese, Scarpa, La Tenaglia, Viarengo.

**GRIOTTE-CHAMBERTIN AC** See Chambertin AC.

**JEAN GRIVOT** *Vosne-Romanée, Côte de Nuits, Burgundy, France* Winemaker Étienne Grivot took time to settle down but has now reconciled both his father's traditional styles and former consultant Accad's experimentation into a high-quality interpretation of his own. He had brilliant results in 1995, especially for RICHEBOURG★★ and NUITS-ST-GEORGES les Boudots★. Expensive. Best years: 1995 93 90 89 88.

**GROS PLANT DU PAYS NANTAIS VDQS** *Loire Valley, France* From the marshy salt-flats around Nantes, Gros Plant can be searing stuff but this acidic wine is well suited to the seafood guzzled in the region. Best producers: Chiron, Guindon, Hallereau, Herbauges, Ch. de la Preuille, Sauvion. Best years: **1996 95**.

**GROSSET** *Clare Valley, South Australia* Jeffrey Grosset is a stubborn perfectionist, crafting tiny quantities of truly hand-made wines in his Auburn winery. A Riesling specialist, he bottles Watervale★★ separately from Polish Hill★★★. Both are supremely good and age well, while Cabernet-blend Gaia★★ is smooth and seamless. Piccadilly (ADELAIDE HILLS) Chardonnay★★ and Pinot Noir★★ are the new buzz. Best years: (Riesling) **1996 95 94 92 90 87 86**.

**GROSSLAGE** German term for a grouping of villages. Some are not too big, and have the advantage of allowing small amounts of higher QmP wines to be made from the grapes from several vineyards. But sometimes the use of vast Grosslage names (for example, Niersteiner Gutes Domtal) only deceives consumers into believing that they are buying something special. After 2004 the term may be abolished – wishful thinking, I'd say. Also an Austrian term, where a single Grosslage refers to an even larger vineyard area than in Germany.

**CH. GRUAUD-LAROSE★★★** *St-Julien AC, 2ème Cru Classé, Haut-Médoc,*
*Bordeaux, France*   One of the largest ST-JULIEN estates and the leading
château of the Cordier group. Throughout the vintages of the 1980s
its brilliant wines were made darker and deeper, sweetened with wood
and toughened with tannin. Less easy to drink young, they should be
even more exciting when they're mature at up to 20 years or so.
Second wine: Sarget de Gruaud-Larose. Best years: (1996) (95) 94 93 **92**
91 90 89 88 **86 85 84 83 82 81 79 78**.

**GRÜNER VELTLINER** Grown in every Austrian wine region with the
exception of Styria. The grape is at its best, however, in KAMPTAL,
KREMSTAL, the WACHAU and the Weinviertel region, where the soil and
slightly damp climate bring out all the lentilly, white-peppery aromas
in the fruit. Also good in Slovakia.

**GUELBENZU** *Navarra DO, Spain*   Small family-owned bodega making
good Guelbenzu Crianza★, blended from Tempranillo, Cabernet
Sauvignon and Merlot, and rich concentrated Evo★★, made mostly
from Cabernet Sauvignon. In 1995 it introduced the unoaked Jardin
cuvée (100% Garnacha) with considerable success. Best years: **1995
94 93 92 90.**

**GUIGAL** *Côte-Rôtie AC, Rhône Valley, France*   Marcel Guigal is among
the most famous names in the Rhône, producing wines from his
company's own vineyards in COTE-ROTIE as well as from purchased
grapes. Guigal's top wines – la Mouline★★★, la Turque★★★ and la
Landonne★★★ – are expensive but superb, if you don't mind an oaky
sweetness masking the wines' fruit for the first few years of its life.
CONDRIEU★★ is also very fine, if oaky, but HERMITAGE★ is merely good,
while the cheaper COTES DU RHONE★★ is a delicious wine outperforming
its humble AC with ease. His GIGONDAS★★ is excellent, too. All reds can
be cellared, the famous trio of Côte-Rôties for perhaps 20 years or
more. Best years: (top reds) (1996) 95 94 91 **90 89 88 85 83 82**.

**CH. GUIRAUD★★** *Sauternes AC, 1er Cru Classé, Bordeaux, France*   A
property that was hauled up from near extinction by the Canadian
Narby family, convinced that Guiraud could be one of SAUTERNES'
greatest wines. Selecting only the best grapes and using 50% new oak
each year, they have returned Guiraud to the top-quality fold. Keep
best vintages for 10 years or more. Second wine (dry): G de Guiraud.
Best years: (1996) (95) **90 89 88 86 83 82 81**.

**GUNDERLOCH** *Nackenheim, Rheinhessen, Germany*   One of the nation's
new stars, producing rich, dramatic wines with explosive fruit aromas.
Makes the best Rieslings★★ anywhere on the Rhine since 1989, and
since 1992 top dessert wines have been ★★★. Best years: 1996 95 94
**93 92 90 89.**

**GUNDLACH-BUNDSCHU** *Sonoma Valley AVA, California, USA*   This family-
owned winery was founded in 1858. Since then it has had its ups and
downs but for the last couple of decades it has been all up. The
Cabernet Sauvignon★★ (Rhine Farm Vineyard) is outstanding, with
lean herbal tones opening up to big, juicy, fruity centres. The Chardonnay is rich but not over the top and a Riesling is delightfully different.
The Zinfandel★ and Cabernet merit at least short-term cellaring.

**GYÖNGYÖS ESTATE** *Gyöngyös, Hungary* The wines from this Hungarian estate appeared on the shelves out of the blue; a British winemaker, Hugh RYMAN, had left his base in France to produce Sauvignon Blanc and Chardonnay in one of the most forward-looking of the old eastern bloc countries. Drink current vintage.

**FRITZ HAAG** *Braunberg, Mosel, Germany* Top MOSEL grower with vineyards in the Brauneberger Juffer and Brauneberger Juffer Sonnenuhr, where vineyard reorganization has temporarily robbed him of his old vines. In spite of this, all wines are at least ★, with Auslese reaching ★★ or ★★★. Best years: 1995 94 **93 92 91 90 88 85**.

**HALBTROCKEN** German for medium dry. In Germany and Austria medium-dry wine has 9–18g per litre of residual sugar, though sparkling wine is allowed up to 50g per litre. But the high acid levels in German wines often make them seem dry and lean.

**HALLAU** *Schaffhausen, Switzerland* Important wine commune situated in German-speaking eastern Switzerland, best known for Müller-Thurgau, fair Blauburgunder (Pinot Noir), especially from Max Baumann, and also Sekt from Hans Schlatter.

**HAMILTON RUSSELL VINEYARDS** *Walker Bay, Overberg WO, South Africa* A passionate and unwavering sense of purpose drive both proprietor Anthony Hamilton-Russell and winemaker Kevin Grant. Ashbourne Pinot Noir★★ and Chardonnay★★ are from single vineyards, the Pinot benefitting from its totally new clone make up. The standard Pinot Noir★ is vegetal

and less inviting, although Chardonnay★★ holds its own. Southern Right is a new label focussing on Pinotage★, Chenin Blanc and Sauvignon Blanc★ from bought-in grapes.

**HANDLEY CELLARS** *Mendocino County, California, USA* Outstanding producer of hand-crafted sparkling wines, including one of California's best Brut Rosés★★ and a delicious, mouth-watering Blanc de Blancs★★. Two bottlings of Chardonnay, one from the DRY CREEK VALLEY★ and an Anderson Valley★, are worth seeking out.

**HANGING ROCK** *Macedon, Victoria, Australia* Highly individual, gutsy sparkling wine, Macedon non-vintage★★ is the stand-out at John and Anne (née Tyrrell) Ellis' ultra-cool-climate vineyard high in the Macedon Ranges. Tangy, high-acid estate-grown Sauvignon Blanc★★ is mouthwatering stuff, while Heathcote Shiraz★, from a warmer neighbouring region, is the best red.

**HARDY** *Southern Vales, South Australia* Fine quality across the board. Siegersdorf Riesling and several varietals under the Nottage Hill label are tasty and affordable; Hardy Collection Chardonnay★ and Cabernet★ are even better – and still affordable. Top of the tree are the commemorative Eileen Hardy Shiraz★★ and Thomas Hardy Cabernet★, both dense reds for hedonists. Eileen Hardy Chardonnay★★ is rich, heady, oak-perfumed and complex. No longer in the hands of the Hardy family, this company was bought by the BERRI RENMANO co-ops, and the group floated as BRL Hardy.

**HARVEST WINE GROUP** *England* An association of various English vineyards and wineries, with all members relinquishing wine-making to Australian John Worontschak of THAMES VALLEY fame. His New World philosophy of inter-vineyard and inter-winery blending has been the backbone behind the heritage-labelled range, and has revolutionized the standard of widely available English wines.

**HARVEYS** *Jerez y Manzanilla DO, Andalucía, Spain* Harveys is the biggest of the sherry firms, thanks to Bristol Cream. The standard range is unexciting, but the up-market 1796 wines are much better.

**HATTENHEIM** *Rheingau, Germany* Fine RHEINGAU village with 13 vine-yard sites, including a share of the famous Marcobrunn vineyard. Best producers: RESS★, SCHLOSS REINHARTSHAUSEN★★, Schloss Schönborn.

**CH. HAUT-BAGES-LIBÉRAL★★** *Pauillac AC, 5ème Cru Classé, Haut-Médoc, Bordeaux, France* This obscure property is fast becoming one of my favourite PAUILLACs: loads of unbridled delicious fruit, positively hedo-nistic style – and I can afford it! The wines will age well but are ready to drink at 5 years. Best years: (1996) (95) 94 **93 90 89 86 85 83 82**.

**CH. HAUT-BAILLY★★** *Pessac-Léognan AC, Cru Classé de Graves, Bordeaux, France* The softest and most charming wines among the GRAVES Classed Growths, which showed welcome improvement in the late 1980s. Drinkable very early, but can age. Second wine: la Parde-de-Haut-Bailly. Best years: (1996) (95) **94 93 90 89 88 86 85 83 82 81**.

**CH. HAUT-BATAILLEY★** *Pauillac AC, 5ème Cru Classé, Haut-Médoc, Bordeaux, France* Despite being owned by the Borie family of DUCRU-BEAUCAILLOU, this small estate has made too many wines that are light and pleasant, attractively spicy, but lacking any real class and con-centration. Recent vintages have improved and it is at last becoming more substantial. Best years: (1996) (95) 94 93 **90 89 85 83 82**.

**CH. HAUT-BRION** *Pessac-Léognan AC, 1er Cru Classé, Graves, Bordeaux, France* The only Bordeaux property outside the MEDOC and SAUTERNES to be included in the great 1855 Classification, when it was accorded First Growth status. The excellent gravel-based vineyard is now part of Bordeaux's suburbs and the red wine★★★ frequently, but by no means always, deserves its exalted status. There is also a small amount of white★★★. At its best it is fabulous wine, magically rich yet marvellously dry, blossoming over 5–10 years. Second wine: (red) Bahans-Haut-Brion. Best years: (reds) (1996) (95) 94 93 90 89 88 86 **85 83 81 78**; (whites) (1996) (95) **94 92 90 89 88 87 85 83 82 81**.

**CH. HAUT-MARBUZET★★** *St-Estèphe AC, Cru Bourgeois, Haut-Médoc, Bordeaux, France* Impressive ST-ESTEPHE wine with great, rich, mouthfilling blasts of flavour and lots of new oak. Best years: (1996) (95) 94 93 **90 89 88 86 85 83 82 81 78**.

**HAUT-MÉDOC AC** *Bordeaux, France* AC for the southern half of the Médoc peninsula. All the finest gravelly soil is here and Haut-Médoc AC covers all the decent vineyard land not included in the 6 separate village ACs (MARGAUX, MOULIS, LISTRAC, ST-JULIEN, PAUILLAC and ST-ESTEPHE). The wines vary somewhat in quality and style. Best pro-ducers: Beaumont★, Belgrave★, Camensac★, CANTEMERLE★★, CISSAC★, Citran★, Coufran★, Hanteillan★, la LAGUNE★★, Lamarque★, LANESSAN★, LAROSE-TRINTAUDON, Ramage-la-Batisse, SOCIANDO-MALLET★★, la Tour-Carnet, la Tour-du-Haut-Moulin. Best years: (1996) 95 **94 90 89 88 86 85**.

**HAUT-MONTRAVEL AC** *South-West France*  Pleasant, sweet white
wines from hillside vineyards at the western limit of the BERGERAC
region. The wines are sweeter than straight MONTRAVEL and COTES DE
MONTRAVEL. Best producers: Gourgueil, Puy-Servain★.

**HAUT-POITOU VDQS** *Loire Valley, France*  Wines from south of the Loire
Valley on the way to Poitiers. Crisp, zingy Sauvignons and Chardonnays, slightly green Cabernet and Gamay reds and fresh rosés; also
good sparkling Diane de Poitiers. In general drink young. The Haut-
Poitou co-op, now run by Georges DUBOEUF, dominates production.

**HAUTE VALLÉE DE L'AUDE, VIN DE PAYS DE LA** *Languedoc-Roussillon,*
*France*  The best still wines from the Limoux sparkling wine district.
Most of the wine is white, with an emphasis on Chardonnay. Barrel-
fermented white wines are entitled to the new LIMOUX AC. Best
producers: l'Aigle★★, Astruc, Buoro, SIEUR D'ARQUES co-op, Vialade.

**HAUTES-CÔTES DE BEAUNE AC** See Bourgogne-Hautes-Côtes de Beaune AC.

**HAUTES-CÔTES DE NUITS AC** See Bourgogne-Hautes-Côtes de Nuits AC.

**HAWKES BAY** *North Island, New Zealand*  One of New Zealand's oldest
and most prestigious wine regions. The high number of sunshine hours, mod-
erately predictable weather during ripening and a complex array of soil
patterns make it ideal for a wide range of wine-making styles. Chardonnay,
Cabernet Sauvignon and Merlot are the area's greatest strengths. Sauvignon
Blanc is generally a bit flat. Best producers: Brookfields, Clearview, Esk
Valley★, MATUA VALLEY★★, MONTANA (Church Road★★), MORTON ESTATE★★,
NGATARAWA★, C J Pask, Sacred Hill, TE MATA★★★, Vidal★, VILLA MARIA★★.

**HEEMSKERK** *Northern Tasmania, Australia*  One of TASMANIA's major
wineries, operating in a severe and marginal climate. Chardonnay,
Pinot Noir and Riesling are erratic but they can be good. Champagne-
method fizz Jansz★ is fine but tart. Heemskerk is now part of a
Tasmanian wine group that includes Rochecombe.

**DR HEGER** *Ihringen, Baden, Germany*  Joachim Heger specializes in
Grauburgunder, Weissburgunder and powerful red Spätburgunder★
with Riesling only a side-line. The Grauburgunder wines from the
Winklerberg★★ are especially worth looking out for. Best years: 1996
**94 93 92 90 89 88**.

**HEIDA** Swiss name for the grape thought to be either the Savagnin of
the French Jura or the Gewürztraminer, which don't taste remarkably similar to me, but there you go. In the Swiss Valais it is known
as the Paien. In Switzerland above the town of Visp at Visperterminen,
Heida is grown at heights of around 1000m (3280ft), the highest-
altitude vineyards in Europe, and the wine is correspondingly
pungent and mountain mad. Best producers: Chanton, St Jodern.

**CHARLES HEIDSIECK** *Champagne AC, Champagne, France*  Under new
owners Rémy Martin, a lot of effort has improved the quality of Heidsieck in recent years. The non-vintage blend★★ is richer than it used
to be, and is now reasonably priced too. The Blanc de Blancs★★ is
now the most reliable of the major brands. Look out for the rosé★ and
the prestige cuvée, Champagne Charlie★. Best years: **1990 89 85**.

139

**HEITZ CELLARS** *Napa Valley AVA, California, USA*  The star attraction here is the Martha's Vineyard Cabernet Sauvignon★★. Heitz recently added a Trailside Vineyard Cabernet and continues offering a Bella Oaks Vineyard Cabernet Sauvignon★, which has its fans, and a straight Cabernet★ that takes time to understand but can be good. Recent problems in the cellar now seem to have been addressed and so future offerings may live up to Heitz's reputation: many in California believe that early bottlings of Martha's Vineyard are among the best wines ever produced in the state. Grignolino Rosé is an attractive picnic wine. Best years: (Martha's Vineyard) 1992 91 **86 85 75**; (Bella Oaks) **1991 87 86 80.**

**HENSCHKE** *Eden Valley, South Australia*  Fifth-generation winemaker Stephen Henschke and his viticulturist wife Prue make some of Australia's grandest reds from old vines in Eden Valley. Hill of Grace★★★, a stunning wine with dark exotic flavours, comes from a single, century-old plot of Shiraz. Mount Edelstone Shiraz★★★ and Cyril Henschke Cabernet★★ are also brilliant wines. The whites★★ are full and intensely flavoured too, despite often coming from unfashionable varieties. Best years: (reds) 1994 93 **92 91 90 88 86 84 82 80 78 72**.

**HÉRAULT, VIN DE PAYS DE L'** *Languedoc, France*  A huge Vin de Pays, covering the entire Hérault *département*. Red wines predominate, based on Carignan, Grenache and Cinsaut, and most of the wine is sold in bulk. But things are changing. There are lots of hilly vineyards with great potential, and MAS DE DAUMAS GASSAC is merely the first of many exciting reds from the region. The whites are improving too. Best producers: du Bosc, Capion, la Fadéze, Grangeneuve, Jany, Limbardie★, MAS DE DAUMAS GASSAC★★, Moulines.

**HERMITAGE AC** *Rhône Valley, France*  Great Hermitage, from steep vineyards above the town of Tain l'Hermitage in the northern Rhône, is revered throughout the world as a rare, rich red wine – expensive, memorable and classic. Not all Hermitage achieves such an exciting blend of flavours because the vineyard area is not large and some merchants will take any grapes just to list Hermitage. But the best growers, with mature red Syrah vines, can create superbly original wine, needing 5–10 years' aging even in a light year and a minimum of 15 years in a ripe vintage. White Hermitage, from Marsanne and Roussanne, is rather less famous but the best wines, made by traditionalists, can outlive the reds, sometimes lasting as long as 40 years. Some winemakers, like JABOULET, are making modern, fruity, fragrant whites that are lovely at 1–2 years old. Best producers: Belle★★, CHAPOUTIER★★ (since 1988), CHAVE★★★, DELAS★★ (single vineyard), Desmeure★, Faurie★★, Fayolle★★, Ferraton★★, Grippat★★, GUIGAL★, JABOULET★★★ (since 1988), Sorrel★★, Viale★★. Best years: (1996) 95 94 92 91 90 89 **88 85 83 82 80 78 76 71 70**.

**JAMES HERRICK** *Vin de Pays d'Oc, Languedoc, France*  When Herrick and his Aussie partners planted 175ha (435 acres) of Chardonnay between Narbonne and Béziers many locals thought he was mad. His neatly trellised rows with drip-feed irrigation are a real contrast to his neighbours' traditionally straggling vines. Chardonnay★ is an attractive blend of exuberant fruit and French elegance. A red, Cuvée Simone, started out well in 1995 but has not fulfilled its early promise.

**THE HESS COLLECTION** *Mount Veeder AVA, California, USA* A NAPA VALLEY producer earning rave reviews for the Cabernet Sauvignon★★ which is showing all the intense lime and black cherry originality of its MOUNT VEEDER fruit, without coating it with impenetrable tannins. Hess Select is an attractive budget label.

**HESSISCHE BERGSTRASSE** *Germany* Small, warm wine region near Darmstadt. Much of the wine-making here is by the local co-op, although the Staatsweindomäne also makes some good wines. There has been less flirtation with new grape varieties here than elsewhere in Germany, and Riesling is still the most prized creation. EISWEINS are a speciality.

**HEURIGER** *Austria* Fresh, young wine drunk in the many taverns in the Viennese hills. Once the wine is a year old it is called *Altwein*, or 'old wine'. No really good wine is sold as Heuriger, yet a few swift jugs of it can make for a great evening – but keep the aspirin handy.

**HEYL ZU HERRNSHEIM** *Nierstein, Rheinhessen, Germany* Top estate on the Rhine practising organic farming. It always produces some fine wines★★ especially from the Brudersberg, Pettenthal, Hipping and Ölberg sites but these are inconsistent lower down the scale. Best years: 1996 95 **93 90 89 88**.

**HIDALGO** *Jerez y Manzanilla DO, Andalucía, Spain* Hidalgo's Manzanilla La Gitana★★ is deservedly the best-selling manzanilla in Spain. Hidalgo is still family-owned, and only uses grapes from its own vineyards. Brands include Mariscal★, Fino Especial and Miraflores, Amontillado Napoleon★★, Oloroso Viejo★★ and Jerez Cortado★★.

**FRANZ HIRTZBERGER** *Wachau, Niederösterreich, Austria* One of the WACHAU's top growers. Hirtzberger's best wines are the Rieslings from Singerriedel★★★ and Hochrain★★. The best Grüner Veltliner comes from the Honivogl site★★. Best years: (Riesling) 1995 94 **93 92 91 90 88**.

**HOCHHEIM** *Rheingau, Germany* Village best known for having given the English the word 'Hock' for Rhine wine, but with good individual vineyard sites, especially Domdechaney, Hölle (or Hell!) and Kirchenstück. On the Königin Victoria Berg there is even a statue of the 19th-century British Queen who swore by the therapeutic qualities of Hock after she'd stopped off there for a picnic. Best producers: Franz KUNSTLER★★, Domdechant WERNER.

**HOGUE CELLARS** *Washington State, USA* Really splendid ripe, brambly Reserve Cabernet Sauvignon★★, often blended with Merlot, and a supple, elegant Reserve Merlot★★ that has hit ★★★ on occasion. The Chardonnay★ looks likely to emulate this high standard. Best years: (reds) **1994 92 91 90 89 87 86**.

**HOLLICK** *Coonawarra, South Australia* Winery making a broader range of good wines than is usually found in COONAWARRA: a much-improved Champagne-method Pinot-Chardonnay★ fizz, subtle Chardonnay★, tobaccoey Cabernet-Merlot★ and a richer Ravenswood Cabernet Sauvignon★★. Spicy Shiraz and limy Riesling go into the second label Terra. Best years: (reds) **1994 93 91 90 88**.

**HOSPICES DE BEAUNE** *Côte de Beaune, Burgundy, France* Scene of a theatrical auction on the third Sunday in November each year, the Hospices is an historic foundation which sells wine from its holdings in the COTE D'OR to finance its charitable works. The quality of the winemaking has increased immeasurably since 1994 thanks to the return of André Porcheret at the helm and the building of a state-of-the-art winery. The wines are matured and bottled by the purchaser, which can cause variations in quality, and pricing reflects charitable status rather than common sense. Best years: (reds) 1995 94 **85**; (whites) 1996 95 **94**.

**HOUGHTON** *Swan Valley, Western Australia* WESTERN AUSTRALIA's biggest winery, with a huge output of 'White Burgundy★' (called Houghton's 'Supreme' in the EU). Also good Sémillon★, Verdelho★, Chardonnay and Chenin Blanc★. With the inclusion of more grapes from the south of the state, the reds have improved, especially Houghton and Moondah Brook Cabernets★.

**VON HÖVEL** *Konz-Oberemmel, Saar, Germany* Jovial Eberhard von Kunow has always made classic Saar Riesling, but since 1993 quality has taken another jump up. The rich, racy new wines are almost all ★★. Best years: 1996 95 94 **93 90 89 88 85**.

**HOWELL MOUNTAIN AVA** *Napa Valley, USA* This mountainous, somewhat magical area in Napa's north-east corner is noted for its extrastrength, powerhouse Cabernet Sauvignon and Zinfandel as well as exotic, full-flavoured Merlot. Best producers: BERINGER (Merlot), DUCKHORN★, DUNN★★★, La Jota.

**HUADONG WINERY** *Shandong Province, China* The first producer of varietal and vintage wines in China, Huadong has received massive investments from its multinational joint owners. But money can't change climates, and excessive moisture from the summer rainy season can cause problems. Riesling and Chardonnay were the first wines to be exported, but most of the noble varieties have been planted.

**GASTON HUET** *Vouvray AC, Loire Valley, France* The grand old man of VOUVRAY who has passed on this famous family estate to his son-in-law, Noël Pinguet, but still takes a keen interest in the wines – complex, traditional Vouvrays which will happily age for up to 50 years in a great vintage. As well as a very good Vouvray Mousseux★★, the estate produces wines from 3 excellent sites – le Haut Lieu★★★, Clos du Bourg★★ and le Mont★★ – which can be dry, medium-dry or sweet, depending on the vintage. Best years: 1996 95 93 **90 89 88 85 76 64 61 59 47**.

**HUGEL ET FILS** *Alsace AC, Alsace, France* Arguably the most famous name in Alsace, thanks to assiduous marketing and (sometimes) the quality of its wines. As well as wines from its own vineyards, Hugel also buys in grapes for basic range wines. Best wines are the sweet ALSACE VENDANGE TARDIVE★★ and SELECTION DE GRAINS NOBLES★★★. Ordinary releases have improved dramatically since 1989. Best years: 1996 **95 94 93 92 90 89 85 83**.

**HUNTER VALLEY** *New South Wales, Australia* NEW SOUTH WALES' oldest wine region overcomes a tricky climate to make fascinating, ageworthy Sémillon and rich, buttery Chardonnay. The reds meet less universal approval. Shiraz is the mainstay, aging well but often developing a leathery overtone. Also some Cabernet and Pinot Noir. Premium region is the Lower Hunter Valley; the Upper Hunter has

142

few wineries but extensive vineyards. Best producers: Allandale, Brokenwood★, LAKE'S FOLLY, LINDEMANS★★, MCWILLIAMS★★, Peterson, ROSEMOUNT★★, ROTHBURY★, TYRRELL'S★★.

**HUNTER'S** *Marlborough, South Island, New Zealand* One of MARLBOROUGH's star winemakers, with superlative Sauvignon★★★, lean and elegant Chardonnay★★, vibrant Riesling★ and a renowned luscious, botrytized Chardonnay★★. Best years: **1996 94 91 89**.

**ICEWINE** *Canada* A speciality of Canada produced from juice squeezed from ripe grapes that have frozen on the vine. Very expensive, very sweet, extremely complex, these are undoubtedly some of the world's greatest dessert wines. Best producers: INNISKILLIN★, Jackson Triggs, MISSION HILL. See also Eiswein.

**HANS IGLER** *Mittelburgenland, Austria* Until his recent death Hans Igler was one of Austria's top red winemakers, particularly renowned for his new oak-aged Blaufränkisch★. His widow continues his work. Best years: **1994 93 92 90 89 86 83**.

**ÎLE DE BEAUTÉ, VIN DE PAYS DE L'** *Corsica, France* Some increasingly good wines are being made here from Syrah, Cabernet Sauvignon, Nielluccio, Sciaccarello and Merlot (for reds); Grenache and Barbarossa (for rosés); Chardonnay and Vermentino (for whites). Best producers: Aleria, Casinca, Marana co-op, Samuletto★, Uval co-op.

**INNISKILLIN** *Niagara Peninsula, Ontario, Canada* Leading Canadian winery producing consistently good Pinot Noir★, a beautifully rounded Klose Vineyard Chardonnay★ full of bananas, vanilla and cinnamon toast, and thick, rich, Vidal ICEWINE★. Winemaker Karl Kaiser is also achieving good results with Cabernet Franc and Merlot.

**IPHOFEN** *Franken, Germany* One of the 2 best towns in FRANKEN (the other is WÜRZBURG) for dry Riesling and Silvaner. Both are powerful, with a pronounced earthiness. Best producers: JULIUSSPITAL★★, Johann Ruck★, Wirsching★.

**IPR (INDICAÇÃO DE PROVENIÊNCIA REGULAMENTADA)** Portuguese classification for regions hoping to qualify for DOC.

**IRANCY AC** *Burgundy, France* Formerly known as Bourgogne-Irancy and labelled simply Irancy from 1996, this northern outpost of vineyards, just south-west of Chablis, is an unlikely champion of the clear, pure flavours of the Pinot Noir grape. But red Irancy can be delicate and lightly touched by the ripeness of plums and strawberries, and can age well. There is also a little rosé. Best producers: Bienvenu, Brocard, Cantin, Colinot, Delaloge, Fort, Simonnet-Febvre. Best years: **1995 93 92 90 89 88**.

**IRON HORSE VINEYARDS** *Sonoma, California, USA* Outstanding sparkling wines with the Brut★★ and the Blanc de Blancs★★★ delicious on release but able to age. A Blanc de Noirs★ called 'Wedding Cuvée' and a Brut Rosé★ complete the line-up. Often overlooked are the Iron Horse table wines including a Cabernets★ (Cabernet Sauvignon-Cabernet Franc blend), a good Pinot Noir★, a barrel-fermented Chardonnay★, a zesty Sauvignon and a vigorous Viognier. Best years: (reds) 1994 **92** 91 **90 88 87** 86 85 84 83; (whites) **1995 93 92 91 90 89**.

**IROULÉGUY AC** *South-West France* A small AC in the Basque Pyrenees, reviving after its virtual disappearance in the 1950s and 60s. There are some spectacular vineyard sites close to the tourist town of

143

St-Jean-de-Pied-Port. Cabernet Sauvignon, Cabernet Franc and Tannat give robust reds that are softer than MADIRAN. Production of white from Courbu and Manseng has recently restarted. Best producers: Abotia, Brana★, Ilarria, Irouléguy co-op, Mignaberry★.

**ISOLE E OLENA** *Chianti Classico DOCG, Tuscany, Italy* One of the pacesetters in CHIANTI CLASSICO, this fine estate is run by Paolo De Marchi. His Chianti Classico★★, characterized by a clean, elegant and spicily perfumed fruit, excels in every vintage. The powerful Super-Tuscan Cepparello★★★, made from 100% Sangiovese, is the top wine, and there is also excellent Syrah★★, Cabernet Sauvignon★★ and Chardonnay★, as well as great VIN SANTO★★★. Best years: (Chianti Classico) (1996) 95 **94 93 91 90 88**.

**ISONZO DOC** *Friuli-Venezia Giulia, Italy* Classy southern neighbour of COLLIO with wines of outstanding value. The DOC covers 20 styles, including Merlot, Chardonnay, Pinot Grigio and Sauvignon. Best producers: Drius★, Silvano Gallo★, Lis Neris-Pecorari★★, Pierpaolo Pecorari★★, Ronco del Gelso★, Villanova★, Vie di Romans★★.

**CH. D'ISSAN**★ *Margaux AC, 3ème Cru Classé, Haut-Médoc, Bordeaux, France* This lovely moated property has rather underperformed over the last few years, although recent vintages show improvement. When successful, the wine can be one of the most elegant but delicate in MARGAUX AC with a fragrant violet and cassis fruit bouquet. Second wine: le Moulin d'Issan. Best years: (1996) (95) **90 89 85 83 82 78**.

**PAUL JABOULET AÎNÉ** *Rhône Valley, France* During the 1970s Jaboulet led the way in raising the world's awareness of the great quality of Rhône wines, yet during the 1980s the quality of wine faltered. But recent vintages, fuller of fruit, less manipulated and proud of their origins, make it look as though Jaboulet is back on the quality bandwagon. Best wines are top red HERMITAGE la Chapelle★★★ and white Chevalier de Stérimberg★★. Also good COTE-ROTIE★, excellent CROZES-HERMITAGE Thalabert★★, fine juicy ST-JOSEPH le Grand Pompée★ and sweet, perfumed MUSCAT DE BEAUMES-DE-VENISE★. Best years: (top reds) (1996) 95 94 91 **90 89 88 78**.

**JACKSON ESTATE** *Marlborough, South Island, New Zealand* Established grapegrower with vineyards in MARLBOROUGH's most prestigious district, Jackson Estate turned its hand to wine-making in 1991 with the help of a local contract winemaker. Unirrigated vineyards help produce a concentrated and very ripe Sauvignon Blanc★★ with an equally concentrated Chardonnay★★ and, more recently, a complex traditional method fizz★. One of New Zealand's most successful 'winemakers without a grape press'. Best years: **1996 94**.

**LOUIS JADOT** *Beaune, Burgundy, France* A leading merchant based in BEAUNE with a broad range only matched by DROUHIN, and with rights to some estate wines of the Duc de Magenta★★. Jadot has particularly extensive vineyard holdings for red wines, but it is the firm's whites which have earned its reputation. Good in Grands Crus like BATARD-MONTRACHET★★ and CORTON-CHARLEMAGNE★★ but it is in lesser ACs like ST-AUBIN★★ and RULLY★ that Jadot really shows what it can do. After leading white Burgundy in quality during the 1970s, the 1980s have been heavier and flatter, impressive, but not thrilling. Best years: (top reds) 1995 93 **92 90 89 88 85**.

**JAFFELIN** *Beaune, Burgundy, France*   Now owned by BOISSET, Jaffelin sells a large range of wine from the Côte d'Or, the Côte Chalonnaise and Beaujolais. The lesser ACs – RULLY★, ST-ROMAIN★, BOURGOGNE Blanc and BEAUJOLAIS – are the best value but don't overlook the CLOS DE VOUGEOT★★ and BEAUNE les Avaux★★. The new owner will have to prove its quality credentials here. Best years: **1995 92 90 89 88**.

**JAMET** *Côte-Rôtie AC, Rhône Valley, France*   Jean-Paul and Jean-Luc Jamet are 2 of the most talented young growers of CÔTE-RÔTIE. If anything, the wines★★ from this excellent estate have improved even further since they took over from their father, Joseph, and they age well for a decade or more. Best years: (1996) 95 94 91 **90 89 88 87 85 83 82**.

**JARDIN DE LA FRANCE, VIN DE PAYS DU** *Loire Valley, France*   This Vin de Pays covers most of the Loire Valley, and production often exceeds 50 million bottles – mostly white, from Chenin and Sauvignon, and very cheap. There is an increasing amount of good Chardonnay, too. The few reds and rosés are generally light and sharp. Best producers: Couillaud, Daviau, des Forges, Hauts de Sanziers, Touche Noire★.

**ROBERT JASMIN** *Côte-Rôtie AC, Rhône Valley, France*   The CÔTE-RÔTIES★★ made by Robert Jasmin and his son Patrick are some of the most intensely aromatic red wines in the Rhône Valley, with a delicious exuberance of gluggable young fruit and a heavenly scent which somehow manage to settle gracefully into middle age. The wines are at their best after 4–5 years, but will keep for much longer. Best years: (1996) 95 94 **91 90 89 88 87 85 83**.

**JASNIÈRES AC** *Loire Valley, France*   A tiny AC north of Tours which usually makes long-lived, bone-dry white from Chenin Blanc. Best producers: Fresneau, Gigou★★. Best years: 1996 95 **93 92 90 89**.

**CH. LA JAUBERTIE** *Bergerac, South-West France*   The most innovative domaine in BERGERAC, run since 1973 by the dynamic RYMAN family, producing fresh, aromatic wines with lots of fruit. The rosé★ and dry white★ should be drunk young, but the red★ can age for up to 5 years. Best years: (red) 1996 **95 94 93 91 90**.

**HENRI JAYER** *Vosne-Romanée, Côte de Nuits, Burgundy, France*   In 1988 the vineyards of this famous estate were divided between MÉO-CAMUZET, Jayer himself and his nephew Emmanuel Rouget. Henri Jayer has kept vineyards in VOSNE-ROMANÉE★★★ and NUITS-ST-GEORGES★★★. Jayer's wines are some of the greatest in Burgundy, showing the heady perfume and exhilarating fruit enriched by oak that top Burgundy is supposed to be all about. Best years: 1993 **92** 90 89 88 **85 80 78**.

**ROBERT JAYER-GILLES** *Côtes de Nuits, Burgundy, France*   A cousin of Henri JAYER, Robert Jayer-Gilles produces expensive but sought-after wines heavily dominated by new oak. He makes good ALIGOTÉ★ and wonderful Hautes-Côtes de Nuits Blanc★★, as well as a range of structured reds, including ÉCHEZEAUX★★ and NUITS-ST-GEORGES les Damodes★★. Best years: 1995 93 **90 88**.

**JEKEL** *Monterey County, California, USA*   A pioneer in MONTEREY in the 1970s, Bill Jekel sold to the distillers Brown-Forman in 1993. Now emphasizing its own vineyard sites, the winery pushes its full-bodied Gravelstone Chardonnay and Bordeaux-blend Sanctuary, although the semi-sweet Riesling continues as its best effort.

# JEREZ Y MANZANILLA DO/SHERRY

*Andalucía, Spain*

The Spanish have won the battle. From 1 January 1996 'British sherry' and 'Irish sherry' ceased to exist. At least in the EU, the only wines that can be sold as sherry come from the triangle of vineyard land between the Andalucian towns of inland Jerez, and Sanlúcar de Barrameda and Puerto de Santa María by the sea.

The best sherries can be spectacular. Three main factors contribute to the high quality potential of wines from this region: the chalky-spongy albariza soil where the best vines grow, the Palomino Fino grape – unexciting for table wines but potentially great once transformed by the sherry-making processes – and a natural yeast called flor. All sherry must be a minimum of 3 years old, but fine sherries age in barrel for much longer. Sherries must be blended through a solera system. About a third of the wine from the oldest barrels is bottled, and the barrels topped up with slightly younger wine from another set of barrels and so on, for a minimum of 3 sets of barrels. The idea is that the younger wine takes on the character of older wine, as well as keeping the blend refreshed.

## MAIN SHERRY STYLES

**Finos, manzanillas and amontillados** These sherries derive their extraordinary, tangy, pungent flavours from flor. Young, newly fermented wines destined for these styles of sherry are deliberately fortified very sparingly to just 15–15.5% alcohol before being put in barrels for their minimum of 3 years' maturation. The thin, soft, oatmeal-coloured mush of flor grows on the surface of the wines, protecting them from the air (and therefore keeping them pale) and giving them a characteristic sharp, pungent tang. Manzanillas are fino-style wines that have matured in the cooler seaside conditions of Sanlúcar de Barrameda, where the flor grows thickest and the fine tang is most accentuated. True amontillados are simply fino sherries that have continued to age after the flor has died (after about 5 years) and so finish their aging period in contact with air. These should all be bone dry. Medium-sweet amontillados are merely concoctions for the export market.

**Oloroso** This type of sherry is strongly fortified after fermentation to deter the growth of flor. Olorosos therefore mature in barrel in contact with the air, which gradually darkens them while they develop rich, intense, nutty, and raisiny flavours.

**Other styles** Palo cortado is an unusual, deliciously nutty, dry style somewhere in between amontillado and oloroso. Sweet oloroso creams and pale creams are almost without exception enriched solely for the export market.

See also INDIVIDUAL PRODUCERS.

146

## BEST PRODUCERS AND WINES

BARBADILLO (Manzanilla Eva, Manzanilla Príncipe, Solear Manzanilla Fina Vieja, Amontillado Príncipe, Amontillado de Sanlúcar, Oloroso del Río, Oloroso Seco).

Delgado Zuleta (Manzanilla La Goya).

Diez Mérito (Don Zoilo Imperial Amontillado and Fino, Victoria Regina Oloroso).

DOMECQ (Amontillado 51-1A, Sibarita Palo Cortado, Venerable Pedro Ximénez).

Garvey (Palo Cortado, Amontillado Tio Guillermo, Pedro Ximénez).

GONZALEZ BYASS (Tio Pepe Fino, Matusalem Oloroso Muy Viejo, Apostoles Oloroso Viejo, Amontillado del Duque Seco y Muy Viejo, Noé Pedro Ximénez, Oloroso Viejo de Añado).

HARVEYS (1796 range).

Herederos de Argües (Manzanilla San Léon, Manzanilla Fina Las Medallas).

HIDALGO (Manzanilla La Gitana, Manzanilla Pasada, Jerez Cortado).

LUSTAU (Almacenista single-producer wines, Old East India Cream, Puerto Fino).

OSBORNE (Fino Quinta, Bailén Oloroso, Solera India Pedro Ximénez).

Sánchez Romate (Pedro Ximénez Cardenal Cisneros).

VALDESPINO (Amontillado Coliseo, Tio Diego Amontillado, Pedro Ximénez Solera Superior).

Williams & Humbert (Pando Fino, Manzanilla Alegria).

**JERMANN** *Friuli-Venezia Giulia, Italy*  Silvio Jermann, though situated in Friuli's COLLIO zone in north-east Italy, produces only Vino da Tavolas from Chardonnay, Pinot Grigio and Riesling, a blend called Vintage Tunina★★, mainly based on Sauvignon and Chardonnay, and a barrel-fermented Chardonnay★★ called 'Where the Dreams have no End', in homage to his favourite pop group U2. The wines are plump and generous but pricy.

**CHARLES JOGUET** *Chinon AC, Loire Valley, France*  A talented artist, sculptor and poet, Charles Joguet is also the leading winemaker in CHINON. His wines demonstrate an impressive richness of flavour which owes more to Bordeaux than to the Loire. There are 4 different reds – Cuvée du Clos de la Curé★★, Clos du Chêne Vert★★, les Varennes du Grand Clos★★ and Clos de la Dioterie★★ – all of which require aging for 5–10 years or more for the full beauty to show. There is also a little rosé. Best years: (1996) 95 **93 92 90 89 88 85 82 81 76**.

**JOHANNISBERG** *Rheingau, Germany*  Just about the most famous of all the Rhine villages with 10 individual vineyard sites, including the very famous Schloss Johannisberg. Best producer: H H Eser.

**KARL-HEINZ JOHNER** *Bischoffingen, Baden, Germany*  Johner specializes in new oak-aged wines from his native BADEN. The vividly fruity Pinot Noir★ and Pinot Blanc★ are very consistent, the rich silky Pinot Noir SJ★★ one of Germany's finest reds. Best years: (reds) 1996 **94 93 92 90 89 88 86**.

**JORDAN** *Alexander Valley AVA, Sonoma, California, USA*  Ripe, fruity Cabernet Sauvignon★★ with a cedary character that is rare in California. The Chardonnay★ has improved markedly, especially the stunning 1992. The sparkling wine, J★★, has also been improving since the 90 vintage. Best years: (reds) 1994 **91 90 87 86**.

**TONI JOST** *Bacharach, Mittelrhein, Germany*  The producer that gives the MITTELRHEIN an international dimension. From the Bacharacher Hahn site Jost makes delicious racy Rieslings★ including well-structured Halbtrockens★ with balmy, pine-scented fruit. The Auslese★★ can add a creaminess without losing its fresh pine needle scent. Best years: 1995 94 **93 90 89 88**.

**JULIÉNAS AC** *Beaujolais, Burgundy, France*  One of the more northerly BEAUJOLAIS Crus, Juliénas makes delicious, 'serious' Beaujolais which can be big and tannic enough to develop in bottle. Best producers: Descombes★, DUBOEUF★, Ch. de Juliénas, Juliénas co-op, Pelletier★. Best years: 1996 **95 94 93 91**.

**JULIUSSPITAL WEINGUT** *Würzburg, Franken, Germany*  A 16th-century charitable foundation which makes dry wines – very good Silvaners, especially from IPHOFEN and WURTZBURG, and the occasional Riesling that's pretty special. Look out for the wines from the estate's holdings in the Würzburger Stein vineyard, sappy Müller-Thurgau, grapefruity Silvaners★★ and petrolly Rieslings★★. Best years: 1995 94 **93 92 90 89**.

**JUMILLA DO** *Murcia and Castilla-La Mancha, Spain*  Jumilla's reputation in Spain is for big alcoholic reds but there are now some fresher, lighter ones, too. Some fruity rosés are made, like the reds, from Monastrell, and there are also a few boring whites. Best producers: Altos de Pio, Señorío del Condestable, Julia Roch Melgares (Casa Castillo), Agapito Rico.

**JURA** See Arbois, Château-Chalon, Côtes du Jura, l'Étoile.

**JURANÇON AC** *South-West France* The sweet white wine made from late-harvested and occasionally botrytized grapes can be heavenly. The rapidly improving dry wine, Jurançon Sec, should be refreshing. Best producers: Bellegarde★, Bru-Baché, CAUHAPE★★, Clos Uroulat★★, Clos Thou★★, Lapeyre, Larredya, de Souch.

**JUVÉ Y CAMPS** *Cava DO and Penedés DO, Catalonia, Spain* Juvé y Camps is ultra-traditional – and expensive. Unusually among the Catalan companies, most of the grapes come from its own vineyards. Fruitiest CAVA is Reserva de la Familia Extra Brut★, but the rosé and the top brand white Cava Gran Juvé are also good.

**KABINETT** Lowest level of QmP wines in Germany, with Oechsle levels ranging from 67 in the Mosel to 85 for a Baden Ruländer. In Austria Kabinett wines must be in the dry style with 17 KMW or 84 Oechsle.

**KAISERSTUHL** *Baden, Germany* A 4000ha (10,000 acre) volcanic stump rising to 600m (1968 feet) and overlooking the Rhine plain and south BADEN. Best producers: BERCHER★, Bickensohl co-op, Dr HEGER★, JOHNER★, Königsschaffhausen co-op, Salwey★.

**KALLSTADT** *Pfalz, Germany* A warm climate combined with the excellent Saumagen site results in the richest dry Rieslings in Germany. These, and the dry Weissburgunder and Muskateller, can stand beside the very best from Alsace, while Pinot Noir is also showing it likes the limestone soil. Best producer: KOEHLER-RUPRECHT★★.

**KAMPTAL** *Niederösterreich, Austria* Wine region centred around the town of Langenlois, making some impressive dry whites, particularly Riesling and Grüner Veltliner. Best producer: BRUNDLMAYER★★.

**KANONKOP** *Stellenbosch WO, South Africa* Beyers Truter is one of South Africa's leading Pinotage exponents. His standard Pinotage★ and lavishly new-oaked Auction Reserve★★ are produced from some of the world's first Pinotage vines (from the 1950s). The Bordeaux-blend Paul Sauer★, Auction Reserve★★ and Cabernet★ uphold an enviable red wine reputation. The Krige brothers, owners of the estate, also have an interest in Truter's other winery, nearby Beyerskloof.

**KARTHÄUSERHOF** *Trier, Ruwer, Germany* Top Ruwer estate which has gone from strength to strength since Christoph Tyrell and winemaker Ludwig Breiling took charge from the 1986 vintage. Since 1993 most wines are ★★, some Auslese and EISWEIN ★★★. Best years: 1996 95 94 93 **92 90 89 88 86**.

**KATNOOK ESTATE** *Coonawarra, South Australia* Expensive but often exceptional Chardonnay★★ and Sauvignon Blanc★★ and improving Cabernet Sauvignon★. The second label Riddoch Estate occasionally throws up a bargain. Best years: (red) 1994 93 **91 90 88**.

**KÉKFRANKOS** See Blaufränkisch.

**KENDALL-JACKSON** *Lake County, California, USA* Jess Jackson founded KJ in bucolic Lake County in 1982 after buying a vineyard there. In 15 years the winery has grown from under 10,000 cases to over 2 million. Early success with Chardonnay was fuelled by a style of wine-making favouring sweetness, but in the 1990s, Jackson redirected energies toward consistency and value. Today's Chardonnays are 100% barrel fermented and oak aged. Most varietals, including ambitious Grand Reserves, are blends from several AVAs. The line-up has experienced

149

a complete quality makeover, exemplified by Cabernet Sauvignon and Pinot Noir. Jackson currently owns a dozen wineries, including Cambria, Stonestreet, Edmeades and Robert Pepi.

**KENWOOD VINEYARDS** *Sonoma Valley AVA, California, USA* One of CALIFORNIA's best Sauvignon Blancs★★ can be found here, but the expanded Zinfandel programme is welcome to Zin fans. Kenwood Zinfandels★ have always been first rate, with the Jack London Ranch★★ often getting rave

reviews for its rich, spicy flavours. In the 1990s, Kenwood released 2 more single-vineyard Zinfandels – Mazzoni Vineyard★ and Nuns Canyon★. Best years: **1994 93 91 90**.

**VON KESSELSTATT** *Trier, Mosel, Germany* Estate making good Riesling★ and the best Spätlese and Auslese★★ wines from some top sites at GRAACH (Josephshöfer) in the MOSEL, Scharzhofberg in the Saar and at Kasel in the Ruwer. Best years: 1996 95 **94 93 91 90 89**.

**KHAN KRUM** *Eastern Region, Bulgaria* Winery producing some of Bulgaria's rare good whites, like oaky Reserve Chardonnay and delicate, apricotty Riesling-Dimiat Country Wine, but below par recently.

**KIEDRICH** *Rheingau, Germany* Small village whose first vineyard is the Gräfenberg, giving extremely long-lived, minerally wines. Wines from Sandgrub and Wasserose are also good. Best producer: WEIL★★.

**KING ESTATE** *Oregon, USA* It took only 3 years for the King Estate to become OREGON's biggest winery and Number 1 producer of Pinot Noir and Pinot Gris. Both wines are made in a user-friendly style. The Reserve Pinot and Reserve Pinot Gris★ offer greater depth. Best years: **1994 93**.

**KIONA** *Yakima Valley AVA, Washington State, USA* A tiny operation in sagebrush country, Kiona has a young but growing reputation for its barrel-fermented Chardonnay★, big, rich Cabernet Sauvignon★★ and excellent sweet Riesling★. Kiona also has a Lemberger, a big juicy red wine that has achieved a cult status in the Pacific Northwest.

**KISTLER** *Sonoma, California, USA* One of CALIFORNIA's hottest Chardonnay producers. Wines are made from 4 different vineyards (Kistler Estate and Dutton Ranch can be ★★★, Durell Vineyard and McCrea Vineyard ★★), and they all possess great complexity with good aging potential. Kistler also makes a number of single-vineyard Pinot Noirs; initial releases have been very good. Best years: (Dutton) **1994 93 92 91 90 87**; (Durell) **1994 93 91 90 89 87**; (Kistler) **1991 90 88**; (McCrea) **1994 93 92 91 90 88**.

**KLEIN CONSTANTIA** *Constantia WO, South Africa* Rescued from alien vegetation and creeping urbanization in 1980 by the Jooste family, this winery is today a South African show-piece. Sauvignon Blanc★★, crisp and vivid, benefits from winemaker Ross Gower's experience in New Zealand; there's also a toasty butterscotch Chardonnay★★, often botrytis-brushed Riesling★ and Vin de Constance★, a beautifully packaged Muscat dessert wine based on the celebrated 18th-century Constantia examples. All have set new standards but reds have yet to rise to the same level. Best years: (whites) **1996 95 93 92 91**.

**KMW** The Austrians use KMW or Klosterneuburger Mostwaage as a scale to determine the must weight or original sugar in freshly picked grapes. Like Oechsle degrees in Germany, each quality category sets a minimum number of KMW (e.g. 19 KMW for Spätlese). 1 KMW is the equivalent of about 5 Oechsle.

**KNAPPSTEIN** *Clare Valley, South Australia* In 1995 Tim Knappstein quit the company, now part of PETALUMA, to focus on his own Lenswood Vineyards, high in the ADELAIDE HILLS. The Knappstein brand remains a leader, with fine Riesling★★ and Traminer★, subtly oaked Fumé Blanc★, Cabernet★, Cabernet-Merlot★ and Chardonnay★. From the 1996 vintage, former Petaluma winemaker Andrew Hardy is pumping new enthusiasm into the wines.

**KOEHLER-RUPRECHT** *Kallstadt, Pfalz, Germany* Bernd Philippi makes dry Rieslings★★★ from the Kallstadter Saumagen site, the oak-aged botrytized Elysium★★ and, since 1991, Burgundian-style Pinot Noirs★★. Best years: (Riesling) 1996 95 94 **93 92 90 89 88 83**.

**ALOIS KRACHER** *Illmitz, Burgenland, Austria* Austria's greatest sweet winemaker. Nouvelle Vague wines are aged in barriques while Zwischen den Seen wines are spared the oak. The Sämling (Scheurebe) Beerenauslesen and Trockenbeerenauslesen, and the Muskat-Ottonels and Chardonnay-Welschrieslings are all ★★★. The Welschrieslings★★ and Bouviers★ are good. Best years: **1995 94 93 91 89 86 81**.

**KREMSTAL** *Niederösterreich, Austria* Wine region on both sides of the Danube around the town of Krems, producing some of Austria's best whites, particularly dry Riesling and Grüner Veltliner. Best producers: Lenz MOSER, Nigl, NIKOLAIHOF★, Salomon.

**KRUG** *Champagne AC, Champagne, France* Krug is a serious (and seriously expensive) Champagne house. The non-vintage is called Grande Cuvée★★★ and knocks spots off most other de luxe brands. This gets more exciting with 1–2 years' extra aging. There is also an excellent vintage wine★★★, a rosé★ and a single-vineyard Clos du Mesnil Blanc de Blancs★★★. Best years: **1989 85 82 81 79**.

**KUENTZ-BAS** *Alsace AC, Alsace, France* A small négociant, with high-quality wines from its own vineyards (labelled Réserve Personnelle) and from purchased grapes (Cuvée Tradition). Look out for the Eichberg Grand Cru★★ and the excellent ALSACE VENDANGE TARDIVE★★ wines. Best years: 1996 **95 94 93 92 90 89 88 86 85**.

**KUMEU/HUAPAI** *Auckland, North Island, New Zealand* A small but significant viticultural area north-west of Auckland. The 9 wineries profit from their proximity to New Zealand's capital. Best producers: COOPERS CREEK★, KUMEU RIVER★, MATUA VALLEY★★, NOBILO, SELAKS★.

**KUMEU RIVER** *Kumeu, Auckland, North Island, New Zealand* This family winery has been transformed by New Zealand's first Master of Wine, Michael Brajkovich, who has created a range of adventurous, high-quality wines. Unconventional oak-aged Sauvignon Blanc★, intense Chardonnay★★★ and softly stylish Merlot-Cabernet Sauvignon★ blend are Kumeu River's most obvious successes. Best years: **1996 95 94 91 90**.

**KUNDE ESTATE** *Sonoma Valley, California, USA*   The Kunde family have been wine-grape growers for at least 100 years in SONOMA COUNTY and in 1990 they decided to start producing wines. The early results have been spectacular, with a powerful, buttery Reserve Chardonnay★★ getting rave reviews and an explosively fruity Viognier★, a real beauty.

**FRANZ KÜNSTLER** *Hochheim, Rheingau, Germany*   Gunter Künstler makes the best dry and sweet Rieslings in the RHEINGAU, although his estate is based in HOCHHEIM on the river Main. They are powerful, minerally wines★★, with everything from the Hölle site worthy of ★★★. In 1996 he bought the run-down Aschrott estate, more than doubling his vineyard area. Best years: 1996 95 **94 93 92** 90 89 88.

**KWV** *Paarl, South Africa*   Converting from a co-op to a company, but retaining its well-known brand name and its legislative authority over the country's wine industry. KWV has an immense range of table wines, fortifieds and brandies and its poor image should wane thanks to new vineyards and cellars and a more international approach from winemakers. Cabernet, Shiraz and Pinotage illustrate new-wave reds, while the Cape's stalwart, Chenin Blanc, has an equally contemporary feel. Best among top-of-the-range Cathedral Cellar is the brambly, soft Bordeaux-style blend Triptych★ and modern, bold Cabernet★. Dessert, sherry- and port-style fortifieds remain superb value: Vintage★★★ and Colheita-style Late Bottled Vintage★★ are particularly memorable.

**LA ROSA** *Cachapoal, Chile*   Old family operation rejuvenated by a new winery and the magic hand of Ignacio Recabarren in the La Palma range. The unoaked Chardonnay is pure apricots and figs, and the Merlot★★ one of the best from the Rapel appellation.

**LABOURÉ-ROI** *Nuits-St-Georges, Burgundy, France*   Price-conscious and generally reliable merchant, yet no longer quite so consistent as before as supply struggles to keep up with demand. The CHABLIS★ and MEURSAULT★ are very correct wines and NUITS-ST-GEORGES★, CHAMBOLLE-MUSIGNY, GEVREY-CHAMBERTIN★, BEAUNE★ and MARSANNAY★ are usually good. Best years: (red) 1995 93 **92 91 90 89 88**.

**LACRYMA CHRISTI DEL VESUVIO DOC** *Campania, Italy*   Since DOC was introduced in 1983, things have improved for the red based on Piedirosso and the white from Coda di Volpe and Verdeca – but the name is still more evocative than the wine. Best producers: Caputo, MASTROBERARDINO, Sorrentino.

**LADOIX AC** *Côte de Beaune, Burgundy, France*   The most northerly village in the COTE DE BEAUNE and one of the least known. The best wines sell under the ACs CORTON, ALOXE-CORTON or Aloxe-Corton Premier Cru, and the less good ones as Ladoix-Côte de Beaune or COTE DE BEAUNE-VILLAGES. There are several good growers in the village and Ladoix wine, mainly red, quite light in colour and a little lean in style, is reasonably priced. Best producers: (reds) Capitain, Chevalier, Cornu★, R Launay, Maillard, Nudant; (whites) Cornu, Maillard. Best years: (reds) 1995 **93 92 90** 89 88.

**CH. LAFAURIE-PEYRAGUEY★★★** *Sauternes AC, 1er Cru Classé, Bordeaux, France*   This was one of the most improved SAUTERNES properties of the 1980s and nowadays is frequently one of the best Sauternes of all. The wines can age well too. Best years: (1996) (95) **90 89** 88 86 85 83.

**CH. LAFITE-ROTHSCHILD★★★** *Pauillac AC, 1er Cru Classé, Haut-Médoc, Bordeaux, France* This PAUILLAC First Growth is frequently cited as the epitome of elegance, indulgence and expense – but the wine can be wretchedly inconsistent. There have been great improvements of late but as the wine often needs 15 years and can take 30 years or more to achieve the magical and unlikely marriage of cedar fragrance and lean but lovely blackcurrant fruit, we won't know for quite a while yet how good these 'new' Lafites are going to be. So it gets its ★★★ rating, but not without reservations. Second wine: les Carruades de Lafite-Rothschild. Best years: (1996) (95) 94 90 89 88 86 **85 82 81 79 76**.

**CH. LAFLEUR★★★** *Pomerol AC, Bordeaux, France* Using some of POMEROL's most traditional wine-making, this tiny estate makes Pomerols that seriously rival those from the great PETRUS for sheer power and flavour, and indeed in recent years has begun to pull ahead of PETRUS for hedonistic richness and concentration. Best years: (1996) (95) 94 93 **90 89 88 86 85**.

**LAFON** *Meursault, Côte de Beaune, Burgundy, France* The leading producer in MEURSAULT and one of Burgundy's current superstars, with a reputation and high prices to match. Dominique Lafon produces rich, powerful Meursaults that spend as long as 2 years in barrel and age superbly in bottle. As well as excellent Meursault, especially Clos de la Barre★★, les Charmes★★★ and les Perrières★★★, Lafon makes a tiny amount of le MONTRACHET★★★ and most individual and exciting reds from VOLNAY★★★ and MONTHELIE★. Best years: 1995 94 93 **92 90 89 88 85**.

**CH. LAFON-ROCHET ★★** *St-Estèphe AC, 4ème Cru Classé, Haut-Médoc, Bordeaux, France* Good-value, affordable Classed Growth claret, usually showing a very attractive, deep, dry, blackcurrant fruit that ages well. Best years: (1996) (95) 94 90 89 88 **86 85 83 82 79**.

**LAGEDER** *Alto Adige DOC, Trentino-Alto Adige, Italy* Leading producer in ALTO ADIGE. Medium-priced varietals under the Lageder label, and pricy estate and single-vineyard wines that steal the show. The Cabernet★ and Chardonnay★★ under the Löwengang label, Sauvignon Lehenhof★★, Cabernet Cor Römigberg★★ and Pinot Grigio Benefizium Porer★★ are the stars. Best years: (premium whites) 1995 **94 93 91 90 88**.

**LAGO DI CALDARO DOC** *Trentino-Alto Adige, Italy* At its best a lovely, delicate, barely red, youthful glugger from the Schiava grape in Italy's mountainous north, tasting of strawberries and cream and bacon smoke. However, much overproduced Caldaro scarcely passes muster as red wine at all. Known in German as Kalterersee. Kalterersee Auslese (or Lago di Caldaro Scelto) is not sweet, but has 0.5% more alcohol. Best producers: Baron Dürfeld de Giovanelli★, Brigl, Castel Ringberg, Hofstätter, LAGEDER★, Karl Martini, Niedermayr, Prima e Nuova co-op★, San Michele Appiano co-op, Schloss Sallegg★.

**CH. LAGRANGE★★** *St-Julien AC, 3ème Cru Classé, Haut-Médoc, Bordeaux, France* Since the Japanese company Suntory purchased this estate in 1983, the leap in quality has been astonishing. No longer an amiable, shambling ST-JULIEN, this has become a single-minded wine of good fruit, meticulous wine-making and fine quality. Second wine: les Fiefs de Lagrange. Best years: (1996) (95) 90 89 **88 86 85**.

153

**LAGREIN** This highly individual black grape variety is planted only in Italy's Trentino-Alto Adige region, where it produces deep-coloured, brambly, chocolaty reds of considerable distinction called Lagrein Dunkel. It also makes a full-bodied yet attractively scented rosé (known as Kretzer). Best producers: Franz Gojer-Glöggelhof★, Gries co-op★, LAGEDER★, Laimburg★, Muri-Gries★, Niedermayr★.

**CH. LA LAGUNE ★★** *Haut-Médoc AC, 3ème Cru Classé, Haut-Médoc, Bordeaux, France* Consistently excellent Classed Growth – full of the charry, chestnut warmth of good oak and a deep, cherry-blackcurrant-and-plums sweetness which, after 10 years or so, becomes outstanding claret. Best years: (1996) (95) 90 89 **88 86 85 83 82 78 76 75**.

**LAKE'S FOLLY** *Hunter Valley, New South Wales, Australia* Erratic wines with an eager following, thanks to the charismatic Dr Max Lake. In the best years, austere Chardonnay★★ ages slowly to a masterly antipodean yet Burgundy-like peak. The Cabernet★★ is supple and beautifully balanced at best but doesn't always live up to its reputation. Best years: (red) 1993 **91 89 87 85 83 81**; (white) **1994 92 91 86**.

**LALANDE-DE-POMEROL AC** *Bordeaux, France* North of its more famous neighbour POMEROL, this AC produces full, ripe wines with an unmistakable mineral edge that are very attractive to drink at 3–4 years old, but age reasonably well too. Even though they lack the concentration of top Pomerols the wines are not particularly cheap. Best producers: Annereaux ★, Belles-Graves, Bertineau-St-Vincent★, Clos de l'Église, la Croix-Chenevelle, la Croix-St-André★, Fougeailles, Garraud★, Grand-Ormeau, Haut-Chaigneau, Haut-Surget, Sergant, Siaurac ★, Tournefeuille, Viaud. Best years: (1996) **95 94 90 89 88 85 83 82**.

**LAMBERHURST** *Kent, England* One of England's steadiest and most reliable producers, and the only triple winner of the Gore-Browne Trophy (England's leading wine award) – twice for a Schönburger and once for a Huxelrebe. Changed hands in 1995.

**LAMBRUSCO** *Emilia-Romagna, Italy* Lambrusco is actually a black grape variety, grown in 4 DOC zones on the plains of Emilia, and 1 around Mantova in LOMBARDY, but it is the red and white screwcap bottles labelled as non-DOC Lambrusco that have made the name famous, even though some of them may contain no wine from the Lambrusco grape at all. Originally a dry or semi-sweet fizzy red wine, whose high acidity naturally partnered the rich local food, good dry Lambrusco (especially Lambrusco di Sorbaia or Grasparossa di Castelvetro) is worth seeking out. However, technology has led to huge quantities of anonymous, sweetened frizzante wines being let loose on the unsuspecting public. Best producers: Venturini Baldini, Barbolini★, Francesco Bellei★, Casali, Cavicchioli★, Chiarli, Ferrari, Giacobazzi, Graziano★, Oreste Lini, Spezia, Riunite.

**LAMOUREAUX LANDING** *Finger Lakes AVA, New York State, USA* The FINGER LAKES region of New York is emerging (along with Long Island) as that state's most important quality wine area. Lamoreaux Landing, established in 1990, has become one of the most important Eastern wineries. Its Chardonnay★★ is a consistent medal winner at competitions and the Pinot Noir improves with each vintage. Also look for the Riesling, Gewürztraminer and a limited-production Blanc de Noirs.

**LANDWEIN** German or Austrian country wine and the equivalent of French Vin de Pays. The wine must have a territorial definition and may be chaptalized to give it more body.

**CH. LANESSAN** ★ *Haut-Médoc AC, Cru Bourgeois, Haut-Médoc, Bordeaux, France* Attractive but occasionally austere Cru Bourgeois from the commune of Cussac-Fort-Médoc. Hardly ever uses new oak barrels, yet often achieves Fifth Growth standard and is never over-priced. Tends to be at its best in top vintages and can easily age for 8–10 years. Second wine: Dom. de Ste-Gemme. Best years: (1996) (95) **90 89 88 85 83 82**.

**CH. LANGOA-BARTON** ★★ *St-Julien AC, 3ème Cru Classé, Haut-Médoc, Bordeaux, France* Owned by the Barton family since the 1820s, Langoa-Barton is usually lighter in style than its St-Julien stablemate LEOVILLE-BARTON, but it is still an extremely impressive and reasonably priced wine. Drink after 7 or 8 years, although it may keep for 15. Second wine: Lady Langoa. Best years: (1996) (95) 94 93 90 89 **88 86 85 83 82 81**.

**LANGUEDOC-ROUSSILLON** *Midi, France* Traditionally a source of undistinguished cheap wine, this area of southern France, running from Nîmes to the Spanish border and covering the *départements* of the Gard, Hérault, Aude and Pyrénées-Orientales, is now turning out some exciting reds. Temperature-controlled vinification and a growing sense of regional pride have wrought the transformation, hand in hand with better grape varieties and ambitious producers, from the heights of MAS DE DAUMAS GASSAC to very good local co-ops. The best wines are the reds, particularly those from CORBIERES, FAUGERES, MINERVOIS and PIC ST-LOUP, and some new wave Cabernets, Merlots and Syrahs, as well as the more traditional Vins Doux Naturels, such as BANYULS, MAURY and MUSCAT DE RIVESALTES; but we are now seeing exciting whites as well, particularly as new plantings of Chardonnay, Marsanne, Viognier and Sauvignon Blanc mature. See also Aude, Bouches-du-Rhône, Collioure, Costières de Nîmes, Coteaux du Languedoc, Côtes du Roussillon, Côtes du Roussillon-Villages, Côtes de Thau, Côtes de Thongue, Faugères, Fitou, Gard, Haute Vallée de l'Aude, Hérault, Muscat de Frontignan, Muscat de Mireval, Oc, St-Chinian, Vallée du Paradis.

**LANSON** *Champagne AC, Champagne, France* A mass-market fizz whose brilliant 'why not?' advertising campaign did so much to democratize Champagne's image. The non-vintage Black Label is reliable stuff, while the rosé ★ and vintage ★★ wines, especially the de luxe blend called Noble Cuvée ★★, aspire to greater things. Recent ownership changes place a question mark over Lanson's future quality. Best years: **1990 89 88 85 83 82 79**.

**CH. LAROSE-TRINTAUDON** *Haut-Médoc AC, Cru Bourgeois, Haut-Médoc, Bordeaux, France* Since it was planted from scratch in 1966, this estate – the largest in the Médoc – has produced substantial amounts of plump, reasonable quality, affordable red Bordeaux. The wines are made to drink at about 5 years but can age for 10. Best years: (1996) (95) **90**.

**CH. LASCOMBES** ★★ *Margaux AC, 2ème Cru Classé, Haut-Médoc,* *Bordeaux, France* This large and important MARGAUX Second Growth has been very inconsistent during the 1970s and early 80s to put it mildly, but the 90 and 89 vintages – showing some of the tantalizing fresh flowers and blackcurrant perfume of which Lascombes is capable – promise a return to form. The Chevalier de Lascombes rosé is rather good, too. Second wine: Ségonnes. Best years: (1996) (95) 94 **90 89 88 86 85.**

**CH. DE LASTOURS** *Corbières AC, Languedoc, France* A large estate in CORBIÈRES, producing some of the most exciting wines in the Midi. The top white is Dry de Lastours★, an interesting blend of Muscat, Malvoisie and Grenache Blanc. But the outstanding wines are the reds – particularly the Cuvée Simon Descamps★★ and the oaky Cuvée Boisée ★★. Best years: (reds) **1995 94 93 90 89 88 86 85.**

**CH. LATOUR** ★★★ *Pauillac AC, 1er Cru Classé, Haut-Médoc, Bordeaux,* *France* Latour's great reputation is based on powerful, long-lasting classic wines. Throughout the 1950s, 60s and 70s the property stood for consistency and a refusal to compromise in the face of financial pressure. Strangely, however, in the early 80s there was an attempt to make lighter, more fashionable wines with mixed results. The late 80s saw a return to classic Latour, much to my relief. Its reputation for making fine wine in less successful vintages is well deserved. After 30 years in British hands, it is now French-owned. Second wine: les Forts de Latour. Best years: (1996) (95) 94 93 90 89 88 **82 79 78 75 70.**

**LOUIS LATOUR** *Beaune, Burgundy, France* Controversial merchant almost as well known for his COTEAUX DE L'ARDÈCHE Chardonnays as for his Burgundies. Latour's white Burgundies are much better than the reds, although the red CORTON-Grancey★ can be good. Latour's oaky CORTON-CHARLEMAGNE ★★, from his own vineyard, is his top wine, but there is also good CHEVALIER-MONTRACHET ★★, BATARD-MONTRACHET ★★ and le MONTRACHET ★★. Even so, as these are the greatest white vineyards in Burgundy, there really should be a higher rating in there somewhere. Best years: (top whites) 1995 93 **92 90 89 88 85.**

**CH. LATOUR-À-POMEROL** ★★ *Pomerol AC, Bordeaux, France* Now directed by Christian Moueix of PÉTRUS fame, this property makes luscious wines, with loads of gorgeous fruit, and enough tannin to age well. Best years: (1996) (95) 94 **90 89 88 85 83 82 81 79.**

**LATRICIÈRES-CHAMBERTIN AC** See Chambertin AC.

**LAUREL GLEN** *Sonoma Mountain AVA, California, USA* Owner-wine-maker Patrick Campbell makes only Cabernet Sauvignon★★★ at his mountaintop winery, with some Merlot and Cabernet Franc blended and bottled there. This is rich wine with deep fruit flavours and it ages after 6–10 years to a perfumed, complex Bordeaux style that is rare in California. Second label: Counterpoint. Two other labels, Terra Rosa and Reds, are made from bought and blended wines. Best years: 1994 93 92 91 **90 87 86 85.**

**LAURENT-PERRIER** *Champagne AC, Champagne, France* A large, family-owned Champagne house, whose wines consistently offer flavour and quality at (fairly) reasonable prices. The non-vintage★ is now leaner and drier, unfortunately, but the Vintage★★ is still delicious, while the top wine, Cuvée Grand Siècle★★★, is among the finest Champagnes of all. There is also very good rosé, as both Non-vintage★ and Vintage Alexandra Grand Siècle★★. Best years: **1990 88 85 82 79**.

**CH. LAVILLE-HAUT-BRION★★★** *Pessac-Léognan AC, Cru Classé de Graves, Bordeaux, France* This is the white wine of la MISSION-HAUT-BRION and is one of the finest white GRAVES, with a price tag to match. The wine is fermented in barrel and needs 10 years' aging or more to reach its savoury but luscious peak. Best years: (1996) (95) 94 **90 89 88 85 83 82 79 78**.

**LAZIO** *Italy* This region is best known for FRASCATI – Rome's white glugger. There are various other bland whites from Trebbiano and Malvasia, such as EST! EST!! EST!!! DI MONTEFIASCONE, and unmemorable red wine from Cesanese, but the region's best are table wines based on Cabernet and Merlot.

**LEASINGHAM** *Clare Valley, South Australia* Another wing of the BRL HARDY group, Leasingham is CLARE VALLEY's biggest winery, with a senior and respected position. Once prostituted on 4-litre casks, the Stanley Leasingham name now stands for rich, chocolaty reds laced with coconutty American oak that are better than ever under the hand of Richard Rowe. Bin 56 Cabernet-Malbec★★ and Bin 61 Shiraz★★ are great bargains, while newly minted Classic Clare Shiraz★★ and Cabernet★★ are high-alcohol blockbusters. Riesling★ can be among the area's best; respectable Chardonnay and Sémillon-Sauvignon as well.

**L'ECOLE NO 41** *Washington State, USA* The velvety and deeply-flavoured Merlot★★ from this fine winery is marvellous. A rich, intense Sémillon★★ is very good and with the 1992 vintage the Chardonnay★★ reaches a similar level.

**LECONFIELD** *Coonawarra, South Australia* Quality here greatly improved following the arrival of winemaker Ralph Fowler. Since 1990, the Cabernet Sauvignon★★ is beautifully crafted, the Merlot★★ a stunner and peppery Shiraz★★ are hot on their heels. The whites have also improved: the Riesling★ is fruitier and the Chardonnay★ more stylish. Best years: (reds) **1995 94 93 91**.

**LEEUWIN ESTATE** *Margaret River, Western Australia* MARGARET RIVER's high-flier, with pricy Chardonnay (at best ★★★) that could be Australia's nearest thing to le MONTRACHET. The Cabernets have been patchy but at best are ★★, blackcurrant yet with a cool lean edge. Best years: (white) **1993 92 91 89 88 87 86 85 82 80**.

**DOM. LEFLAIVE** *Puligny-Montrachet, Côte de Beaune, Burgundy, France* The most famous white Burgundy producer of all, with extensive hold-ings in some of the world's greatest vineyards (BATARD-MONTRACHET, Chevalier-Montrachet and, since 1990, le MONTRACHET itself). The price of the wines is correspondingly high, but 1986–92 produced a number of disappointing wines. A new wine-making team, led by Anne-Claude Leflaive and including the talented Pierre Morey, and a move to bio-dynamic growing, herald a change for the better. The top wines here – Pucelles★★, Chevalier-Montrachet★★ and Bâtard-Montrachet★★★ – are consistently delicious. They are capable of aging for up to 20 years. Best years: 1995 94 93 **85 83**.

**OLIVIER LEFLAIVE FRÈRES** *Puligny-Montrachet, Côte de Beaune, Burgundy, France* Former co-manager of Dom. LEFLAIVE, négociant Olivier Leflaive specializes in crisp, modern white wines from the Côte d'Or and the Côte Chalonnaise that are good examples of international-standard Chardonnay. The best-value wines are those from lesser ACs – ST-ROMAIN, MONTAGNY★, ST-AUBIN★ and RULLY★ – but the rich, oaky BATARD-MONTRACHET★★ is the star turn of talented winemaker Franck Grux. Best years: **1995 93 92 90 89 88**.

**PETER LEHMANN** *Barossa Valley, South Australia* Lehmann buys grapes from hundreds of BAROSSA smallholders, but we can no longer say he owns no vineyards, as he bought the superb Stonewell plot in 1994, source of his best Shiraz★★. The company, public since 1993, makes splendidly juicy reds, old-fashioned but packed with fruit. Also tasty Chardonnay★, lemony Sémillon★ and dry, long-lived Riesling★.

**LENZ VINEYARDS** *Long Island AVA, New York State, USA* Leading Long Island winery going from strength to strength. Merlot★ is elegant and powerful with soft, balanced tannins; dry Gewürztraminer★ is spicy and tasty – a good apéritif. In good vintages the Pinot Noir★ has deep, ripe fruit. Chardonnay is mostly excellent and a new Cabernet Franc is appealing. The brut-style sparkler★ is hard to find, but worth the search.

**JEAN LEÓN** *Penedés DO, Catalonia, Spain* Jean León, who died in 1996, established vineyards to supply wine for his Californian restaurant, before selling to TORRES in 1995. The style is Californian, the reds★★ rich and blackcurranty, made from Cabernet Sauvignon with Cabernet Franc and Merlot, the Chardonnay★★ rich, biscuity and pineappley, fermented in oak. Best years: (reds) 1990 **87 85 82 79**.

**LEONETTI CELLAR** *Washington State, USA* Cabernet Sauvignon★★★ and Merlot★★★ have won high praise from many critics and the tiny production is sold out within hours. The wines are immense with very concentrated fruit and enough tannin to chew on but not be blasted by. Best years: 1994 93 **92 91 90 89 88 87**.

**CH. LÉOVILLE-BARTON★★★** *St-Julien AC, 2ème Cru Classé, Haut-Médoc, Bordeaux, France* Made by Anthony Barton, whose family has run this ST-JULIEN property since 1821, this excellent claret is a traditionalist's delight. Dark, dry and tannic, the wines are difficult to taste young and therefore often underestimated, but over 10–15 years they achieve a lean yet sensitively proportioned classical beauty rarely equalled in Bordeaux. Moreover, they are extremely fairly priced. Praise be. Best years: (1996) (95) 94 93 90 89 88 86 **85 82 81 78**.

**CH. LÉOVILLE-LAS-CASES★★★** *St-Julien AC, 2ème Cru Classé, Haut-Médoc, Bordeaux, France* This is the largest of the 3 Léoville properties and probably now the most exciting of all the ST-JULIEN wines. A direct neighbour of the great LATOUR, there are certain similarities in the wines. Since 1975 Las-Cases has been making wines of startlingly deep, dark concentration. From a good year the wine really needs 15 years of aging and should last happily for up to 30 years. Second wine: Clos du Marquis. Best years: (1996) (95) 94 93 90 89 88 86 **85 83 82 81 79 78 75**.

**CH. LÉOVILLE-POYFERRÉ**★★ *St-Julien AC, 2ème Cru Classé, Haut-Médoc, Bordeaux, France*  Until comparatively recently, this was the least good of the 3 Léoville properties. The 1980s saw a marked improvement with a string of excellent wines produced under Didier Cuvelier, who has gradually increased the richness of the wine without wavering from its austere style. Since the 1986 vintage these are approaching the top level and need 8–10 years' aging to blossom. Second wine: Moulin-Riche. Best years: (1996) (95) 93 90 89 **86 85 83 82**.

**DOMAINE LEROY** *Vosne-Romanée, Côte de Nuits, Burgundy, France*  In 1988 Lalou Bize-Leroy bought the former Domaine Noëllat in VOSNE-ROMANEE, renaming it Domaine Leroy. Here she produces some fiendishly expensive, though fabulously concentrated, wines with bio-dynamic methods and almost ludicrously low yields from top vineyards such as CLOS DE VOUGEOT★★, RICHEBOURG★★★ and ROMANEE-ST-VIVANT★★. Best years: 1995 93 **92** 91 90 **89** 88.

**MAISON LEROY** *Auxey-Duresses, Côte de Beaune, Burgundy, France*  A négociant tucked away in the back streets of AUXEY-DURESSES, Leroy also co-owns Domaine de la ROMANEE-CONTI, although is no longer involved in the distribution of the wines. However, its own cellar contains an extraordinary range of gems, often terrifyingly expensive, dating back to the early years of the century. Best years: **1971** 59 49 **47 45 37**.

**LIEBFRAUMILCH** *Pfalz, Rheinhessen, Nahe and Rheingau, Germany*  A branded wine from the PFALZ, RHEINHESSEN, NAHE or the RHEINGAU that must be made of 70% Riesling, Silvaner, Müller-Thurgau or Kerner grapes. Liebfraumilch is sweetish, low in acidity and designed for drinking on its own without food. At best it is a well-constructed wine that appeals to the uninitiated wine drinker. Liebfraumilch was a crucially important factor in introducing millions to wine during the 1980s, but since then it has had a relentlessly down-market image. Best producers: Sichel (Blue Nun), Valckenberg (Madonna).

**LIGURIA** *Italy*  Thin coastal strip of north-west Italy, running from the French border at Ventimiglia to the Tuscan border. The best-known wines are the RIVIERA LIGURE DI PONENTE, CINQUETERRE and ROSSESE DI DOLCEACQUA DOCs.

**LIMOUX AC** *Languedoc, France*  The first AC in the Languedoc where producers are allowed to use Chardonnay and Chenin Blanc, which must be vinified in oak. Production is dominated by the SIEUR D'ARQUES co-op, whose best wines, Toques et Clochers★, fetch high prices at the annual charity auction.

**LINDEMANS** *Murray River, Victoria, Australia*  Large, historic company now part of Southcorp Wines Pty Ltd. Best wines are old-fashioned HUNTER VALLEY Shiraz★★ ('burgundy' and Steven Vineyard), Chardonnay★★ and Sémillons★★★ (labelled 'chablis', 'white burgundy' and Sémillon!). There is a trio of rather variable and oaky COONAWARRA reds: St George Cabernet★, spicy Limestone Ridge Shiraz-Cabernet★★ and multi-variety Pyrus★. PADTHAWAY Chardonnay is no longer the star it was but a new flagship trio of Coonawarra whites was released in 1995 – a Chardonnay, Riesling★ and Sauvignon★.

The mass-market Bin 65 Chardonnay★ is a flagship for affordable Australian Chardonnay abroad. Best years: (Hunter Shiraz) 1993 **91 87 86 83 82 80 79 73 70 65**; (Sémillon) 1996 95 93 91 **90 89 87 86 80 79 78 75 72 70 68**; (Coonawarra reds) 1994 93 **91 90 88 86 85 82**.

**LINGENFELDER** *Grosskarlbach, Pfalz, Germany* Rainer Lingenfelder's talent is indisputable, but there have been worrying quality problems here since 1994. At best, the Grosskarlbacher Burgweg Spätlese Trocken★★ is crisp and aromatic, the 92 Freinsheimer Spätlese★★ full of grapefruit, pine and apricots aromas; his Spätburgunder★★ can be one of Germany's best red wines (the 89 was rich in cocoa and raspberry flavours but the 91 disappointing), and he also makes delightful Dornfelder★. To top it all the Riesling is heavenly, especially from his 89 Freinsheimer Goldberg site★★★. Best years: **1993 91 90 89 88 83**.

**JEAN LIONNET** *Cornas, Rhône Valley, France* Jean Lionnet produces dense, tannic CORNAS★★ in a fairly modern style. The emphasis here is on new oak aging, and the wines can seem closed when young. It's worth waiting for 6–7 years, especially for his Domaine de Rochepertuis★★. Lionnet also produces impressive COTES DU RHONE★ from his younger Cornas vines, and a little white ST-PERAY. Best years: (1996) 95 94 **91 90 89 88 85 83**.

**LIRAC AC** *Rhône Valley, France* An excellent but underrated AC between TAVEL and CHATEAUNEUF-DU-PAPE. The reds have the dusty, spicy fruit of Châteauneuf without quite achieving the intensity of the best examples. They age well but are delicious young. The rosé is refreshing with a lovely strawberry fruit and the white can be good – drink them both young before the perfume goes. Best producers: Aquéria★, Assémat, Devoy, Fermade, la Genestière, Maby★, la Mordurée★, St-Roch, Ségriès, la Tour. Best years: **1995 94 91 90**.

**LISTEL** *Golfe de Lion, Languedoc, France* Listel is best known for its Gris de Gris (a rather dull rosé), Brut de Listel, an equally dull fizz, and a sweet grapy concoction called Pétillant de Listel. Its varietal wines, particularly Sauvignon and Cabernet Sauvignon, are much better. Now part of the VAL D'ORBIEU group.

**LISTRAC-MÉDOC AC** *Haut-Médoc, Bordeaux, France* Set back from the Gironde and away from the best gravel ridges, Listrac is 1 of the 6 specific ACs within the HAUT-MEDOC. The wines can be good without ever being thrilling, and are marked by solid fruit, a slightly coarse tannin and an earthy flavour. Best producers: CLARKE, Ducluzeau, Fonréaud, Fourcas-Dupré, Fourcas-Hosten, Fourcas-Loubaney, Grand Listrac co-op, Mayne-Lalande, Saransot-Dupré. Best years: (1996) (95) **90 89 88 86 85 83**.

**LOCOROTONDO DOC** *Puglia, Italy* Nutty, crisp, dry white from the south. Drink young. Best producers: Borgo Canale, Candido, Leone de Castris, Locorotondo co-op.

**LOIRE VALLEY** *France* The Loire river cuts right through the heart of France. The upper reaches are the home of world-famous SANCERRE and POUILLY-FUME. The region of Touraine makes good Sauvignon Blanc, while at VOUVRAY and MONTLOUIS the Chenin Blanc makes some pretty good fizz and still whites, ranging from sweet to very dry. The Loire's best reds are made in SAUMUR-CHAMPIGNY, CHINON and BOURGUEIL, mainly from Cabernet Franc, with ANJOU-VILLAGES improving fast. Anjou is famous for ROSE D'ANJOU but the best wines are white, either sweet from the Layon Valley or very dry Chenin from SAVENNIERES. Near the mouth of the river around Nantes is MUSCADET. See also Anjou Blanc, Anjou Mousseux, Anjou Rouge, Bonnezeaux, Cabernet d'Anjou, Cheverny, Côte Roannaise, Coteaux de l'Aubance, Coteaux du Layon, Crémant de Loire, Gros Plant du Pays Nantais, Haut-Poitou, Jardin de la France, Menetou-Salon, Muscadet des Coteaux de la Loire, Muscadet Côtes de Grand Lieu, Muscadet de Sèvre-et-Maine, Pouilly-sur-Loire, Quarts de Chaume, Quincy, Rosé de Loire, St-Nicolas-de-Bourgueil, Saumur, Saumur Mousseux, Touraine, Touraine Mousseux.

**LOMBARDY** *Italy* Lombardy, the richest and most populous of Italian regions, is a larger consumer than producer of wine, with its capital Milan drinking vast quantities from the OLTREPO PAVESE zone, as well as imports from France. Many of its best grapes go to provide base wine for Italy's thriving Spumante industry. However, there are some interesting wines in Oltrepò Pavese, VALTELLINA, LUGANA and high-quality sparkling and still wines in FRANCIACORTA.

**DR LOOSEN** *Bernkastel, Mosel, Germany* Loosen's St Johannishof estate has portions of some of the MOSEL's most famous vineyards: Treppchen and Prälat in ERDEN, Würzgarten in URZIG, Sonnenuhr in WEHLEN, Himmelreich in GRAACH and Lay in BERNKASTEL. Young Ernst Loosen took over in 1988 and since then the wines have gone from strength to strength, with most wines achieving ★★, and Spätlese and Auslese from Wehlen, Ürzig and Erden frequently ★★★. One of Germany's foremost protagonists of organic methods, his simple Riesling is very good, year in year out. Best years: 1996 95 **94 93 92 90 89 88 85 76**.

**LÓPEZ DE HEREDIA** *Rioja DOC, Rioja, Spain* A charmingly old-fashioned, family-owned RIOJA company, who still age wines for a long time in old oak casks. Reds and traditional, oaky whites are excellent – the younger wines are called Viña Cubillo★ or Viña Bosconia★, and the mature wines Viña Tondonia★ and Viña Bosconia. Good, oaky whites, especially the younger Cuvée Viña Gravonia. Best years: (reds) **1991 90 89 87 86 85 78 76 73**.

**LOS LLANOS** *Valdepeñas DO, Castilla-La Mancha, Spain* A huge, scrupulously clean and well-equipped winery in central Spain, renowned for its excellent value, mature, oak-aged red Señorío de Los Llanos★ in both Reserva and Gran Reserva qualities. Best years: (reds) **1992 87 85 84 83 82**.

**CH. LOUDENNE** *Médoc AC, Cru Bourgeois, Bordeaux, France* This lovely pink château on the banks of the Gironde river has been owned by the English firm Gilbeys since 1875. The wines, both red and white, are gentle in style, but tend to lack excitement. Recent vintages are showing more character. Best years: (1996) (95) **90 89 88 86**.

**LOUISVALE** *Stellenbosch WO, South Africa* Chardonnay, the sole variety on this farm, is produced in 3 guises: a barrel-fermented version★ impresses with buttery, biscuity richness and oak balance; Chavant (lightly oaked) and Chavant (unwooded) complete the line-up. Best among the reds, from bought-in grapes, is dense, spicy-minty Cabernet-Merlot★.

**LOUPIAC AC** *Bordeaux, France*   A sweet wine area across the Garonne
♀ river from BARSAC. The wines are attractively sweet without being
gooey. Drink young in general, though they can age. Best producers:
du Chay, Clos Jean, du Cros, Loupiac-Gaudiet, Mazarin, Dom. du Noble,
de Ricaud. Best years: (1996) **95 90 89 88 86 85 83**.

**CH. LA LOUVIÈRE** *Pessac-Léognan AC, Bordeaux,*
🍷 *France*   This property is one of the GRAVES' rising
stars and its growing reputation is almost entirely
due to the presence of André Lurton, who has revitalized the property over the last 30 years. The
well-structured reds★★ and fresh, Sauvignon-
based whites★★ are excellent value for money.
Best years: (reds) (1996) (95) 94 93 **90 89 88 86 85**;
(whites) (1996) **95 94 90 89 88**.

**LUGANA DOC** *Lombardy, Italy*   Medium-bodied white (occasionally
♀ sparkling) from the Trebbiano di Lugana grape. Well-structured wines
from the better producers can develop excitingly over several years.
Best producers: Ca' dei Frati★★, Premiovini, Provenza, Roveglia★,
Visconti★, Zenato.

**PIERRE LUNEAU** *Muscadet de Sèvre-et-Maine AC and Muscadet des*
🍷 *Coteaux de la Loire AC, Loire Valley, France*   Meticulous Muscadet
producer who specializes in unoaked Muscadets for the long haul – his
top wine, le 'L' d'Or★★, ages brilliantly – but his oak-fermented wines,
although interesting, are disconscertingly variable.

**LUNGAROTTI** *Torgiano DOC, Umbria, Italy*   Leading producer of TORGIANO.
🍷 Also makes fine red San Giorgio★★ (Cabernet-Sangiovese), white Torgiano, Chardonnays Miralduolo and Vigna Palazzi★, and even a good
sherry-style Solleone. His Torgiano Riserva Rubesco★★ is now DOCG.

**LUSSAC-ST-ÉMILION AC** *Bordeaux, France*   One of the ST-EMILION
🍷 satellite ACs. Much of the wine, which tastes like a lighter St-Émilion,
is made by the first-rate local co-op and should be drunk within
4 years of the vintage. However, certain properties are worth seeking
out. Best producers: Barbe-Blanche★, Bel-Air, Courlat, Croix-de-
Rambeau, la Grenière, Haut-Milon, Lyonnat, Vieux-Ch.-Chambeau,
Villadière. Best years: 1996 **95 90 89 88**.

**EMILIO LUSTAU** *Jerez y Manzanilla DO, Andalucía, Spain*   Specializes in
♀ supplying 'own label' wines to supermarkets. Quality is generally good,
and there are some real stars at the top, especially the Almacenista
range★★, very individual dry sherries from small, private producers.

**CH. LYNCH-BAGES** *Pauillac AC, 5ème Cru Classé, Haut-Médoc, Bordeaux,*
🍷 *France*   I am a great fan of Lynch-Bages red★★★ – with its almost
succulent richness, its gentle texture and its starburst of flavours, all
butter, blackcurrants and mint, and it is now one of PAUILLAC's most
popular wines. Because of its Fifth Growth status, it was inclined to be
underpriced; I couldn't say that now, but it's still excellent value. It is
impressive at 5 years, beautiful at 10 years and irresistible at 20. The
Second wine: Haut-Bages-Avérous. White wine: Blanc de Lynch-
Bages★★. Best years (reds): (1996) (95) 94 90 89 88 **87** 86 **85 83 82 81**.

**MACÉRATION CARBONIQUE** Vinification method used mainly in the
BEAUJOLAIS region, but increasingly in the south of France and the
Loire, to produce fresh fruity reds for drinking young. Bunches of

grapes are fermented whole in closed containers – a process which extracts lots of fruit and colour, but little tannin.

**MÂCON AC** *Mâconnais, Burgundy, France*   The basic Mâcon AC, but most whites in the region are labelled under the superior MACON-VILLAGES AC. The wines are rarely exciting. Chardonnay-based Mâcon-Blanc, especially, is a rather expensive basic quaffer. Drink young. Mâcon Supérieur has a slightly higher minimum alcohol level. Best producers: Bertillonnes, Bruyère, DUBOEUF. Best years: **1996 95**.

**MÂCON-VILLAGES AC** *Mâconnais, Burgundy, France*   Mâcon-Villages should be an enjoyable, fruity, fresh wine for everyday drinking at a fair price, but because it comes from Chardonnay, the wines are often overpriced. Forty-three villages in the region can call their wine Mâcon-Villages or add their own name, as in Mâcon-Viré. Best villages: Chardonnay, Chaintré, Charnay, Clessé, Davayé, Igé, Lugny, Prissé, la Roche Vineuse, St-Gengoux-de-Scissé, Uchizy, Viré. Best producers: Bonhomme★, de Chervin, Clessé co-op, Deux Roches, Manciat-Poncet, Merlin★, Prissé co-op, de Roally, St-Gengoux co-op, Thévenet★★, Tissier, Valette, Verget★, Vincent★, Viré co-op. Best years: 1996 **95 94 93**.

**MACULAN** *Breganze DOC, Veneto, Italy*   Fausto Maculan makes an impressive range of BREGANZE DOC led by Cabernet Fratta★★ and Palazzotto★★, along with excellent non-DOC reds from the Ferrata vineyards, but his most impressive wines are sweet Torcolato★★ and Acininobili★★★ made from botrytized Vespaiola grapes.

**MADEIRA DOC** *Madeira, Portugal*   The sub-tropical island of Madeira seems an unlikely place to find a serious wine. However, Madeiras are very serious indeed and the best can survive to a great age. Internationally famous by the 17th century, modern Madeira was shaped by the phylloxera epidemic 100 years ago, which wiped out the vineyards. Replantation was with hybrid vines inferior to the 'noble' and traditional Malvasia (or Malmsey), Boal (or Bual), Verdelho and Sercial varieties. There are incentives to replant with noble grapes, but progress is slow. The typically burnt, tangy taste of inexpensive Madeira comes from the process of heating in huge vats. The better wines are aged naturally in the sub-tropical warmth. All the wines are fortified early on and may be sweetened with fortified grape juice before bottling. Basic 3-year-old Madeira is made mainly from Tinta Negra Mole, whereas higher quality Reserves (5 years old), Special Reserves (10 years old) and Vintage wines (from a single year, aged in cask for at least 20 years) tend to be made from 1 of the 4 'noble' grapes. Under European labelling restrictions any wine with a varietal designation must be made from the grape stated on the label. The best Madeira can survive to a great age but it's a rare beast in modern times. Best producers: Artur Barros e Souza, MADEIRA WINE COMPANY (Blandy's, Cossart Gordon), Henriques & Henriques, d'Oliveira.

**MADEIRA WINE COMPANY** *Madeira DOC, Madeira, Portugal*   This company ships more than half of all Madeira exported in bottle. Among the brand names are Blandy's, Cossart Gordon, Leacock, Lomelino and Rutherford & Miles. Now controlled by the Symington family from the mainland. Big improvements are taking place especially at 3- and 5-year-old levels.

**MADIRAN AC** *South-West France* In the gentle hills of Vic-Bilh, north of Pau, there has been a steady revival of the Madiran AC as viticulturalists have gradually discovered ways to propagate the difficult Tannat vine successfully. Several of the best producers are now using new oak and this certainly helps to soften the rather aggressive wine. Best producers: Aydie★, Barréjat, Bouscassé★★, Caves de Crouseilles★, Chapelle-Lenclos★, Laffitte-Teston★, MONTUS★★, Mouréou★, Union des Producteurs PLAIMONT. Best years: 1995 **94 93 92 90 89 88 85**.

**CH. MAGDELAINE**★★ *St-Émilion Grand Cru AC, 1er Grand Cru Classé, Bordeaux, France* Owned by the quality-conscious company of MOUEIX, these are dark, rich, aggressive wines, yet with a load of luscious fruit and oaky spice. In lighter years the wine has a gushing, easy, tender fruit and can be enjoyed at 5–10 years. Best years: (1996) (95) 94 90 89 **88 86 85 83 82 75**.

**MAIPO VALLEY** *Chile* Birthplace of the Chilean wine industry and closest wine-making region to the capital city of Santiago. Cabernet is king in this valley and most of Chile's premium-priced reds come from here. Good Chardonnay is produced from vineyards close to the Andes. Best producers: CANEPA★, CARMEN★★, CONCHA Y TORO★★.

**MÁLAGA DO** *Andalucía, Spain* Málaga is a curious blend of sweet wine, alcohol and juices (some boiled up and concentrated, some fortified, some made from dried grapes) and production is dwindling. The label generally states colour and sweetness. The best Málagas are intensely nutty, raisiny and caramelly. The traditional, much-admired Scholtz Hermanos, ceased operations in 1996. Best producer: Larios.

**CH. MALARTIC-LAGRAVIÈRE** *Pessac-Léognan AC, Cru Classé de Graves, Bordeaux, France* This is one of the few GRAVES Classed Growths whose reputation has been upheld by its white wine (though the red is good too and ages beautifully). The tiny amount of white★ is made from 100% Sauvignon Blanc and usually softens after 3–4 years into a lovely nutty wine. Best years: (reds) (1996) (95) **89 88 85 83 82 81 78**; (whites) (1996) **95 94**.

---

**MALVASIA** This grape is widely planted in Italy and is found there in many guises, both white and red. In Friuli, it is known as the Malvasia Istriana and produces tight, fragrant wines of great charm, while in Tuscany, Umbria and the rest of central Italy, it is used to improve the blend for wines like ORVIETO and FRASCATI. On the islands, Malvasia is used in the production of rich, dry or sweet wines in Bosa and Cagliari (in Sardinia) and in Lipari off the coast of Sicily to make really tasty, apricotty sweet wines. As a black grape, Malvasia Nera is blended with Negroamaro in southern Puglia, while in Piedmont a paler-skinned relation produces frothing light reds in Castelnuovo Don Bosco, just outside Turin. Variants of Malvasia also grow in Spain and mainland Portugal. On the island of Madeira it produces sweet, varietal fortified wine, often known by its English name Malmsey.

---

**LA MANCHA DO** *Castilla-La Mancha, Spain* Spain's vast central plateau is Europe's biggest delimited wine area. Whites are never exciting (the dominant Airén grape has little character) but nowadays are often fresh and attractive. Reds, from Cencibel (Tempranillo), and without the traditional addition of white grapes, can be light and fruity, or richer, sometimes with a dash of Cabernet Sauvignon. New DO regulations in 1995 allow for much-needed irrigation and the planting of new grape varieties, including Viura, Chardonnay and Merlot. There is still much rough, old-style wine, but progress is fast. Best producers: Casa de la Viña, Fermin Ayuso Roig (Viña Q, Estola), Nuestra Señora de la Cabeza co-op (Casa Gualda), Nuestra Señora de Manjavacas co-op, Rodriguez y Berger (Viña Santa Elena★), Julian Santos Aguado (Don Fadrique), Torres Filoso (Arboles de Castillejo★), Vinícola de Castilla (Castillo de Alhambra, Señorío de Guadianeja★).

**MANZANILLA** See Jerez y Manzanilla DO.

**MARANGES AC** *Côte de Beaune, Burgundy, France* AC created in 1989 to cover the little-used Cheilly, Dezize and Sampigny ACs in the southern COTE DE BEAUNE. Attractive light wines, though many growers still sell them as COTE DE BEAUNE-VILLAGES. Best producers: Jean-Claude Bachelet, Charleux, Contat-Grange, DROUHIN, Duchemin. Best years: (reds) 1995 **93 92 90**.

**MARCHE** *Italy* The Adriatic region makes good white VERDICCHIO and reds from Montepulciano and Sangiovese led by ROSSO CONERO and ROSSO PICENO, which can be excellent.

**MARCILLAC AC** *South-West France* Strong, dry red wines (there is a little rosé), largely made from the local grape Fer. The reds are rustic but full of fruit and should be drunk between 2 and 5 years. Best producers: Marcillac-Vallon co-op, Philippe Teulier.

**MARGARET RIVER** *Western Australia* The first Australian region planted on the advice of scientists, in the late 1960s. Very quickly established its name as a leading quality area for Cabernet, with marvellously deep, structured reds sometimes recalling Classed Growth Bordeaux. Now Chardonnay, concentrated and opulent, is arguably the star turn, but there is also fine grassy Sémillon, tropical Sauvignon and spicy Verdelho. Best producers: CAPE MENTELLE★★, CULLENS★★, EVANS & TATE★, LEEUWIN ESTATE★★★ (Chardonnay), MOSS WOOD★★, PIERRO★★★ (Chardonnay), VASSE FELIX★★.

**MARGAUX AC** *Haut-Médoc, Bordeaux, France* AC centred on the village of Margaux but including Soussans and Cantenac, Labarde and Arsac in the south. The gravel banks dotted through the vineyards mean that the wines are rarely heavy and should have a divine perfume when mature at 7–12 years. Best producers: (Classed Growths) Ferrière★★★, d'ISSAN★, LASCOMBES★★, MARGAUX★★★, PALMER★★, RAUZAN-SEGLA★★★, du TERTRE★★; (others) d'ANGLUDET★★, Labégorce-Zédé, Monbrison★★, SIRAN★. Best years: (1996) (95) 94 90 89 **88 86 85 83 82**.

**CH. MARGAUX★★★** *Margaux AC, 1er Cru Classé, Haut-Médoc, Bordeaux, France* The greatest wine in the Médoc. 1978–90 produced flawless wines as great as any MARGAUX ever made. Recent ownership changes should not affect the wine as inspired winemaker Paul Pontallier remains in charge. There is also some delicious white, Pavillon Blanc, made from Sauvignon Blanc, but it must be the most expensive wine sold under the BORDEAUX AC label by a mile. Second wine: (red) Pavillon Rouge. Best years: (reds) (1996) (95) 94 93 90 89 88 86 **85 83 82 81 80 79 78**; (whites) (1996) **95 94 90 89 88 86 85**.

**MARLBOROUGH** *South Island, New Zealand* Marlborough has enjoyed such spectacular success as a quality wine region that it is difficult to imagine that the first vines were planted as recently as 1973. Long, cool and relatively dry ripening and free-draining stony soils are the major assets. Its snappy, aromatic Sauvignon Blanc first brought the region fame worldwide. Fine-flavoured Chardonnay, steely Riesling, elegant Champagne-method fizz and luscious botrytized wines are the other successes. Best producers: CELLIER LE BRUN, CLOUDY BAY★★, CORBANS★ (Stoneleigh), DELEGAT'S (Oyster Bay★), Fromm, Grove Mill, HUNTER'S★, JACKSON ESTATE★★, MONTANA, NAUTILUS★★, Alan Scott, VAVASOUR★★, Wairau River, Whitehaven, Wither Hills.

**MARNE ET CHAMPAGNE** *Champagne AC, Champagne, France* Family firm, the second-largest producer in Champagne, selling over 20 million bottles, mainly for supermarkets, under dozens of different labels. The best known is Alfred Rothschild, which is the second-biggest selling Champagne in France.

**MARQUÉS DE CÁCERES** *Rioja DOC, Rioja, Spain* Go-ahead RIOJA winery making crisp, aromatic, modern whites★ and rosés★, and fleshy, fruity reds★ with the emphasis on aging in bottle, not barrel. Best years: (reds) 1993 92 91 90 89 87 85 82 78.

**MARQUÉS DE GRIÑÓN** *Rioja DOC, Rioja and Rueda DO, Castilla y León, Spain* From his home estate at Malpica, near Toledo and Madrid, Carlos Falcó (the eponymous Marqués de Griñón) has expanded into RUEDA and now into RIOJA, after selling a stake in his company to BERBERANA and forming a partnership with the giant concern. Minty Cabernet de Valdepusa★★ and Durius red★ (blended from TORO and RIBERA DEL DUERO) have been joined by a barrel-fermented Chardonnay and a Syrah from his own estate, 2 Marqués de Griñón red Riojas (a lightly oaked young wine★ and a Reserva★), and white Durius Rueda Sauvignon. Best years: (reds) 1995 94 93 92 91 90 89 86.

**MARQUÉS DE MONISTROL** *Cava DO and Penedés DO, Catalonia, Spain* Martini & Rossi owns this beautiful winery. The young Brut Selección★ is the freshest and fruitiest CAVA. The still whites, Blanc de Blancs★ and Blanc en Noirs★, are good, the reds, long unexceptional, have gained from the introduction of a young Merlot. Drink the youngest available.

**MARQUÉS DE MURRIETA** *Rioja DOC, Rioja, Spain* The RIOJA bodega that most faithfully preserves the traditional style of long aging. Ultra-conservative, yet sporting glistening new fermentation vats and a Californian bottling line. The latest move has been to release more wines under their splendidly ornate Castillo de Ygay★★ label. No longer do these wait 20 years for release, so the Marqués de Murrieta★ label is now kept for younger wines. Whites are dauntingly oaky, reds packed with savoury, mulberry fruit. Best years: (reds) 1992 91 89 87 85 68 64; (whites) 1992 91 86 85 78.

**MARQUÉS DE RISCAL** *Rioja DOC, País Vasco, and Rueda DO, Castilla y León, Spain* When the families who own RIOJA's oldest bodega recaptured control of management in 1988 they installed one of their own as cellar master: Francisco Hurtado de Amézaga, who had been behind the huge success of Riscal's RUEDA winery. Old musty vats were promptly cleared out, and the classic pungent reds★★ reappeared. The expensive, Cabernet-based Barón de Chirel cuvée is an important addition. In Rueda, the consultancy of Hugh RYMAN has translated into increasingly aromatic whites★. Best years: (reds) **1992 91 90 89**.

**MARSALA DOC** *Sicily, Italy* Fortified wines, more sought after these days for confectionery or sauces, but once as esteemed as sherry or Madeira. A taste of an old Vergine (unsweetened) Marsala, fine and complex, will show why. Today most is sweetened. Purists would say this mars its delicate nuances, but DOC regulations allow for sweetening Fine and Superiore versions. Best producers: (Vergine) Florio★, Pellegrino; also De Bartoli (VECCHIO SAMPERI★★, and Il Marsala Superiore★).

**MARSANNAY AC** *Côte de Nuits, Burgundy, France* Village almost in the Dijon suburbs and best known for its rosé, which can be quite pleasant but a little too austere and dry. The red is rapidly proving itself to be one of Burgundy's most fragrant wines, if never very full in texture. There is very little white but it is dry and nutty and good. Best producers: Bouvier, Charlopin, Bruno CLAIR★, Coillot, Collotte, Fougeray, JADOT, LABOURE-ROI★, Trapet. Best years: (red) 1995 **93 90 88 85**.

**MARSANNE** Undervalued grape which produces rich, nutty wines in the northern Rhône (HERMITAGE, CROZES-HERMITAGE, ST-JOSEPH and ST-PERAY), often with the more lively Roussanne. Also planted in Switzerland, and performs brilliantly in Australia at CHATEAU TAHBILK★★ and MITCHELTON★.

**MARTINBOROUGH** *Wairarapa, North Island, New Zealand* A moderately cool, dry climate, free-draining infertile soils and an uncompromising attitude toward quality are this tiny region's greatest assets. Makes some of the country's top Pinot Noirs but can also turn out big, complex Chardonnay, intense, ripe Cabernet Sauvignon blends, full-flavoured yet elegant Sauvignon Blanc and honeyed, botrytized Riesling. Best producers: ATA RANGI★★, Dry River★★, MARTINBOROUGH VINEYARD★★, PALLISER ESTATE★.

**MARTINBOROUGH VINEYARD** *Martinborough, North Island, New Zealand* Since 1986 many of the country's best Pinot Noirs come from here, although they now have many challengers. Winemaker Larry McKenna's heart may be in Pinot Noir★★ but he also makes impressive Chardonnay★★, strong spicy Riesling★, and luscious botrytized styles★★ when vintage conditions allow. Best years: 1996 **94 91 90 89**.

**MARTÍNEZ BUJANDA** *Rioja DOC, País Vasco, Spain* Family-owned firm that makes some of the best 'modern' RIOJAS. Whites and rosés are young and crisp, reds★ are full of fruit *and* age very well. Best years: (reds) **1994 92 91 90 87 86 85**.

**LOUIS M MARTINI** *Napa Valley, California, USA* During the 1980s the wines from this well-respected NAPA winery changed from being deep and rich to relatively light, though pleasant and cheap. Recently it has turned to a more concentrated style based on single vineyards and a range of Reserve wines, so far with mixed results. The Monte Rosso Cabernet Sauvignon★ can be very good, the Chardonnays are coming along nicely and a budget-priced Carneros Pinot Noir is delicious.

**MARTINSTHAL** *Rheingau, Germany* Situated next door to the village of RAUENTHAL, Martinsthal makes medium-bodied spicy Rieslings that offer good value for money in a region where this is hard to come by. Best producers: J B Becker, Diefenhart.

**MARZEMINO** This red grape of northern Italy's TRENTINO province makes deep-coloured, plummy and zesty reds that are best drunk within 3–5 years. Best producers: Bossi Fedrigotti, Casata Monfort, Letrari★, Spagnolli★, De Tarczal★, Vallarom★.

**MAS DE DAUMAS GASSAC** *Vin de Pays de l'Hérault, Languedoc, France* Ebullient Aimé Guibert is the best-known producer in the Languedoc, proving that the HERAULT, normally associated with cheap table wine, is capable of producing great red wines that can age in bottle. The Daumas Gassac rosé is dull; however, the tannic yet rich Cabernet Sauvignon-based red★★ and the fabulously scented white★★★ (Viognier, Muscat, Chardonnay and Petit Manseng) are brilliant, if expensive. Best years: (reds) 1995 94 93 92 91 **90 89 88 87 85**.

**MAS JULLIEN** *Coteaux du Languedoc AC, Languedoc, France* Olivier Jullien makes some of the most exciting wines in France from traditional Midi varieties with such success that bottles have to be strictly rationed. Reds include les Cailloutis★ and les Depierre★★. White les Vignes Oubliées★★ (Terret Bouret, Carignan and Grenache) is memorable. Also late-harvest Clairette Beaudille. Best years: **1995 94 93 91**.

**MASCARELLO** *Barolo DOCG, Piedmont, Italy* Two first-rate producers sport this famous BAROLO name. The old house of Giuseppe Mascarello (now run by grandson Mauro) is renowned for dense, chunky Dolcetto★ and intense BARBERA★ (particularly Ginestra), but the pride of the house is Barolo from the Monprivato★★★ vineyard. The other, Bartolo Mascarello, is one of the great old-fashioned producers of Barolo★★★, yet his wines have an exquisite perfume and balance as well. Both his Dolcetto★★ and Freisa★ are excellent, too. Best years: (Barolo) (1996) (95) 93 90 89 **88 85**.

**MASI** *Veneto, Italy* Family firm, headed by Sandro Boscaini, that is one of the driving forces in VALPOLICELLA★ and SOAVE★. Campo Fiorin★, a Ripasso Valpolicella, is worth looking out for, as is AMARONE★ from the Mazzano vineyard. The oaky Toar is a blend of Corvina and other native grape varieties. The wines of Serègo Alighieri are also produced by Masi.

**MASTROBERARDINO** *Campania, Italy* This family firm has long flown the flag for southern Italy. Best known for red TAURASI★ and white Greco di Tufo★ and Fiano di Avellino★.

**MATANZAS CREEK** *Sonoma Valley AVA, California, USA* Sauvignon Blanc★★ is taken very seriously here and the results show in a complex, pleasing wine; Chardonnay★★ is rich and toasty but not overblown. Limited edition Chardonnay and Merlot under the Journey label are opulent but pricy and controversial. In recent years, Merlot★★★ has steadily improved, with a silky richness that fills the mouth with ripe flavour. Best years: (Chardonnay) **1994 93 92 91 90**; (Merlot) **1993 92 91 90 88**.

**MATUA VALLEY** *Waimauku, Auckland, North Island, New Zealand* Ross and Bill Spence have explored many options to produce their present range of stylish, high-quality wines. Best wines include the sensuous, scented Ararimu Chardonnay★★★, lush and strongly varietal Gewürz-traminer, a creamy oak-aged Sauvignon Blanc★★, tangy MARLBOROUGH Shingle Peak Sauvignon Blanc★★, fine Merlot★★ and thrilling Ararimu Cabernet Sauvignon★★★. Best years: (reds) 1996 **94 93 91 90 89**.

**CH. MAUCAILLOU★** *Moulis AC, Cru Bourgeois, Haut-Médoc, Bordeaux, France* Maucaillou shows that you don't have to be a Classed Growth to make high-quality claret. Expertly made by the Dourthe family, it is soft but classically flavoured. It matures quickly but ages well for 10–12 years. Best years: (1996) (95) **90 89 88 86 85 83 82 81**.

**MAURY AC** *Roussillon, France* A Vin Doux Naturel made mainly from Grenache Noir. This strong, sweetish wine can be made in either a young, fresh style or the locally revered old rancio style. Best producers: Mas Amiel★★, Maury co-op★, Pleiade★.

**MAXIMIN GRÜNHAUS** *Grünhaus, Ruwer, Germany* The best estate in the Ruwer valley and one of Germany's greatest. Carl von Schubert vinifies separately the wines of his 3 monopoly vineyards (Abtsberg, Bruderberg and Herrenberg), making chiefly dry and medium-dry wines of great subtlety and distinction. In good vintages the wines are easily ★★★ and will age for decades. Best years: 1996 95 94 93 **92 90 89 88 85 83 79 76 75 71**.

**MAZIS-CHAMBERTIN AC** See Chambertin AC.

**MAZOYÈRES-CHAMBERTIN AC** See Chambertin AC.

**McWILLIAMS** *Riverina, New South Wales, Australia* Large family winery whose best wines are the Mount Pleasant range from the Lower HUNTER VALLEY: classic bottle-aged Sémillons, including Elizabeth★★★ and Lovedale★★★, buttery Chardonnays★★ and special-vineyard Shirazes★ – Old Paddock, Old Hill and Rose Hill. Also classy liqueur Muscat★★ and 'sherries'★ from Riverina, and exciting table wines from Barwang★ vineyard near COWRA. Best years: (Hunter Sémillon) 1996 95 93 **91 90 87 86 84 82 80 79**.

**MÉDOC AC** *Bordeaux, France* The Médoc peninsula north of Bordeaux on the left bank of the Gironde river produces a good fistful of the world's most famous reds. These are all situated in the Haut-Médoc, the southern, more gravelly half of the area. The Médoc AC, for reds only, covers the northern part. Here, in these flat clay vineyards, the Merlot grape dominates. The wines can be attractive, dry but juicy and most are best to drink at 3–5 years old. Best producers: Greysac, Lacombe-Noaillac, LOUDENNE, les Ormes-Sorbet, Patache d'Aux, Plagnac, POTENSAC★★, Rollan-de-By, la Tour-de-By★, la Tour-Haut-Caussan★, la Tour-St-Bonnet, Vieux-Robin. Best years: (1996) 95 **94 90 89 88 86 85 83 82 81**.

**MEERLUST** *Stellenbosch WO, South Africa* Eight generations of Myburghs have lived on this beautiful farm. Current owner Hannes Myburgh maintains his late father's faith in the Bordeaux varieties; his complex Rubicon★★ was one of the Cape's first Bordeaux blends. Italian cellarmaster Giorgio Dalla Cia's passion is Merlot★, elegantly and classically styled. Much-heralded experiments with Chardonnay★★ have resulted in the first commercial release, a rich toasty-spicy 1995.

**MENDOCINO COUNTY** *California, USA* The northernmost county of the North Coast AVA. The best growing areas are Anderson Valley AVA, a cool east–west valley opening up to the Pacific Ocean and a good area for sparkling wines and the occasional Pinot Noir; and Redwood Valley AVA, a warmer area with good results from Zinfandel and Cabernet. Best producers: FETZER, HANDLEY CELLARS★★, Hidden Cellars, Jepson, Lazy Creek★★, McDowell Valley★, Navarro★★, Parducci, Pepperwood Springs, ROEDERER★★, Scharffenberger★★.

**MENDOZA** *Argentina* The most important wine region in Argentina, accounting for about 90% of fine wine production. Situated in the eastern foothills of the Andes on a similar latitude to Chile's Santiago, the region's bone-dry continental climate produces powerful, high-alcohol reds. High-altitude sub-regions like Tupungato are now producing better whites, particularly Chardonnay. Further from the mountains, the sub-regions of Maipú and Luján are proving ideal for Malbec, Syrah and Cabernet. Best producers: ARIZU, CATENA★, NORTON★.

**MENETOU-SALON AC** *Loire Valley, France* Extremely attractive, chalky-clean Sauvignon whites and cherry-fresh Pinot Noir reds and rosés from just west of SANCERRE. Best producers: de Chatenoy★, Chavet★, Denis, Gilbert, A Mellot, Pellé★, Roger, Teiller★. Best years: 1996 **95 93 90 89**.

**MÉO-CAMUZET** *Vosne-Romanée, Côte de Nuits, Burgundy, France* Super-quality estate, thanks in no small measure to the advice of Henri JAYER, a third of whose property it gained in 1988. The style is heavily influenced by Jayer – new oak barrels and luscious, rich fruit combining to produce superb wines, which also age well. The CORTON★★★ and CLOS DE VOUGEOT★★★ are the top wines here, but don't miss the 2 VOSNE-ROMANEE Premiers Crus, aux Brulées★★ and les Chaumes★★. Best years: 1995 93 **92 90 89 88**.

**MERCUREY AC** *Côte Chalonnaise, Burgundy, France* Most important of the 4 main COTE CHALONNAISE villages. The red is usually pleasant and strawberry-flavoured, and can take some aging. There is not much white but I like its buttery, even spicy taste. It is best drunk at 3–4 years old. Best producers: (reds) Chanzy, FAIVELEY★, Juillot★★, Yves de Launay★, Maréchal★, RODET★, Saier, de Suremain, Voarick; (whites) FAIVELEY (Clos Rochette)★★, Genot-Boulanger★, Juillot, RODET (Chamirey). Best years: (red) 1995 **93 90 89 88**.

**MERLOT** See pages 172–3.

**GEOFF MERRILL** *Southern Vales, South Australia* A high-profile wine-maker who combines an instinctive feel for wine with canny market-ing ability. Under the Geoff Merrill brand he fields nicely bottle-aged Cabernet and Chardonnay-Sémillon★. The cheaper Mount Hurtle brand has a moreish Grenache rosé★ and a wacky new Who Cares? label was introduced in 1996.

**LOUIS MÉTAIREAU** *Muscadet de Sèvre-et-Maine AC, Loire Valley, France* Classic Muscadets with considerable intensity, due to low yields and careful wine-making. Styles range from lighter Petit Mouton to concentrated Cuvée LM★ and Cuvée One★★.

**MÉTHODE CHAMPENOISE** See Champagne method.

**MEURSAULT AC** *Côte de Beaune, Burgundy, France* The biggest and most popular white wine village in the COTE D'OR. There are no Grands

Crus, but a whole cluster of Premiers Crus. The general standard of wine is variable due to the worldwide demand. The deep-golden wine is lovely to drink young but better aged for 5–8 years. Only a little Meursault red is made. Best producers: Ampeau★, Michel Bouzereau, Boyer-Martenot★, COCHE-DURY★★★, DROUHIN, Fichet★★, JADOT, Javillier★★, François Jobard★★, LAFON★★★, Matrot★★, Michelot-Buisson★, Pierre Morey★★, Potinet-Ampeau★, Prieur★, Ropiteau-Mignon★, Roulot★★. Best years: 1995 94 93 **92 90 89**.

**JOS MEYER ET FILS** *Alsace AC, Alsace, France*  Traditional company making excellent wine, whether as a merchant or as a producer in its own right. The top wines are Gewürztraminer (particularly les Archenets★★) and Pinot Blanc (les Lutins★). Best years: 1996 **95 94 93 92 90 89 86 85 83**.

**CH. MEYNEY★** *St-Estèphe AC, Cru Bourgeois, Haut-Médoc, Bordeaux, France*  One of the most reliable ST-ESTEPHES, producing broad-flavoured wine with dark, plummy fruit. Second wine: Prieur de Meyney. Best years: (1996) (95) 94 **90 89 88 86 85 83 82 81 78 75**.

**LOUIS MICHEL & FILS** *Chablis AC, Burgundy, France*  The prime exponents of unoaked CHABLIS. The top Crus – les Clos★★, Montmains★★ and Montée de Tonnerre★★ – are fresh-flavoured and long-lived. Best years: 1995 93 **92 90 89 88**.

**MIDI** *France*  A loose geographical term, virtually synonymous with LANGUEDOC-ROUSSILLON, covering the vast, sunbaked area of southern France between the Pyrenees and the RHONE VALLEY.

**MILDARA** *Murray River, Victoria, Australia*  Based on the Murray River, but the best wines are from large COONAWARRA vineyards and include the hugely popular and fairly priced Jamieson's Run★ (blended red and Chardonnay and Sauvignon Blanc whites). Also owns Balgownie, Wolf BLASS, Andrew Garrett, Ingoldby, Krondorf, Tisdall, YELLOWGLEN, and was itself bought in 1996 by Fosters the lager lads.

**MILLTON** *Gisborne, North Island, New Zealand*  Organic vineyard using biodynamic methods, whose top wines include the sophisticated and individual Clos St Anne Chardonnay★★, botrytized Opou Vineyard Riesling★★ and ambitiously complex barrel-fermented Chenin Blanc★. Best years: 1996 **95 94 91 90**.

**MINERVOIS AC** *Languedoc, France*  Attractive mostly red wines from north-east of Carcassonne. The area's great strength is organization, and big companies like Nicolas have worked hard with local co-ops to produce good-quality, juicy, quaffing wine at reasonable prices. The best wines are made by the estates: full of ripe, red fruit and pine-dust perfume, for drinking young. It can age, especially if a little new oak has been used. Best producers: (reds) CLOS CENTEILLES★★, Fabas★, Festiano, de Gourgazaud★, Meyzonnier, Nicolas, Paraza, Piccinini★, Ste-Eulalie★, la Tour Boisée★, Vassière, Villerambert-Julien★, Violet★.

**MISSION** *Hawkes Bay, North Island, New Zealand*  New Zealand's oldest winery is owned by the Society of Mary. Established in HAWKES BAY 142 years ago, the Mission has a history of producing much mediocre and a small amount of excellent wine. Recently, however, quality and consistency have improved. The best wine is a stylish Jewelstone Chardonnay★★, best value is a spicy, medium-dry Gewürztraminer★. Best years: **1996 95 94 91 90**.

# MERLOT

Red wine without tears. That's the reason Merlot has vaulted from being merely Bordeaux's red wine support act, well behind Cabernet Sauvignon in terms of class, to being the darling of the 1990s, planted like fury all over the world. It is able to claim some seriousness and pedigree, but – crucially – can make wine of a fat, juicy character mercifully low in tannic bitterness, which can be glugged with gay abandon almost as soon as the juice has squirted from the press. Yet this doesn't mean that Merlot is the jelly baby of red wine grapes. Far from it.

*WINE STYLES*

**Bordeaux Merlot** The great wines of Pomerol and St-Émilion are largely based on Merlot and the best of these can mature for 20–30 years. In fact there is more Merlot than Cabernet Sauvignon planted in Bordeaux, and I doubt if there is a single red wine property that does not have some growing, because the variety ripens early, can cope with cool conditions and is able to bear a heavy crop of fruit. In a cool, damp area like Bordeaux Cabernet Sauvignon cannot always ripen, so the soft, mellow character of Merlot is a fundamental component of the blend even in the best Médoc estates.

**Other European Merlots** The south of France has briskly adopted the variety, but in the hot Languedoc the grape often ripens too fast to express its full personality and can seem a little simple and even raw-edged. Italy has long used very high-crop Merlot to produce a simple, light quaffer in the north, particularly in the Veneto, though Friuli and Alto Adige make fuller styles and there are some impressive Tuscan examples. The Italian-speaking Swiss canton of Ticino is often unjustly overlooked for concentrated, oak-aged versions. Eastern Europe should provide fertile pastures for Merlot and so far the most convincing, albeit simple, styles have come from Hungary and Bulgaria, although the younger examples are almost invariably better than the old. The improvement in Merlots has been one of the most striking developments in Spain in the mid-1990s.

**New World Merlots** Youth is also important in the New World, nowhere more so than in Chile. Chilean Merlot has leapt to the front of the pack of New World examples with gorgeous garnet-red wines of unbelievable crunchy fruit richness that cry out to be drunk virtually in their infancy. California Merlots often have more serious pretensions, but the nature of the grape is such that its soft, juicy quality still shines through. The cooler conditions in Washington State have produced some thrilling wines, and even the east coast of the US has produced good examples from places such as Long Island. With some French input, South Africa is starting to get Merlot right, and in New Zealand, despite the cool, damp conditions, some gorgeous rich examples have been made. Only Australia seems to find Merlot problematic – but there's so much other ripe fruit in Australian reds that maybe Merlot isn't a necessity there.

## BEST PRODUCERS

### France
*Bordeaux* (St-Émilion) l'ANGELUS, AUSONE, BEAU-SEJOUR-BECOT, CANON, MAGDELAINE, le TERTRE-ROTEBOEUF, Troplong-Mondot; (Pomerol) BON PASTEUR, la FLEUR-PETRUS, LAFLEUR, PETRUS, le PIN, TROTANOY; *Bergerac* la JAUBERTIE.

### Other European Merlots
*Italy* (Veneto) MACULAN; (Trentino) Bossi Fedrigotti; (Tuscany) AVIGNONESI, CASTELLO DI AMA, ORNELLAIA (Masseto); (Lazio) Falesco.

*Spain* (Somontano) Viñas del Vero; (Valdeorras) Joaquin Rebolledo.

*Switzerland* Zündel.

### Eastern European Merlots
*Bulgaria* RUSSE, Sakar, Stambolovo, SUHINDOL.

### New World Merlots
*USA* (California) ARROWOOD, BERINGER, CUVAISON, FERRARI-CARANO, MATANZAS CREEK, NEWTON, SHAFER, Swanson; (Washington) ANDREW WILL, Columbia Winery, HOGUE, L'ECOLE NO 41, LEONETTI; (New York) BRIDGEHAMPTON.

*Australia* LECONFIELD, PETALUMA, Yarra Ridge.

*New Zealand* DELEGAT'S (Proprietor's Reserve), Esk Valley, MONTANA (Church Road), Waitakere Road.

*South Africa* FAIRVIEW, Morgenhof.

*Chile* CARMEN, CASA LAPOSTOLLE, ERRAZURIZ, LA ROSA.

**MISSION HILL** *British Columbia, Canada* British Columbia's most progressive producer, employing the full-time services of New Zealand winemaker John Simes. Antipodean style is clearly evident in the passion fruit aromas of the Chardonnay★★, and the Pinot Blanc★ shows equally good fruit retention. Slightly oxidized Pinot Noir★★ is a real stunner in reds. Best years: 1995 94.

**CH. LA MISSION-HAUT-BRION★★** *Pessac-Léognan AC, Cru Classé de Graves, Bordeaux, France* I always find la Mission wines powerful but, unlike its neighbour HAUT-BRION, never charming. Their strength is in massive, dark fruit and oak flavours and they often need 20 years' age or so. Best years: (1996) (95) 94 93 90 89 **88 85 82 81 79 78 75**.

**MITCHELL** *Clare Valley, South Australia* The effervescent Jane and winemaker husband Andrew Mitchell turn out some of CLARE VALLEY's fruitiest but most cellarable Riesling★★ and a much-improved barrel-fermented Sémillon★★ which both deserve a wider audience. Peppertree Vineyard Shiraz★ and Cabernet Sauvignon★ are plump, chocolaty and typical of the region. Best years: **1995** 94 93 92 90.

**MITCHELTON** *Goulburn Valley, Victoria, Australia* Victoria's most consistently fine Riesling★★. Oaked Marsanne★, released at 4 years old, is a speciality; new Mitchelton III red★★ and white★★ are character-filled blends designed to partner Mediterranean food. Reds from Shiraz★★ and Cabernet★ are increasingly deep and structured.

**MITTELRHEIN** *Germany* Small, unsung (as far as great wine is concerned, that is) northerly wine region. About 75% of the wine here is Riesling but, unlike other German regions, the Mittelrhein has been in decline over the last few decades. The vineyard sites are steep and difficult to work – although breathtaking. Some wines are successfully turned into Sekt and most of WEGELER-DEINHARD's Lila Imperial comes from the region. The best growers (like Toni JOST★★) cluster around BACHARACH in the south, and produce wines of a striking mineral tang and dry, fruity intensity.

**MOELLEUX** French for soft or mellow, used to describe sweet or medium-sweet wines.

**MOËT & CHANDON** *Champagne AC, Champagne, France* Moët & Chandon's enormous production of more than 25 million bottles a year dominates the Champagne market. Good non-vintage can be absolutely delightful – soft, creamy and a little spicy, and consistency is improving, at last. The vintage★ is more consistent, and usually has a strong style to it, while the rosé★ shows a Pinot Noir floral fragrance depressingly rare in modern Champagne. Dom Pérignon★★★ is the de luxe cuvée. It can be one of the greatest Champagnes of all, but you've got to age it for a number of years or else you're wasting your money on the fancy bottle. Best years: **1992 90 88 86 85 83 82**.

**MONBAZILLAC AC** *South-West France* Bergerac's leading sweet wine. Most of it is light, vaguely sweet and entirely forgettable, usually from the efficient but unadventurous co-op. This style won't age, but a real, truly rich, late-harvested Monbazillac can happily last 10 years. Best producers: la Borderie★, le Fage, Haut-Bernasse, Hébras★★, Ch. Monbazillac (made by the co-op), Theulet★, Treuil-de-Nailhac★. Best years: 1996 **95 93 91 90 89 88 86**.

**ROBERT MONDAVI** *Napa Valley, California, USA* Robert Mondavi is a Californian institution, spreading the gospel of California wine from his NAPA home base. Best known for the regular bottling Cabernet Sauvignon★, open and fruity with the emphasis on early drinkability, and the Reserve Cabernet★★★, possessing enormous depth and power. Winemaker Tim Mondavi has put a great deal of energy into Pinot Noir over the past few years and the results are beginning to pay off. A regular bottling of Pinot Noir★ and a Reserve Pinot Noir★★★ are improving with every vintage: velvety smooth and supple wines with great style, perfume and balance. For many years the Mondavi trademark wine was Fumé (Sauvignon) Blanc, but in recent years Chardonnay has become the winery leader (the Reserve★★ can be superb), although the quality is inconsistent. The Mondavis also own Byron Winery in SANTA BARBARA COUNTY, Vichon Winery in Napa, OPUS ONE in Napa in partnership with the Rothschilds, as well as the Mondavi Woodbridge winery, where inexpensive varietal wines are produced. A new line of alternative wines, aimed at a younger market and based chiefly on Italian varietals, was released in 1994. Has an interest in CALITERRA of Chile and is making wines in France's LANGUE-DOC to be sold under the Vichon Mediterranean label. Best years: (Cabernet Sauvignon Reserve) 1993 92 **91 88 87 86 85 84 82**; (Pinot Noir Reserve) **1994 92 91 90 88 87**; (Chardonnay Reserve) **1994 92 91 90 88 87**.

**MONT TAUCH, LES PRODUCTEURS DU** *Fitou, Languedoc-Roussillon, France* A big, quality-conscious co-op based in the Fitou region, but producing a large range of MIDI wines, from good gutsy FITOU★★ and CORBIERES★ to rich MUSCAT DE RIVESALTES★ and light but gluggable Vin de Pays du Torgan. Its top red wine, called Terroir de Tuchan★★, is one of the most exciting in the Midi. Best years: (whites and rosés) **1995 94**; (reds) **1995 94 93 91 90 89**.

**MONTAGNE-ST-ÉMILION AC** *Bordeaux, France* A ST-EMILION satellite which can produce rather good red wines. The wines are normally ready to drink in 4 years but age quite well in their slightly earthy way. Best producers: Bonneau, Calon, Corbin, Faizeau, des Laurets, des Moines★, Montaiguillon, Négrit, Roc-de-Calon, Roudier, Vieux-Ch.-St-André. Best years: 1995 **94 90 89 88 85 83 82**.

**MONTAGNY AC** *Côte Chalonnaise, Burgundy, France* The most southerly of the 4 Côte Chalonnaise village ACs. The wines are dry and rather lean, but now that some producers are aging their wines for a few months in new oak, there has been a great improvement. Generally best with 2 years' age or more. Best producers: Arnoux, BUXY co-op★, FAIVELEY, Louis LATOUR, Olivier LEFLAIVE★, B Michel★, Roy, Steinmaier, Vachet★. Best years: **1995 93 92**.

**MONTALCINO** See Brunello di Montalcino DOCG.

**MONTANA** *Auckland, Gisborne, Hawkes Bay and Marlborough, New Zealand* Montana is easily the country's largest winemaker, and it has consistently made some of New Zealand's best-value wines. The Sauvignon Blanc★★ and Chardonnay★ are in a considerable way to thank for putting New Zealand on the international map. The company now wants to prove that big can be best. To achieve that goal it has established The McDonald Winery, a small (by Montana standards) winery in HAWKES BAY from which it produces top

Chardonnay★★, Merlot★★ and Cabernet Sauvignon-Merlot★★. Church Road Reserve Chardonnay★★ and Cabernet★★ are among New Zealand's finest. Montana's Special 'Estate' bottlings, particularly Ormond Estate Chardonnay★★★ in GISBORNE, also bode well. Montana make excellent Lindauer fizz★ and, with the help of the Champagne house DEUTZ, produce the austere, yet full-bodied Deutz MARLBOROUGH Cuvée NV Brut★★. Best years: **1996 94 93 91 90**.

**MONTECARLO DOC** *Tuscany, Italy* Both reds (Sangiovese with Syrah) and whites (Trebbiano with Sémillon and Pinot Grigio) are distinctive. But other non-DOC wines can include Cabernet, Merlot, Pinot Bianco, Vermentino and even Roussanne. Best producers: Buonamico★, Carmignani★, Michi.

**MONTECILLO** *Rioja DOC, Rioja, Spain* Owned by sherry firm OSBORNE, Montecillo makes high-quality RIOJAS in young and mature styles. Red and white Viña Cumbrero★ is young and fruity. Rich, fruity Viña Monty★★ red Gran Reservas are aged in French oak barrels and combine delicacy with flavour. Best years: (reds) **1993 91 88 87 86 82 81 78 73**.

**MONTEFALCO DOC** *Umbria, Italy* The often good Sangiovese-based Montefalco Rosso is outclassed by the dry Sagrantino di Montefalco (now DOCG) and Sagrantino Passito, a glorious sweet red made from dried grapes. Best producers: ADANTI★★, Antonelli, Caprai★. Best years: (1996) **95 93 91 90 88 85**.

---

**MONTEPULCIANO** This grape, grown mostly in eastern Italy (and unconnected with Tuscany's Sangiovese-based wine VINO NOBILE DI MONTEPULCIANO) can produce deep-coloured, fleshy, spicy wines with moderate tannin and acidity. Besides MONTEPULCIANO D'ABRUZZO, it is used in ROSSO CONERO and ROSSO PICENO in the Marche and also in Umbria.

---

**MONTEPULCIANO D'ABRUZZO DOC** *Abruzzo, Italy* The Montepulciano grape's most important manifestation. Quality varies from the insipid or rustic to concentrated and characterful. Best producers: Cantina Tollo★, Cornacchia★, Filomusi Guelfi★, Illuminati★, Masciarelli★, Nicodemi★, Umani Ronchi★, Valentini★★★, Zaccagnini★★.

**MONTEREY COUNTY** *California, USA* Large CENTRAL COAST county south of the San Francisco Bay. The most important AVAs are Arroyo Seco, Chalone, Carmel Valley and Salinas Valley. Best grapes are Chardonnay, Riesling and Pinot Blanc, with some good Cabernet Sauvignon, Merlot in Carmel Valley and Pinot Noir in the cool north of the county. Best producers: Bernardus, CHALONE★★, Durney, JEKEL★, The Monterey Vineyard★, Morgan★, Smith & Hook★, Ventana★.

**MONTES** *Curicó, Chile* One of Chile's most frustratingly erratic producers but the new Malbec★★ shows Aurelio Montes at his best. Sauvignon Blanc★ has improved dramatically and Montes Alpha Cabernet Sauvignon★ continues to be a solid performer.

**MONTEVERTINE** *Tuscany, Italy* Based in the heart of CHIANTI CLASSICO, Montevertine is famous for its non-DOC wines, particularly Le Pergole Torte★★★. This was the first of the new-style Super-Tuscans made solely with Sangiovese, and remains one of the best. Owner Sergio Manetti includes a little Canaiolo in the excellent Il Sodaccio★★ and Montevertine Riserva★★. Best years: (1996) 95 94 **93 90 88 86 85**.

**MONTHELIE AC** *Côte de Beaune, Burgundy, France* Attractive, mainly red wine village lying halfway along the COTE DE BEAUNE behind the more famous communes of MEURSAULT and VOLNAY. The wines generally have a lovely, cherry fruit and make pleasant drinking at a good price. Best producers: J F COCHE-DURY★★, Garaudet, LAFON★, Olivier LEFLAIVE, Maison LEROY, Monthelie-Douhairet★, Parent, Potinet-Ampeau, Roulot★, Suremain★, Thévenin-Monthelie★. Best years: (reds) 1995 **93 90 89 88**; (whites) **1995 92 90**.

**MONTICELLO CELLARS** *Napa Valley AVA, California, USA* In the early 1980s owner Jay Corley produced some very good, full-fruited Chardonnays★, and in the mid-80s he began buying in Cabernet Sauvignon and Merlot for a range of reds that has now overtaken the whites. There are 2 Cabernet Sauvignons, the Corley Reserve★ in a big, classic California style and the Jefferson Cuvée, a softer, more approachable wine. Also some fairly impressive yeasty fizz under the Montreaux★ label. In some years a sweet wine from Sémillon, called Chateaux M, is made.

**MONTILLA-MORILES DO** *Andalucía, Spain* Sherry-style wines that are sold almost entirely as lower-priced sherry substitutes. However, the wines *can* be superb, particularly the top dry amontillado, oloroso and rich Pedro Ximénez styles. And if you think top sherry is underpriced, they're almost giving this stuff away. Also light, fruity but uncharacterful dry whites. Best producers: Toro Albalá★, Alvear★ (top labels only), Aragón, Gracia Hermanos, Pérez Barquero★.

**HUBERT DE MONTILLE** *Volnay, Burgundy, France* Estate producing some of the most concentrated, ageworthy red wines on the COTE DE BEAUNE. If you're willing to wait for 10 years or more, de Montille's VOLNAYS and POMMARDS are very rewarding wines. The Volnay Champans★★, Pommard les Épenots★★★ and Pommard les Pezerolles★★ are all well worth their high prices. Best years: 1995 93 92 90 89 88 **85 83**.

**MONTLOUIS AC** *Loire Valley, France* Situated on the opposite bank of the Loire river to the VOUVRAY AC, Montlouis wines are made from the same Chenin grape and in similar styles (dry, medium and sweet and Champagne-method fizz) but tend to be a touch more rustic than its neighbour's since the grapes rarely ripen quite as well. Two-thirds of the production is Mousseux, a green, appley fizz which is best drunk young. The still wines need aging for 5–10 years, particularly the sweet or Moelleux version. Best producers: Berger★, Chidaine, Delétang★, Levasseur, Moyer★, Taille aux Loups★★. Best years: 1996 95 93 **90 89 88 86 85 83 82 78 76 70**.

**MONTRACHET AC** *Côte de Beaune, Burgundy, France* This world-famous Grand Cru straddles the boundary between the villages of CHASSAGNE-MONTRACHET and PULIGNY-MONTRACHET, with another Grand Cru, Chevalier-Montrachet, immediately above it on the slope. Le Montrachet produces wines with a unique combination of concentration, finesse and perfume – white Burgundy at its most sublime.

177

Chevalier's higher elevation yields a slightly leaner wine that is less explosive in its youth, but good examples will become ever more fascinating over 20 years or more. Best producers: COLIN★★★, DROUHIN★★★, LAFON★★★, Laguiche★★, Dom. LEFLAIVE★★, RAMONET★★★, Dom. de la ROMANEE-CONTI★★★, Thénard★★. Best years: 1995 93 **92** 90 **89 88 86 85**.

**MONTRAVEL AC** *South-West France* Dry, medium-dry and sweet white wines from the western end of the Bergerac region. Production is declining. Best producers: de Gouyat, de Krevel★, le Raz, de Roque Peyre.

**CH. MONTROSE★★** *St-Estèphe AC, 2ème Cru Classé, Haut-Médoc, Bordeaux, France* Used to be thought of as the leading ST-ESTEPHE property, famous for its dark, brooding wine that would take around 30 years of aging before it was at its prime. Following a period in the late 1970s and early 80s when the wines became lighter and easier, Montrose has now returned to its original firm, dense, powerful style. Recent vintages have been exceptional. Second wine: la Dame de Montrose. Best years: (1996) 95 94 93 90 89 86.

**CH. MONTUS** *Madiran AC, South-West France* Alain Brumont has led MADIRAN's revival using 100% Tannat and deft public relations. He ages his top wine in new oak and they need time to show their best. Brumont has 3 properties: Montus★★★, Bouscassé★★ and Meinjarre★. Montus and Bouscassé make a very drinkable dry PACHERENC DU VIC-BILH★, while Bouscassé has a series of fine Moelleux★★.

**MOREY-ST-DENIS AC** *Côte de Nuits, Burgundy, France* Morey has 5 Grands Crus (Clos des Lambrays, CLOS DE LA ROCHE, CLOS DE TART, CLOS ST-DENIS and a share of BONNES-MARES) as well as some very good Premiers Crus. Basic village wine tends to be dilute and dull, but from a good grower the wine has good strawberry or redcurrant fruit and acquires an attractive depth as it ages. A tiny amount of startling nutty white wine is also made. Best producers: Pierre Amiot, Castagnier-Vadey★, Charlopin★, Charvet★, CLAIR★★, DROUHIN, DUJAC★★, FAIVELEY★, Georges Lignier★★, Hubert Lignier★★, Marchand★, Perrot-Minot★, Ponsot★★, Rossignol-Trapet★, J Tardy★. Best years: 1995 93 **90 89** 88.

**MORGON AC** *Beaujolais, Burgundy, France* A BEAUJOLAIS Cru around the commune of Villié-Morgon. Most of the wine produced has a soft, cherry fruit for very easy drinking but from a good grower and from the slopes of the Mont du Py the wine can be thick and dark, acquiring a perfume of cherries as it ages. Classic Morgon is the most tannic of the Beaujolais crus. Best producers: Aucoeur, Georges Brun, la Chanaise, Charvet★, Descombes★★, Desvignes★, DUBOEUF, Lapierre★, Paquet, Savoye★, Vincent. Best years: 1996 **95 93 91 90 88**.

**MORNINGTON PENINSULA** *Victoria, Australia* Exciting new cool, maritime region dotted with small vineyards often owned by monied Melbourne hobbyists. Chardonnay is tantalizing and honeyed, and Pinot Noir shows great promise. Best producers: Craig Avon, DROMANA★, King's Creek, Massoni, Moorooduc Estate, STONIER'S★★, T'gallant.

**MORRIS** *Rutherglen, Victoria, Australia* Historic winery, ORLANDO-owned, making traditional regional favourites like liqueur Muscat★★ and Tokay★★ (Old Premium is ★★★), 'ports', 'sherries' and robust table wines from Shiraz★, Cabernet★, Durif and Blue Imperial (Cinsaut). Mick Morris retired in 1993, handing over the reins to his son David.

**MORTON ESTATE** *Katikati, North Island, New Zealand* Katikati is the tiny town where Morton Estate built their winery in Dutch Cape of Good Hope style. Their vineyards, however, are in HAWKES BAY. Best wines are the robust, complex Black Label Chardonnay★★★, nectarine/tropical fruit Black Label Fumé Blanc★, intense berries and cedar Black Label Cabernet Sauvignon-Merlot★★, as well as a highly successful fizz★★. Best years: (whites) **1996 95 94 91 90**.

**MOSCATO D'ASTI DOCG** *Piedmont, Italy* The Moscato (Muscat) grape comes in a seemingly infinite number of styles, but not one is as beguiling as this delicately scented and gently bubbling version, made from Moscato Bianco grapes grown in the hills between Asti and Alba in north-west Italy. The DOCG is the same as for ASTI Spumante, but only select grapes go into this wine, which is frizzante (semi-sparkling) rather than spumante (fully sparkling). The best are thrillingly grapy and low in alcohol. Drink the wines while still bubbling with youthful fragrance. Best producers: ASCHERI★, Bera★, Braida★, Cascina Pian d'Or★, Caudrina★★, Piero Gatti★, Icardi★, Marenco★, Beppe Marino★, La Morandina★, Perrone★, Saracco★★, La Spinetta★★, I Vignaioli di Santo Stefano★; (Moscato del Piemonte) Marco Negri★.

**MOSCATO PASSITO DI PANTELLERIA DOC** *Sicily, Italy* The Muscat of Alexandria grape is used to make this powerful dessert wine. Pantelleria is a small island south-west of SICILY, closer to Africa than it is to Italy. The grapes are picked in mid-August and laid out in the hot sun to dry and shrivel for a fortnight. They are then crushed and fermented to give an amber-coloured, intensely flavoured sweet Muscat that is one of the best produced. The wines are best drunk within 5–7 years of the vintage, though they can age gracefully for a decade or more. Best producers: De Bartoli (Bukkuram★★), Murana (Martingana★★, Khamma★), Nuova Agricoltura co-op, Pellegrino★.

**MOSEL-SAAR-RUWER** *Germany* Not a coherent wine region, but a collection of vineyard areas on the Mosel and its tributaries, the Saar and the Ruwer. The Mosel river itself rises in the French Vosges before forming the border between Germany and Luxembourg. In its first German incarnation in the Upper Mosel the fairly dire Elbling grape holds sway but with the Middle Mosel begins a series of villages responsible for some of the world's very best Riesling wines: Piesport, Brauneberg, Bernkastel, Graach, Ürzig and Erden. The wines are not big or powerful, but in good years they have tremendous 'slaty' breed and an ability to blend the greenness of perfumes and fruits with the golden warmth of honey. Great wines are rarer in the lower part of the valley as the Mosel swings round into Koblenz. The Saar can produce wonderful, piercing wines in villages such as Serrig, Ockfen and Wiltingen. The Ruwer is north of Trier and produces slightly softer wines; if no village names stand out here there are a few estates (MAXIMIN GRUNHAUS, KARTHAUSERHOF) which are on every list of the best in Germany. See also Ayl, Bernkastel, BraLineberg, Erden, Graach, Ockfen, Piesport, Ürzig, Wehlen.

**LENZ MOSER** *Rohrendorf-bei-Krems, Kremstal, Austria* Important merchant buying growers' wines and bottling them as 'Selection'. Also fine Burgenland wines from the Klosterkeller Siegendorf and

Weinviertel wines (including Cabernet Sauvignon!) from the Malteser Ritterorden estate.

**MOSS WOOD** *Margaret River, Western Australia* Winery producing outstanding silky smooth, rich but structured Cabernet★★. The Chardonnay★★ can be rich and peachy and the Pinot Noir★ erratic but magical at best. Sémillon★★, both oaked and unoaked, is a consistently fascinating wine. Best years: (reds) 1993 92 **91 90 88 86 85 83 80 75**.

**J P MOUEIX** *Bordeaux, France* As well as owning PETRUS, la FLEUR-PETRUS, MAGDELAINE, TROTANOY and other properties, the Moueix family runs a thriving merchant business specializing in the wines of the right bank, particularly POMEROL and FRONSAC. Quality is generally high. Christian Moueix (son of Jean-Pierre) also runs a California winery called DOMINUS.

**MOULIN-À-VENT AC** *Beaujolais, Burgundy, France* The BEAUJOLAIS Cru that can sometimes resemble a full, chocolaty Burgundy, tasting more of Pinot Noir than Gamay, if you leave the wine to age for 6–10 years. Best producers: Brugne, Champagnon★, Charvet★, Chastel, Chauvet★, DUBOEUF (single domaines★), Janodet★, Lapierre, Ch. du Moulin-à-Vent★★, Siffert, la Tour du Bief★★, Trichard. Best years: 1996 95 **93 91 90 88 85**.

**MOULIS AC** *Haut-Médoc, Bordeaux, France* The smallest of the specific ACs within the HAUT-MEDOC area. Much of the wine is excellent – delicious at 5–6 years old, though good examples should age 10–20 years – and not overpriced. Best producers: Anthonic, Biston-Brillette, Brillette★, CHASSE-SPLEEN★★, Duplessis, Dutruch-Grand-Poujeaux, Gressier-Grand-Poujeaux, MAUCAILLOU★, Moulin-à-Vent★, POUJEAUX★★. Best years: (1996) (95) **94 90 89 88 86 85 83 82**.

**MOUNT LANGI GHIRAN** *Grampians, Victoria, Australia* Rapidly rising star turning out powerful, peppery Shiraz★★★, well-structured Cabernet★★, fragrant Riesling★★ and decent unwooded Chardonnay. New is Pinot Gris; Sangiovese is among the new plantings. Best years: (red) **1994** 93 **92 91 90 88 86 84**.

**MOUNT MARY** *Yarra Valley, Victoria, Australia* Classic property which uses Bordeaux as a model, with dry white 'Triolet'★ blended from Sauvignon Blanc, Sémillon and Muscadelle, and 'Cabernets'★★ from all 5 Bordeaux red grapes (Cabernet Sauvignon, Cabernet Franc, Merlot, Petit Verdot and Malbec) that ages beautifully. The Pinot Noir★★ is almost as good. Best years: ('Cabernets') 1994 **92 91 90 88 84 80**.

**MOUNT VEEDER AVA** *Napa Valley, USA* Cabernet Sauvignon and Zinfandel wines, made in a typical rough-hewn style, come from this small mountain AVA in NAPA's south-west corner. Best producers: Chateau Potelle★, HESS COLLECTION★★, Mount Veeder Vineyards★, Mayacamas.

**MOUNTADAM** *Eden Valley, South Australia* The late David Wynn and his Bordeaux-educated son Adam selected this property on one of the highest points of the Mount Lofty Ranges and planted the vineyards from scratch. Mountadam's rich, buttery Chardonnay★★ has a worldwide reputation. There is also sumptuous Pinot★★, leaner Cabernet★, and fruity David Wynn unoaked and Eden Ridge organic labels. Best years: (Cabernet) 1994 93 **91 90 87 84**.

**MOURVÈDRE** This southern French grape variety needs lots of sunshine to ripen, which is why it performs well on the Mediterranean coast at BANDOL, producing wines that can age for 20 years or more. It is increasingly important as a source of colour, body and tarry, pine-needle flavour in the wines of CHATEAUNEUF-DU-PAPE and parts of the MIDI. It is now beginning to make a reputation in Australia and California, where it is occasionally known as Mataro.

**MOUSSEUX** French for sparkling wine.

**MOUTON-CADET** *Bordeaux AC, Bordeaux, France* The most widely sold red Bordeaux in the world was created by Baron Philippe de Roth-schild in the 1930s. The wine is blended and comes from the entire Bordeaux region, is perfectly correct but uninspiring – and never cheap. There is also a white and rosé.

**CH. MOUTON-ROTHSCHILD** *Pauillac AC, 1er Cru Classé, Haut-Médoc, Bordeaux, France* Baron Philippe de Rothschild died in 1988 after 65 years of managing Mouton-Rothschild, raising it from being a run-down Second Growth to its promotion to First Growth status in 1973 and a reputation as one of the greatest wines★★★ in the world. The most magnificently rich and indulgent of the great Bordeaux reds when young, the wine takes 15–20 years to open up fully to its brilliant blackcurrant and cigar box  best. White wine: Aile d'Argent. Best years: (1996) (95) 94 93 91 89 88 86 **85 83 82 78 70**.

**MUDGEE** *New South Wales, Australia* Small, long-established but over-looked region neighbouring HUNTER VALLEY, but with higher altitude and cooler temperatures. Major new plantings are giving it a fresh lease of life. ROSEMOUNT has just introduced an impressive Shiraz-Cabernet called Mountain Blue. Best producers: Huntington, Miramar, Montrose, Thistle Hill.

**MUGA** *Rioja DOC, Rioja, Spain* A traditional family winery making high-quality, elegant, rich red RIOJAS★, especially the Gran Reserva, Prado Enea★. It is the only bodega in Rioja where every step of red wine-making, from fermentation to aging, is still carried out in oak containers. In recent years, the whites and rosés have been good too. Best years: (reds) **1992 90 89 87 85 82 81**.

**MULDERBOSCH** *Stellenbosch WO, South Africa* A sleek, gooseberry-infused Sauvignon Blanc★★ shot this farm into the spotlight in 1991; equally successful subsequent vintages have conferred cult status. Purity with intensity are also the hallmarks of Chardonnay★★ and new Steen-op-Hout★ (Chenin brushed with oak). Faithful Hound, a friendly Cabernet-Merlot★ blend, is the sole red. The estate changed hands in 1996 but dedicated winemaker Mike Dobrovic remains.

**EGON MÜLLER** *Scharzhofberg, Saar, Germany* Not only some of the greatest German wines but also the most expensive. The ultimate sweet versions are the estate's Auslese, Beerenauslese, Trockenbeeren-nauslese and Eiswein, all ★★★. Regular Kabinett and Spätlese wines are pricy but classic. Best years: 1995 94 93 **91 90 89**.

**MÜLLER-CATOIR** *Neustadt-Haardt, Pfalz, Germany*  Müller-Catoir is an eye-opener for those who are sceptical about Germany's ability to make wines in a more international idiom. From vineyards in the PFALZ region he produces wine of a piercing fruit flavour and powerful structure unexcelled in Germany – or anywhere else for that matter – including Riesling, Grauburgunder, Scheurebe, Gewürztraminer, Rieslaner (all frequently ★★★), Muskateller★★ and Weissburgunder★. Best years: 1996 **95 94 93 92 90 89 88**.

**MÜLLER-THURGAU**  The workhorse grape of Germany, largely responsible for LIEBFRAUMILCH. Once thought to be a crossing of Riesling and Sylvaner, new research proves that it is, in fact, Sylvaner x Chasselas, which explains its saltiness and non-Riesling aromas. When yields are low it produces pleasant floral wines; but this is rare since it was bred for productivity. It is occasionally better in England – though the odd good examples, with a slightly green edge to the grapy flavour, come from Austria, Switzerland, Luxembourg and northern Italy. New Zealand used to (and probably still does) pride itself on making the world's best Müller-Thurgau, although acreage is in rapid decline.

**G H MUMM** *Champagne AC, Champagne, France*  Mumm's top-selling non-vintage brand, Cordon Rouge, is usually one of the least impressive Grande Marque Champagnes, frequently out-performed by its Californian counterpart, MUMM NAPA. The de luxe cuvée, René Lalou, is slightly better, but the best wine is the elegant Mumm de Cramant★★. Best years: **1989 88 85**.

**MUMM NAPA** *Napa Valley AVA, California, USA*  The French Champagne house MUMM and Seagram Classic Wines of California started Mumm Napa in 1983. Some reports have it that the French owners are sorry they did because the bubbly coming out of California has been superb. Cuvée Napa Brut Prestige★★ is one of California's classiest sparklers, although the more expensive Vintage Reserve★ runs a close second. A Blanc de Noirs★ is far better than most pink Champagnes. A Tête de Cuvée DVX has righted itself after a weak debut vintage.

**MURFATLAR** *Romania*  Lying to the west from the Black Sea, Murfatlar produces excellent late-harvest wines from Chardonnay, Muscat Ottonel and, in particular, Pinot Gris★. Sparkling wines are now being made, too. The maritime influence can create the problem of warm nights with resultant low acidity levels, often a fault in the Cabernet Sauvignon and Merlot made here. When they work it out, Murfatlar should be a good source of ripe, soft reds. Best producer: Murfatlar Winery.

**MUSCADET AC** *Loire Valley, France*  All change in 1994 with Muscadet becoming the base AC for the whole region with 3 high-quality zones: MUSCADET DES COTEAUX DE LA LOIRE, MUSCADET COTES DE GRAND LIEU, and MUSCADET DE SEVRE-ET-MAINE. Producers who make basic Muscadet AC are allowed higher yields but cannot use the term *sur lie* on the labels. Inexpensive and best drunk young and fresh. Best producers: Chereau-Carré, Donatien-Bahaud, Ch. de la Preuille★, Sauvion.

**MUSCADET DES COTEAUX DE LA LOIRE AC** *Loire Valley, France*  East of Nantes and on both sides of the Loire river, this is the smallest of the 3 high-quality zones. Yields are lower than for basic MUSCADET AC and producers can use *sur lie* on their labels. Best producers: Guindon, Luneau-Papin.

**MUSCADET CÔTES DE GRAND LIEU AC** *Loire Valley, France*   A new AC for the best vineyards around Lac de Grand Lieu, south-west of Nantes. The vines have to be 7 years old before they merit the AC. Some of these wines can age for up to 5 years. The first vintage was 1994. Best producers: Batard, Bel-Air, Herbauges.

**MUSCADET DE SÈVRE-ET-MAINE AC** *Loire Valley, France*   The Maine and Sèvre rivers converge south of Nantes in north-west France and give their name to this AC. Look out for the term *sur lie* on a label as it describes the traditional method of bottling – the wine is bottled directly off its sediment or lees, retaining a creamy, yeasty flavour and a slight prickle of carbon dioxide. Good Muscadet perfectly matches the local seafood. Most is drunk young but the best can age for several years. Best producers: Michel Bahuaud★ (estate bottlings), Bideau-Giraud, Bossard★★, Chasseloir★, Chéreau-Carré★, Couillaud★, Dubois, Marquis de Goulaine, LUNEAU★★, METAIREAU★★, Sauvion★, Touche★. Best years: **1996 95 93 89**.

**MUSCAT** See pages 184–5.

---

**MUSCAT OF ALEXANDRIA**   Not to be confused with the superior Muscat Blanc à Petits Grains, Muscat of Alexandria rarely shines in its own right but performs a useful job worldwide, adding perfume and fruit to what would otherwise be dull, neutral white wines. It is common for sweet and fortified wines throughout the Mediterranean basin and in South Africa (where it is also known as Hanepoot), as well as being a fruity, perfumed bulk producer there and in Australia.

---

**MUSCAT DE BEAUMES-DE-VENISE AC** *Rhône Valley, France*   Some of the best Muscat Vin Doux Naturel in France comes from the attractive village of BEAUMES-DE-VENISE in the southern Rhône. In the 1980s the wine achieved phenomenal success as a 'sophisticated' dessert wine though you'll find the locals supping it on the way home from work. It is certainly sweet but with a fruity acidity and a bright fresh feel to it. Best drunk young to get all that lovely grapy perfume at its peak. Best producers: BEAUMES-DE-VENISE CO-OP★, Coyeux★, Durban★★, JABOULET★, Vidal-Fleury.

**MUSCAT BLANC À PETITS GRAINS** See Muscat.

**MUSCAT DE CAP CORSE AC** *Corsica, France*   New, fortified wine AC covering 17 communes on the island of CORSICA. Muscat à Petits Grains is the only permitted grape variety.

**MUSCAT DE FRONTIGNAN AC** *Languedoc, France*   The well-known Muscat Vin Doux Naturel on the Mediterranean coast. With colours ranging from bright gold to deep orange, it is quite impressive but can seem rather cloying. Best producers: Cave du Muscat de Frontignan, la Peyrade★, Robiscau.

**MUSCAT DE MIREVAL AC** *Languedoc, France*   An AC for Vin Doux Naturel, a little further inland to the much better-known MUSCAT DE FRONTIGNAN. The wines, while still sweet and ripe, can have a little more acid freshness, and quite an alcoholic kick as well. Best producers: la Capelle, Mas des Pigeonniers, Moulinas.

# MUSCAT

It's strange, but there's hardly a wine grape in the world which makes wine that actually tastes of the grape itself. Yet there's one variety which is so joyously, exultantly grapy that it more than makes up for all the others – the Muscat, generally thought to be the original wine vine. In fact there seem to be about 200 different branches of the Muscat family, but the one that always makes the most exciting wine is called Muscat à Petits Grains. These berries can be crunchily green, golden yellow, pink or even brown, and the wines they make can be either really pale and dry, fresh, rich and golden, subtly aromatic or as dark and sweet as treacle.

## WINE STYLES

**France** Muscat is grown from the far north-east right down to the Spanish border, yet is rarely accorded great respect in France. This is a pity because the dry, light, hauntingly grapy Muscats of Alsace are some of France's most delicately beautiful wines. (These are sometimes blended with the crossbreed Muscat Ottonel.) It pops up sporadically in the Rhône Valley, especially in the sparkling wine enclave of Die. Mixed with Clairette, the Clairette de Die Tradition is a fragrant grapy fizz that should be better known.

Muscat de Beaumes-de-Venise could do with being less well known because quality has suffered in recent years. But its success has encouraged the traditional fortified winemakers of Languedoc-Roussillon, especially in Frontignan and Rivesaltes, to make fresher, more perfumed wines rather than the usual flat and syrupy ones.

**Italy** Muscat is grown in Italy for fragrantly sweet or (rarely) dry table wines in the north and for fortified wines (though the less fine Muscat of Alexandria makes most of the rich southern Moscato). Yet the greatest Muscats in Italy are those of Asti, where it is called Moscato Bianco. As either Asti Spumante or Moscato d'Asti this brilliantly fresh, grapy fizz can be a blissful drink. Italy also has red varieties: the Moscato Nero for rare sweet wines in Lazio, Lombardy and Piedmont; and Moscato Rosa for delicately sweet, cherry-coloured wines in Trentino-Alto Adige and Friuli-Venezia Giulia.

**Other regions** Hungary still grows some Muscat, Crimea has shown how good it can be in the Massandra fortified wines, and Greece's finest wines are the Muscats of Samos and Patras. As Muskateller in Austria and Germany it makes both sweet and dry subtly aromatic wines. In Spain, Moscatel de Valencia is sweet, light and sensational value. Moscatel de Grano Menudo is on the resurgence in Navarra and has been introduced in Mallorca. California grows Muscat, often calling it Muscat Canelli, but South Africa and Australia make better use of it. With darker berries, and called Brown Muscat in Australia and Muscadel in South Africa, it makes some of the world's most luscious, fortified wines, especially in north-east Victoria in Australia.

## BEST PRODUCERS

**Sparkling Muscat**

*France* (Clairette de Die) Achard-Vincent, Clairette de Die co-op.

*Italy* (Moscato d'Asti) Bera, Braida, Caudrina, Saracco, La Spinetta.

**Dry Muscat**

*Austria* F X PICHLER, TEMENT.

*France* (Muscat d'Alsace) J Becker, Dirler, TRIMBACH, ZIND-HUMBRECHT.

*Germany* (Muskateller) BERCHER, MULLER-CATOIR, Rebholz.

*Spain* (Mallorca) Miguel Oliver; (Alicante) Bocopa.

*Italy* (Goldenmuskateller) Conti Martini, Tiefenbrunner.

**Sweet Muscat**

*Australia* (Liqueur Muscat) ALL SAINTS, BAILEY'S, CHAMBERS, MCWILLIAMS, MORRIS, SEPPELT, Stanton & Killeen, YALUMBA.

*France* (Muscat d'Alsace) ZIND-HUMBRECHT; (Muscat de Beaumes-de-Venise) Coyeux, Durban, Paul JABOULET; (Muscat de Frontignan) Peyrade; (Muscat de Rivesaltes) CAZES, de Jau.

*Greece* Samos co-op.

*Italy* (Moscato di Pantelleria) De Bartoli, Murana; (Moscato di Strevi Passito) Ivaldi; (Moscato Rosa/Rosenmuskateller) Schloss Sallegg.

*South Africa* KWV, Nuy Co-op, Weltevrede.

*Spain* (Moscatel de Valencia) Castillo de Liria; (Navarra) CHIVITE, OCHOA.

**MUSCAT DE RIVESALTES AC** *Roussillon, France*   Made from Muscat Blanc à Petits Grains and Muscat of Alexandria, the wine can be very good indeed, especially since several go-ahead producers are now allowing the skins to stay in the juice for longer periods, thereby gaining perfume and fruit. Best producers: CAZES★★, des Chênes★, Destavel★, Forca Real, de Jau★★, Laporte★, Mas Rous★, MONT TAUCH co-op★, de Pena★, Piquemal, Sarda-Malet★.

**MUSCAT DE ST-JEAN-DE-MINERVOIS AC** *Languedoc, France*   Up in the remote and wild Minervois hills is the little village of St-Jean-de-Minervois with its small appellation for fortified Muscat, made only from the superior Muscat à Petits Grains. It is less cloying than some Muscats from the plains of LANGUEDOC-ROUSSILLON, more tangerine and floral. Best producers: Barroubio★, Vignerons de Septimanie★.

**MUSIGNY AC** *Grand Cru, Côte de Nuits, Burgundy, France*   One of the handful of truly great Grands Crus, combining power with an exceptional depth of fruit and lacy elegance – an iron fist in a velvet glove. Understandably expensive. A tiny amount of white Musigny is produced by de Vogüé. Best producers: DROUHIN★★, Groffier★★, JADOT★★, Mugnier★★★, Prieur, Roumier★★, de Vogüé★★★. Best years: 1995 93 90 **89** 88 **85**.

**NAHE** *Germany*   Wine region named after the River Nahe which rises below Birkenfeld and joins the Rhine by BINGEN, just opposite RUDESHEIM in the RHEINGAU. Riesling, Müller-Thurgau and Silvaner are the main grapes, but the Rieslings from this geologically complex region are considered some of Germany's best. The finest vineyards are those of Niederhausen and SCHLOSSBÖCKELHEIM, situated in the dramatic, rocky Upper Nahe Valley. See also Bad Kreuznach.

**CH. NAIRAC**★★ *Barsac AC, 2ème Cru Classé, Bordeaux, France*   This Second Growth estate is an established star in BARSAC which, by dint of enormous effort and considerable investment, produces a wine sometimes on a par with the First Growths. The influence of aging in new oak casks, adding spice and even a little tannin, makes this sweet wine a good candidate for aging 10–15 years. Best years: (1996) (95) **90** 89 88 86 83 82 81 80 76.

**NALLE WINERY** *Dry Creek Valley AVA, California, USA*   Owner and wine-maker Doug Nalle is one of the leading producers of Zinfandel in California. He is one of that rare breed that would rather not talk to the press. 'All I'm doing is making the best Zinfandel I can make', he once explained. Nalle's superb Zinfandel★★★ just keeps getting better and more expensive. Best years: **1994 93 92 91 90**.

**NAPA COUNTY** *California, USA*   Home to some of California's best traditional wineries as well as many of its more determined newcomers, Napa has made itself synonymous with quality California wine. The county is viticulturally diverse, with about 20 major sub-areas already identified, but no proof as yet that they offer 20 genuinely diverse styles. Napa's reputation rests on its Cabernet, Merlot and Chardonnay, with Pinot Noir important in the CARNEROS district. Many feel that in the long run, Chardonnay will become less important in Napa and plantings of Cabernet and Merlot will increase. See also Napa Valley.

**NAPA VALLEY AVA** *California, USA* An AVA designed to be so inclusive that it is almost completely irrelevant. It includes vineyards that are outside the Napa River drainage system – such as Pope Valley and Chiles Valley. Because of this a number of sub-AVAs have been and are in the process of being created, but few of them have any real claim to being discernibly different from their neighbours, and many fear that these sub-AVAs will simply serve to dilute the magic of Napa's name. Best producers: BEAULIEU★, BERINGER★, CAIN★, CAYMUS★★, CHATEAU MONTELENA★★, CHIMNEY ROCK★★, Clos Pegase★, CLOS DU VAL★, CUVAISON, DIAMOND CREEK★★, DOMAINE CHANDON★, DUCKHORN★, DUNN★★, FLORA SPRINGS★★, FRANCISCAN★, FROG'S LEAP★, HEITZ CELLARS★, HESS COLLECTION★★, MONDAVI★★, MONTICELLO, MUMM NAPA★, NEWTON★★, OPUS ONE★★, Joseph PHELPS★, SCHRAMSBERG★, SHAFER★★, SILVERADO★★, STAG'S LEAP★★, STERLING★, TREFETHEN, Turley★. See also Carneros, Howell Mountain, Mount Veeder, Oakville, Rutherford.

**NAUTILUS** *Marlborough, South Island, New Zealand* An Australian-owned company controlled by S Smith & Sons (YALUMBA) with vineyards, a retail outlet and a share in the winery Raupara Vintners. Nautilus makes one of the better examples of MARLBOROUGH Sauvignon Blanc★★, stylish Chardonnay★★ and superb fizz★★★. Best years: **1996 94 91 89**.

**NAVARRA DO** *Navarra, Spain* This buzzing region is Spain's answer to the New World, with growing numbers of vineyards planted to Cabernet Sauvignon, Merlot and Chardonnay in addition to Tempranillo, Garnacha and Moscatel de Grano Menudo (Muscat à Petits Grains). This translates into a wealth of juicy reds, barrel-fermented whites, unoaked young Garnacha reds and modern sweet Muscats. Best producers: Camilo Castilla, Julian CHIVITE★, GUELBENZU★, Magaña, Alvaro Marino, Castillo de Monjardin, Nekeas co-op, OCHOA★, Palacio de la Vega, Piedemonte Olite co-op, Príncipe de Viana (formerly Cenalsa), Sada co-op, Señorío de Sarría★, Vicente Malumbres, Vinícola Navarra.

**NEBBIOLO** See pages 188–9.

**NEBBIOLO D'ALBA DOC** *Piedmont, Italy* Red wine from Nebbiolo grown around Alba, but excluding the BAROLO and BARBARESCO zones. The vineyards in the Langhe and Roero hills on either side of the Tanaro river are noted for sandy soils that produce a fragrant, fruity style for early drinking, though some growers make wines of real character that improve for 5 years or more. Best producers: Alario★, ALTARE★, ASCHERI★, CERETTO, Correggia★★, Bruno GIACOSA★, PRUNOTTO★, Ratti★, Vietti★. Best years: **1995 94 93 91 90**.

**NÉGOCIANT** French term for a merchant who buys and sells wine. In Bordeaux a négociant refers to a commercial stock-holding operation. In Burgundy and elsewhere a négociant-éleveur is a merchant who buys, makes, ages and sells wine.

**NELSON** *South Island, New Zealand* A range of mountains separates Nelson from MARLBOROUGH at the northern end of the South Island. Nelson is made up of a series of small hills and valleys with a wide range of meso-climates, which support most of the grape varieties grown in New Zealand. Best results are from Chardonnay, Riesling and Sauvignon Blanc. Best producers: NEUDORF★★★, Ruby Bay, SEIFRIED★★ (Redwood Valley).

# NEBBIOLO

It seems almost bizarre that the grape that makes such great red wines as Nebbiolo should be so limited in its geographical spread. Yet the variety that is responsible for the majestic wines of Barolo and Barbaresco is found almost nowhere outside north-west Italy. Its name derives from the Italian for fog, *nebbia*, because it ripens late when the hills are shrouded in autumn mists. It needs a thick skin to withstand this fog, so often gives wines with a very tannic character that needs years to soften. When grown in the limestone soils of the Langhe hills around Alba, Nebbiolo produces wines that are seldom deep in colour but have a wonderful array of perfumes and an ability to develop great complexity with age – rivalled only by Pinot Noir and Syrah.

So far efforts to grow Nebbiolo elsewhere haven't been that successful, partly because high, cool, fog-shrouded vineyards are rare in the New World, where most producers like to have their harvest safely gathered long before autumn mists descend. Even so, because of the fame of Barolo and Barbaresco, and because many vineyards were created by Italian emigrants, there are a few examples.

## WINE STYLES

**Barolo** Usually considered the best and longest-lived of the Nebbiolo wines, though the myth that it needs a decade or more to be drinkable has been dispelled by new-style Barolo that is better balanced, softer and ready sooner.

**Barbaresco** Barolo's neighbour is somewhat more approachable though styles vary between the traditional and the new.

**Nebbiolo d'Alba and Roero** Lighter types of Nebbiolo are produced here, as well as under the new Langhe DOC. The variety is also used for special Super-Tuscans in the Alba area, such as Altare's Vigna Arborina and Aldo Conterno's Il Favot.

**Nebbiolo-Barbera blends** The 2 varieties go together in table wines such as Clerico's Arte, Rocche dei Manzoni's Bricco Manzoni and Roberto Voerzio's Vignaserra.

**Northern Piedmont** Nebbiolo is also the principal grape for reds of northern Piedmont – Carema, Gattinara and Ghemme.

**Lombardy** Known locally as Chiavennasca, it is the main variety of the Valtellina and Valtellina Superiore DOC wines.

**New World** Mexico produces an adequate Nebbiolo in Baja California, and several Argentine producers make a fairly rustic version. But the most likely successes will be in California – not all from Italian/American families but from new wave Italian enthusiasts like Randall Grahm of Bonny Doon and Jim Clendenen of Au Bon Climat. Australia, too, has its enthusiasts, such as Gary Crittenden of Dromana Estate.

See also BAROLO, BARBARESCO, CAREMA, GATTINARA, GHEMME, NEBBIOLO D'ALBA, VALTELLINA; AND INDIVIDUAL PRODUCERS.

## BEST PRODUCERS

**Italy**

*Barolo* ALTARE, Azelia, CERETTO, Chiarlo, CLERICO, Aldo CONTERNO, Giacomo CONTERNO, Conterno-Fantino, Riccardo Fenocchio, GAJA, Bruno GIACOSA, Elio Grasso, Bartolo MASCARELLO, Giuseppe MASCARELLO, Pio Cesare, PRUNOTTO, Ratti, Rocche dei Manzoni, Sandrone, Paolo Scavino, Vajra, Vietti, Roberto VOERZIO.

*Barbaresco* Barbaresco co-op, Cantina del Glicine, Castello di Neive, CERETTO, Cigliuti, GAJA, Bruno GIACOSA, I Paglieri, Marchesi di Gresy, Bruno Rocca-Rabaja.

*Nebbiolo d'Alba and Roero* Alario, ASCHERI, Correggia, Deltetto, Malvirà, PRUNOTTO, Ratti, Vietti.

*Northern Piedmont* (Carema) Ferrando; (Gattinara) Antoniolo, Le Colline, Travaglini; (Ghemme) Antichi Vigneti di Cantalupo.

*Valtellina* Conti Sertoli Salis, Enologica Valtellinese, Fay, Nino Negri, Rainoldi, Triacca.

**New World Nebbiolos**

*USA* (California) AU BON CLIMAT, BONNY DOON, Martin Brothers, Il Podere dell'Olivos, Viansa.

*Mexico* L A CETTO.

**NEUCHÂTEL** *Switzerland* Swiss canton with high-altitude vineyards, mainly Chasselas for whites and Pinot Noir for reds. Three small areas (Schloss Vaumarcus, Hôpital Poutalès and Domaine de Champrevèyres) have the right to a special AC. Best producers: Ch. d'Auvernier, Porret.

**NEUDORF** *Nelson, South Island, New Zealand* Owners Tim and Judy Finn make stylish and often innovative wines and have resisted the temptation to expand production, preferring instead to fine-tune the quality of their wines by careful vineyard and winery management. Best wines are Chardonnay★★★, Sauvignon Blanc★, Pinot Noir★★ and Riesling★★. Best years: **1996 94 91**.

**NEW SOUTH WALES** *Australia* Australia's most populous state. The RIVERINA, a vast, hot irrigated area of 4700ha (11,600 acres) grows 14% of Australia's grapes and makes oceans of basic-quality table wine but is definitely showing signs of improvement. The HUNTER VALLEY, MUDGEE, COWRA, and Hilltops are smaller, premium-quality regions hugging the coastal highlands. Orange is a high-altitude, up-and-coming inland district. The CANBERRA district is a burgeoning area of tiny vineyards at chilly altitudes.

**NEW WORLD** When used as a geographical term, New World includes all the Americas, South Africa, Australia and New Zealand. By extension, it is also a term used to describe the clean, fruity, upfront style now in evidence all over the world, but pioneered by winemakers in the USA, Australia and New Zealand.

**NEW YORK STATE** *USA* Wine grapes were first planted on Manhattan Island in the mid-17th century but it wasn't until the early 1950s that a serious wine industry began to develop in the state as vinifera grapes were planted to replace natives such as *Vitis labrusca*. The most important region is the FINGER LAKES in the north of the state, with the Hudson River also showing some form, but Long Island is the most exciting area; the maritime climate seems ideal for Chardonnay, Merlot and Pinot Noir, along with a scattering of Riesling sometimes made into a very successful sweet version. The wines, in general, have well-developed varietal fruit character and show good balance, but the erratic weather patterns of the East Coast can still pose ripeness problems. Best producers: (Long Island) BRIDGEHAMPTON★★, Gristina, Hargrave★★, LENZ★, Palmer, PECONIC BAY, Pindar; (others) Benmarl, Brotherhood, Four Chimneys Farm Winery, FOX RUN, Heron Hill, LAMOUREAUX LANDING★, Millbrook, Vinifera, Wagner, Wiemer Vineyard.

**NEWTON VINEYARDS** *Napa Valley AVA, California, USA* Spectacular winery and vineyards set into steep mountain slopes above St Helena. Estate Cabernet Sauvignon★★ and Merlot★★ are some of California's most balanced and ageworthy examples of the varietals. Recent release of an unfiltered, unfined Chardonnay★★★ played to rave reviews. Newtonian★ is the excellent second label for Cabernet blend and Chardonnay and sold chiefly in export markets. Age the Chardonnays for up to 5 years, reds for 10–15. Best years: (Cabernet Sauvignon) 1992 91 **90 85**; (Merlot) 1993 92 91 **90 88 87 86**; (Chardonnay) 1994 **93 91 90**.

**NGATARAWA** *Hawkes Bay, North Island, New Zealand*  Small producer of premium wines. Chardonnay★ and botrytized Riesling★★ have produced the best results. Cabernet Sauvignon-Merlot can also be good but lacks consistency. Special Selections are bottled under the Glazebrook label★ (Chardonnay and Cabernet-Merlot) and are generally delicious, although they are best drunk relatively young. Best years: **1996 95 94 91**.

**NIAGARA PENINSULA** *Ontario, Canada*  Sandwiched between lakes Erie and Ontario, the Niagara Peninsula benefits from regular through-breezes created by the Niagara escarpment, the cool climate bringing out distinctive characteristics in the wine. Chardonnay leads the way in dry whites, with Riesling and Vidal making good ICEWINE. Pinot Noir is proving the most successful red grape, but Merlot and Cabernet Franc have made leaps in quality in recent vintages. Best producers: Cave Spring, Chateau des Charmes, Henry of Pelham, INNISKILLIN★, Southbrook Farm.

**NIEPOORT** *Port DOC, Douro, Portugal*  Small port shipper of Dutch origin, now run by the fifth generation of the Niepoort family. Produces outstanding vintage ports★★★, old tawnies★★★ and a new single-quinta wine: Quinta do Passadouro★★★. Unfiltered LBVs★★ are among the best in their class – intense and complex. Best years: (vintage ports) 1994 92 91 87 83 **82 80 77 70 66 63 55 45 27**.

**NIERSTEIN** *Rheinhessen, Germany*  Both a small town and a large Bereich which includes the infamous Grosslage Gutes Domtal. The town boasts 23 vineyard sites and the top ones (such as Ölberg, Orbel, Hipping and Pettenthal) are some of the best in the whole Rhine Valley. Best producers: GUNDERLOCH★★, HEYL ZU HERRNSHEIM★★, St Antony★★.

**NIKOLAIHOF** *Wachau, Niederösterreich, Austria*  The Saahs family of Mautern makes some of the best wines in the WACHAU as well as in nearby Krems-Stein in KREMSTAL. These include small amounts of one of Austria's most highly prized Rieslings from their small plot in the famous Steiner Hund vineyard★★. Best years: 1995 **94 92 91 90 86 83 79 77**.

**NOBILO** *Kumeu/Huapai, Auckland, North Island, New Zealand*  A family winery which produces a wide range of wines from popular medium-dry White Cloud to single-vineyard varietals. Dixon Vineyard Chardonnay★★, a lush, intensely flavoured wine, is Nobilo's 'prestige' label. Sleek Sauvignon Blanc★★ and Chardonnay★ from Nobilo's newly developed MARLBOROUGH vineyard are rapidly moving toward centre-stage. Best years: **1996 95 94 91 89**.

**NOBLE ROT** English term for *Botrytis cinerea*, which the French call *pourriture noble* and the Germans *Edelfäule*, the fungus which attacks grapes under certain climatic conditions, shrivelling the bunches and intensifying their sugar through dehydration. A vital ingredient in the finest dessert wines, such as SAUTERNES and TROCKENBEERENAUSLESE.

**NORTON** *Mendoza, Argentina*  Austrian-owned winery, with one of the country's best viticulturists, Carlos Tizio Mayer, delivering superb quality fruit. Good new aromatic Torrontés and clean, crisp Sémillon-Chenin Blanc blend★. A thumping blockbuster Malbec★★ heads the reds with top-of-the-range Privada★ blend needing at least 5 years' cellaring.

191

**NUITS-ST-GEORGES AC** *Côte de Nuits, Burgundy, France* This large AC for mainly red wine is one of the few relatively reliable 'village' names in Burgundy. Although it has no Grands Crus many of its Premiers Crus (it has 38!) are extremely good. The red can be rather slow to open out, often needing at least 5 years. There are also minuscule amounts of white made by Gouges, Domaine l'Arlot and RION. Best producers: Chauvenet★, R Chevillon★★, Confuron★, Domaine l'Arlot★★, R Dubois★★, FAIVELEY★, Gouges★★, GRIVOT★★, JAYER★★★, JAYER-GILLES★★, LABOURE-ROI★, Michelot★★, Moillard★, Remoriquet★, RION★★. Best years: (reds) 1995 93 **92 90 89 88 85**.

**OAKVILLE AVA** *Napa Valley, USA* Made official in 1996, this region is similar in just about every respect to RUTHERFORD, which lies immediately to the north. Planted primarily to Cabernet Sauvignon, the area contains some of the best vineyards (MONDAVI, Martha's Vineyard, OPUS ONE), but no discernible regional style has made itself known.

**OC, VIN DE PAYS D'** *Languedoc-Roussillon, France* Increasingly exciting Vin de Pays concentrating on New World-style red and white wines. Local producers such as SKALLI-FORTANT and VAL D'ORBIEU have been complemented by the arrival of talented winemakers from Australia, England and Switzerland. Best producers: Dom. de la BAUME★, Grange de Quatre Sous★, HERRICK, Lalaurie, Lurton★, RYMAN, SKALLI-FORTANT, VAL D'ORBIEU★ (top reds), Virginie★.

**OCHOA** *Navarra DO, Navarra, Spain* Javier Ochoa has clearly taken his own advice as the former chief winemaker of the experimental wine research station by completely modernizing the family bodega and his 68ha (168 acres) of vineyards. The resulting wines are fresh, clean and fruity, with particularly good Cabernet Sauvignon★, Tempranillo★ and sweet Muscat★. Best years: (reds) **1993** 92 91 90 89 87 86 85.

**OCKFEN** *Saar, Germany* Village with one famous individual vineyard site, the Bockstein. The wines can be superb in a sunny year, never losing their cold steely streak but packing in delightful full-flavoured fruit as well. Best producers: Dr Fischer, Heinz Wagner★★, ZILLIKEN★★.

**OECHSLE** German scale measuring must-weight based on specific gravity. This scale is more familiar to beer fanatics in Britain and the USA. To get the Oechsle figure you take the specific gravity of water, 1000, and for every unit of specific gravity above that – in the case of grapes this refers to units of sugar in the grape's juice – you add 1. So grape juice with a specific gravity of 1130 (130 parts of sugar over and above the basic 1000) has the first 1000 lopped off and we're left with an Oechsle of 130, indicating a fairly ripe, sugar-filled grape, likely to give a full, potentially quite alcoholic wine.

**OESTE** A colloquialism for the ESTREMADURA region of Portugal.

**OISLY-ET-THÉSÉE, CONFRÉRIE DES VIGNERONS D'** *Touraine, Loire Valley, France* Founded in 1960, this innovative co-op established itself as one of the leading names in TOURAINE under the directorship of the late Jacques Choquet. Choquet's vision lives on in the fresh, but richly flavoured wines, especially the Sauvignon-based whites★, Gamay-based reds and CREMANT DE LOIRE★, all sold under the Baronnie d'Aignan label. Except for their Sauvignon Cuvée Excellence★★, the best single varietals come from Château de Vallagon★. Best years: **1996** 95 94 93 90 89.

**OKANAGAN VALLEY** *British Columbia, Canada* The most important wine-producing region of British Columbia and first home of Canada's rich, honeyed ICEWINE. The Okanagan Lake's warmth helps temper the bitterly cold nights but October frosts can be a problem here. Pinot Blanc and Pinot Noir are the top performing grapes. Best producers: Blue Mountain, Gray Monk, MISSION HILL★★, Quail's Gate.

**OLOROSO** See Jerez y Manzanilla DO/Sherry.

**OLTREPÒ PAVESE DOC** *Lombardy, Italy* This hilly zone of south-west Lombardy makes 14 different types of wine under its DOC. Oltrepò Pavese is Italy's main source of Pinot Nero, used mainly for sparkling wines that may be called Classese when made by the Champagne method here, though base wines supply Spumante industries elsewhere. The hills have long furnished Milan with daily wines, often fizzy, though still reds from Barbera, Bonarda and Pinot Nero and whites from the Pinots, Riesling and, lately, Chardonnay can be impressive. Best producers: Anteo, Le Fracce★, Frecciarossa★, Fugazza, Mazzolino, Monsupello★, Piccolo Bacco dei Quaroni, Santa Maria della Versa co-op★, Vercesi del Castellazzo★, Bruno Verdi★.

**OMAR KHAYYAM** *Maharashtra, India* Champagne-method sparkling wine produced from a blend of Chardonnay, Ugni Blanc, Pinot Noir, Pinot Meunier – and Thompson Seedless. The Thompson is now being used less and less as plantings of the other varieties come on stream. Technology, thanks to  Champagne consultants PIPER-HEIDSIECK, together with high-sited, irrigated vineyards, generally produce a firm, fresh, chunky sparkler – though quality is somewhat erratic.

**OPPENHEIM** *Rheinhessen, Germany* Village whose reputation has suffered from the sale of much inferior wine under the Oppenheimer Krötenbrunnen label. In its steepest sites, such as Sackträger, it can be one of the best villages in RHEINHESSEN, where the vineyards line the left bank of the Rhine, giving relatively earthy, but full-flavoured wines. Best producers: Guntrum, Koch, Kühling-Gillot.

**OPUS ONE** *Napa Valley AVA, California, USA* Widely publicized joint venture between Robert MONDAVI and the late Baron Philippe de Rothschild of MOUTON-ROTHSCHILD. The first vintage (1979) was released in 1983. At that time, the $50 price was the most expensive for any California wine, though others have reached beyond it now. The various Opus bottlings since 1979 have been in the ★★ range but have rarely reached the standard of the Mondavi Reserve Cabernet – and the price still seems too high. Best years: 1993 92 91 **90 88 87 84 80**.

**OREGON** *USA* Oregon shot to international stardom in the early 1980s following some perhaps overly generous praise of its Pinot Noir, but the state has failed to consolidate this position. Not that Oregon Pinot Noir can't be attractive but, at its best (like the 1994), it offers a black cherry fruit generally without much complexity. Chardonnay can be quite good in an austere, understated style. The rising star is Pinot Gris which, in

Oregon's cool climate, can be delicious with surprising complexity. The Willamette Valley is considered the best growing region and the Dundee hills area the best sub-region. Best producers: ADELSHEIM★★, AMITY★★, Argyle, Arterberry, BEAUX FRERES, Bethel Heights★, Cameron★, DOM. DROUHIN★★, Elk Cove★, Eola Hills, ERATH, EYRIE★★, Henry Estate, King Estate, PONZI★, Rex Hill★★, SOKOL BLOSSER★★, Tualatin, Yamhill Valley★.

**ORLANDO** *Barossa Valley, South Australia* Australia's second-biggest wine company is now owned by Pernod-Ricard, and encompasses MORRIS, Wickham Hill, Gramps, Richmond Grove and WYNDHAM ESTATE. Top wines under the Orlando name are consistent COONAWARRA reds St Hugo★ and Jacaranda Ridge★; individualistic Eden Valley Rieslings St Helga★ and Steingarten★★; and spicy Flaxmans Traminer★. Jacobs Creek basics are deservedly Australia's most successful brand abroad, but these days Orlando lacks strength at the premium end.

**ORNELLAIA, TENUTA DELL'** *Bolgheri, Italy* This beautiful property was developed by Lodovico Antinori, brother of Piero, after he left the family firm, ANTINORI, to strike out on his own. The red Ornellaia★★★, a Cabernet-Merlot blend, can be interestingly compared with neighbouring SASSICAIA. The white Poggio alle Gazze★★ is made solely with Sauvignon. An outstanding Merlot, Masseto★★★, is produced in small quantities. Best years: (1996) (95) 94 93 **92 91** 90 **88**.

**ORVIETO DOC** *Umbria, Italy* Traditionally a lightly sweet ABBOCCATO white wine, Orvieto is now usually a dry characterless white. In the superior Classico zone, however, the potential for richer and more biscuity wines exists. Not generally a wine for aging, Palazzone's Riserva★★ is an exception. Best producers: Antica Selva di Meana, Barberani★, CASTELLO DELLA SALA★, Decugnano dei Barbi★, Palazzone★, Salviano★, Conte Vaselli★, Le Valette★.

**OSBORNE** *Jerez y Manzanilla DO, Andalucía, Spain* The biggest drinks company in Spain, Osborne does most of its business in brandy and other spirits. Its sherry arm in Puerto de Santa María specializes in the light Fino Quinta★. Amontillado Coquinero★, rich, intense Bailén Oloroso★★ and Solera India★ are very good indeed.

**OVERBERG WO** *South Africa* South Africa's most southerly wine region, embracing the upland area of Elgin as well as the coastal ward of Walker Bay. Much prized for cool-climate viticulture, Sauvignon, Chardonnay, Riesling and Pinot Noir vindicate the decision to replace valuable apple orchards. Walker Bay was opened up (at the time illegally) by HAMILTON RUSSELL in the mid-1970s, who remained the only producer until BOUCHARD FINLAYSON started in the early 90s – the 2 have now become 9. Pinot Noit is the holy grail of the majority, although Pinotage is also being pursued successfully. Best producers: (Walker Bay) BOUCHARD FINLAYSON★, HAMILTON RUSSELL★★, Wildekrans★.

**PAARL WO** *South Africa* Paarl vineyards cover nearly 19% of South Africa's entire plantings; the many soils and climates in this basically warm area create anything from Cap Classique sparkling to sherry-style. Wineries are also varied: KWV's 22-ha (55-acre) complex is said to be the largest winery facility in the world; Claridge represents the boutique end. Wellington and Franschhoek are smaller designated areas within the Paarl region. Best producers: (Paarl) BACKSBERG★,

BOSCHENDAL★, FAIRVIEW★★, GLEN CARLOU★★, KWV, STELLENBOSCH FARMERS' WINERY (Plaisir de Merle★★, Nederburg), Veenwouden★★, VILLIERA★★, Welgemeend★; (Wellington) Claridge★.

**PACHERENC DU VIC-BILH AC** *South-West France*  Small amount of individual whites from an area overlapping the MADIRAN AC in north-east Béarn. The wines are mainly dry but there are some medium-sweet/sweet late-harvest wines. Most Pacherenc is best drunk young. Best producers: Aydie, Brumont★★, Crampilh, Damiens★, Laffitte-Teston, MONTUS★, PLAIMONT co-op.

**PADTHAWAY** *South Australia*  This wine region has always been the alter-ego of nearby COONAWARRA, growing whites to complement Coonawarra's reds. But today some excellent reds are made, and even PENFOLDS Grange now has some Padthaway grapes. HARDY'S Eileen Hardy★★★ and Collection★ Chardonnays and LINDEMANS' Padthaway Chardonnay are the best examples. Padthaway Sauvignon Blanc is also some of Australia's tastiest. Best producers: Browns of Padthaway, HARDY, LINDEMANS, SEPPELT.

**BODEGAS PALACIO** *Rioja DOC, País Vasco, Spain*  Founded in 1894 by Don Cosme Palacio, then the owner of VEGA SICILIA. Relaunched in the late 1980s by new owner Jean Gervais and POMEROL winemaker Michel Rolland, whose Cosme Palacio Hermanus★★ has become a cult wine in Spain. Best years: **1994 92 91 90 89**.

**ALVARO PALACIOS** *Priorato DO, Catalonia, Spain*  Although he was only in his 20s, Alvaro Palacios was already a veteran with Bordeaux and Napa experience when he launched his boutique winery in the rough hills of southern CATALONIA in the late 1980s. He is now one of the driving forces of the area's sensational rebirth. His expensive, highly concentrated reds★★★ from old Garnacha vines and a dollop of Cabernet Sauvignon, Merlot and Syrah have won a cult following. Best years: 1994 93 92 **90**.

**PALETTE AC** *Provence, France*  Tiny AC just east of Aix-en-Provence. Even though the local market pays high prices, I find the reds and rosés rather tough and charmless. However, Ch. Simone, the only producer of white Palette, manages to achieve a wine of some flavour from basic southern grapes. Best producers: Crémade, Ch. Simone.

**PALLISER ESTATE** *Martinborough, North Island, New Zealand*  State-of-the-art winery producing some of New Zealand's best Sauvignon★★ (certainly the best outside MARLBOROUGH) and Riesling, with some impressive but less consistent Pinot Noir★. Exciting botrytized dessert wines appear in favourable vintages. It may be small but it's still one of the largest in MARTINBOROUGH. Best years: **1996 94 91**.

**CH. PALMER★★** *Margaux AC, 3ème Cru Classé, Haut-Médoc, Bordeaux, France*  This estate was named after a British major-general who fought in the Napoleonic Wars. Palmer was the leading property in MARGAUX AC during the 1960s and 70s until the Mentzelopolous family took over at Ch. MARGAUX in 1977. Although only a Third Growth, the wine, with its wonderful perfume and irresistible plump fruit, often manages to be as good as the top Second Growths but sometimes would benefit from rather more body and intensity. The very best vintages can age for 30 years or more. Second wine: Réserve-du-Général. Best years: (1996) (95) 90 89 88 **86 85 83 82 79 78 75 70**.

**PALOMAS** *Rio Grande do Sul, Brazil* Winery just north of the Uruguay border, in the one area of Brazil where the climate at least tolerates the cultivation of classic vinifera varieties. Its simple, ramshackle wines satisfy curiosity rather than titillate.

**CH. PAPE-CLÉMENT** *Pessac-Léognan AC, Cru Classé de Graves, Bordeaux, France* This expensive and famous GRAVES Classed Growth mainly for red wine★★★ has not always been as consistent as it should be – but things have looked up considerably since the exciting 1986 vintage. In style it is mid-way between the refinement of  HAUT-BRION and the firmness of its MISSION-HAUT-BRION. There is also a small production of steadily improving white wine. Second wine (red): Clémentin. Best years: (1996) (95) 94 93 90 89 88 **86 85**.

---

**PARELLADA** This Catalan exclusivity is the lightest of the trio of simple white grapes that go to make CAVA wines in north-eastern Spain. It also makes still wines, light, fresh and gently floral, with good acidity and (for Spain) lowish alcohol (between 9 and 11%). Drink it as young as possible – and I mean *young* – while it still has the benefit of freshness.

---

**PARKER ESTATE** *Coonawarra, South Australia* Recent arrival on the premium market, a red specialist impressing with its first efforts made by the experienced Ralph Fowler at Leconfield. The top label is the cheekily named Terra Rossa First Growth★★, which has excellent cellar potential, although the 1994 is a bit on the green side. Whether style and quality will be maintained under its new winemaker from 1995 is as yet unknown.

**PARRINA DOC** *Tuscany, Italy* On the coast in southern Tuscany, the Sangiovese-Canaiolo red is minty and robust; the white is from Trebbiano and Ansonica. Drink within 3–5 years. Riserva★ will keep a little longer. Best producer: La Parrina. Best years: **1996 95 94 93**.

**PASSITO** Italian term indicating that the wine is made from dried grapes. The result is usually a sweet wine with a raisiny intensity of fruit. See also Moscato Passito di Pantelleria, Recioto della Valpolicella, Vin Santo.

**LUIS PATO** *Bairrada, Beira Litoral, Portugal* Leading 'modernist' in BAIRRADA, passionately convinced of the Baga grape's ability to make great reds★★ on clay soil. Best years: 1995 **92 91 88 85**.

**PATRIMONIO AC** *Corsica, France* Good, underrated wines from the northern end of the island. The reds and rosés, based on the local Nielluccio grape, are your best bet, but look out for the fresh Vermentino whites and the fortified Muscat. Best producers: Arena, Gentile, Leccia. Best years: (reds) **1995 94 93 92 91 90 89**.

**PAUILLAC AC** *Haut-Médoc, Bordeaux, France* The deep gravel banks around the town of Pauillac in the HAUT-MEDOC are the true heartland of Cabernet Sauvignon. For many wine lovers, the king of red wine grapes finds its ultimate expression in the 3 Pauillac First Growths (LATOUR, LAFITE-ROTHSCHILD and MOUTON-ROTHSCHILD). The large AC also contains 15 other Classed Growths, including world-famous PICHON-LONGUEVILLE-LALANDE, PICHON-LONGUEVILLE and LYNCH-BAGES. The uniting characteristic of Pauillac wines is their intense blackcurrant fruit flavour and heady cedar and pencil-shavings perfume. These are the longest-lived of Bordeaux's great red wines. Best producers: BATAILLEY★, Fonbadet★, GRAND-PUY-DUCASSE★, GRAND-PUY-LACOSTE★★, HAUT-BAGES-LIBERAL★★, HAUT-BATAILLEY★, LAFITE-ROTHSCHILD★★★, LATOUR★★★, LYNCH-BAGES★★★, MOUTON-ROTHSCHILD★★★, Pibran★, PICHON-LONGUEVILLE★★★, PICHON-LONGUEVILLE-LALANDE★★★, PONTET-CANET★★. Best years: (1996) (95) 94 90 89 88 86 **85 83 82 81 79 78**.

**CH. PAVIE★★** *St-Émilion Grand Cru AC, 1er Grand Cru Classé, Bordeaux, France* The second-biggest of the ST-EMILION Premiers Grands Crus (after FIGEAC), Pavie is one of the most improved properties in the AC. The wines will happily evolve for a decade yet never lose the soft, unctuous charm of the fruit and the sweet oak. Best years: (1996) (95) **90 89 88 86 85 83 82 81**.

**PÉCHARMANT AC** *South-West France* Lovely red wines from this small AC north-east of BERGERAC. The wines are quite light in body but have a delicious, full, piercing flavour of blackcurrants and a most attractive grassy acidity. Good vintages will easily last 10 years and end up indistinguishable from a good HAUT-MEDOC wine. Best producers: Bertranoux, Champarel★, Clos Peyrelevade★, Corbiac, Costes, Haut-Pécharmant★, la Métairie, Tiregand★. Best years: 1996 **95 90 89 88 86 85 83**.

**PECONIC BAY VINEYARDS** *Long Island AVA, New York State, USA* Peconic Bay has a well-deserved reputation for Chardonnay, which it makes in a light, unoaked style called Petite Chardonnay, and a barrel-fermented Reserve Chardonnay★★, which is complex and filled with buttery, ripe flavours. But don't neglect the Merlot, which emphasizes soft, fresh fruit or the intense Cabernet Sauvignon. Cabernet Franc has also been added.

**PEDROSA** *Ribera del Duero DO, Castilla y León, Spain* Delicious, elegant reds★, both young and oak-aged, from a family winery in the little hill village of Pedrosa del Duero. The wines are not cheap, but far less pricy than some stars of this fashionable region. Best years: (reds) 1994 **92 91 90 89 86**.

**PEÑAFLOR** *Mendoza, Argentina* The biggest producer of wine in Argentina sends millions of litres of cheap Termidor brand to Buenos Aires each month. Investment in its fine wine arm, Trapiche, along with the recent hiring of Bordeaux oenologist Michel Rolland, is beginning to deliver results. Grassy Chenin Blanc★, rich, melony Chardonnay and punchy Sauvignon★ from high-altitude vineyards show promise. Oak-aged Cabernet-Malbec blend★ is a mouthfilling red.

**PENEDÉS DO** *Catalonia, Spain* The wealthy CAVA industry is based in Penedés, and the majority of the still wines are white, made from the Cava trio of Parellada, Macabeo and Xarel-lo, clean and fresh when young, but never exciting. Better whites are made from Chardonnay. The reds are variable, the best made from Cabernet Sauvignon and/or Tempranillo and Merlot. Best producers: Albet i Noya, Can Feixes, Can Ráfols dels Caus, Cavas Hill, JUVÉ Y CAMPS, Jean LEON★★, MARQUÉS DE MONISTROL★, Masía Bach★, Albert Milá i Mallofré, Puig y Roca, TORRES★, Vallformosa, Jané Ventura.

197

**PENFOLDS** *Barossa Valley, South Australia* Part of Australia's Southcorp Wines group, Penfolds proves that quality *can* go in hand with quantity and is regarded as the dominant force in Australian wine. Makes the country's greatest red wine, Grange★★★, and a welter of superbly rich, structured reds from Magill Estate★ through St Henri★, Bin 707 Cabernet★★★, Bin 389 Cabernet-Shiraz★★, Bin 28 Kalimna★★ and Bin 128 Coonawarra Shiraz★ to Koonunga Hill★. Still very much a red wine name, although toasty Chardonnay★★, oaky Sémillon★★ and lemony Sémillon-Chardonnay★★ are all leaders in their styles. Best years: (reds) **1994 93 92 91 90 88 86 84 83 82 80 78 76 71**.

**PENLEY ESTATE** *Coonawarra, South Australia* Launched in 1991 with immediate impact, the first wines are from bought-in grapes, while its large but unproven COONAWARRA vineyard is planned to be the eventual source. The quality of the Cabernet Sauvignon★★★ is outstanding and matches its lavish packaging. Shiraz and Chardonnay are ★★.

**PERLWEIN** German for lightly sparkling wine.

**PERNAND-VERGELESSES AC** *Côte de Beaune, Burgundy, France* The little-known village of Pernand-Vergelesses contains a decent chunk of the great Corton hill, including much of the best white CORTON-CHARLEMAGNE Grand Cru vineyard. The red wines sold under the village name are very attractive when young with a nice raspberry pastille fruit and a slight earthiness, and will age for 6–10 years. As no-one ever links poor old Pernand with the heady heights of Corton-Charlemagne, the whites sold under the village name can be a bargain – quite a rarity in Burgundy. The wines can be a bit lean and dry to start with but fatten up beautifully after 2–4 years in bottle. Best producers: (reds) Besancenot-Mathouillet★, Chandon de Briailles★, Cornu★, Denis★, Dubreuil-Fontaine★★, Laleure-Piot★, Rapet★, Rollin★; (whites) Dubreuil-Fontaine★, GERMAIN★, Guyon★, JADOT★, Laleure-Piot★, Pavelot★, Rapet★, Rollin★. Best years: (reds) 1995 **93 90 89 88 85**; (whites) 1995 **92 90 89 88**.

**JOSEPH PERRIER** *Champagne AC, Champagne, France* This is the sole Champagne house left in Châlons-en-Champagne (previously called Châlons-sur-Marne) and is still family-run. The NV Cuvée★ is biscuity and creamy, the Prestige Cuvée Josephine★★ has length and complexity, but the much cheaper Cuvée Royale Vintage★★ is the best deal. Best years: **1990 89 88 85 82**.

**PERRIER-JOUËT** *Champagne AC, Champagne, France* This is supposedly the best of the Champagne houses owned by the Canadian multinational Seagram. The non-vintage is variable, but the vintage is still a good rich style★★. A de luxe cuvée, Belle Époque★★, famous for its embossed Art Nouveau label has, for once in the image-obsessed world of Champagne, an exciting flavour to match the exterior fol-de-rols. The Belle Époque rosé★★ is excellent, too. Best years: **1990 89 88 85 82**.

**PESQUERA** *Ribera del Duero DO, Castilla y León, Spain* Viña Pesquera reds, richly coloured, firm, fragrant and plummy-tobaccoey, are among Spain's most expensive – and best. Made by the small firm of Alejandro Fernández, they are 100% Tempranillo, and sold as Crianzas★★, with Reservas★★ and Gran Reserva Janus★★★ in the best years. Best years: 1994 93 **92 91 90 89 86 85**.

**PESSAC-LÉOGNAN AC** *Bordeaux, France*   New AC, created in 1987, for the northern (and best) part of the GRAVES region and including all the Graves Classed Growths. The supremely gravelly soil tends to favour red wines over the rest of the Graves. Now one of the most exciting areas of France for top-class white wines, the standard is fast improving thanks to the advent of cool fermentation, controlled yeast selection and the use of new oak barrels. Best producers: (reds) CARBONNIEUX★, Dom. de CHEVALIER★★★, de FIEUZAL★★, HAUT-BAILLY★★, HAUT-BRION★★★, la LOUVIERE★★, MALARTIC-LAGRAVIERE★, la MISSION-HAUT-BRION★★, PAPE-CLEMENT★★★, de Rochemorin, SMITH-HAUT-LAFITTE★, la Tour-Haut-Brion, la TOUR-MARTILLAC★; (whites) CARBONNIEUX★, Dom. de CHEVALIER★★★, Couhins-Lurton★★, de FIEUZAL★★★, HAUT-BRION★★★, LAVILLE-HAUT-BRION★★★, la LOUVIERE★★, MALARTIC-LAGRAVIERE★, de Rochemorin★, SMITH-HAUT-LAFITTE★★, la TOUR-MARTILLAC★★. Best years: (reds) (1996) (95) 94 90 89 88 **86 85 83 82 81 79 78**; (whites) (1996) **95 94 90 89 88 86 85 83 82**.

**PETALUMA** *Adelaide Hills, South Australia*   Run by Brian Croser, probably Australia's most influential and thoughtful winemaker. Champagne-method Croser★★ is fine but very dry and lean. The Chardonnay★★★ and COONAWARRA Cabernet-Merlot★★★ are consistently outstanding and CLARE Riesling★★★ is fuller and longer lasting than most of its peers. Best years: (reds) 1994 93 **92 91 90 88**.

**PÉTILLANT**   French for a slightly sparkling wine, often one which has been purposely bottled with a bit of carbon dioxide.

**PETIT CHABLIS AC** *Chablis, Burgundy, France*   Once this denoted the outlying parts of the CHABLIS region. Then the vineyards were upgraded to full Chablis. Now more land has been planted even further away. The wine is often thin but can be appealing when drunk young. Too close to regular Chablis in price, though.

**PETIT VERDOT**   A rich, tannic red variety, grown mainly in Bordeaux's HAUT-MEDOC to add depth, colour and fabulous violet-fragrance to top wines. Late-ripening and erratic yield limits its popularity, but warmer-climate plantings in Australia and California are giving exciting results.

**CH. PETIT-VILLAGE★★** *Pomerol AC, Bordeaux, France*   This top POMEROL wine, traditionally much sterner in style than its neighbours, is now made by Jean-Michel Cazes, who also runs PICHON-LONGUEVILLE in PAUILLAC. In general it is worth aging the wine for 8–10 years at least. Best years: (1996) 90 89 88 **85 83 82 81 79 78**.

**PETITE SIRAH**   Long used as a blending grape in California but used also for varietal wines, Petite Sirah is supposed to be the Durif of southern France, although there is now some doubt about that. At its best in California and Mexico, the wine has great depth and strength; at worst it can be monstrously huge and unfriendly. Best producers: L A CETTO★ (Mexico), FETZER, Foppiano, RIDGE★, Turley.

**CH. PÉTRUS★★★** *Pomerol AC, Bordeaux, France*   Now one of the most expensive red wines in the world, but only 30 years ago Pétrus was virtually unknown. The powerful, concentrated wine is the result of the caring genius of Pétrus' co-owners since 1962, the MOUEIX family, who have maximized the potential of the vineyard of almost solid clay and remarkably old vines, which is, in places, up to 70 years of age. Drinkable for its astonishingly rich, dizzying blend of fruit and spice flavours after a decade, but top years will age for much longer, developing exotic scents of tobacco and chocolate and truffles as they mature. Best years: (1996) (95) 94 93 90 89 88 **86 85 82 79 75 71**.

**CH. DE PEZ**★★ *St-Estèphe AC, Cru Bourgeois, Haut-Médoc, Bordeaux, France* One of ST-ESTÈPHE's leading non-Classed Growths, de Pez makes mouthfilling, satisfying claret with sturdy fruit. Slow to evolve, good vintages often need 10 years or more to mature. Best years: (1996) (95) 94 90 89 88 86 **85 83 82 79 78 75**.

**PFALZ** *Germany* Germany's most productive wine region makes a lot of mediocre wine but the quality estates are capable of matching the best that Germany has to offer. The Mittelhaardt has a reputation for Riesling, especially round the villages of WACHENHEIM, FORST and Deidesheim, though Freinsheim, Ungstein, KALLSTADT, Gimmeldingen and Haardt also produce fine Riesling as well as Scheurebe, Pinot Gris and Dornfelder. In the Südliche Weinstrasse the warm climate makes the area an ideal testing ground for the so-called Burgunders (Pinot Noir, Pinot Blanc and Pinot Gris), as well as Gewürztraminer, Scheurebe, Muscat and Dornfelder, usually made dry but rich. See also Bad Dürkheim, Burrweiler, Kallstadt.

**JOSEPH PHELPS** *Napa Valley AVA, California, USA* Joseph Phelps' Insignia★★ red (Cabernet, Merlot and Cabernet Franc) is consistently one of California's top wines, strongly fruit-driven with a lively spicy background. Phelps makes 2 Cabernets: Napa Valley★, a medium-weight wine, and Backus Vineyard★; each has solid fruit with good balance. Attractive Eisele Vineyard was discontinued after 1991. Best years: (Insignia) 1993 92 91 **89 87 85 84 80**; (Cabernet) 1994 **92 91 90 89**.

**PIAT D'OR** An inexorably popular, off-dry Vin de Table, dull and ludicrously over-priced – but then someone had to pay for the extremely effective advertising. Now also playing the MIDI varietal card.

**PIAVE DOC** *Veneto, Italy* The Piave plains, north of Venice, churn out vast quantities of Merlot, Cabernet, Rabosa and Tocai. Under the DOC 8 different varieties are permitted, but much is bought up by Veronese merchants and sold simply as Merlot del Veneto. Best producers: Collalto, Ornella Molon★, Rechsteiner, Roncade.

**PIC ST-LOUP** *Coteaux du Languedoc AC, Languedoc, France* The vineyards of this Cru, arranged around a steep outcrop of limestone north of Montpellier, produce some of the best reds in the Languedoc. This is one of the coolest growing zones in the MIDI. Syrah does particularly well and, along with Grenache and Mourvèdre, it is the dominant variety. Whites from Marsanne, Roussanne, Rolle and Viognier are beginning to show promise. Best producers: Mas Bruguière★, l'Hortus★★, Lascaux, de la Roque★. Best years: **1995 94 93 91**.

**FRANZ X PICHLER** *Wachau, Niederösterreich, Austria* A leading WACHAU superstar whose Kellerberg and Steinertal Rieslings★★★ are extremely concentrated. There are also excellent Grüner Veltliners★★ from the Loibner Berg. Best years: 1995 **94 92 91 90 86 75**.

**CH. PICHON-LONGUEVILLE★★★** *(since 1988) Pauillac AC, 2ème Cru Classé, Haut-Médoc, Bordeaux, France*  Despite its superb vineyards with the potential for making great PAUILLAC, Pichon-Longueville (called Pichon-Baron until 1988) wines were 'also-rans' for a long time. In 1987 the management was taken over by Jean-Michel Cazes of LYNCH-BAGES and, since then, there has been a remarkable change in fortune. Recent vintages have been of First Growth standard, with firm tannic structure and rich dark fruit. Cellar for at least 10 years, although it is likely to keep for 30. Second wine: les Tourelles de Pichon. Best years: (1996) (95) 94 90 89 88 **86 82**.

**CH. PICHON-LONGUEVILLE-LALANDE★★★** *(on recent form) Pauillac AC, 2ème Cru Classé, Haut-Médoc, Bordeaux, France*  Pichon-Longueville-Lalande has been run since 1978 by the inspirational figure of Madame de Lencquesaing, who has led the property ever upwards on a wave of passion and involvement, through her superlative vineyard management and wine-making sensitivity. Divinely scented and lush at 6–7 years, the wines usually last for 20 at least. Things dipped at the end of the 1980s, but recent efforts look exciting again. Second wine: Réserve de la Comtesse. Best years: (1996) (95) 94 **89 88 86 85 83 82 81 79 78 75**.

**PIEDMONT** *Italy*  This is the most important Italian region for the tradition of quality wines. In the north, there is CAREMA, GHEMME and GATTINARA. To the south in the Langhe hills, there's BAROLO and BARBARESCO, both masterful examples of the Nebbiolo grape, and other wines from Dolcetto and Barbera grapes. In the Monferrato hills, in the provinces of Asti and Alessandria, the Barbera, Moscato and Cortese grapes hold sway. Recent changes in the system have created the broad new DOCs of Colline Novaresi in the north, Langhe and Monferrato in the south and the region-wide Piemonte appellation designed to classify all wines of quality from a great range of grape varieties. See also Asti, Erbaluce di Caluso, Gavi, Moscato d'Asti, Nebbiolo d'Alba, Roero.

**PIEROPAN** *Veneto, Italy*  Leonildo and Teresita Pieropan produce excellent SOAVE Classico★ and, from 2 single vineyards, Calvarino★★ and La Rocca★★, the definitive wines of this zone. There is an excellent Recioto di Soave Le Colombare★★, a good Riesling Italico and an opulent Passito della Rocca★★, a barrique-aged blend of Garganega, Sauvignon and Riesling Italico.

**PIERRO** *Margaret River, Western Australia*  Yet another of MARGARET RIVER's wine-making doctors, Mike Peterkin makes Pierro Chardonnay★★★ by the hatful, but it is a masterpiece of power and complexity. The Sémillon-Sauvignon blend★ is full and less grassy than most, while Pinot Noir is just okay. Fire Gully is the second label with bought-in grapes. Best years (Chardonnay): **1994 93 92 90 89 87 86**.

**PIESPORT** *Mosel, Germany*  Best known for the generic Piesporter Michelsberg wines that are soft, sweet and easy-drinking, but also capable of producing excellent Rieslings from the top Goldtröpfchen site. With their intense blackcurrant and peach aromas they are unique among Mosel wines. Best producers: Grans-Fassian, Reinhold Haart★★, Kurt Hain★, von KESSELSTATT★, Weller-Lehnert.

# PINOT NOIR

There's this myth about Pinot Noir that I think I'd better lay to rest. It goes something like this. Pinot Noir is an incredibly tricky grape to grow; in fact Pinot is such a difficult customer that the only place that regularly achieves magical results is the thin stretch of land known as the Côte d'Or, between Dijon and Chagny in France, where mesoclimate, soil conditions and 2000 years of experience weave an inimitable web of pleasure.

This just isn't so. The thin-skinned, early-ripening Pinot Noir is undoubtedly more difficult to grow than other great varieties like Cabernet or Chardonnay, but that doesn't mean that it's impossible to grow elsewhere – you just have to work at it with more sensitivity and flexibility. And although great red Burgundy is a hauntingly beautiful wine, most Burgundians completely fail to deliver the magic, and the glorious thing about places like New Zealand, California, Australia and Germany is that we are seeing an ever increasing number of wines that are thrillingly different to anything produced in Burgundy, yet with flavours that are unique to the Pinot Noir.

## WINE STYLES

**France** All France's great Pinot Noir wines do come from Burgundy's Côte d'Or. Rarely deep in colour, they should nonetheless possess a wonderful fruit quality when young – raspberry, strawberry, cherry or plum that becomes more scented and exotic with age, the plums turning to figs and pine, and the richness of chocolate mingling perilously with truffles and well-hung game. Strange, challenging, hedonistic. France's other Pinots – in north and south Burgundy, the Loire, Jura, Savoie, Alsace and now occasionally in the South of France – are lighter and milder, and in Champagne its pale, thin wine is used to make sparkling wine.

**Other European regions** The great 1993, 90 and 89 vintages have allowed German winemakers to produce impressive, perfumed wines (generally called Spätburgunder). Italy, where it is called Pinot Nero, and Switzerland (where it is known as Blauburgunder) both have fair success with the variety. Austria and Spain have produced a couple of good examples, and Romania, the Czech Republic and Hungary produce significant amounts of variable quality.

**New World** Light, fragrant wines have bestowed upon Oregon in America's Pacific Northwest the greatest reputation for being 'another Burgundy'; but I get more excited about the marvellously fruity, erotically scented wines of California's Carneros and Russian River Valley regions, and the original offerings from the outposts south of San Francisco. New Zealand is the most important southern hemisphere producer with wines of thrilling fruit and individuality, while Australia is slowly finding its way and even South Africa and Chile have a few fine producers.

## BEST PRODUCERS

### France

*Burgundy* (growers) Comte Armand, DUJAC, Engel, GRIVOT, Henri JAYER, Lafarge, LAFON, Dom. LEROY, MEO-CAMUZET, de MONTILLE, Denis Mortet, Ponsot, Dom. de la ROMANEE-CONTI, Roumier, ROUSSEAU, TOLLOT-BEAUT; (merchants) DROUHIN, FAIVELEY, JADOT, LABOURE-ROI, Maison LEROY, RODET; (co-ops) BUXY, Caves des Hautes-Côtes.

### Germany
BERCHER, Huber, K-H JOHNER, KOEHLER-RUPRECHT.

### Switzerland Gantenbein.

### New World Pinot Noirs

*USA* (California) ACACIA, AU BON CLIMAT, CALERA, CHALONE, DEHLINGER, Lane Tanner, MONDAVI (Reserve), RASMUSSEN, J Rochioli, SAINTSBURY, SANFORD, WILLIAMS SELYEM; (Oregon) ADELSHEIM, AMITY (Winemakers Reserve), BEAUX FRERES, DOMAINE DROUHIN, ERATH.

*Australia* BANNOCKBURN, Bass Phillip, COLDSTREAM HILLS, Diamond Valley, Freycinet, Giaconda, MOUNT MARY, MOUNTADAM, Scotchman's Hill, TARRAWARRA, YARRA YERING.

*New Zealand* ATA RANGI, COLLARDS, Dry River, MARTINBOROUGH VINEYARD, NEUDORF, Rattray, ST HELENA, Te Kairanga.

*South Africa* HAMILTON RUSSELL (Ashbourne).

*Chile* CONO SUR, VALDIVIESO.

**CH. LE PIN★★★** *Pomerol AC, Bordeaux, France* Now one of the most expensive wines in the world, with prices at auction overtaking those for PETRUS. The 1979 was the first vintage and the wines, which are concentrated but elegant, are produced from 100% Merlot. The tiny 2ha (5 acres) vineyard lies close to those of TROTANOY and VIEUX-CH.-CERTAN. Best years: (1996) (95) 94 **90 89 88 86 85 83 82 81**.

**PINOT BIANCO** See Pinot Blanc.

**PINOT BLANC** Wine made from the Pinot Blanc grape has a clear, yeasty, appley taste and good examples can age to a delicious honeyed fullness. In France its chief power-base is in Alsace, where it is taking over the 'workhorse' role from Sylvaner and Chasselas. In fact, most CREMANT D'ALSACE now uses Pinot Blanc as the principal variety. Important in northern Italy as Pinot Bianco, in Germany and Austria as Weissburgunder and is successful in Hungary, Slovakia, Slovenia and the Czech Republic. Promising new plantings in California, Oregon and Canada.

**PINOT GRIGIO** See Pinot Gris.

**PINOT GRIS** Found mainly in France's Alsace, where it is now called Tokay-Pinot Gris. With a low acidity and a deep colour the grape produces fat, rich wines that will often mature wonderfully. It is occasionally used in Burgundy to add fatness to a wine. As Pinot Grigio it is also grown in northern Italy, where it produces some of the country's most popular dry whites. Also successful in Austria and Germany as Ruländer or Grauer Burgunder, and as Malvoisie in the Swiss Valais. There are some fine Romanian and Czech examples, as well as good spirited ones in Hungary (as Szurkebarat). Made in a crisp style, it is very successful in Oregon in the USA.

**PINOT MEUNIER** The most widely planted grape in the Champagne region. A vital ingredient in Champagne, along with the other permitted varieties – Pinot Noir and Chardonnay – though it is the least well known of the three.

**PINOT NERO** See Pinot Noir.
**PINOT NOIR** See pages 202–3.

**PINOTAGE** A Pinot Noir x Cinsaut cross, conceived in South Africa in 1925 but not widely planted until the 1950s. Despite show successes and its current popularity on the international market, it remains a love-or-hate grape among Cape winemakers. Recently, the variety's champion and driving force behind the Pinotage Producers' Association, Beyers Truter of KANONKOP, showed that the estery character so disliked by many could be tamed. A whole new breed of Pinotages, both wooded and unwooded, is now emerging from the Cape: opulent with plummy, summer-pudding succulence shot with redcurrant freshness. Also found in tiny quantities in New Zealand, California (rarely), Germany and Zimbabwe. **Best producers:** Avontuur, BACKSBERG, Beyerskloof★, Clos Malverne, FAIRVIEW★, GRANGEHURST★, KANONKOP★, (Reserve★★), Hugh RYMAN, SIMONSIG★, WARWICK★★, Wildekrans.

**RAUENTHAL** *Rheingau, Germany* This most famous wine village of the RHEINGAU produces some of the region's most overpriced wines from the great Baiken and Gehrn sites. Sadly few of the Rieslings made here today have the intense spice and mineral character for which they are renowned. Best producers: August Eser★, J B Becker, Georg BREUER★★.

**CH. RAUZAN-SÉGLA★★★** *Margaux AC, 2ème Cru Classé, Haut-Médoc, Bordeaux, France* A dynamic change of wine-making regime in 1982 brought about a startling change for the better. This has been further improved by new owners Chanel from 1994. Now the wines have a rich blackcurrant fruit, almost tarry, thick tannins and weight, excellent woody spice and superb concentration. Second wine: Ségla. Best years: (1996) (95) 94 93 90 89 88 86 **85 83**.

**JEAN-MARIE RAVENEAU** *Chablis AC, Burgundy, France* The outstanding grower in CHABLIS producing beautifully nuanced wines from 3 Grands Crus (Blanchot★★, les Clos★★★ and Valmur★★★) and 4 Premiers Crus (Montée de Tonnerre★★, Vaillons★★, Butteaux★★ and Chapelots★★), using a combination of oak and stainless steel fermentation. The wines can easily age for a decade or more. Best years: 1995 93 **92** 90 **89 88** 86 75 71.

**RAVENSWOOD** *Sonoma Valley AVA, California, USA* Joel Peterson, one of California's leading Zin masters, established Ravenswood in 1976 with the sole purpose of making Zinfandel. During the lean years, when most California Zinfandel was pink and sweet, Peterson added a serviceable Chardonnay, a sometimes very good Cabernet Sauvignon★ and a tasty Merlot. But Zinfandel remains the trump card here. Peterson makes several, varying the menu from year to year: the Dickerson Vineyard★★, Old Hill★★ and Old Vines★★★ are super Zins, with ripe, concentrated fruit – bold and beautiful wines. Most should be drunk 5–15 years from the vintage. Best years: 1994 **92 91** 90 87 86 **85**.

**CH. RAYAS** *Châteauneuf-du-Pape, Rhône Valley, France* The most famous estate in CHATEAUNEUF-DU-PAPE. The eccentric Jacques Reynaud produces big, alcoholic, exotically rich reds★★ and whites★★ which also age well. However, prices are not cheap and the wines are not consistent, but at its best Rayas is worth the money. The red is made entirely from low-yielding Grenache vines – the only such wine in the AC – while the white is a blend of Clairette, Grenache Blanc and (so rumour has it) Chardonnay. The COTES DU RHONE Ch. de Fonsalette★ is wonderful stuff. Best years: (Châteauneuf-du-Pape) 1995 94 93 91 90 89 88 **86**; (whites) 1995 94 **93 91** 90 89 **86**.

**RECIOTO DELLA VALPOLICELLA DOC** *Veneto, Italy* The great sweet wine of VALPOLICELLA, made from grapes picked earlier than usual and left to dry on straw mats until the end of January. The wines are deep in colour, with a rich, bitter-sweet cherryish fruit. They age well for 5–8 years, but are best drunk young. As with Valpolicella, the Classico tag is all important. SOAVE makes its own version of Recioto. Best producers: Corte Aleardi★, ALLEGRINI★, Brigaldara★, Brunelli★, Dal Forno★★★, MASI (Serègo Alighieri★★), QUINTARELLI★★, Le Ragose★, Le Salette★, Speri★, Tedeschi★. Best years: **1995 93 90 88 85**.

**DOM. DE LA RECTORIE** *Banyuls AC and Collioure AC, Roussillon, France*
Parcé is a famous name in BANYULS. For many years Dr A Parcé (Mas Blanc) kept the Banyuls flag flying. Now his distant relations Marc and Thierry Parcé are leading the way. Their COLLIOURE★★ is made for keeping, while the Banyuls Cuvée Léon Parcé can be enjoyed for its youthful fruit or kept for future pleasure. The Vin de Pays Cuvée l'Argile★★ made from Grenache Blanc is one of the best whites in ROUSSILLON. Best years: (reds) 1995 94 **93**.

**REGALEALI** *Sicily, Italy* The estate of the Conte Tasca d'Almerita in the highlands of central SICILY makes some of Italy's most admired wines, although all are Vino da Tavolas. From native grape varieties come Rosso del Conte★★ (based on Nero d'Avola) and white Nozze d'Oro★ (based on Inzolia), but the range extends to Chardonnay★★ and Cabernet Sauvignon★★ of extraordinary intensity and elegance. Conte d'Almerita Crémant Brut★ (Chardonnay and Pinot Nero) may well be the finest Champagne-method sparkler south of the Alpine regions.

**RÉGNIÉ AC** *Beaujolais, Burgundy, France* In 1988 the village of Régnié and its neighbour Durette were promoted to BEAUJOLAIS' 10th Cru. The wines are generally light and attractive but in poor years not up to scratch. Best producers: Bel-Air, Cinquin, Crêt des Bruyères, DUBOEUF★, Laforest, Magrin, Rampon, Trichard. Best years: **1996 95**.

**REGUENGOS DOC** *Alentejo, Portugal* One of the most promising of the new ALENTEJO DOCs with good, flavoursome reds epitomizing the excitingly juicy flavours of southern Portugal. Best producers: ESPORAO★★, FONSECA SUCCESSORES (J S Rosado Fernandes★★), Reguengos de Monsaraz co-op.

**REMELLURI** *Rioja DOC, País Vasco, Spain* Organic RIOJA estate producing wines with far more fruit than usual and good concentration for aging. Best are ★★. Best years: **1993 91 89**.

**RESERVA** Spanish wines of above-average quality that have fulfilled certain aging requirements: reds must have at least 3 years' aging before sale, of which one must be in oak barrels; whites and rosés must have at least 2 years' aging, of which 6 months must be in oak.

**RÉSERVE** French for what is, in theory at least, a winemaker's finest wine. The word has no legal definition in France.

**BALTHASAR RESS** *Eltville-Hattenheim, Rheingau, Germany* Stefan Ress has cleared out his cellar and replaced all his wooden casks with stainless steel and fibre glass. Although his wines continue to exhibit some of the cleanest, purest fruit of any RHEINGAU producer, for a time vintages lost some individuality. There was a partial return to form with the 92 vintage. Basically a Riesling producer, he also produces delicious Scheurebe★. Best years: **1993 92 90**.

**RETSINA** *Greece* Resinated white and rosé wine now common all over Greece. The best retsinas are deliciously oily and piny, while the resin provides (as mint does) a mild cooling effect on the tongue. For this reason, retsina need not be overchilled. The younger the better is a good rule here. Best producers: Achaia-Clauss, Botrys, Cambas, Kourtakis.

**REUILLY AC** *Loire Valley, France* Extremely dry but attractive Sauvignon from west of the world-famous SANCERRE. Also some pale Pinot Noir red and Pinot Gris rosé. Best producers: Beurdin★, Cordier, Lafond, Malbête, Martin, Sorbe. Best years: **1996 95 93 90**.

**RHEINGAU** *Germany* Wine region occupying a south-facing stretch of the Rhine flanking the city of Wiesbaden. Considered Germany's most aristocratic wine region, both in terms of the racy, slow-maturing 'breed' of the wines and because of the number of noble estate owners. Unfortunately the most famous names here are no longer a guarantee of top quality, and a new generation of winemakers now makes the best wines. See also Eltville, Geisenheim, Hattenheim, Hochheim, Johannisberg, Kiedrich, Martinsthal, Rüdesheim, Winkel.

**RHEINHESSEN** *Germany* Large wine region to the south and west of Mainz. On the Rheinterrasse between Mainz and Worms are a number of very famous top-quality estates, especially at Nackenheim, NIERSTEIN, OPPEN-HEIM and Bodenheim. BINGEN, to the north-west, also has a fine vineyard area along the left bank of the Rhine.

**RHÔNE VALLEY** *France* The Rhône starts out as a river in Switzerland, ambling through Lake Geneva before hurtling southwards into France. In the area south of Lyon, between Vienne and Avignon, the valley becomes one of France's great wine regions. In the northern part, where vertigo-inducing slopes overhang the river, there is not much wine produced but the little that is made is of remarkable individuality. The Syrah grape reigns here in COTE-ROTIE and on the great hill of HERMITAGE. ST-JOSEPH, CROZES-HERMITAGE and CORNAS also make excellent reds, while the white Viognier grape yields perfumed, delicate wine at CONDRIEU and at the tiny AC CHATEAU-GRILLET. In the southern part the steep slopes give way to wide plains, where the vines swelter in the hot sun, with hills both in the west and east. Most of these vineyards are either COTES DU RHONE or COTES DU RHONE-VILLAGES, reds, whites and rosés, but there are also specific ACs. The most well known of these are CHATEAUNEUF-DU-PAPE and the luscious, golden dessert wine, MUSCAT DE BEAUMES-DE-VENISE. See also Clairette de Die, Coteaux de l'Ardèche, Coteaux du Tricastin, Côtes du Lubéron, Côtes du Vivarais, Gigondas, Lirac, St-Péray, Tavel, Vacqueyras.

**RÍAS BAIXAS DO** *Galicia, Spain* The best of the 5 DOs of Galicia, Rías Baixas is making increasing quantities of Spain's best whites (apart perhaps from a few Chardonnays in the north-east). The magic ingredient is the characteristic Albariño grape, making creamy-rich, fruity whites with a glorious fragrance. Drink young or exceptionally with short aging. Best producers: Adegas das Eiras★★, Agro de Bazan★★, Aldea de Abaixo, Dominguez Borrajo, Granxa Fillaboa★, Lagar de Fornelos★ (La RIOJA ALTA ), Pazo de Barrantes★ (MARQUES DE MURRIETA), Pazo de Señorans★, Quinta de Couselo★★, Robaliño, Bodegas Salnesur★★, Santiago Ruiz★★ (Lan), Valdamor, Vilariño-Cambados★★.

**RIBATEJO** *Portugal* Portugal's second-largest wine region straddles the river Tagus (Tejo) upstream from Lisbon. Prolific vineyards on the fertile soils alongside the river are producing large volumes of increasingly good everyday reds. There are 5 IPRs, of which Almeirim, with its giant co-op, is probably the best known. The Ribatejo is also the traditional source of some good GARRAFEIRAS. Best producers: Almeirim co-op, BRIGHT BROTHERS, Quinta do Casal Branco★, Falua.

**RIBERA DEL DUERO DO** *Castilla y León, Spain* The dark elegant reds in this DO, from Tinto Fino (Tempranillo) sometimes with Cabernet Sauvignon and Merlot, are as good as those of RIOJA. Also a few light rosés. New names are rising to join the top ranks of quality. Best producers: Alión, Ismael ARROYO★★★, Victor Balbás, Hijos de Antonio Barceló, Felix Callejo★, Carraovejas★, Dehesa de los Canonigos, PEDROSA★, PESQUERA★★, VEGA SICILIA★★★.

**DOMAINE RICHEAUME** *Côtes de Provence AC, Provence, France* German-owned property close to Mont Ste-Victoire, much painted by Cézanne. The estate is run on organic principles and is planted with a mix of Mediterranean varieties (Cinsaut, Grenache, Syrah) and Cabernet Sauvignon, which produce impressively deep-coloured wines★ full of smoky spice and power. Best years: 1995 **93 92 91 90 89 88**.

**RICHEBOURG AC** *Grand Cru, Côte de Nuits, Burgundy, France* Rich, fleshy wine from the northern end of VOSNE-ROMANEE. Most domaine-bottlings are exceptional. Best producers: GRIVOT★★, Jean Gros★★★, JAYER★★★, Dom. LEROY★★★, Noëllat★★, Dom. de la ROMANEE-CONTI★★★. Best years: 1995 93 **92** 90 **89** 88 **85** 78.

**RICHOU** *Loire Valley, France* One of the leading domaines in the Loire, producing a large consistently good range of wines. The best are the ANJOU-VILLAGES Vieilles Vignes★★ and the sweet COTEAUX DE L'AUBANCE Cuvée les Trois Demoiselles★★. Best years: 1996 **95 94 93 90 89 88**.

**MAX FERD RICHTER** *Mülheim, Mosel-Saar-Ruwer, Germany* Dr Richter makes Riesling wines in some of the best sites in the MOSEL, including Wehlener Sonnenuhr★★, Brauneberger Juffer★★ and Graacher Domprobst★★. His wines are marked out by splendid racy acidity balanced by fragrant Riesling fruit. His Mülheimer Helenenkloster vineyard is unique in Germany for producing a magical Eiswein★★★ virtually every year. Best years: 1996 **95 94 93 92 90 89 88**.

**RIDGE VINEYARDS** *Santa Clara, California, USA* Established as a Zinfandel-only winery in 1962, winemaker Paul Draper moved into Cabernet Sauvignon★★ and Petite Sirah★ in the late 1960s. The Zinfandels★★★, made with grapes from various sources, have great intensity and long life, and all the reds display ageability, impressive concentration of fruit and originality. There is some Chardonnay★, too. Best years: (Zinfandel) **1994 93 92 91 90 88 85 84**.

**RIECINE** *Chianti DOCG, Tuscany, Italy* John Dunkley's small estate in Gaiole makes some of the most exquisite CHIANTI. Yields are low, so there is a great intensity of fruit and a superb definition of spiced cherry flavours. Both the CHIANTI CLASSICO★★ and Riserva★★★ are outstanding, while the barrique-aged La Gioia★★★ is equally impressive. Best years: (1996) 95 94 93 **90 88 86 85**.

**RIESLING** See pages 220–1.

**RIESLING ITALICO** Known as Welschriesling in the rest of Europe, and not in any way related to the great Riesling of the Rhine, this grape is widely planted in Italy, especially in the north, where it produces decent dry whites. In Austria it makes some of the very best sweet wines. Watch out for a revival in Hungary where, as Olaz Rizling, it is highly esteemed.

**CH. RIEUSSEC**★★ *Sauternes AC, 1er Cru Classé, Bordeaux, France*
♀ Apart from the peerless and scarcely affordable Ch. d'YQUEM, Rieussec often used to be the richest, most succulent wine of SAUTERNES. However, recent vintages have displayed a rather 'correct' style for what was always a wine that walked on the wild and wonderful side. Happily the 1990 is magnificent. Cellar for at least 10 years, though it may be kept for another decade or more. The dry white wine, called 'R', is inexplicably dull. Second wine: Clos Labère. Owned since 1984 by LAFITE-ROTHSCHILD. Best years: (1996) (95) **90 89 88 86 85 83 81 75**.

**RIO GRANDE DO SUL** *Brazil* High rainfall and humidity in this southern-most region of Brazil mean that fungal diseases and ripening can be a problem for winemakers, and most of the vines planted are hybrids. Flying winemaker John Worontschak has made progress with Cabernet Sauvignon and Merlot at Vinicola Aurora, but Chardonnay is still his most drinkable wine.

**RIOJA DOC** *Rioja, Navarra, País Vasco and Castilla y León, Spain* Rioja, in
🏢 the centre of northern Spain, is not all oaky, creamy whites and elegant, barrel-aged reds, combining oak flavours with wild straw-berry and prune fruit. Over half Rioja's red wine is sold young, never having seen the inside of a barrel, and most of the white is fairly anonymous. With the award of Spain's first DOC and 2 good harvests in 1989 and 90, grape prices dropped and Rioja seemed set to return to the popularity it had previously enjoyed in the 1970s. But wine quality is still maddeningly inconsistent (though the best producers are improving all the time), and prices for grapes – and wine – have shot up in the last 2 years, despite a large harvest in 1995. Stick with the good guys. Best producers: (reds) Amézola de la Mora, BARON DE LEY, BERBERANA★, Berceo, Beronia, BRETON★★, CAMPILLO★★, CAMPO VIEJO★, Luis Cañas, CONTINO★★, El COTO★, Cosecheros Alaveses, CVNE, DOMECQ★, FAUSTINO MARTINEZ★, Herencia Lasanta, LOPEZ DE HEREDIA★, MAR-QUES DE CACERES★, MARQUES DE GRINON★, MARQUES DE MURRIETA★, MARQUES DE RISCAL★★, Marqués de Vargas, MARTINEZ BUJANDA★, MONTECILLO★, MUGA★, Navajas, PALACIO★★, REMELLURI★★, La RIOJA ALTA★★, RIOJANAS★, Sierra Cantabria, Torre de Oña, Viña Ijalba; (whites) Beronia, BRETON★★, CAMPO VIEJO★, CVNE★, LOPEZ DE HEREDIA★, MARQUES DE CACERES★, MARQUES DE MURRIETA★, MONTECILLO★, La RIOJA ALTA★, RIOJANAS★.

**LA RIOJA ALTA** *Rioja DOC, Rioja, Spain* One of the very best of the old-
🏢 established RIOJA producers, making almost entirely Reservas and Gran Reservas. Its only Crianza, Viña Alberdi★, fulfils the minimum age requirements for a Reserva anyway. There is a little good, lemony-oaky Viña Ardanza Reserva★ white. Red Reservas, Viña Arana★ and Viña Ardanza★★, age splendidly, and Gran Reservas, Reserva 904★★ and Reserva 890★★★ (made only in exceptional years) are among the very best of Rioja wines. Best years: (reds) **1994 92 89 88 87 86 85 82 81 78 76 73**.

**RIOJANAS** *Rioja DOC, Rioja, Spain* This quality winery makes Reservas
🏢 and Gran Reservas in 2 styles: elegant Viña Albina★ and richer Monte Real★. The white, Monte Real Blanco Crianza★, is one of RIOJA's best. The whites and Reservas can be kept for 5 years after release, Gran Reservas for 10 or more. Best years: (reds) **1994 91 90 89 87 83 82 73 64**.

# RIESLING

I'm sad to have to make this bald statement at the start, but I feel I must. If you have tasted wines with names like Laski Riesling, Olasz Riesling, Welschriesling, Gray Riesling, Riesling Italico and the like and found them unappetizing – do not blame the Riesling grape. These wines have filched Riesling's name, but have nothing whatsoever to do with the great grape itself.

Riesling is Germany's finest contribution to the world of wine – and herein lies the second problem. German wines have fallen to such a low level of general esteem through the proliferation of wines like Liebfraumilch that Riesling, even true German Riesling, has been dragged down with it.

So what *is* true Riesling? It is a very ancient German grape, probably the descendant of wild vines growing in the Rhine Valley. It certainly performs best in the cool vineyard regions of Germany's Rhine and Mosel Valleys, but also does well in New Zealand and cool parts of Australia; yet it is widely planted in California, South Africa and Italy, and the warmer parts of Australia also grow it to good effect.

## WINE STYLES

**Germany** These wines are based on a marvellous perfume and an ability to hold on to a piercing acidity, even at high ripeness levels, so long as the ripening period has been warm and gradual rather than broiling and rushed. German Rieslings can be bone dry, through to medium and even lusciously sweet, but if they are dry, they must be made from fully ripe grapes, otherwise the acidity is excessive and the wine's body insufficient.

Young Rieslings often show a delightful floral perfume, sometimes blended with the crispness of green apples, often lime, sometimes even peach, raisin or honey, depending upon the ripeness of the grapes. As the wines age, the lime often intensifies, and a flavour perhaps of slate, perhaps of petrol/kerosene intrudes.
**Other regions** The rather heavier, petrolly style is typical of Australia's warmer areas, while California generally produces a grapy style which is usually best when sweet. In the valleys of the Danube in Austria, Riesling gives stunning dry wines that combine richness with elegance. The mountain vineyards of northern Italy, and the cool vineyards of the Czech Republic, Slovakia and Switzerland can show a floral sharp style, but the most fragrant wines come from Germany, from France's Alsace, and from New Zealand, with some success from America's Pacific Northwest and New York State, and from the odd cool spot in Australia. South Africa's cooler regions produce delicate drier styles; there are also good late harvest and botrytized Rieslings.

In general Rieslings are best drunk young, but dry Alsace wines can improve for many years, and the truly sweet German styles can age for generations.

## BEST PRODUCERS

### Dry Rieslings

*Austria* BRUNDLMAYER, FREIE WEINGARTNER WACHAU, HIRTZBERGER, Knoll, NIKOLAIHOF, F X PICHLER, PRAGER.

*France* (Alsace) Kreydenweiss, Ostertag, Schlumberger, TRIMBACH, ZIND-HUMBRECHT.

*Germany* J BIFFAR, Georg BREUER, GUNDERLOCH, JULIUSSPITAL, KOEHLER-RUPRECHT, Franz KUNSTLER, J LEITZ, LINGENFELDER, LOOSEN, MAXIMIN GRÜNHAUS, MÜLLER-CATOIR, St Antony.

### Non-dry Rieslings

*Germany* BURKLIN-WOLF, Christoffel, DONNHOFF, GUNDERLOCH, HAAG, Johannishoff, JOST, KARTHAUSERHOF, von KESSELSTATT, Franz KUNSTLER, LINGENFELDER, LOOSEN, Egon MULLER, MULLER-CATOIR, J J PRUM, RICHTER, Willi Schaefer, SCHLOSS REINHARTSHAUSEN, SCHLOSSGUT DIEL, SELBACH-OSTER, WEIL, ZILLIKEN.

*France* (Alsace) HUGEL, TRIMBACH, ZIND-HUMBRECHT.

### New World Rieslings

*Australia* Wolf BLASS, Leo Buring, DELATITE, GROSSET, HENSCHKE, Howard Park, MITCHELL, MITCHELTON, ORLANDO, PETALUMA, Pikes, PIPERS BROOK.

*New Zealand* COOPERS CREEK, CORBANS (Stoneleigh), Dry River, Giesen, Grove Mill, MARTINBOROUGH VINEYARD, MONTANA, NEUDORF, Pegasus Bay, SEIFRIED (Redwood Valley).

*South Africa* BUITENVERWACHTING, KLEIN CONSTANTIA, SIMONSIG, STELLENZICHT, THELEMA, VILLIERA.

*USA* (Oregon) AMITY; (New York) BRIDGEHAMPTON.

221

**R** **DANIEL RION**

**DANIEL RION** *Nuits-St-Georges, Côte de Nuits, Burgundy, France* One of Burgundy's most consistent performers, producing supple, concentrated but sometimes slightly 'serious' reds from Pinot Noir and a little bit of crisp, white Aligoté. Also white NUITS-ST-GEORGES les Terres Blanches from 1994. The best wines are the VOSNE-ROMANEE les Beaux Monts★★ and les Chaumes★★, Nuits-St-Georges Clos de Argillières★★ and the village level VOSNE-ROMANEE★. Best years: 1995 94 93 **92 90 89 88 85**.

**RISERVA** An Italian term, recognized in many DOCs and DOCGs, for a special selection of superior-quality wine that has been aged longer before release. Quite often, it is also destined for longer aging. It is only a promise of a more pleasurable drink if the wine had enough fruit and structure in the first place. Losing favour in BAROLO, it is still important in CHIANTI.

**RIVERA** *Puglia, Italy* One of southern Italy's most dynamic producers. In the traditional mould, the CASTEL DEL MONTE Riserva Il Falcone★ is an excellent, full-blooded southern red. There is also a series of varietals sold under the Terre al Monte label, best of which are Aglianico, Pinot Bianco and Sauvignon Blanc.

**RIVERINA** *New South Wales, Australia* Along with South Australia's RIVERLAND, this extensive irrigated region, fed by the Murrumbidgee River, provides the bulk of Australia's basic table wines. Many of Australia's best-known brands, from companies like PENFOLDS, HARDY, ORLANDO and MCWILLIAMS, though not mentioning either Riverina or Riverland on the label, will in fact be based on wines from these areas. There are also some remarkable sweet wines such as the botrytis Sémillon★★★ from DE BORTOLI, McWilliams★, Miranda★ and Wilton Estate★★.

**RIVERLAND** *South Australia* This is a vast irrigated region along the Murray River, producing 27% of the national grape crush. Mainly given over to bulk and cheaper bottles of table and fortified wine, although BERRI RENMANO can produce some high-quality special selections. Best producers: ANGOVES, BERRI RENMANO, Kingston Estate, Trentham Estate, YALUMBA (Oxford Landing).

**RIVESALTES AC** *Languedoc-Roussillon, France* Vin Doux Naturel from a large area around the town of Rivesaltes. These fortified wines are some of southern France's best and can be made from an assortment of grapes, mainly white Muscat (when it is called MUSCAT DE RIVESALTES) and Grenache Noir, Gris and Blanc. There is also a Rancio style which ages well. Best producers: Ch. Cap de Fouste, Vignerons CATALANS, CAZES★★, des Chênes★, Ch. de Corneilla, Forca Real★, Ch. de Jau★, Laporte, Mas Rancoure★, Rivesaltes co-op, Sarda-Malet★, Terrats co-op, Troillas co-op.

**RIVIERA LIGURE DI PONENTE DOC** *Liguria, Italy* This DOC zone stretches from Genoa westwards through stunning scenery to Ventimiglia on the French border, and north to PIEDMONT. The major grapes grown here are the bold white Pigato and the more delicate Vermentino, and the red Ormeasco (Piedmont's Dolcetto, producing soft, plummy wines) and more fragile Rossese. Best producers: Maria Donata Bianchi★, Bruna, Colle dei Bardellini, Fèipu dei Massaretti★, Foresti, Lupi★, Maccario, Terre Rosse★, La Vecchia Cantina.

**ROBERTSON WO** *South Africa*   Hot, dry inland area with lime-rich soils, uncommon in the Cape, that are ideal for vines. Chenin Blanc and Colombard are the major varieties in this predominantly white wine region; used mainly for distilling, they also produce tasty everyday wines. Chardonnay performs very well, as does the traditional Muscadel (Muscat Blanc à Petits Grains) but Sauvignon Blanc and reds generally have yet to prove themselves. Best producers: Bon Courage, Graham BECK★, DE WETSHOF★, Robertson Winery, Springfield, Van Loveren, Zandvliet.

**ROCKFORD** *Barossa Valley, South Australia*   Wonderfully nostalgic wines from the stone winery of Robert 'Rocky' O'Callaghan, who has a great respect for the old vines so plentiful in the Barossa, and delights in using antique machinery. Produces masterful Basket Press Shiraz★★, 1886 Vine Vale Riesling★, Dry Country Grenache★ and red sparkling cult wine, Black Shiraz★★. Best years: (reds) 1994 93 **92 91 90 87 85**.

**ANTONIN RODET** *Mercurey, Côte Chalonnaise, Burgundy, France*   Merchant based in the village of MERCUREY, specializing in Côte Chalonnaise, but also producing an excellent range from throughout Burgundy. Now controlled by LAURENT-PERRIER, Rodet owns or co-owns 4 domaines – Ch. de Rully★★, Ch. de Chamirey★, Ch. de Mercurey★★ and Jacques Prieur★★ – which are the source of the best wines. Don't miss the BOURGOGNE Vieilles Vignes★, one of the best inexpensive Chardonnays available. Best years: **1995** 93 92 90 89 88.

**LOUIS ROEDERER** *Champagne AC, Champagne, France*   Good-quality firm making some of the best, full-flavoured Champagnes around. As well as the excellent non-vintage★★ and pale rosé★ it also makes a big, exciting vintage★★, and the famous Roederer Cristal★★, a de luxe cuvée which is usually, but not always, delicious. Both the vintage version and Cristal can usually be aged for 10 years or more, depending on its characteristics. Best years: **1991 90 89 88 86 85**.

**ROEDERER ESTATE** *Anderson Valley AVA, California, USA*   Californian off-shoot of French Champagne house Louis ROEDERER. The Brut★★ (sold in the UK as Quartet) is somewhat austere, a step back from the upfront fruit of many California sparklers, but it should age well if you can wait. L'Ermitage★★, a tête de cuvée first released in 1994, is a stunning addition to the range of California fizz.

**ROERO DOC** *Piedmont, Italy*   The Roero hills lie across the Tanaro River from the Langhe hills, home of BAROLO and BARBARESCO. Long noted as a source of Nebbiolo in supple, fruity red wines to drink in 2–5 years, Roero has made its mark with the white Arneis grape. The red wine is called simply Roero and the white Roero Arneis. Best producers: Almondo★, Cantina del Glicine★, CERETTO, Cornarea, Correggia★, Deltetto★, Bruno GIACOSA★, Malabaila, Malvirà★, Monchiero Carbone★, Negro★, Porello★, PRUNOTTO★, Rabino, Enrico Serafino, Vietti★.

**ROMAGNA** *Emilia-Romagna, Italy*   Romagna's wine production is centred on 4 DOCs and 1 DOCG. The whites are from Trebbiano (ineffably dull), Pagadebit (showing promise as both a dry and sweet wine) and Albana (ALBANA DI ROMAGNA was upgraded to DOCG in 1987 and can be made in either dry or sweet versions). The reds are dominated by the Sangiovese grape, which ranges from young and fresh through to wines that can rival a good CHIANTI. Castelluccio makes outstanding Sangiovese, such as Ronco delle Ginestre★★ or Ronco dei Ciliegi★★. Best producers: (Sangiovese) Le Calbane★, Casetto dei Mandorli★, Castelluccio★★, Celli, Conti★, Ferrucci★, La Palazza★, Paradiso★, Spalletti, Tre Monti★, Zerbina★★.

**LA ROMANÉE-CONTI AC**★★★ *Grand Cru, Côte de Nuits, Burgundy, France* For many extremely wealthy wine lovers this is the pinnacle of red Burgundy. It is an incredibly complex wine with great structure and pure, clearly defined fruit flavour, but you've got to age it two dozen years to see what all the fuss is about. The vineyard covers only 1.8ha (4½ acres), which is one reason for the high prices. Wholly owned by Dom. de la ROMANÉE-CONTI. Best years: 1995 93 90 89 88 85 **78 76 71 69**.

**DOM. DE LA ROMANÉE-CONTI** *Vosne-Romanée, Côte de Nuits, Burgundy, France* This famous red wine domaine owns a string of Grands Crus in VOSNE-ROMANÉE (la TACHE★★★, RICHEBOURG★★★, ROMANÉE-CONTI★★★, ROMANÉE-ST-VIVANT★★, ECHEZEAUX★★) and Grands-Échézeaux★★) as well as a small parcel of le MONTRACHET★★★. The wines are all ludicrously expensive but they can be quite sublime – full of fruit when young, but capable of aging for 15 years or more to an astonishing marriage made in heaven and hell of richness and decay. Recent vintages seem to show a necessary return to consistency. At these prices they'd better! Best years: 1995 93 90 89 88 85 **78 71 69**.

**ROMANÉE-ST-VIVANT AC** *Grand Cru, Côte de Nuits, Burgundy, France* By far the largest of VOSNE-ROMANÉE's 6 Grands Crus. At 10–15 years the wines should reveal the keenly balanced brilliance of which the vineyard is capable but a surly, rough edge sometimes gets in the way. Best producers: Arnoux★, DROUHIN★★, JADOT, LATOUR, Dom. LEROY★★, Noëllat★★, Dom. de la ROMANÉE-CONTI★★. Best years: 1995 93 90 89 88 **85 78 76**.

**RONGOPAI** *Te Kauwhata, Auckland, North Island, New Zealand* Small winery whose greatest success has been with bunch- and berry-selected sweet botrytis styles, which include Riesling, Müller-Thurgau and Chardonnay★★. There is also distinctive dry Sauvignon Blanc, Chardonnay★, Riesling and Cabernet Sauvignon. Best years: **1996 94 93 91 90**.

**ROSÉ D'ANJOU AC** *Loire Valley, France* AC for cheap ANJOU rosé that is usually somewhere between off-dry and reasonably sweet. Produced predominantly from the Groslot grape, which doesn't give much colour or flavour. Most of the top producers prefer to use ROSE DE LOIRE or CABERNET D'ANJOU titles. Drink young. Best producer: Caves de la Loire.

**ROSÉ DE LOIRE AC** *Loire Valley, France* AC for dry rosé wine from SAUMUR and TOURAINE but mainly from ANJOU. It can be a lovely grassy drink but drink as young as possible and chill well. Best producers: Cailleau, de l'Echalier, Haute Perche, de Passavant, RICHOU.

**ROSÉ DES RICEYS AC** *Champagne, France* This is a curiosity and an expensive one at that. It's a still, dark pink wine made from Pinot Noir grapes in the southern part of the Champagne region. Best producers: Alexandre Bonnet, Horiot.

**ROSEMOUNT ESTATE** *Hunter Valley, New South Wales, Australia* Model winery buying grapes from several regions to produce some of Australia's best and most popular wines. Top wines are complex, weighty Roxburgh★★★ and Show Reserve★★ Chardonnays; blackcurranty COONAWARRA Cabernet★★ and gutsy Balmoral Shiraz★★★. New Rose label

single-vineyard wines are promising: Chardonnay★★ from the Orange region, McLaren Vale Syrah★, and Yarrawa Sauvignon from the HUNTER. Mountain Blue Shiraz-Cabernet is the most exciting new wine to come out of MUDGEE for a long time. 'Split label' Sémillon-Chardonnay and Shiraz-Cabernet★ are among Australia's best inexpensive gluggers. Best years: (whites) **1995 94 93 91 90 89 87**.

**ROSSESE DI DOLCEACQUA DOC** *Liguria, Italy* A small area producing red wines from the Rossese grape. Styles range from light and fresh to more structured wines. Drink within 3–5 years. Best producers: Cane★, Foresti, Guglielmi, Lupi, Maccario, Perinaldo★.

**ROSSO** Italian for red.

**ROSSO CONERO DOC** *Marche, Italy* The best wines in this zone, on the Adriatic coast just south of Ancona, are made solely from Montepulciano, for they have a wonderfully spicy richness undiluted by the addition of Sangiovese. Wine-making has improved greatly in recent years. Best producers: Leopardi Dittajuti★, Garofoli★★, Mecella (Rubelliano★), Moroder★ (Dorico★★), Le Terrazze (Sassi Neri★), Umani Ronchi★ (Cumaro★★). Best years: 1996 **95 94 93 92 90**.

**ROSSO DI MONTALCINO DOC** *Tuscany, Italy* The little brother of BRUNELLO DI MONTALCINO spends much less time in wood, so retaining a wonderful exuberance of flavour that Brunello loses through its longer cask-aging. Best producers: ALTESINO★, ARGIANO★, BANFI★, Barbi★, Canalicchio di Sopra★, Caparzo★, Casanova di Neri★, Castelgiocondo★, Ciacci Piccolomini d'Aragona★★, Col d'Orcia★, Costanti★★, Fuligni★, La Gerla★, Maurizio Lambardi★★, Lisini★, Siro Pacenti★★, Poggio Antico★, Il Poggiolo★, Il Poggione★, San Filippo★, Talenti★, Valdicava★, Val di Suga★. Best years: 1996 **95 94 93 91 90**.

**ROSSO DI MONTEPULCIANO DOC** *Tuscany, Italy* This DOC, created in only 1989, gives producers the option of honing the production of their grander VINO NOBILE DI MONTEPULCIANO DOCG by diverting some of the younger, juicier vats into bottle at an earlier stage. Some producers turn out a fresh, jammy, rather innocuous style, but the best give the drinker a mouthful of plummy, chocolaty flavours that is pure delight. Best producers: AVIGNONESI, La Braccesca★, Buracchi, Le Casalte★, Contucci★, Dei★, POLIZIANO★, Valdipiatta★. Best years: **1996 95 94 93**.

**ROSSO PICENO DOC** *Marche, Italy* Though related to ROSSO CONERO, this red is often considered a poor relative, since the basic Sangiovese tends to be lean and harsh in the Marche. But when the full complement of Montepulciano is used at 40%, Rosso Piceno can be rich and seductive. Best producers: Boccadigabbia★, Cocci Grifoni★, Velenosi★, Villa Pigna★, Villamagna. Best years: **1996 95 94 93 91 90**.

225

**ROTHBURY ESTATE** *Hunter Valley, New South Wales, Australia* After a protracted fight, Len Evans' brainchild was sold in 1996 to the Fosters brewery, which adds it to its MILDARA-BLASS group of brands. What effect this will have on its wines is uncertain, but Rothbury has a great name for sturdy HUNTER Shiraz★ (Reserve★★) and barrel-fermented Chardonnay★★ as well as quaffing COWRA Chardonnay★ and some of the Hunter's greatest Sémillons★★★. Best years: (whites) **1996 95 93 91 90 86 84 79**; (reds) **1995 93 91 89 87 86 83 81 79**.

**ROUGE** French for red.

**ROUGE HOMME** *Coonawarra, South Australia* Came to the Southcorp stable as part of LINDEMANS, which bought it from the pioneer Redman family (red-man, geddit?) in 1965. Now blossoming in the hands of winemaker Paul Gordon, a whiz with reds. He's smartened up the Cabernet Sauvignon★, Shiraz-Cabernet★ and Pinot Noir★ so they're among the best value for money in the country. New Cabernet blend Richardson's Red Block★★ is a moreish award-winning drop; the white version is fair to middling. Best years: **1994 93 91 90 88 86**.

**ROUSSANNE** The RHONE VALLEY's best white grape variety, Roussanne is frequently blended with Marsanne. Roussanne is the more aromatic and elegant of the two, less prone to oxidation and with better acidity, but growers usually prefer Marsanne due to its higher yields. Now being planted in the MIDI.

**ARMAND ROUSSEAU** *Côte de Nuits, Burgundy, France* One of the most highly respected and important CHAMBERTIN estates, with vineyards in Clos-de-Bèze, Mazis-Chambertin and Charmes-Chambertin as well as CLOS DE LA ROCHE★★ in MOREY-ST-DENIS and GEVREY-CHAMBERTIN Clos St-Jacques★★. The outstandingly harmonious, elegant, yet rich wines are made in a traditional style and enjoy an enviable reputation for longevity. The Chambertin★★★ is exceptionally fine. Best years: 1995 93 **92** 91 90 **89** 88 **85**.

**ROUSSILLON** *France* The snow-covered peaks of the Pyrenees form a spectacular backdrop to the ancient region of Roussillon, now the Pyrénées-Orientales *département*. The vineyards produce a wide range of fairly priced wines, mainly red, ranging from the ripe, raisin-rich Vins Doux Naturels to light, fruity-fresh Vins de Pays. After spending several years in the shadow of the LANGUEDOC renaissance, there are now some really exciting table wines, both white and red, being made in Roussillon, especially by individual estates. See also Banyuls, Collioure, Côtes du Roussillon, Côtes du Roussillon-Villages, Maury, Muscat de Rivesaltes, Rivesaltes.

**RUCHOTTES-CHAMBERTIN AC** See Chambertin AC.

**RÜDESHEIM** *Rheingau, Germany* Village producing silky, aromatic wines from some famous sites (Schlossberg, Berg Rottland, Berg Roseneck and Bischofsberg). Not to be confused with the NAHE village of the same name. Best producers: Georg BREUER★★, Johannishof, J Leitz.

**RUEDA DO** *Castilla y León, Spain* The RIOJA firm of MARQUES DE RISCAL launched the reputation of this white-wine-only region in the 1970s, first by rescuing the almost extinct local grape, Verdejo, then by introducing Sauvignon Blanc. Fresh young whites have been joined by barrel-fermented wines aiming for a longer life, particularly those made by an immigrant from Bordeaux, Brigitte Lurton. Best producers: Alvarez y Diez, Castilla La Vieja (Mirador), Cerro Sol (Doña Beatriz), Belondrade y Lurton★★, Hermanos Lurton★★, MARQUES DE GRINON★, MARQUES DE RISCAL, Angél Rodríguez Vidal (Martinsancho), Vinos Sanz.

**RUFFINO** *Tuscany, Italy*   Huge wine-making concern, whose main business is still centred on basic CHIANTI, though it has succeeded in establishing some fine wines. CHIANTI CLASSICO comes from estates at Zano★, Nozzole★ and Santedame★★, though the classic is Riserva Ducale★★. Vino da Tavolas include Chardonnay Cabreo La Pietra★★, Cabernet Cabreo Il Borgo★★, Pinot Noir Nero del Tondo★ and the unique blend of Colorino and Prugnolo in Romitorio di Santedame★.

**RUINART** *Champagne AC, Champagne, France*   This is one of the oldest Champagne houses. Ruinart has a surprisingly low profile, given the quality of its wines. The non-vintage★ is good, but the top wines here are the excellent, classy Dom Ruinart Blanc de Blancs★★★ and the Dom Ruinart Rosé★★. Best years: **1992 90 88 86 85 83 82.**

**RULLY AC** *Côte Chalonnaise, Burgundy, France*   One of Burgundy's most improved ACs with good-quality, reasonably priced wine. Originally famous for sparkling wines, it is now best-known for its still whites, increasingly aged in oak. Reds are light, with a fleeting strawberry and cherry perfume. Best producers: (whites) Brelière, Chanzy, Delorme, DROUHIN★, Duvernay, FAIVELEY★★, JADOT★, JAFFELIN★, Olivier LEFLAIVE★, RODET★★, de Suremain; (reds) Chanzy, Delorme, Duvernay, la Folie, Jacqueson★. Best years: (whites) **1995 94 92 90**; (reds) **1995 93 90.**

**RUSSE** *Northern Region, Bulgaria*   An up-and-coming star, achieving vibrant, zesty results with Cabernet Sauvignon★ and Merlot★. The low-priced 'country' blends are good.

**RUSSIAN RIVER VALLEY AVA** *Sonoma, USA*   Beginning south of Healdsburg along the Russian River as it flows south-west, this wine valley becomes progressively cooler and foggier toward the south. Seemingly coming from nowhere, it is now challenging Carneros as the top spot for Pinot Noir and Chardonnay. Best producers: DEHLINGER★★★, De Loach★, IRON HORSE★★, Rochioli★★, SONOMA-CUTRER, Rodney Strong★, Joseph SWANN★★, Marimar TORRES★★, WILLIAMS SELYEM★★.

**RUST-EN-VREDE** *Stellenbosch WO, South Africa*   Owner, former Springbok Jannie Englebrecht, and cellarmaster Kevin Arnold produce a range of tailored reds. Recent vintages of Shiraz★ show increasingly pronounced berries-and-spice fruit. Rust-en-Vrede★★, a Cabernet-Shiraz-based blend, is designed to express vintage and estate's terroir. Best years: **1992 91 89.**

**RUSTENBERG** *Stellenbosch WO, South Africa*   This magnificent estate, a national monument, underwent the start of an extensive overhaul in 1996. The new winemaker, New Zealander Rod Easthope, immediately made his mark with 2 stylish Sauvignons, a sleek, steely Rustenberg★★ and broader, nettly Brampton★★, the latter from grapes from owner Simon Barlow's other estate on the Helderberg. Two Chardonnays, similarly labelled, are also good, but it will be red variations on the Cabernet Sauvignon/Franc/Merlot theme which promise to restore the estate to the ranks of the Cape super-league.

**RUTHERFORD AVA** *California, USA*   This recently defined viticultural area in mid-NAPA VALLEY has inspired endless hours of argument and acrimony. The heart of the area – known as the Rutherford Bench – does seem to be a prime Cabernet Sauvignon production zone and many of the traditional old Napa Cabernets have come from Rutherford and exhibit the 'Rutherford Dust' flavour.

**RUTHERGLEN** *Victoria, Australia*   This district in north-east Victoria is the home of heroic reds from Shiraz, Cabernet and Durif, and luscious, world-beating fortifieds from Muscat and Tokay (Muscadelle). There are also good sherry-style and ultra-ripe vintage port-style wines. The whites from Chardonnay and Sémillon are tasty but unsubtle. Best producers: ALL SAINTS★★, Campbells, CHAMBERS★★, MORRIS★★ (fortifieds), St Leonards (whites), Stanton & Killeen.

**HUGH RYMAN** *Bordeaux, France*   One of the most important influences on wine-making in the south and south-west of France, Hugh Ryman, a young English-born winemaker, trained in Australia and Bordeaux, and now makes large quantities of keenly priced wine for the British market. He manages to bolt a fine Australian-type technique on to dry snappily flavoured French fruit. Ryman formed Rystone with Esme Johnson (ex-Majestic) in 1993, which now owns la JAUBERTIE (his family's BERGERAC property), Ch. de Sours and has a 50% share in Vignelaure in Provence. Ryman makes wine all over the south of France and, since 1991, in Spain, Hungary, Moldova, South Africa, California and South America, too. In 1996 he even made Muscadet. He produces sharply fruity wines under a variety of labels. His Vin de Pays d'OC Chardonnay★ and COTES DE GASCOGNE Dom. le Puts★ white are good value for money, as are his GYONGYOS Estate Hungarian Sauvignon and Chardonnay. Also good southern reds including Vin de Pays d'OC Cabernet★.

**SAALE-UNSTRUT** *Germany*   Region located in the former East Germany. In the old days Saale-Unstrut wines were virtually reserved for Party members and their chief reputation was for rarity. But there has been considerable improvement since reunification in 1989. Best producers: Lützkendorf.

**SACHSEN** *Germany*   Until recently one of Europe's forgotten wine regions on the river Elbe in former East Germany. During the last couple of years some good wines have started coming out of Sachsen. Best producers: Schloss Proschwitz, Klaus Seifert, Zimmerling.

**CH. ST-AMAND★** *Sauternes AC, Bordeaux, France*   One of the few non-Classed Growth properties that regularly manages to produce big, rich, classic SAUTERNES, although the price is verging on the high side. The wine is also sold as Ch. la Chartreuse. Best years: (1996) (95) **90 89 88 86 83**.

**ST-AMOUR AC** *Beaujolais, Burgundy, France*   What a lovely name for the northernmost BEAUJOLAIS Cru, producing juicy, soft-fruited wine which lasts well for 2–3 years. Best producers: Billards★, Dom. du Paradis, DUBOEUF, Patissier★, Poitevin, Revillon★, Saillant, Ch. de St-Amour, Spay★. Best years: **1996 95**.

**ST-AUBIN AC** *Côte de Beaune, Burgundy, France* Some of Burgundy's best-value wines. Good reds, especially from Premiers Crus like les Frionnes and les Murgers des Dents de Chien. Also reasonably priced, oak-aged white wines. Best producers: Jean-Claude Bachelet, Clerget★, COLIN, DROUHIN★★, GERMAIN★, JADOT★★, JAFFELIN, Lamy★, Lamy-Pillot★, Olivier LEFLAIVE★, Albert Morey★, Prudhon, RAMONET★★, Roux★, Thomas. Best years: **1995 93 92 90.**

**ST-CHINIAN AC** *Languedoc, France* Large AC for strong, spicy red wines with more personality than run-of-the-mill HÉRAULT, especially when carbonic maceration has been used to extract lots of fruit and colour from the grapes. Best producers: Berlou★ co-op, Cazal-Viel★, Clos Bagatelle, Coujan, la Dournie, Jougla, Maurel Fonsalade★★, Roque-brun★ co-op, St-Chinian co-op. Best years: **1995 94 93 91 90 89.**

**ST-DÉSIRAT, CAVE CO-OPERATIVE DE** *St-Joseph, Rhône Valley, France* St-Désirat is the largest single producer of ST-JOSEPH wines and one of the best co-ops in the RHÔNE VALLEY. The intense, smoky red St-Joseph★★ is a fantastic bargain, as are local Vins de Pays. Best years: **1992 91 90 89.**

**ST-ÉMILION AC** *Bordeaux, France* The Roman hill town of St-Émilion is the centre of Bordeaux's most historic wine region. The finest vineyards are on the côtes, or steep slopes, around the town, although a second large area to the west, called the *graves*, contains 2 of St-Émilion's most famous properties, CHEVAL-BLANC and FIGEAC. It is a region of smallholdings, with over 1000 different properties, and consequently the co-op is important. The dominant Merlot grape gives wines with a 'come hither' softness and sweetness rare in red Bordeaux. St-Émilion AC is the basic generic AC, with 4 so-called satellites (LUSSAC, MONTAGNE, PUISSEGUIN, ST-GEORGES) allowed to annexe their name to it. The best producers, including the Classed Growths, are found in the more controlled ST-EMILION GRAND CRU AC category. Best years: **1995 94 90 89 88 86 85.**

**ST-ÉMILION GRAND CRU AC** *Bordeaux, France* St-Émilion's top-quality AC, which includes the estates classified as Grand Cru Classé and Premier Grand Cru Classé. The 1996 classification lists 55 Grands Crus Classés. Top wines in this category are better value than Premiers Grands Crus Classés and can age for 10–15 years. Best producers: l'ARROSEE★, BALESTARD-LA-TONNELLE★, Canon-la-Gaffelière★, la Dominique★★, Pavie-Decesse★, TERTRE-ROTEBOEUF★★, Soutard★, Troplong-Mondot★★. Best years: (1996) (95) 94 **90 89 88 86 85 83 82.** See also St-Émilion Premier Grand Cru Classé.

**ST-ÉMILION PREMIER GRAND CRU CLASSÉ** *Bordeaux, France* The St-Émilion élite level, divided into 2 categories – 'A' and 'B', with only the much more expensive CHEVAL-BLANC and AUSONE in category 'A'. There are 11 'B' châteaux, with l'ANGELUS and BEAU-SEJOUR-BECOT added in the 1996 Classification. Best producers: l'ANGELUS★★★, AUSONE★★, BEAU-SEJOUR-BECOT★★, Beauséjour★★, BELAIR★, CANON★★, CHEVAL-BLANC★★★, Clos Fourtet★★, FIGEAC★★, MAGDELAINE★★, PAVIE★★. Best years: (1996) (95) 94 90 89 **88 86 85 83 82 79 78 75.**

**ST-ESTÈPHE AC** *Haut-Médoc, Bordeaux, France* Large AC north of PAUILLAC with 5 Classed Growths. St-Estèphe wines have high tannin levels but given time (10–20 years for full development) those sought-after flavours of blackcurrant and cedarwood do peek out. Best producers: CALON-SEGUR★, COS D'ESTOURNEL★★★, Cos Labory★, HAUT-MARBUZET★★, LAFON-ROCHET★★, Lilian-Ladouys★, Marbuzet★, MEYNEY★, MONTROSE★★, les Ormes-de-Pez★★, de PEZ★★. Best years: (1996) (95) 94 90 89 88 86 **85 83 82 78 75**.

**ST-GEORGES-ST-ÉMILION AC** *Bordeaux, France* The best satellite ST-EMILION, with lovely, soft wines that can nevertheless age for 6–10 years. Best producers: Calon, Ch. St-Georges★, Maquin St-Georges★, Tour-du-Pas-St-Georges★, Vieux-Montaiguillon. Best years: 1995 **94 90 89 88 85 83**.

**ST HALLETT** *Barossa Valley, South Australia* Bob McLean manages this revitalized winery which makes Old Block Shiraz★★★, one of BAROSSA's best reds, using very old vines and open fermenters. Sémillon-Sauvignon Blanc★★ and Chardonnay★ are excellent modern whites. Best years: (reds) **1994 93 92 91 90 88 86**.

**ST HELENA** *Canterbury, South Island, New Zealand* This winery achieved fame with New Zealand's first outstanding Pinot Noir in 1982. Finally found form again with 89★★ and 90★★. Also good Pinot Blanc★ and Pinot Gris★. Best years: (Pinot Noir) **1996 95 94 91 90 89**.

**ST HUBERTS** *Yarra Valley, Victoria, Australia* A proud old YARRA VALLEY name dating back to the 1860s. Now its future is up in the air following Fosters' takeover of ROTHBURY, although the brand will continue for the present. Has been respected for crystal-clean Chardonnay★, fragrant Pinot Noir★ and elegant, modern Cabernet★ and Cabernet-Merlot★. Best years: (Cabernet) 1994 **93 92 91 90 88 87 82**.

**ST-JOSEPH AC** *Rhône Valley, France* Large, mainly red AC, on the opposite bank of the Rhône to HERMITAGE. Made from Syrah, the reds have mouthfilling fruit with irresistible blackcurrant richness. Brilliant at 1–2 years, they can last for up to 8. There is only a little white made and, with up-to-date wine-making, these are usually pleasant, flowery wines for drinking without too much ceremony at a year old or so. FLORENTIN makes a rare, hefty, old-style gobsmacker. Best producers: (reds) CHAPOUTIER★, CHAVE★★, COURSODON★★, FLORENTIN★, Gaillard★★, Gonon★, GRAILLOT★, Gripa★★, Grippat★★, JABOULET★, Pinchon★, ST-DESIRAT CO-OP★★; (whites) Cuilleron★, FLORENTIN★, Gripa★★, Grippat★★. Best years: (reds) 1996 **95 92 91 90 89**; (whites) **1996 95 94 92**.

**ST-JULIEN AC** *Haut-Médoc, Bordeaux, France* For many, St-Julien produces perfect claret, with an ideal balance between opulence and austerity and between the brashness of youth and the genius of maturity. It is the smallest of the HAUT-MEDOC ACs but almost all is first-rate vineyard land and quality is high. Best producers: BEYCHEVELLE★★, BRANAIRE★, DUCRU-BEAUCAILLOU★★, GLORIA★★, GRUAUD-LAROSE★★★, LAGRANGE★★, LANGOA-BARTON★★, LEOVILLE-BARTON★★★, LEOVILLE-LAS-CASES★★★, LEOVILLE-POYFERRE★★, ST-PIERRE★★, TALBOT★★. Best years: (1996) (95) 94 93 90 89 88 86 **85 83 82 81 79 78**.

**ST-NICOLAS-DE-BOURGUEIL AC** *Loire Valley, France* An enclave of just under 500ha (1250 acres) within the larger BOURGUEIL AC. Almost all the wine is red and with the same piercing red fruit flavours of

Bourgueil, but a little less weight. They are drinkable at 2–3 years, but are much better after 7–10 years, especially in warm vintages. Best producers: Audebert, P Jamet★★, Lorieux, Mabileau★, Taluau★, Vallée★. Best years: 1995 **93 90 89 88 86 85**.

**ST-PÉRAY AC** *Rhône Valley, France* Rather hefty, Champagne-method fizz from Marsanne and Roussanne grapes from vineyards across the river from Valence. There is also a little still white, which is usually dry and stolid. Best producers: Chaboud, CLAPE, DELAS, Fauterie★, Juge, LIONNET, Thiers★★, Voge. Best years: **1996 95 94**.

**CH. ST-PIERRE★★** *St-Julien AC, 4ème Cru Classé, Haut-Médoc, Bordeaux, France* Small ST-JULIEN property making wines that have become much lusher and richer since 1982, with far more new oak spice. Drinkable early, but top vintages can improve for 20 years. Best years: (1996) (95) 94 93 **90 89 88 86 83 81 79 78 75**.

**ST-ROMAIN AC** *Côte de Beaune, Burgundy, France* Out-of-the-way village producing red wines with a firm, bitter-sweet cherrystone fruit and flinty-dry whites varying between the austerely acid and the quirkily old-style. Both are usually good value by Burgundian standards, and may take at least 5 years to open out. Best producers: (reds) Gras, Thévenin-Monthélie★; (whites) Bazenet★, Buisson, Gras★, JAFFELIN★, Olivier LEFLAIVE, Taupenot, Thévenin-Monthélie★. Best years: (reds) 1995 **93 90**; (whites) 1995 **93 92 90**.

**ST-VÉRAN AC** *Mâconnais, Burgundy, France* Often thought of as a POUILLY-FUISSE understudy. This is gentle, fairly fruity, normally unoaked Mâconnais Chardonnay at its best and the overall quality is good. The price is fair, too. Best to drink young. Best producers: Chagny, Corsin★★, Deux Roches, J-M Drouin★, DUBOEUF★, Grégoire, Loron, Luquet, Lycée Agricole de Davayé, Merlin★, Prissé co-op, Tissier★, Vincent★. Best years: **1996 95 94 93 92**.

**DOM. STE-ANNE** *Côtes du Rhône AC, Rhône Valley, France* Top-notch COTES DU RHONE and COTES DU RHONE-VILLAGES produced by Burgundian expatriate Guy Steinmaier. There are several reasonably priced and marvellously full-throttle reds – COTES DU RHONE★, COTES DU RHONE-VILLAGES★★, Cuvée Notre Dame des Cellettes★★ and Cuvée St-Gervais★★ – as well as good Viognier★. Best years: **1995** 94 93 91 90 89.

**STE-CROIX-DU-MONT AC** *Bordeaux, France* This is the best of the 3 sweet wine ACs that gaze jealously at SAUTERNES and BARSAC across the Garonne river (the others are Cadillac and LOUPIAC). Usually the wine is mildly sweet rather than splendidly rich, and is best drunk as an apéritif or with hors d'oeuvre. The top wines can age for at least a decade. Best producers: Bertranon, Crabitan-Bellevue, Loubens, Lousteau-Vieil★, des Mailles, du Mont, la Rame★. Best years: 1996 **95 90 89 88 86 85 83**.

**SAINTSBURY** *Carneros AVA, California, USA* New wave, deeply committed winery using only CARNEROS fruit. Its Pinot Noirs★★★ are brilliant examples of the perfume and fruit quality of Carneros. The Reserve★★★ is deeper and oakier, while Garnet★ is a delicious, lighter style. Chardonnay★ and Reserve Chardonnay★★ are also impressive, best drunk after 2–3 years. Best years: (Chardonnay) **1994 93 92 91 90**; (Chardonnay Reserve) **1994 93 92 90**; (Pinot Noir Reserve) **1992 91 90**; (Pinot Noir Carneros) **1994 93 92 91 90 87**.

**CH. DE SALES★** *Pomerol AC, Bordeaux, France*  POMEROL's largest property. Tucked in the north-western tip of the AC where the soil is sandier, the wines never have the tingling excitement of the best Pomerols but are reasonably priced. Quick to mature, they are still capable of aging for 10 years in bottle. Best years: (1996) (95) 94 **90 89 88 82**.

**SALICE SALENTINO DOC** *Puglia, Italy*  Probably the best of the DOCs in the Salento peninsula, turning out wines that are deep-coloured, ripe and chocolaty, acquiring hints of roast chestnuts and prunes with age. The wine is made from the ubiquitous Negroamaro grape, tempered by a dash of the perfumed Malvasia Nera. Drink after 3 or 4 years, although they may last as long again. Best producers: Candido★, De Castris★, Taurino★, Vallone★.

**SAMOS** *Greece*  The island of Samos was granted an appellation and a Grand Cru in 1982 but its reputation for producing rich, sweet dessert wines from the Muscat grape stretches back centuries. The 2 wineries of the Samos co-op make wines almost identical in style. Pale green Samena dry white★ made from early-picked Muscat, deep gold, honeyed Samos Nectar★★ and the seductively complex Samos Anthemis★★, cask-aged for up to 5 years.

**SAN LUIS OBISPO COUNTY** *California, USA*  Central Coast county best known for Chardonnay, Pinot Noir, a bit of old-vine Zinfandel and Cabernet Sauvignon. There are 5 AVAs – Edna Valley, Paso Robles, SANTA MARIA VALLEY (shared with SANTA BARBARA COUNTY), Arroyo Grande Valley and York Mountain, each of which has already grown some outstanding grapes and will surely grow a lot more. Best producers: Clairborne & Churchill, Corbett Canyon, Creston Vineyards, Eberle★★, Edna Valley, Maison Deutz, Martin Brothers, Meridian, Talley, Wild Horse.

**SAN PEDRO** *Curicó, Chile*  A take-over by Chile's biggest brewer, along with the arrival of Jacques Lurton as consultant, has turned the fortunes of San Pedro around. The quality of Gato Negro Cabernet Sauvignon and Cabernet-Merlot has leapt in the last 2 vintages; but the Castillo de Molina range shows just what a little more money can buy. Crisp, clean Sauvignon Blanc★★, Chardonnay Reserve★ and Merlot★ are the wines to watch.

**SANCERRE AC** *Loire Valley, France*  Sancerre mania broke out in the 1970s, firstly with the white wine which can provide the perfect expression of the bright green tang of the Sauvignon grape, then with the reds and rosés which are made from Pinot Noir. Consequently the wine is rather expensive and of variable quality. The whites, from a good grower in one of the best villages like Bué, Chavignol, Verdigny or Ménétréol in the chalky rolling land around the hill town of Sancerre, can be deliciously refreshing, so too can the rare Pinot Noir rosé. Reds, also from Pinot Noir, really need hot years like 1989 and 90 to be good. Drink the wines young. Best producers: Bailly-Reverdy★, Bourgeois★, Cotat★★, Crochet★★, Daulny, Alain & Pierre Dezat★, André Dezat, Fouassier, Gitton★★, A Mellot★, Midgeon, Milliérioux★, Natter★, Pellé, Reverdy★, Jean-Max Roger★, Vacheron★, Vatan★. Best years: 1996 **95 93 90 89**.

**SANDEMAN** *Port DOC, Douro, Portugal and Jerez y Manzanilla DO, Spain*
No longer one of the 'First Growths' of port, Sandeman says it is trying to improve quality. We'll wait and see. Partners is a reliable ruby. Best at the moment are the aged tawnies, 10-year-old★ and 20-year-old★★. Sandeman's major sherry export markets are Germany and the Netherlands. Best years: (vintage ports) **1980 77 67 66 63**.

**SANFORD** *Santa Ynez Valley AVA, California, USA* Richard Sanford was one of the first Californians to appreciate the importance of matching specific vineyard sites with suitable grape varieties, and one of the first to seek out cool, slow-ripening conditions especially for Pinot Noir. He planted the great Benedict vineyard in the Santa Ynez Valley in 1971, thus establishing Santa Ynez and SANTA BARBARA as potentially top-quality vineyard regions. Sanford is now one of the leading Santa Barbara wineries, making sharply focussed, green-edged Pinot Noir★★, Chardonnay★★ and Sauvignon Blanc★. A new series of 'Signature' Pinot Noir★★ is especially impressive.

**SANGIOVESE** The Sangiovese rivals Trebbiano Toscano as the most widely planted grape variety in Italy. It is grown throughout the country from LOMBARDY in the north through ROMAGNA, the MARCHE and UMBRIA to PUGLIA and SICILY in the deep south, but reaches its greatest heights in central TUSCANY. This grape has produced a wide variety of clones that make generalization difficult. Furthermore, recent research has shown that there is no close correlation between grape size and quality. After widespread planting with inferior but high-yielding clones produced in Romagna in the late 1960s and early 70s, much care is being taken in the current wave of replanting, whether in CHIANTI CLASSICO, BRUNELLO DI MONTALCINO or VINO NOBILE DI MONTEPULCIANO. Styles range from pale, lively and cherryish through the vivacious, mid-range Chiantis to the top Riservas and Super-Tuscans. At the latter level, Sangiovese shows itself to be one of the great grapes of the world. California producers like ATLAS PEAK, FETZER, Robert Pepi and Seghesio are now working some of their magic on this grape. There are one or two quite interesting examples from Argentina. See also Super-Tuscans.

**SANTA BARBARA COUNTY** *California, USA* Central Coast county, just north of Los Angeles, which is best known for Chardonnay, Riesling and Pinot Noir. The main AVAs are Santa Ynez Valley and most of SANTA MARIA VALLEY (the remainder is in SAN LUIS OBISPO COUNTY), both leading areas for Pinot Noir. Best producers: AU BON CLIMAT★, Babcock★, Byron★, CAMBRIA, Firestone, Foxen★★, Lane Tanner (Pinot Noir★★★), QUPE★★, SANFORD★★, Whitcraft, Zaca Mesa★.

**SANTA MADDALENA DOC** *Alto Adige, Italy* Light, delicate wine from the Schiava grape grown in the hills above Bolzano. It has an attractive perfume of black cherries, cream and bacon smoke, and can be improved no end with the addition of up to 10% of Lagrein. The best wines are generally from the original Classico zone. Drink young but some vintages can age. Best producers: Franz Gojer-Glögglhof★, Gries co-op, LAGEDER★, Hans Rottensteiner★, Heinrich Rottensteiner★, Santa Maddalena co-op, Thurnhof.

**SANTA MARIA VALLEY AVA** *California, USA*   Cool Santa Maria Valley is coming on strong as a producer of Chardonnay and Pinot Noir. Look for wines made from grapes grown in Bien Nacido and Sierra Madre vineyards by several small wineries. Best producers: AU BON CLIMAT★, Byron★, CAMBRIA, Foxen★★, Lane Tanner (Pinot Noir★★★), QUPE★★.

**SANTA RITA** *Maipo, Chile*   Signs are emerging that this MAIPO giant is climbing out of the doldrums. CANEPA's Andrés Ilabaca has joined up as winemaker and has some great fruit to work with. Juicy, plum-packed CASABLANCA Merlot★★ shows what he can do. Medalla Real range is currently more reliable than the 120 portfolio.

**SANTENAY AC** *Côte de Beaune, Burgundy, France*   There are some good wines here. The reds often promise good ripe flavour, but are usually disappointing, although worth aging for 4–6 years in the hope that the wine will open out. The best whites, as with the reds, come from les Gravières Premier Cru on the border with CHASSAGNE-MONTRACHET, one of Burgundy's top white wine villages. Best producers: (reds) Belland, Clair, COLIN★, Fleurot-Larose, GERMAIN, J Girardin★, V Girardin★, Mestre, Bernard Morey★, Pousse d'Or★, Prieur-Brunet, Roux★; (whites) JAFFELIN, Lequin-Roussot, Maufoux, Prieur-Brunet. Best years: (reds) 1995 **93 90 89 88 85**; (whites) 1993 **92 90 89 88 85**.

**SARDINIA** *Italy*   Grapes of Spanish origin, like the white Vermentino and Torbato and the red Monica, Cannonau and Carignano, dominate production on this huge, hilly Mediterranean island, but they vie with a Malvasia of Greek origin and natives like Nuragus and Vernaccia. The cooler northern part favours whites, especially Vermentino, while the southern and eastern parts are best suited to reds from Cannonau and Monica. The wines were powerful, alcoholic monsters, but the current trend is for a lighter style. See also Carignano del Sulcis, Vermentino, Vernaccia di Oristano.

**SASSICAIA DOC★★★** *Tuscany, Italy*   This Cabernet Sauvignon-Cabernet Franc blend from the coast has done more than any other wine to gain credibility abroad for Italy. Vines were planted in 1944 to satisfy the Marchese Incisa della Rochetta's thirst for fine red Bordeaux, which was in short supply during the war. The wine remained purely for family consumption until nephew Piero Antinori (of ANTINORI) and winemaker Giacomo Tachis persuaded the Marchese to refine production practices and to release several thousand bottles from the 1968 vintage. Since then, Sassicaia's fame has increased as it consistently proved itself to be one of the world's great Cabernets, combining a blackcurrant power of blistering intensity with a heavenly scent of cigars. It is the first Italian single-owner estate wine to have its own DOC, within the BOLGHERI appellation, from the 1994 vintage. Best years: (1996) (95) 94 93 92 91 90 88 **85 82 81 78 75 71 68**.

**SAUMUR AC** *Loire Valley, France*   Improving dry whites from around Saumur, made mainly from Chenin Blanc, but 20% of Chardonnay can be added. The reds are lighter than those of SAUMUR-CHAMPIGNY. There is a little dry to off-dry Cabernet rosé and sweet Coteaux de Saumur in good vintages. Best producers: Beauregard, Fourrier, de la Paleine, Reclu, de la Renière★, St-Cyr-en-Bourg co-op, Tessier, Vatan★★, Villeneuve★★. Best years: (red) 1996 **95 94 93 90 89**.

**SAUMUR-CHAMPIGNY AC** *Loire Valley, France*   Saumur's best red wine. Cabernet Franc is the main grape and in hot years the wine can be superb, with a piercing scent of blackcurrants and raspberries easily overpowering the earthy finish. Delicious young, it can age for 6–10 years. Best producers: Cordeliers★, Drouineau★, FILLIATREAU★★, Foucault★★, T Germain★★, Neau★, Val Brun★, Vatan★★, Villeneuve★★. Best years: **1996 95 94 93 90 89**.

**SAUMUR MOUSSEUX AC** *Loire Valley, France*   Reasonable Champagne-method sparkling wines made mainly from Chenin Blanc. Adding Chardonnay and Cabernet Franc makes Saumur Mousseux softer and more interesting. Usually non-vintage. Small quantities of rosé are also made. Best producers: BOUVET-LADUBAY★, GRATIEN & MEYER★, Grenelle★, St-Cyr-en-Bourg co-op★.

**SAUTERNES AC** *Bordeaux, France*   The name Sauternes is synonymous with the best sweet wines in the world. Sauternes and BARSAC both lie on the banks of the little river Ciron and are 2 of the very few areas in France where noble rot occurs naturally. Production of these intense, sweet, luscious wines from botrytized grapes is a risk-laden and extremely expensive affair and the wines are never going to be cheap. From good producers (most of which are Crus Classés) the wines are worth their high price – with 14% alcohol they have a richness full of flavours of pineapples, peaches, syrup and spice. Good vintages should be aged for 5–10 years and they can often last twice as long. Best producers: BASTOR-LAMONTAGNE★★, de FARGUES★★, GILETTE★★, GUIRAUD★★, les Justices★, LAFAURIE-PEYRAGUEY★★★, Lamothe-Guignard★, de Malle, Rabaud-Promis★, Rayne-Vigneau★, RIEUSSEC★★, ST-AMAND★, SUDUIRAUT★★, la Tour-Blanche★, d'YQUEM★★★. Best years: (1996) (95) **90 89 88 86 83 81 80 76 75 71 70**. See also Noble Rot.

**SAUVIGNON BLANC** See pages 236–7.

**SAVENNIÈRES AC** *Loire Valley, France*   The AC for wines from Chenin Blanc, produced on steep vineyards above the Loire south of Anjou and which have always been thought of as steely and dry. They also used to appear in semi-sweet and sweet styles, and with the great 1989 and 90 vintages, we've seen a revival of these. The top wines usually need at least 8 years to mature, and can age for longer. There are 2 extremely good Grand Cru vineyards with their own ACs, la Coulée-de-Serrant and la Roche-aux-Moines. Best producers: Baumard★★, Clos de la Coulée-de-Serrant★★, Closel★★, d'Épiré★★, Laroche★, Pierre-Bise, Soulez★, Tijou. Best years: (1996) 95 93 91 **90 89 88 85 83 82 78 76 71 70 69 66**.

**SAVIGNY-LÈS-BEAUNE AC** *Côte de Beaune, Burgundy, France*   This is a large village that concentrates its production mainly on red wines. The reds are usually middle weight and are best drunk at 4–10 years from the vintage. The top Premiers Crus are more substantial yet rarely shed their rather earthy core. The white wines manage to show a bit of dry, nutty class after 3–4 years. All the wines are generally reasonably priced. Best producers: Bize, Camus-Bruchon★, Capron-Charcousset★, Écard★, Girard-Vollot★, V Girardin★, Guillemot, Jacob★, Maréchal★, Pavelot★★, TOLLOT-BEAUT★★. Best years: (reds) 1995 **93 92 90 89 88**; (whites) **1995 93 92 90**.

# SAUVIGNON BLANC

Of all the world's grapes, the Sauvignon Blanc is leader of the 'love it or loathe it' pack. It veers from being wildly fashionable to totally out of favour depending upon where it is grown and which country's consumers are being consulted. But Sauvignon is always at its best when full rein is allowed to its very particular talents because this grape does give intense, sometimes shocking flavours, and doesn't take kindly to being put into a straitjacket.

*WINE STYLES*

**Sancerre-style Sauvignon** Although initially used largely as a blending grape in Bordeaux, where its characteristic green tang injected a bit of life into the blander, waxier Sémillon, Sauvignon first became trendy as the grape used for Sancerre, a bone-dry Loire white whose green gooseberry fruit and slightly smoky perfume inspired the winemakers of other countries to try to emulate, then often surpass the original model.

But Sauvignon is only successful where it is respected. The grape is not as easy to grow as Chardonnay, and the flavours are not so adaptable. Yet the range of styles Sauvignon produces is as wide, if less subtly nuanced, as those of Chardonnay. It is highly successful when picked not too ripe, fermented cool in stainless steel, and bottled early. This is the Sancerre model followed by growers elsewhere in France, in Italy, Portugal, Spain and Eastern Europe, increasingly in South Africa and Chile, but above all in New Zealand.

**Using oak** Sauvignon also lends itself to fermentation in barrel and aging in new oak, though less happily than does Chardonnay. This is the model of the Graves region of Bordeaux, although generally here Sémillon would be blended in with Sauvignon to good effect.

New Zealand again excels at this style, though there are good examples from California, Australia, northern Italy and South Africa. In southern Styria (Steiermark) a handful of producers makes powerful, aromatic versions with a touch of oak. In all these regions the acidity that is Sauvignon's great strength should ideally remain, but there should be a dried apricots kind of fruit and a spicy, biscuity softness from the oak. These oaky styles are best drunk either within about a year, or after aging for 5 years or so, and can produce remarkable, strongly individual flavours that you'll either love or loathe.

**Sweet wines** Sauvignon is also a crucial ingredient in the great sweet wines of Sauternes and Barsac from Bordeaux, though it is less susceptible than its partner Sémillon to the sweetness-enhancing 'noble rot' fungus or botrytis.

Sweet wines from the USA, South Africa, Australia and, inevitably, New Zealand range from the interesting to the outstanding – but the characteristic green tang of the Sauvignon should stay in the wine even at ultra-sweet levels.

## BEST PRODUCERS

**Top-class Sauvignons**

*France* (Pouilly-Fumé) Didier DAGUENEAU, André Dezat; (Sancerre) Bourgeois, Cotat, Crochet, Jean-Max Roger; (Pessac-Léognan) Couhins-Lurton, SMITH-HAUT-LAFITTE.

*New Zealand* Allan Scott, CLOUDY BAY, COOPERS CREEK, Highfield Estate, HUNTER'S, Isabel, Jackson Estate, MATUA VALLEY, PALLISER, SELAKS, VAVASOUR, VILLA MARIA, Wairau River.

**Other good Sauvignons**

*Australia* Bridgewater Mill, Brookland Valley, DELATITE, HANGING ROCK, KATNOOK, Pikes, SHAW & SMITH, STAFFORD RIDGE, Yarra Ridge.

*Austria* Polz, Gross, TEMENT.

*Chile* VINA CASABLANCA.

*France* (Bergerac) la JAUBERTIE; (Touraine) OISLY-ET-THESEE co-op.

*Hungary* GYONGYOS ESTATE.

*Italy* Edi Kante, LAGEDER, ORNELLAIA, SCHIOPETTO, Vie di Romans, Villa Russiz.

*New Zealand* Lawson Dry Hills, MONTANA, Rothbury (Marlborough), SEIFRIED.

*South Africa* BUITENVERWACHTING, Neil ELLIS (Elgin), KLEIN CONSTANTIA, MULDERBOSCH, SAXENBURG, THELEMA, VILLIERA.

*USA* (California) KENWOOD, MATANZAS CREEK, Murphy-Goode.

**SAVOIE** *France* Savoie's high alpine vineyards, which are scattered between Lake Geneva and Grenoble and on the banks of the Rhône and Isère rivers, produce fresh, snappy white wines with loads of flavour, when made from the Altesse (or Roussette) grape. There are some attractive light reds and rosés, too, mainly from a group of villages south of Chambéry and, in hot years, some positively Rhône-like reds from the Mondeuse grape. Most of the better wines use the VIN DE SAVOIE AC. See also Crépy, Seyssel.

**SAXENBURG** *Stellenbosch WO, South Africa* Two harvests a year are a feature of winemaker Nico van der Merwe's life. He creates some of the Cape's most sought-after reds, led by a headily scented, burly Private Collection Shiraz★★★; hardly a grape pip's breath behind in the same line are Cabernet★★, Merlot★★, as well as whites Sauvignon★★ and Chardonnay★★. Nico is aiming for the same magic at Swiss-owner Adrian Bührer's other estate, Ch. Capion in the LANGUEDOC.

**SCHEUREBE** Very popular Silvaner x Riesling crossing most widespread in Germany's Rheinhessen and Pfalz. Also planted in Austria, where it is frequently sold under the name Sämling 88. Suitable for higher Prädikat wines such as Trockenbeerenauslese and Eiswein. When ripe it has a marvellous flavour of honey and the pinkest of pink grapefruit.

**SCHIOPETTO** *Friuli-Venezia Giulia, Italy* Mario Schiopetto is one of the legends of Italian viniculture, pioneering the development of scented varietals and, above all, high-quality, intensely concentrated white wines from COLLIO. Most outstanding are Tocai★★ and Pinot Bianco★★, both of which begin life as intense but closed wines, opening out with age to display a myriad range of flavours.

**SCHLOSS REINHARTSHAUSEN** *Erbach, Rheingau, Germany* Estate formerly wholly owned by the Hohenzollern family, which ruled Prussia and then Germany until 1918. There are several fine vineyard sites, including the great Erbacher Marcobrunn. There is an interesting organic Weissburgunder-Chardonnay blend from its vines in Erbacher Rheinhell, an island in the middle of the Rhine. Superb Rieslings★★ (some ★★★) and good Sekt★. Best years: 1995 94 **93 92 90 89**.

**SCHLOSS SAARSTEIN** *Serrig, Saar, Germany* This estate makes some of the best wines in the Saar. The Riesling Dry can taste a little austere; better balanced are wines like the Serriger Riesling Kabinett★ or Spätlese★ and Auslese★★, which keep the startling acidity but coat it with fruit, often with the aromas of slightly unripe white peaches. Saarstein makes the occasional spectacular EISWEIN★★★. Best years: 1995 **93 92 90 89 88 86 85**.

**SCHLOSS VOLLRADS** *Oestrich-Winkel, Rheingau, Germany* Now jointly managed by Graf Matuschka-Greiffenclau and his nephew Markus Matuschka. Although there have been persistant rumours about the impending sale of the estate, present ownership continues. The Graf has been making it his business for some years now to tell people how to drink his wines with food. To anyone brought up in France his ideas would sound decidedly weird, but Matuschka does have his followers, though few of them live outside his native Germany. Most of his wines are angular, austere and lean, but he occasionally produces

Spätlese and Auslese beauties as good as any in the Rhine Valley. Keep the best vintages for 5–10 years. Best years: 1995 **90 89 88 85 83**.

**SCHLOSSBÖCKELHEIM** *Nahe, Germany* This NAHE village's best-known sites are the Felsenberg and Kupfergrübe but good wines come from Mühlberg and Königsfels. Best producers: Paul Anheuser, CRUSIUS★, Hermann DONNHOFF★★, Staatlichen Weinbaudomänen Niederhausen-Schlossböckelheim.

**SCHLOSSGUT DIEL** *Burg Layen, Nahe, Germany* One of the NAHE's best estates, where Armin Diel used to attract publicity by making unconventional wines. Diel was in the vanguard of the move towards 'dry' wines in Germany. Possibly the first man in Germany to use oak fermentation for wines like his Tafelwein Grauburgunder 1984. Some may find the oakiness exaggerated. He produces more traditional wines from his Dorsheimer Goldloch site, where in 1990 and 93 he made excellent Spätlese★★ and Auslese★★ wines, as well as imposing EISWEIN★★★. Best years: **1995 93 92 90 89 88**.

**SCHRAMSBERG** *Napa Valley AVA, California, USA* The first California winery to make Champagne-method sparklers from the classic Champagne grapes. Though all releases do not achieve the same heights, the best can be unequalled in California – and in most of CHAMPAGNE too. The Crémant★ is an attractive sweetish sparkler, the Blanc de Noirs★ and the Blanc de Blancs★★ stand out. Top of the line is the Reserve Brut★★★, which is frequently world class. A recent release called J Schram was initially disappointing but later releases have achieved ★★ status.

**SEAVIEW** *Southern Vales, South Australia* Best known for good, mass-market fizz★ and excellent Pinot-Chardonnay★★ and Blanc de Blancs★★ but, along with commercial-quality reds and whites, occasionally produces super export selection Cabernet★. Impressive new premium brand is Edwards & Chaffey★★.

**SEIFRIED ESTATE** *Nelson, South Island, New Zealand* Established in 1974 by Austrian Hermann Seifried and his New Zealand wife Agnes. The best wines include botrytized Riesling★★ and Gewürztraminer★ and Sauvignon Blanc★★. The Redwood Valley label is used in export markets. Best years: **1996 94 91**.

**SEKT** German for sparkling wine. The wine will be entirely German only if it is called 'Deutscher Sekt' or 'Sekt bA'. The best wines are Champagne method and will occasionally be 100% Riesling. Best producers: Bergdolt, KOEHLER-RUPRECHT, Max Ferd RICHTER, SCHLOSS REIN-HARTSHAUSEN★, WEGELER-DEINHARD (Lila).

**SELAKS** *Kumeu/Huapai, Auckland, North Island, New Zealand* A long-established winery making New Zealand's best Sauvignon Blanc-Sémillon★★★ and an increasingly good Sauvignon Blanc★★; also Chardonnay★ and Riesling★. Best years: **1996 94 91**.

**SELBACH-OSTER** *Zeltingen, Mosel, Germany* Johannes Selbach is one of the MOSEL's new generation of star winemakers, producing very pure, elegant Riesling★★. Best years: 1995 94 **93 92 91 90 89 88 85**.

**SÉLECTION DE GRAINS NOBLES** *Alsace AC, Alsace, France* This term is used for late-harvest wines made exclusively from super-ripe Muscat, Riesling, Gewürztraminer or Pinot Gris grapes. Usually sweet or medium-sweet and should be affected by noble rot, they are among

Alsace's finest, but are very expensive to produce (and to buy). Best producers: HUGEL★★★, Schlumberger★★, TRIMBACH★★, ZIND-HUMBRECHT★★★. Best years: 1995 92 **90 89 83 76**.

**SELLA & MOSCA** *Sardinia, Italy* Apart from the rich, port-like Anghelu Ruhu★ made from semi-dried Cannonau grapes, this much-modernized old firm produces excellent dry whites, Terra Bianche★ (Torbato), La Cala★ (Vermentino) and oak-aged reds, Marchese di Villamarina★ (Cabernet) and Tanca Farrà★★ (Cannonau-Cabernet). Best years: (reds) 1995 94 **93 90 89 88**.

**SELVAPIANA** *Chianti DOCG, Tuscany, Italy* This 25-ha (62-acre) estate in CHIANTI RUFINA has always produced excellent, refined wines that are typical of the zone. But from 1990 it has vaulted into the top rank of Tuscan estates, particularly with the Riserva★★ and single-vineyard Riserva, Vigna Bucerchiale★★★. Best years: 1996 95 94 **93 91 90 88 86 85**.

---

**SÉMILLON** Found mainly in south-west France, especially in the sweet wines of SAUTERNES and BARSAC where, because of its thin skin, it is prone to NOBLE ROT. Also blended with Sauvignon to make dry wine – almost all the great GRAVES Classed Growths are based on this blend. Performs well in Australia (aged Sémillon, particularly from the HUNTER VALLEY, can be wonderful) on its own or as a blender with Chardonnay. It is blended with Sauvignon in New Zealand, Australia, CALIFORNIA and WASHINGTON STATE. Enjoying a revival in the South African Cape, where it is primarily a bulk blender, but barrel-fermented varietals and blends with Sauvignon produce outstanding results.

---

**SEPPELT** *Barossa Valley, South Australia and Grampians, Victoria* Leading Australian fizz factory, from mass-produced Great Western 'champagne' up to excellent Fleur de Lys★, and on to Drumborg★, Harpers Range★ and Salinger★★, all made by the Champagne method from Pinot Noir and Chardonnay. They are pristine and fruity with minor yeast influence. A Sauvignon fizz called Rhymney is the latest addition. Table wines are generally good, especially Great Western Shiraz★ and Chardonnay★, Dorrien Cabernet★, Partalunga Riesling★, and wines from super-cool Drumborg. Also wonderful sparkling red Show Reserve Shiraz★★ (the 85 is ★★★) and top-notch fortifieds (some ★★★).

**SETÚBAL DOC** *Terras do Sado, Portugal* Fortified wine from the Setúbal Peninsula south of Lisbon, which is called 'Moscatel de Setúbal' when made from at least 85% Moscatel, and 'Setúbal' when it's not. Best producers: José Maria da FONSECA SUCCESSORES★, J P VINHOS.

**SEYSSEL AC** *Savoie, France* Known for its feather-light, sparkling wine, Seyssel Mousseux. With the lovely sharp, peppery bite of the Molette and Altesse grapes smoothed out with a creamy yeast, it is an ideal summer gulper. The still white is light and floral. Best producers: Mollex, Varichon & Clerc★.

---

**SEYVAL BLANC** Hybrid grape (Seibel 5656 x Rayon d'Or) whose disease resistance and ability to continue ripening in a damp autumn make it a useful variety in England, Canada and NEW YORK STATE and other areas in the eastern US. Gives clean, sappy, grapefruit-edged wines that are sometimes a very passable imitation of bone-dry CHABLIS.

240

**SHAFER** *Stags Leap AVA, California, USA* One of the best of the newer NAPA wineries, making unusually fruity Stags Leap district Cabernet★★ and a Reserve-style Hillside Select★★★. Merlot★★ is increasingly important; now from the Red Shoulder Vineyard in CARNEROS, Chardonnay is greatly improved. Best years: (Cabernet Stags Leap) **1994 92 90 87**; (Cabernet Hillside Select): **1993 92 91 90 85 84**.

**SHAW & SMITH** *Adelaide Hills, South Australia* Cousins Michael Hill Smith – Australia's first MW and operator of a noted wine bar – and Martin Shaw, an ex-flying wine-maker, had a runaway success with their deep, tangy Sauvignon★★

from the first vintage in 1989. Not a pair to rush in, they have gradually added a wooded Reserve★★ and unwooded Chardonnay★ to the list but, as yet, no red. Best years: **1995 94 93 92 91**.

**SHERRY** See Jerez y Manzanilla DO.

**SHIRAZ** See Syrah.

**SICILY** *Italy* It is very hot on the island, and the traditional wines are the high-strength examples that make use of these conditions, and those that are fortified (MARSALA). Yet classy table wines can be produced in the cooler uplands. Grillo, Cataratto and Inzolia are the best white grapes, but the boring Trebbiano is becoming far too common. The best reds come from Calabrese (or Nero d'Avola), Perricone and Nerello Mascalese. See also Alcamo, Corvo, Etna, Moscato Passito di Pantelleria, Vecchio Samperi.

**SIEUR D'ARQUES, LES CAVES DU** *Limoux AC and Blanquette de Limoux AC, Languedoc, France* This well-organized and modern co-op dominates the production of the still and sparkling wines of LIMOUX, making around 90% of the area's wines. The BLANQUETTE DE LIMOUX and CREMANT DE LIMOUX★ are both reliable but the real excitement comes with the Toques et Clochers Chardonnays★. The co-op also makes a range of white and red varietal Vins de Pays.

**SILVER OAK CELLARS** *Napa Valley, California, USA* One of California's best Cabernet Sauvignon producers, with bottlings from ALEXANDER VALLEY★★ grapes and NAPA VALLEY★★ as well as a superlative limited release Bonny's Vineyard★★★, last produced in 1991. Forward, generous, fruity wines, impossible not to enjoy young, yet with great staying power. Best years: (Alexander Valley) **1994 93 92 91 90 88 87 85**; (Napa Valley) **1994 93 92 91 90 88 87 86 85 84 82**; (Bonny's Vineyard) **1991 90 86**.

**SILVERADO** *Napa Valley AVA, California, USA* Owned by a branch of the Disney family, there's nothing Mickey Mouse about the splendid Cabernet Sauvignon★★ and Chardonnay★★ from this estate winery. The regular bottling of Cabernet has intense yet playful fruit and is drinkable fairly young. A Limited Reserve bottling has more depth and is capable of some aging. The Chardonnay has soft, inviting fruit and a silky finish and is best within 2–3 years of the vintage. A fruity Merlot and Super-Tuscan-style Sangiovese are also much in demand. Best years: (Reserve) **1993 91 90 87 86**.

**SIMI** *Alexander Valley AVA, California, USA* Historic winery which was revitalized by the arrival of Zelma Long as winemaker in 1979 and the purchase by current owner Moët-Hennessy in 1981. Long has brought the Cabernet Sauvignon★, Chardonnay★★ and Sauvignon Blanc★ up to high standards, and the Chardonnay Reserve has occasionally reached ★★★.

**SIMONSIG** *Stellenbosch WO, South Africa* A family-owned estate with winemaker Johan Malan showing nimble ability in the cellar. The extensive, varied range contains many top-notch wines: Tiara★, a Bordeaux blend; a fruitily concentrated unwooded Pinotage★; dry Riesling★, Chardonnay★★, Gewürztraminer dessert wine★ and the Cape's first commercially produced Cap Classique sparkler, Kaapse Vinkel★★, are the most noteworthy.

**SION** *Valais, Switzerland* Considered one of the top wine villages in the VALAIS and best known for its pure Chasselas Fendant. Best producers: Michel Clavien★, Domaine du Mont d'Or★.

**CH. SIRAN★** *Margaux AC, Cru Bourgeois, Haut-Médoc, Bordeaux, France* Consistently good claret, approachable young, but with enough structure to last for as long as 20 years. Second wine: Ch. Bellegarde. Best years: (1996) (95) **90 89 86 85 83 82**.

**SKALLI-FORTANT DE FRANCE** *Languedoc-Roussillon, France* Robert Skalli produces modern, varietal wines under the Vins de Pays d'OC label. The oak-influenced Chardonnay★, Sauvignon Blanc and Syrah★ are Skalli's best wines. The cheaper range is called Fortant; Fortant de France is reserved for the more expensive wines. Best years: **1995 94 93**.

**SLIVEN** *Southern Region, Bulgaria* This winery is now providing some of Bulgaria's best, cleanest Chardonnay. The reds, like the juicy Merlot-Pinot Noir Country Wine, deliver the goods, too.

**CH. SMITH-HAUT-LAFITTE** *Pessac-Léognan AC, Cru Classé de Graves, Bordeaux, France* Large property best known for its reds★, now one of the most improved and innovative estates in PESSAC-LEOGNAN AC since a change of ownership in 1990. There is only a little white★★ (from 100% Sauvignon) but it is a shining example of tip-top modern white Bordeaux. Best years: (reds) (1996) (95) 94 90 **89 88 86 85 83**; (whites) (1996) **95 94 92 90**.

**SMITH WOODHOUSE** *Port DOC, Portugal* Underrated but consistently satisfying port from this shipper. The Smith Woodhouse vintage★★ is worth looking out for, and its Late Bottled Vintage Port★★ is the rich and characterful, figgy, unfiltered type. Best years: (vintage ports) 1994 91 85 83 **80 77 70 63**.

**SOAVE DOC** *Veneto, Italy* In the hilly Soave Classico zone near Verona, the Garganega and Trebbiano di Soave grapes can produce ripe, nutty, scented wines of great quality. However, 70% of all Soave comes from the flat fertile plains and much of this is cynically blended by merchants into a limp, tasteless white. Since 1992, the legal addition of 30% of Chardonnay should help. The DOC also applies to Recioto di Soave, made from dried grapes, a sweet wine that is outstanding from ANSELMI and PIEROPAN. Luckily, the dominant local co-op can produce good wine. Best producers: ANSELMI★★, Bertani★, BOLLA★, La Cappuccina, Gini★, Inama, MASI★, PIEROPAN★★, Prà★, Soave co-op, Suavia★.

**CH. SOCIANDO-MALLET★★** *Haut-Médoc AC, Cru Bourgeois, Haut-Médoc, Bordeaux, France*   Owner Jean Gautreau has made this one of Bordeaux's star Crus Bourgeois now worthy of classification. The wine is dark and tannic with every sign of great classic red Bordeaux flavours to come if you can hang on for 10–15 years. Best years: (1996) (95) 94 93 90 89 88 86 **85 83 78**.

**SOGRAPE** *Portugal*   Sogrape proves that it is possible to be the biggest *and* among the best and can be credited with revolutionizing quality in some of Portugal's most reactionary wine regions. Mateus Rosé is still the company's golden egg. but Sogrape makes good to very good wines in BAIRRADA★, DAO★, DOURO (reds★) and VINHO VERDE as well. and subsidiary FERREIRA provides top-flight ports and BARCA VELHA★★, one of Portugal's best reds. Bairrada Reserva Branco★ is a nutty, oaky white, previously unparalleled in Portugal. First signs from the new winery in Dão are hopeful; Grão Vasco is set to improve; Quinta dos Carvalhais Branco★ is oaky, marmalady and characterful; the Duque de Viseu red★★ is crammed with ripe, oaky, mulberry fruit. Excellent new red from the ALENTEJO: Vinha do Monte★. Offley-Forrester (formerly owned by Martini) now belongs to Sogrape.

**SOKOL BLOSSER WINERY** *Willamette Valley AVA, Oregon, USA*   Consistently good Chardonnay★★ (Redland) and sometimes outstanding, though not as consistent, Pinot Noir★★ (Redland). The Chardonnay tends to the buttery, toasty style, while the several versions of Pinot Noir emphasize a soft, rather elegant fruit.

**SOLAIA, VINO DA TAVOLA★★★** *Tuscany, Italy*   ANTINORI's stylish blend of Cabernet Sauvignon and Cabernet Franc, together with about 20% Sangiovese. comes from a vineyard adjacent to TIGNANELLO in CHIANTI CLASSICO. Some consider the opulent, elegant Solaia to be the top rival to SASSICAIA among Cabernet-based Super-Tuscans. Best years: (1996) (95) 94 93 90 88 **86 85 82 79 78**.

**SOLERA** Traditional Spanish system of blending fortified wines, especially sherry and MONTILLA-MORILES. See also Jerez y Manzanilla DO/Sherry.

**SOMONTANO DO** *Aragón, Spain*   In the foothills of the Pyrenees, this region is an up-and-coming star. Reds and rosés from the local grapes (Moristel and Tempranillo) can be light, fresh and flavourful, and new plantings of international varieties such as Chardonnay and Gewürztraminer are already yielding promising wines. An interesting development is the rediscovery of the soft native red grape, Moristel. Best producers: COVISA★★, VCAA★ (Enate), Bodega Pirineus★.

**SONOMA COUNTY** *California, USA*   Sonoma's vine-growing area is big and sprawling, with dozens of soil types and mesoclimates, from the fairly warm SONOMA VALLEY/ALEXANDER VALLEY region to the cool Green Valley and lower RUSSIAN RIVER VALLEY. The best wines are from Chardonnay, Sauvignon Blanc, Cabernet Sauvignon and Zinfandel. Catching up with rival NAPA in quality and originality of flavours. See also Carneros, Dry Creek Valley.

**SONOMA-CUTRER** *Russian River Valley AVA, California, USA*   Crisp, pleasant but often overrated Chardonnay from 3 vineyards. Les Pierres is the most complex and richest of the 3, often worth ★★. Cutrer★ can also have a complexity worth waiting for but the Russian River Ranches is usually rather flat and ordinary.

**SONOMA VALLEY AVA** *Sonoma, USA*   The oldest wine region north of San Francisco, Sonoma Valley is situated on the western side of the Mayacamas Mountains, which separate it from NAPA VALLEY. Though similar, the climate is somewhat drier, and present plantings favour red varieties. **Best producers:** ARROWOOD★★, BUENA VISTA, CHATEAU ST JEAN★, CARMENET★★, B R Cohn, Fisher★, GUNDLACH-BUNDSCHU★, KENWOOD★, KISTLER★★, KUNDE★, LAUREL GLEN★★★, MATANZAS CREEK★★, RAVENSWOOD★★, St Francis★, Sebastiani.

**SOUTH AUSTRALIA**   Australia's biggest grape-growing state, with 25,000ha (62,000 acres) of vineyards. Covers many climates and most wine styles from bulk wines to the very best. Old established areas are BAROSSA, CLARE and Eden valleys, SOUTHERN VALES, Langhorne Creek, COONAWARRA and RIVERLAND. Newer districts creating excitement are ADELAIDE HILLS and PADTHAWAY, Koppamurra and Limestone Coast.

**SOUTH-WEST FRANCE**   As well as the world-famous wines of Bordeaux, south-west France has many lesser-known, inexpensive ACs, VDQS and VdPs, over 10 different *départements* from the Atlantic coast to Languedoc-Roussillon. Bordeaux grapes (Cabernet, Merlot and Cabernet Franc for reds; Sauvignon, Sémillon and Muscadelle for whites) are common, but there are lots of interesting local varieties as well, such as Tannat (in MADIRAN), Petit Manseng (in JURANCON) and Mauzac (in GAILLAC). See also Bergerac, Cahors, Côtes de Duras, Côtes du Frontonnais, Côtes de Montravel, Gaillac, Irouléguy, Monbazillac, Montravel, Pacherenc du Vic-Bilh.

**SOUTHERN VALES** *South Australia*   Sunny maritime region just south of Adelaide, with about 45 mainly small wineries, and big boys HARDY and SEAVIEW. Once a 'port' area, nowadays it is good for full-bodied whites and reds from Chardonnay, Sauvignon Blanc, Shiraz, Grenache and Cabernet. **Best producers:** CHAPEL HILL★★, CHATEAU REYNELLA★★, Coriole, D'Arenberg, Andrew Garrett, HARDY★★, Ingoldby, Geoff MERRILL★, Normans, SEAVIEW★, WIRRA WIRRA★★, Woodstock.

**SPÄTBURGUNDER**   See Pinot Noir.

**SPÄTLESE**   German for literally 'late-picked' and therefore riper grapes, but this is a question of must weight of the juice. In Germany the Oechsle level runs from 76 for a Mosel Riesling to 92 for a Baden Ruländer. In Austria a Spätlese must be 19 KMW or 94 Oechsle.

**SPUMANTE**   Italian for 'sparkling'. Bottle-fermented wines are often referred to as *metodo classico* or *metodo tradizionale*.

**SQUINZANO DOC** *Puglia, Italy*   The name today evokes memories of deep-coloured, high-strength wines, for it was the Italian blending wine par excellence. A blend of Negroamaro and Malvasia Nera grapes, the wines are too often clumsy, though potential undoubtedly exists. **Best producer:** Santa Barbara co-op.

**STAFFORD RIDGE** *Adelaide Hills, South Australia*   Geoff Weaver, who put many runs on the board as chief winemaker at HARDY, dedicates himself to crafting fine wines from grapes grown only on his 10-ha planting at Lenswood. He uses the PETALUMA winery to vinify his deliciously limy Riesling★, crisply gooseberryish Sauvignon★★ and pungently tropical, fruit-driven Chardonnay★★. Cabernet-Merlot is only a mild success.

**STAG'S LEAP WINE CELLARS** *Stags Leap AVA, California, USA* The winery's fame was made when the Cabernet Sauvignon 1973 came first at the Paris tasting of 1976. At its best, Cabernet Sauvignon★★ can be a stunning wine, particularly the SLV Reserve★★★ from estate vineyards; the Cask 23 Cabernet Sauvignon★ is good, sometimes very good, but is overhyped. Recent vintages haven't measured up to earlier standards. A lot of work has gone into the Chardonnay and from the 89 vintage★★ the style is one of NAPA's most successful. Best years: (reds) 1993 **92 91 90 89 88 84 81 79**; (whites) **1993 91 90**.

**STAPLE ST JAMES** *Kent, England* A small but well-run vineyard near the Kent coast, whose vibrantly fruity Huxelrebe★ is consistently one of England's best bone-dry whites.

**STEELE WINES** *Lake County, California, USA* Owner and winemaker Jed Steele is a master blender. He sources grapes from vineyards all over California and shapes them into exciting wines, usually featuring vivid fruit with supple mouthfeel. But he also offers single-vineyard wines and has, in current release, 4 Chardonnays★. His Zinfandels★ are often superb and his Pinot Noirs (CARNEROS, SANTA MARIA VALLEY) are better than most. Shooting Star is a budget second label, which provides remarkable value in a ready-to-drink style.

**STEIERMARK** *Austria* Known as Styria in English, this wine region in south-east Austria formerly covered much of Slovenia's vineyards, too. The best wines are Morillon (unoaked Chardonnay, though oak is catching on here as well), Sauvignon Blanc and Gelber Muskateller. Best producers: Gross★, Polz★, Sattlerhof, TEMENT★★.

**STELLENBOSCH WO** *South Africa* Considered the hub of the South African wine industry, this fine red wine region boasts the greatest concentration of wineries in the Cape, with vineyards straddling valley floors and stretching up the many mountain slopes. Climates and soils are as diverse as wine styles; the renowned reds are matched by some excellent Sauvignon Blanc and Chardonnay. The major wholesalers and the Oenological and Viticultural Research Station have their headquarters here. Best producers: Avontuur, BERGKELDER, Beyerskloof★, Blaauwklippen, Clos de Ciel★★, Delheim, Eikendal, Neil ELLIS★★, GRANGEHURST★, Hartenberg, Jordan★, KANONKOP★★, L'Avenir★, Le Bonheur, Lievland★, LOUISVALE★, MEERLUST★★, Morgenhof★, MULDERBOSCH★★, Neethlingshof★, Overgaauw★, RUST-EN-VREDE★, RUSTENBERG★★, SAXENBERG★★, SIMONSIG★, STELLENZICHT★★, THELEMA★★★, Uiterwyk, Vergelegen★, Vriesenhof, WARWICK★★.

**STELLENBOSCH FARMERS' WINERY** *Stellenbosch, South Africa* South Africa's largest producer, buying in wine and grapes and with leading brands in every sector. Whites generally have a more modern touch than reds in top-of-the-range Zonnebloem. Two wineries in PAARL also fall under SFW's wing: Nederburg and Plaisir de Merle. Nederburg's standard range is sound if unexciting. Its outstanding botrytised dessert, Edelkeur★★, is sold only through annual auction. Plaisir de Merle is the company's showpiece winery: winemaker Neil Bester was tutored at Ch. MARGAUX's by Paul Pontallier, who still advises here. In only two vintages, the soft yet beautifully structured Cabernet Sauvignon★★ has shot to the top of the rankings; the Merlot★★ looks likely to follow.

# SUPER-TUSCANS

*Tuscany, Italy*

The term 'Super-Tuscans', first used by English and American writers, has now been adopted by Italians themselves to describe the new-style red wines of Tuscany. The 1970s and 80s were a time when enormous strides were being made in Bordeaux, Australia and California, yet these changes threatened to bypass Italy completely because of its restrictive wine laws. A group of winemakers, led by Piero Antinori, abandoned tradition to put their best efforts and best grapes into creative wines styled for modern tastes, replacing old casks with barriques, while planting Cabernet and other trendy varieties, such as Merlot, Pinot Noir and Syrah, alongside Sangiovese in vineyards that emerged with sudden grandeur as crus. Since the DOC specifically forbade such innovations, producers were forced to label their wines as plain Vino da Tavola. The 'Super-Tuscan' Vino da Tavolas, as they were quickly dubbed, were a phenomenal success: brilliant in flavour with an approachable, upfront style, although foreigners find it hard to believe that table wines with no official credentials could outrank DOCG Chianti in prestige and price.

## WINE STYLES

**Renaissance wines** The phenomenon began in the 1970s with Sassicaia, the Cabernet from the coast, soon followed by Antinori's Tignanello, the prototype blend of Sangiovese with Cabernet grown in Chianti Classico and raised in the requisite French barrels.

**Traditional wines** Some producers kept their faith in the natives. Montevertine produced Le Pergole Torte in 1976 as the first pure Sangiovese aged in French oak. Sangiovese has regained eminence among Super-Tuscans, though critics outside Italy often prefer wines based on French varietals.

## CLASSIFICATIONS

A law passed in 1992 should bring most Super-Tuscans into line with official classifications. Sassicaia now has its own DOC under Bolgheri; Chianti Classico's newly independent DOCG would cover many a Sangiovese-based Super-Tuscan; and plans for a regional Toscana DOC would create niches for superior wines from the international varieties. A consortium of producers uses the name Capitolato to specify 4 types of table wine, followed by an identifying term: Biturica (mainly Cabernet), Cardisco (mainly Sangiovese), Selvante (mainly Sauvignon) and Muschio (mainly Chardonnay or Pinot Bianco).

---

See also BOLGHERI, CHIANTI CLASSICO, SASSICAIA, SOLAIA, TIGNANELLO, VINO DA TAVOLA; AND INDIVIDUAL PRODUCERS.

LA GIOIA
di Riecine
PRODUCT OF ITALY
1993

VINO DA TAVOLA DI TOSCANA
IMBOTTIGLIATO ALL'ORIGINE DA
JOHN ABBAGNANO-DUNKLEY
GAIOLE IN CHIANTI - ITALIA
750 ML ℮          13% VOL.
NON DISPERDERE IL VETRO NELL'AMBIENTE

(1996) 95 94 93 **90 88 86 85**

BEST PRODUCERS

**Sangiovese and other Tuscan
varieties** ALTESINO (Palazzo
Altesi), Badia a Coltibuono
(Sangioveto), BOSCARELLI
(Boscarelli), Castellare (I Sodi
di San Niccolò), FELSINA
BERARDENGA (Fontalloro), Fontodi
(Flaccianello della Pieve),
ISOLE E OLENA (Cepparello),
MONTEVERTINE (Le Pergole Torte,
Il Sodaccio), Poggio Scalette
(Il Carbonaione), POLIZIANO
(Elegia), Querceto (La Corte),
RIECINE (La Gioia), San Giusto a
Rentennano (Percarlo), VOLPAIA
(Coltassala).

**Sangiovese-Cabernet blends**
ANTINORI (Tignanello), AVIGNONESI
(Grifi), Fonterutoli (Concerto),
Querciabella (Camartina),
RAMPOLLA (Sammarco), VOLPAIA
(Balifico).

**Cabernet** ANTINORI (SOLAIA), Col
d'Orcia (Olmaia), ISOLE E OLENA
(Collezione), Nozzole (Il Pareto),
POLIZIANO (Le Stanze).

**Merlot** AVIGNONESI, CASTELLO DI
AMA (Vigna L'Apparita),
ORNELLAIA (Masseto).

**Cabernet-Merlot blends**
Capezzana (Ghiaie della Furba),
ORNELLAIA (Ornellaia), Terriccio
(Lupicaia, Tassinaie).

**STELLENZICHT** *Stellenbosch WO, South Africa* Dynamic and hugely talented winemaker Andre van Rensburg is totally dedicated to quality. In his first vintage, he produced Syrah★★★, which beat PENFOLDS Grange in the controversial 1995 South Africa/Australia wine test match; he tackles underrated Sémillon with the same fervour. Botrytized desserts★★ (Riesling and Sémillon-Sauvignon) are rivalled only by those from sister winery Neethlingshof.

**STERLING VINEYARDS** *Napa Valley AVA, California, USA* After more than 20 vintages as winemaker, Bill Dyer was replaced by Greg Fowler of MUMM NAPA. Reserve Cabernet★★ is good to very good, while the regular bottling is improving. Winery Lake Pinot Noir★ is now beginning to hit its stride. The NAPA VALLEY Chardonnay★ is rich and intense but balanced. Best years: (reds) 1994 **92 91 90 87 86 85**.

**STONIER'S** *Mornington Peninsula, Victoria, Australia* Book publisher Brian Stonier's winery is the peninsula's biggest and a quality leader, with occasionally stunning Reserve Chardonnay★★ and Reserve Pinot★★ as well as fine standard bottlings, although nothing is cheap. Cabernets are rather herbaceous, in the greenish regional style.

**STONYRIDGE** *Waiheke Island, Auckland, North Island, New Zealand* A leading winery on WAIHEKE ISLAND, Stonyridge specializes in reds made from Cabernet Sauvignon, Merlot and Cabernet Franc. The top label, Larose★★, is a remarkably Bordeaux-like red of real intensity. Best years: 1996 94 93 **91 89 87**.

**CH. SUDUIRAUT★★** *Sauternes AC, 1er Cru Classé, Bordeaux, France* Together with RIEUSSEC, Suduiraut is regarded as a close runner-up to d'YQUEM. Although the wines are delicious at only a few years old, the richness and excitement increase enormously after a decade or so. Very expensive and seemed to be under-performing since the mid-1980s but now owned by AXA of PICHON-LONGUEVILLE fame, so watch out! Best years: (1996) **90 89 88 82 79 76**.

**SUHINDOL** *Northern Region, Bulgaria* The old warhorse among Bulgarian wineries, and the first to be privatized. It perfected the creamy, curranty, throat-soothing style of Cabernet Sauvignon now synonymous with Bulgaria, and it does a good Cabernet-Merlot blend too.

**SUPER-TUSCANS** See pages 246–7.

**SUPÉRIEUR** French for a wine with a higher alcohol content than the basic AC. Bordeaux Supérieur, for example, has a minimum of 10.5% alcohol by volume, compared with 10% for straight Bordeaux.

**SUPERIORE** Italian for DOC wines with higher alcohol or more aging than the norm.

**SUTTER HOME** *Napa Valley AVA, California, USA* Now known for White Zinfandel, Sutter Home still makes a very drinkable Amador County Zinfandel, although it doesn't achieve the intensity and richness of its Zins of the 1970s and early 80s.

**SWAN VALLEY** *Western Australia* The original WESTERN AUSTRALIA wine region and the hottest stretch of vineyards in Australia, spread along the torrid, fertile silty flats of Perth's Swan River. It used to specialize in fortified wines, but SOUTH AUSTRALIA and north-east VICTORIA both do them better. New wave whites and reds, especially from Moondah Brook and Houghton, are encouraging. Best producers: Paul Conti, EVANS & TATE, HOUGHTON★, Moondah Brook, Westfield.

**JOSEPH SWAN VINEYARDS** *Russian River Valley AVA, California, USA*
Joseph Swan made legendary Zinfandel in the 1970s and was one of the first to age Zinfandel★★ in French oak. In the 1980s he turned to Pinot Noir★★ which is now probably the winery's best offering. After Swan's death in 1989, his son-in-law, Rod Berglund, took over as winemaker. Best years: 1994 **93 92 91**.

**SYRAH** See pages 250–1.

**LA TÂCHE AC**★★★ *Grand Cru, Côte de Nuits, Burgundy, France* Along with la ROMANEE-CONTI, la Tâche is the greatest of the great VOSNE-ROMANEE Grands Crus and it is similarly owned by Dom. de la ROMANEE-CONTI. The wine has the rare ability to provide layer on layer of flavours. Keep it for 10 years or you'll only experience a fraction of the pleasures you paid big money for. Best years: 1995 93 90 **89** 88 **85 78**.

**TAFELWEIN** German for table wine.

**TAITTINGER** *Champagne AC, Champagne, France* One of the few large independently owned Champagne houses. The top wine, Comtes de Champagne Blanc de Blancs★★, used to be memorable for its creamy, foaming pleasures, but hasn't been so hot recently. Ordinary non-vintage★ is soft and honeyed and shows the relatively high percentage of Chardonnay used by Taittinger in the blend. The Comtes de Champagne rosé★★ is elegant and always enjoyable. Another de luxe cuvée, called Vintage Collection★, is certainly good, but sells at a silly price. Best years: **1991 90 89 88 86 85 82 79**. See also Bouvet-Ladubay.

**CH. TALBOT**★★ *St-Julien AC, 4ème Cru Classé, Haut-Médoc, Bordeaux, France* A fine Fourth Growth: chunky, soft-centred but sturdy, capable of aging extremely well for 10–20 years. Second wine: Connétable Talbot. Best years: (1996) (95) 94 90 89 88 **86 85 83 82 81 79 78**.

**TALTARNI** *Pyrenees, Victoria, Australia* Biggest winery in this region, specializing in classic, deep-flavoured, European-style Cabernet★, Syrah★★, Merlot and Malbec; also good and improving fizz, especially new Clover Hill★ from Tasmania. Fumé Blanc★★ is full yet tangy and gooseberry-like. Best years: (reds) 1994 93 **92 91 90 88 86 84 82**.

**TANNIN** Harsh, bitter element in red wine, derived from grape skins and stems, and from oak barrels. Tannins soften with age and are essential for long-term development in reds.

**TARRAWARRA** *Yarra Valley, Victoria, Australia* Clothing magnate and arts patron Marc Besen wanted to make a le MONTRACHET, and hang the expense. His winemakers are on the right track: Tarrawarra Chardonnay★★ is deep and multi-faceted, but Pinot Noir★★ is just as good, with almost COTE DE NUITS flavour and concentration. Tunnel Hill is a less costly brand of both, but no other varieties are planted or planned. Best years: **1994 92 90 89 88**.

---

**TASMANIA** *Australia* Situated off the southern coast of Australia, Tasmania is a minor state viticulturally, with only 400ha (1000 acres) of vines. The very cool climate has attracted seekers of greatness in Pinot Noir and Chardonnay, but doesn't always deliver. Top Pinots are great but they're a minority, Chardonnay is usually good and often superbly refined, and there is some delicious Riesling. An important supplier of grapes for sparkling wine. Best producers: Delamere, Freycinet, HEEMSKERK, Moorilla, Notley Gorge, PIPERS BROOK★★, Rowella, Spring Vale, Stoney.

# SYRAH/SHIRAZ

Syrah so far produces world-class wines in only 2 countries. In France, where Hermitage and Côte-Rôtie are 2 of the world's great reds; and in Australia, where as Shiraz it produces some of the New World's most remarkable reds. And wherever Syrah appears it trumpets a proud and wilful personality based on loads of flavour and unmistakable originality.

Perhaps it is exactly this proud and wilful personality that has thus far limited its spread round the warmer wine regions of the world, but there may be another reason. Syrah's heartland – Hermitage and Côte-Rôtie in the Rhône Valley – comprise a mere 270ha (670 acres) of steeply terraced vineyards producing hardly enough wine to make more than a very rarefied reputation for themselves. Growers in countries like Italy, Spain, California or Eastern Europe simply had no idea as to what kind of flavour the Syrah grape produced, so didn't copy it.

*WINE STYLES*
**French Syrah** The flavours of Syrah are most individual, but with modern vineyard practices and modern wine-making techniques they are far less daunting than they used to be. Traditional Syrah had a savage, almost coarse, throaty roar of a flavour. And from the very low-yielding Hermitage vineyards, the small grapes often showed a bitter tannic quality.

But better selections of clones in the vineyard, and the replacement of old, dirty equipment and antediluvian wine-making practices with stainless steel, clean, new wood, and scientifically correct wine-making, have revealed that Syrah in fact gives a wine with a majestic depth of fruit, all blackberry and damson, loganberry and plum, some quite strong tannin, and some tangy smoke, but also a warm creamy aftertaste, and a promise of chocolate and occasionally a scent of violets. It is these characteristics that have made Syrah increasingly popular throughout the south of France as an 'improving' variety for its rather rustic red wines.

**Australian Shiraz** Australia's most widely planted red variety is often used for light, soft, bulk wines. But it can give spectacularly good results when taken seriously – especially in the Clare, Eden Valley and Barossa regions of South Australia, in Victoria's warmer vineyards (especially those in the Grampians region), and in New South Wales' Hunter Valley. The flavours are rich, intense, thick sweet fruit coated with chocolate, and seasoned with leather, herbs and spice. It is frequently blended with Cabernet Sauvignon to add a little richness to Cabernet's more angular frame.

**Other regions** In California more producers are turning out superb southern-Rhône-like blends as well as varietal examples modelled closely on Côte-Rôtie or Hermitage. In South Africa, too, some exciting wines are appearing from the small band who have put their faith in Shiraz.

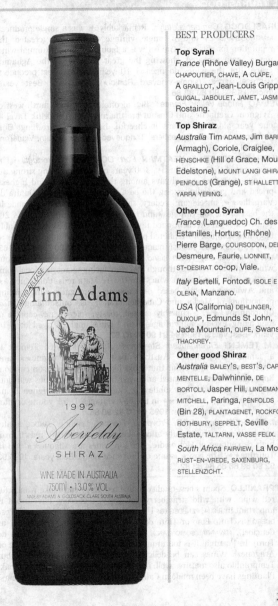

## BEST PRODUCERS

**Top Syrah**

*France* (Rhône Valley) Burgaud, CHAPOUTIER, CHAVE, A CLAPE, A GRAILLOT, Jean-Louis Grippat, GUIGAL, JABOULET, JAMET, JASMIN, Rostaing.

**Top Shiraz**

*Australia* Tim ADAMS, Jim BARRY (Armagh), Coriole, Craiglee, HENSCHKE (Hill of Grace, Mount Edelstone), MOUNT LANGI GHIRAN, PENFOLDS (Grange), ST HALLETT, YARRA YERING.

**Other good Syrah**

*France* (Languedoc) Ch. des Estanilles, Hortus; (Rhône) Pierre Barge, COURSODON, DELAS, Desmeure, Faurie, LIONNET, ST-DESIRAT co-op, Viale.

*Italy* Bertelli, Fontodi, ISOLE E OLENA, Manzano.

*USA* (California) DEHLINGER, DUXOUP, Edmunds St John, Jade Mountain, QUPE, Swanson, THACKREY.

**Other good Shiraz**

*Australia* BAILEY'S, BEST'S, CAPE MENTELLE, Dalwhinnie, DE BORTOLI, Jasper Hill, LINDEMANS, MITCHELL, Paringa, PENFOLDS (Bin 28), PLANTAGENET, ROCKFORD, ROTHBURY, SEPPELT, Seville Estate, TALTARNI, VASSE FELIX.

*South Africa* FAIRVIEW, La Motte, RUST-EN-VREDE, SAXENBURG, STELLENZICHT.

251

**TAURASI DOCG** *Campania, Italy* Remarkably, it was a single producer, MASTROBERARDINO, and a single vintage, 1968, that created the reputation for this red. The 68 was a fabulous, deep autumnal wine, never again repeated, showing the great potential of the Aglianico grape. But the wines do need 5–10 years' aging. Best producers: MASTROBERARDINO (single-vineyard Radici★), Struzziero. Best years: (recent) 1993 90 **89 88 86**.

**TAVEL AC** *Rhône Valley, France* Big, alcoholic rosé from north-west of Avignon. Grenache and Cinsaut are the main grapes. Drink Tavel at one year old if you want it cheerful, heady, yet refreshing. Best producers: Aquéria, Genestière, Trinquevedel, Vieux Moulin, Vignerons de Tavel.

**TAYLOR FLADGATE & YEATMAN** *Port DOC, Douro, Portugal* The aristocrat of the port industry, 300 years old and still going strong. Its vintage ports★★★ are always among the longest-lived and highest-priced and generally among the best. The second wine is Quinta de Vargellas★★, an elegant, cedary, single-quinta vintage port made in the best of the 'off-vintages' and released when mature. Taylor's 20-year-old★ is an excellent aged tawny, and Taylor's LBV is reasonably figgy and complex for a filtered port. Keep the best vintage ports for at least 25 years. Best years: (vintage ports) 1994 92 85 83 **80** 77 **75 70 66** 63.

**TE MATA** *Hawkes Bay, North Island, New Zealand* HAWKES BAY's glamour winery and still its best, though it is now facing increasing local competition. The best-known wines are the Te Mata reds, Coleraine★★★ and Awatea★★, both based on Cabernet Sauvignon with varying proportions of Merlot and Cabernet Franc. Also outstanding Elston Chardonnay★★★, a superbly crafted, toasty, spicy wine, capable of long aging. Exceptional vintages of all 3 wines might be aged for 5–10 years. Best years: 1996 **94 91 90 89 83 82**.

**E & M TEMENT** *Ehrenhausen, Steiermark, Austria* Manfred Tement is a fanatic who makes Austria's best Sauvignon Blanc★★ and Chardonnay★★ in a cellar that looks like a Heath Robinson cartoon. Both varieties are fermented and aged in oak, giving wines with lots of power and depth but subtle oak character. The Sauvignon Blanc from the Zieregg site is ★★★ in the best vintages. Drink young or after short keeping. Best years: **1995 94 93 92 90 88**.

**DOM. TEMPIER** *Bandol AC, Provence, France* Leading BANDOL estate, run by the Péyraud family and making rich, ageworthy reds from a high percentage of Mourvèdre. The top wines are Migoua★★ and la Tourtine★★. The rosé★ is one of Provence's best. Best years: 1995 **93 92 90 89 88 85 84 83 82**.

---

**TEMPRANILLO** Spain's best-quality native red grape can make wonderful red wine, with wild strawberry and spicy, tobaccoey flavours. It is important in RIOJA, PENEDES (as Ull de Llebre or Ojo de Liebre), RIBERA DEL DUERO (as Tinto Fino or Tinta del País), LA MANCHA and VALDEPENAS (as Cencibel), NAVARRA, SOMONTANO, UTIEL-REQUENA and TORO (as Tinto de Toro). In Portugal it is found in the DOURO and DAO (as Tinta Roriz or Aragonez). Wines can be deliciously fruity for drinking young, but Tempranillo also matures well, and its flavours blend happily with oak. Plantings have been made in California and Oregon in the past 2 years.

**TERLANO DOC** *Trentino-Alto Adige, Italy* Primarily white wine DOC
zone, to the north and east of Bolzano, which is especially good for
Chardonnay, Pinot Bianco and Sauvignon. Best producers: LAGEDER
(Sauvignon Lehenhof★★), Schwanburg, Terlano co-op★.

**TEROLDEGO ROTALIANO DOC** *Trentino-Alto Adige, Italy* Teroldego is a
native TRENTINO variety, producing deep-coloured, grassy, blackberry-
flavoured wine on the gravel soils of the Rotaliano plain. Best
producers: Barone de Cles★, Conti Martini★, Dorigati★, Foradori★★,
Gaierhof, A & R Zeni★.

**TERRA NOBLE** *Maule, Chile* Small Talca-based winery making only 2
wines: a grassy, mineral-edged Sauvignon Blanc and a light Nouveau-
style Merlot. Loire wizard Henri Marionnet acts as consultant.

**TERRAS DO SADO** *Setúbal Peninsula, Portugal* Area south of Lisbon
with 2 IPR regions, Arrábida and Palmela. SETUBAL – decent enough fortified wine – is the local celebrity but is fast being outstripped by excellent
table wines, particularly red from Periquita with Cabernet and Merlot. Best
producers: FONSECA SUCCESSORES★, J P VINHOS★.

**CH. DU TERTRE★★** *Margaux AC, 5ème Cru Classé, Haut-Médoc,
Bordeaux, France* Obscure MARGAUX property at last gaining the
recognition it deserves. With lots of fruit and tannin, the wine is
usually delicious at 5–6 years old, but will happily age for 10–15
years. Best years: (1996) (95) 94 **93 90 89 88 86 85 82 80 79 78**.

**CH. LE TERTRE-RÔTEBOEUF★★** *St-Émilion Grand Cru AC, Bordeaux,
France* ST-EMILION's most exceptional unclassified estate. The richly
seductive, Merlot-based wines sell at the same price as the Premiers
Grands Crus Classés. Best years: (1996) (95) 94 90 89 **88 86 85**.

**THACKREY & CO.** *Marin County, California, USA* A tiny winery (1500
cases) with a cult following for huge Rhône-style red wines, especially
the Orion★★, made from Syrah grapes grown in NAPA, and a
Mourvèdre called Taurus★. The wines are well thought of by those
who prefer power over elegance. All can age for 5 years or more.

**THAMES VALLEY** *Berkshire, England* Eighteen grape varieties planted
over 13ha (32 acres) from which 2 Aussies, viticulturist Jon Leighton
and consultant winemaker John Worontschak, produce full-flavoured
wines, many with antipodean-style use of oak. Fumé★ is a remarkable
Graves-lookalike, and won the Gore-Brown Trophy in 1993.
Worontschak, the force behind the HARVEST WINE GROUP, is also mad keen
on sweet wine★ and fizz★ (Heritage Brut won the Gore Brown trophy
in 1996). My feeling is: we ain't seen nothing yet.

**H THANISCH** *Bernkastel, Mosel, Germany* This is the rump of the original Thanisch estate. The labels remain substantially the same, so look
out for the VDP eagle, which will tell you that you have the wine
which is still in family hands. The Thanisch heirs have kept a chunk
of the famous DOCTOR vineyard too. Quality improved up to 1992 but
has been problematic since. Best years: **1992 90 89 88 76**.

**THELEMA MOUNTAIN VINEYARDS** *Stellenbosch WO, South Africa* This
family-owned winery, like its mountainside vineyards, continues to
scale dizzy heights. In the 1996 SAA wine list awards, winemaker
Gyles Webb repeated his red/white trophy successes of 1995 and then

went on to take his second Diner's Club Award with a rich, blackcurranty 94 Cabernet Sauvignon★★★. The vineyards, too, win prizes, which shows where Webb's priorities lie. A Cabernet-Merlot★★★ blend laced with violet perfume, barrel-fermented Chardonnay★★★, poised Sauvignon Blanc★★ and less-hyped Riesling★ are all excellent. Best years: (reds) **1994 93 92 91**; (whites)**1996 95 94 93 92 91**.

**THERMENREGION** *Niederösterreich, Austria* This region, to the south of Vienna, derives its name from the thermal spa towns of Baden and Bad Vöslau. Just south of Vienna is the village of Gumpoldskirchen with its rich and often sweet wines. The red wine area around Baden produces large amounts of Blauer Portugieser together with a couple of good examples of Pinot Noir and Cabernet. Best producer: Stadlmann★.

**THREE CHOIRS** *Gloucestershire, England* Martin Fowke makes the wine at this 28-ha (68-acre) vineyard. The impressive range includes zingy New Release, sold at the same time as BEAUJOLAIS NOUVEAU. Estate Premium Medium Dry★, from Seyval Blanc, Reichensteiner and Müller-Thurgau, is the main seller, and he has been making a sparkling wine★ since 1990.

**PAUL THOMAS** *Washington State, USA* Now on the rebound since being acquired by Associated Vintners (owners of Columbia Winery) a few years ago. A new 100-ha (220-acre) vineyard is the source of both a very successful Chardonnay★ and the Cabernet-Merlot★ blend. These show a judicious oak influence given by the intelligent use of oak chips – something the winery is refreshingly open about. At least a dozen other wines are made in the constantly changing line-up, but the Sémillon★ is particularly noteworthy. Best years: **1995 94 93**.

**TICINO** *Switzerland* Italian-speaking, southerly canton of Switzerland. The most important wine of the region is Merlot del Ticino, usually soft and highly gluggable, but sometimes fuller and more serious with some oak barrel-aging. Best producers: Daniel Huber, Werner Stucky, Christian Zündel★.

**TIGNANELLO, VINO DA TAVOLA★★** *Tuscany, Italy*
The wine that broke the mould in Tuscany. Piero ANTINORI, who took control of his family company in the 1960s when CHIANTI's reputation was rock bottom, admired Bordeaux reds and set out to imitate them, with advice from Bordeaux's leading winemaker Professor Émile Peynaud. He employed the previously unheard of practice of aging in small French oak barrels and used Cabernet Sauvignon in the blend with

Sangiovese. Because of this the wine could only be labelled as simple Vino da Tavola, but the quality was superb and Tignanello's success sparked off the Super-Tuscan movement outside DOC regulations that has produced many of Italy's most exciting wines. Grapes are said to come entirely from the Tignanello property in CHIANTI CLASSICO in a blend of 80% Sangiovese and 20% Cabernet Sauvignon. Top vintages are truly great wines: lesser vintages are of decent Chianti Classico quality. Best years: (1996) (95) 94 93 **91** 90 **88 86 85**. See also Super-Tuscans.

**TINTA RORIZ** See Tempranillo.

**TOCAI FRIULANO** Unrelated to Hungary's or Alsace's Tokay, the Tocai Friulano is a north-east Italian grape producing dry, nutty, oily whites of great character in COLLIO and COLLI ORIENTALI and good wines in the Veneto's COLLI EUGANEI, as well as lots of neutral stuff in PIAVE. Best producers: Borgo del Tiglio★, Dorigo★, PUIATTI★, Russiz Superiore★, SCHIOPETTO★★, Specogna★, La Viarte★, Vie di Romans★, Villa Russiz★.

**TOKAJI** *Hungary and Slovakia* Strange, fascinating and unique, Tokaji wine has a sweet-sour-sweet, sherry-like tang. On the Hungarian-Slovak border, mists from the Bodrog river ensure that noble rot or botrytis on the Furmint, Hárslevelü and Muscotaly (Muscat Ottonel) grapes is a fairly common occurrence. Old single-vineyard Museum wines★★ from the Tokaji Wine Trust demonstrate the area's potential and recent French and Spanish investments are currently exploiting it. Quality is very much on the up. Tokaji should be sold ready to drink, though the oxidized nature of most old-style releases made you think you'd missed the boat a bit. Best producers: Megyer, Pajzos Disznókö, Royal Tokaji Wine Company.

**TOLLOT-BEAUT & FILS** *Chorey-lès-Beaune, Burgundy, France* High-quality COTE DE BEAUNE reds with lots of fruit and a pronounced new oak character. The village-level CHOREY-LES-BEAUNE★, ALOXE-CORTON★★ and SAVIGNY-LES-BEAUNE★★ wines are all excellent, as is the top-notch BEAUNE Premier Cru Clos du Roi★★. Best years: 1995 93 **92 90 89 88**.

**TORGIANO DOC & DOCG** *Umbria, Italy* A zone near Perugia dominated by LUNGAROTTI. In the 1960s and 70s, while most central Italian red was harsh and fruitless, Lungarotti's Rubesco Torgiano was always ripe and plummy. It is no longer so good but the Riserva Vigna Monticchio★★ is a fine black cherry-flavoured wine. Torgiano Riserva Rosso has been accorded DOCG. Best producer: LUNGAROTTI.

**TORO DO** *Castilla y León, Spain* Toro makes mainly reds, which are strong, robust, full of colour and tannin, and pretty high in alcohol. The main grape, Tinto de Toro, is a local deviant of Tempranillo, and there is some Garnacha. Whites from the Malvasia grape are generally heavy. Best producers: Fariña★ (reds), Vega Saúco.

**TORRES** *Penedés DO, Catalonia, Spain* Large family winery led by visionary Miguel Torres, making good wines with local grapes, Parellada and Tempranillo, but also renowned for French varieties. Viña Esmeralda★ (Muscat d'Alsace and Gewürztraminer) is grapy and spicy, Fransola★ (Parellada and Sauvignon Blanc) is richly grassy, and Milmanda★★ is a delicious, expensive Chardonnay from a CONCA DE BARBERA vineyard, although it sports the PENEDES DO. Successful reds are Gran Coronas★, soft, oaky and blackcurranty (Tempranillo and Cabernet); fine, relatively rich Mas la Plana★★ (Cabernet Sauvignon); floral, perfumed Mas Borras★ (Pinot Noir); and raisiny Las Torres★ (Merlot). Best years (Mas la Plana): **1989 88 87 83 81 76 75 73**.

**MARIMAR TORRES ESTATE** *Sonoma, California, USA* The sister of Spanish winemaker Miguel Torres has established her own winery in the cool Green Valley region of SONOMA COUNTY, only a few miles from the Pacific Ocean. The first Chardonnays★★ were big, intense wines, perhaps a shade heavy on the oak, best with 2–4 years' age. The first few Pinot Noirs approach ★★★ quality.

**MIGUEL TORRES** *Curicó, Chile* The man who brought innovation, fresh ideas and technology to Chile in 1979 sadly hasn't sustained his momentum, while the rest of the competition has rushed past. Best of a disappointing range is the hefty but well-structured Manso de Valasco Cabernet★ from old vines.

**CH. LA TOUR-MARTILLAC** *Pessac-Léognan AC, Cru Classé de Graves, Bordeaux, France* A GRAVES Classed Growth that for many years positively cultivated an old-fashioned image but which is now a property to watch. Organic practice is strictly followed in the vineyard, which has many ancient vines. In the past, the reds★ were deep, dark and well-structured but they lacked charm. Things improved considerably in the 1980s. Since 1986 new-style vinification has also transformed the whites★★. Best years: (reds) (1996) (95) 90 88 **86 85 83 82**; (whites) (1996) **95 94 93 90 89 88**.

**TOURAINE AC** *Loire Valley, France* The general AC for Touraine wines in the central LOIRE. There are 6140ha (15,170 acres) of AC vineyards, divided half and half between red or rosé and white. Most of the Touraine reds are from the Gamay and in hot years these can be juicy, rough-fruited wines. There is a fair amount of red from Cabernets Sauvignon and Franc, too, and some good Côt (Malbec). The reds are best drunk young. Fairly decent whites come from the Chenin Blanc but the best wines are from Sauvignon Blanc. These can be a good SANCERRE substitute at half the price. Drink at one year old, though Chenin wines can last longer. As well as generic Touraine wine, there are 3 more ACs, Touraine-Amboise and Touraine-Mesland for reds, rosés and whites, and Touraine-Azay-le-Rideau for whites and rosés only. Best producers: (reds and rosés) Dom. de la Charmoise★, Corbillières, Octavie, OISLY-ET-THESEE co-op, Roche Blanche★; (whites) Barbou, Baron Briare★, Bougrier, Dom. de la Charmoise★, Ch. de Chenonceau★, Delaunay, Frissant, Marcadet★, Octavie★, OISLY-ET-THESEE co-op★, Roche Blanche★. Best years: (reds) **1996 95 93 90 89 88**; (whites) **1996 95 93 90 89 88**.

**TOURAINE MOUSSEUX AC** *Loire Valley, France* A sparkling wine AC covering the entire Touraine region. The wines are rarely as good as the best VOUVRAY and CREMANT DE LOIRE. Best producers: Ch. de Chenonceau★, Delaunay, Monmousseau.

---

**TOURIGA NACIONAL** High-quality red Portuguese grape which is rich in aroma and fruit. It is prized for port production as it is also contributes deep colour and tannin to the blend. Slowly increasing in importance for table wines elsewhere in Portugal, such as the DAO.

---

**TRADITIONAL METHOD** See Champagne method.

**TRAS-OS-MONTES** *Portugal* Impoverished north-eastern province, traditionally a supplier of grapes for Mateus Rosé, but with 3 IPR regions, Valpaços, Chaves and Planalto-Mirandês, still producing pretty rustic stuff. Best producer: Valle Pradinhos.

---

**TREBBIANO** The most widely planted white Italian grape variety – far too widely, in fact, for Italy's good. As the Trebbiano Toscano, it is used as the base for GALESTRO and any number of other neutral, dry whites, as well as in VIN SANTO. But there are also a number of grapes masquerading under the Trebbiano name that aren't anything like as neutral. The most notable are the Trebbiano from LUGANA and ABRUZZO – both grapes capable of full-bodied, fragrant wines. Called Ugni Blanc in France, and primarily used for distilling, as it should be.

**TREFETHEN VINEYARDS** *Napa Valley AVA, California, USA* An off-dry Riesling★ is one of the best wines from this NAPA estate, although the Chardonnay has won more renown. The Cabernet is haphazard, and a Merlot has been added. Two good-value wines, Eshcol Chardonnay and Eshcol Cabernet Sauvignon, are frequently the most attractive wines made here.

**TRENTINO** *Italy* This northern region is officially linked with ALTO ADIGE, but they are completely different. The wines rarely have the verve or perfume of Alto Adige examples, but can make up for this with riper softer flavours, where vineyard yields have been kept in check. The Trentino DOC covers 20 different styles of wine, including white Pinot Bianco and Grigio, Moscato Giallo, Müller-Thurgau and Nosiola, and red Schiava, Lagrein, Marzemino, Teroldego and Cabernet. Trento Classico is a special DOC for sparkling wines made by the Champagne method. Best producers: Bossi Fedrigotti, Castel Noarna, Cavit co-op, Conti Martini★, Dorigati, Ferrari★★, Foradori★★, Maso Cantanghel★★, Pojer & Sandri★, San Leonardo★, De Tarczal★, Vallarom★★, La Vis co-op. See also Teroldego Rotaliano.

**DOM. DE TRÉVALLON** *Provence, France* Iconoclastic Parisian Eloi Dürrbach makes brilliant reds★★★, mixing the wildness of Mediterranean herbs with a sweetness of blackberry, blackcurrant and black, black plums. Dürrbach's tradition-busting blend of Cabernet Sauvignon and Syrah, no longer accepted (since the 94 vintage) by the appellation les BAUX-DE-PROVENCE, is the finest wine to come out of Provence in the last decade. The wines age extremely well, but are surprisingly drinkable in their youth. Best years: 1995 **94 92 90 89 87 86 85 83 82**.

**F E TRIMBACH** *Alsace AC, Alsace, France* Excellent grower/merchant whose trademark is a beautifully structured, subtly perfumed elegance. Riesling and Gewürztraminer are the specialities, but the Pinot Gris and Pinot Blanc are first-rate too. Top wines are Gewürztraminer Cuvée des Seigneurs de Ribeaupierre★★★, Riesling Cuvée Frédéric Émile★★★ and Riesling Clos St-Hune★★★. Also very good ALSACE VENDANGE TARDIVE★★ and SELECTIONS DES GRAINS NOBLES★★. Best years: 1996 95 **93 92 90 89 88 85**.

**TRITTENHEIM** *Mosel, Germany* An important MOSEL wine village with several excellent vineyard sites, most notably the Apotheke (pharmacy) and Leiterchen (or little ladder). The wines are sleek and with crisp acidity, balanced by plenty of fruit. Best producers: Clüsserath, Grans-Fassian, Milz.

**TROCKEN** German for dry. In most parts of Germany and Austria Trocken means less than 9g per litre residual sugar. Trocken wines have become a fashion in Germany, but have not made great strides in other countries.

**TROCKENBEERENAUSLESE** German for 'dry berry selected', denoting grapes affected by noble rot (*Edelfäule* in German) – the wines will be lusciously sweet. Required Oechsle levels for Trockenbeerenauslese are 150 Oechsle for a Mosel Riesling or 154 for a south Baden Ruländer. An Austrian Trockenbeerenauslese must be 30 KMW or 156 Oechsle.

**CH. TROTANOY★★** *Pomerol AC, Bordeaux, France* Another POMEROL estate (along with PETRUS, LAFLEUR, LATOUR-A-POMEROL and others) which has benefited from the brilliant touch of the MOUEIX family. After a dip in the mid-1980s, recent vintages are getting back on form. Best years: (1996) (95) 94 93 90 89 88 **82 81 79 78 76 75 71 70 67 66 64 61**.

**TURSAN VDQS** *South-West France* Wine of local interest only, made on the edge of les Landes, the sandy coastal area south of Bordeaux. The white is the most interesting: made from the Baroque grape it is clean, crisp and refreshing. Best producers: de Bachen★, Tursan co-op.

**TUSCANY** *Italy* Tuscany's rolling hills, clad with vines, olive trees and cypresses, have produced wine since at least Etruscan times, and today Tuscany leads the way in promoting the new image of Italian wines. Its 26 DOCs and DOCGs are based on the red Sangiovese grape and are led by CHIANTI, BRUNELLO DI MONTALCINO and VINO NOBILE DI MONTEPULCIANO, as well as famous Super-Tuscans like ORNELLAIA and TIGNANELLO. White wines, despite sweet VIN SANTO, and the occasional excellent Chardonnay and Sauvignon, do not figure highly. See also Bolgheri, Carmignano, Galestro, Montecarlo, Parrina, Pomino, Rosso di Montalcino, Rosso di Montepulciano, Sassicaia, Super-Tuscans, Vernaccia di San Gimignano.

**TYRRELL'S** *Hunter Valley, New South Wales, Australia* Family-owned company with prime Lower Hunter vineyards, whose wines usually taste splendid on their home patch but, until recently, have been inconsistent on the export market. Makes superb Vat 1 Sémillon★★, intermittently excellent Vat 47 Chardonnay★★, and Vat 5 and 9 Shiraz which can be fine. Vat 6 Pinot Noir is variable. Best years: (Sémillon) 1995 94 93 **91 86 79 76 74 72**; (Chardonnay) **1995 94 93 92 91 90 87 86 79 77 73**; (reds) **1993 92 91 87 85 83 75 65**.

**UGNI BLANC** See Trebbiano.

**UMBRIA** *Italy* Wine production in this land-locked, central Italian region is dominated by ORVIETO, which accounts for almost 70% of DOC production. However, some of the most characterful wines are the reds from TORGIANO and MONTEFALCO. Other zones, like Colli del Trasimeno, Colli Altotiberini and Colli Perugini, produce more basic forgettable reds and whites.

**ÜRZIG** *Mosel, Germany* Middle MOSEL village with a very famous vineyard site – the Würzgarten (spice garden) – that tumbles spectacularly down to the river banks and produces marvellously spicy Riesling wines from its red slate and sandstone soil. Drink with 5 years' age or more. Best producers: J J Christoffel★, LOOSEN★★★.

**UTIEL-REQUENA DO** *Valencia, Spain* Inland from Valencia, Utiel-Requena is renowned for its rosés, mostly made from the Bobal grape. A lot of Tempranillo has been planted recently, making better, longer-lasting reds. Best producers: Campo de Requena, Torre Oria, Vinival.

**VACQUEYRAS AC** *Rhône Valley, France* The most important and consistently successful of the COTES DU RHONE-VILLAGES communes was promoted to its own AC in 1989. The reds have a lovely dark colour, a round, warm, spicy bouquet and a rich deep flavour that seems infused with the herbs and pine dust of the south. They are lovely to drink at 2–3 years and good wines will age for 5 years or more. Best producers: Clos des Cazaux★★, Combe★, Couroulu★, la Fourmone★★, JABOULET, des Lambertins, de Montmirail★, Pascal★, des Roques, Vacqueyras co-op★. Best years: **1995 94 93 91 90 89**.

**VAL D'ORBIEU, LES VIGNERONS DU** *Languedoc-Roussillon, France* Dynamic but erratic growers' association that sells in excess of 20 million cases a year and is France's largest wine exporting company. Recently acquired LISTEL. Membership includes several, but by no means all, of the Midi's best co-ops (Cucugnan, Cuxac, Ribauté and Montredon) and individual producers (Dom. de Fontsainte, Ch. la Voulte-Gasparets and Ch. St-Auriol). Now developing a range of blended wines (Cuvée Chouette★, Chorus★, Pas de Deux and la Cuvée Mythique★★), which are a judicious mix of traditional Mediterranean varieties and Cabernet or Merlot from Bordeaux. Also has a joint venture with PENFOLDS. In 1995 it released Laperouse 1994; the white was exotically good but the red hard and disappointing. Best years: **1995 94 93 91 90 89 88**.

**VALAIS** *Switzerland* Swiss canton flanking the Rhône above Lake Geneva. Between Martigny and Sierre the valley turns north-east creating an Alpine suntrap, and this short stretch of terraced vineyard land provides the majority of Switzerland's most individual wines

from Fendant, Pinot Noir and Gamay, and including Syrah and Chardonnay which are recent innovations. Best producers: Caves Imesch, Michel Clavien, J Germanier, Gilliard, Mathier, Mont d'Or★, Raymond, Zufferey.

**VALDEPEÑAS DO** *Castilla-La Mancha, Spain* Valdepeñas offers some of Spain's best inexpensive oak-aged reds, but these are a small drop in a sea of less exciting stuff. In fact there are more whites than reds, at least some of them now modern, fresh and fruity. Drink young, although the best reds from Tempranillo will last 10 years. Best producers: Casa de la Viña, LOS LLANOS★, Luís Megía, Real, Félix Solís.

**VALDESPINO** *Jerez y Manzanilla DO, Andalucía, Spain* Old-fashioned, very high-quality family sherry business. Delicious wines include Inocente Fino★, Tio Diego Amontillado★★, the expensive but concentrated Palo Cortado Cardenal★★, dry amontillados Coliseo★★★ and Don Tomás★★, Don Gonzalo Old Dry Oloroso★★ and Pedro Ximénez Solera Superior★★.

**VALDIVIESO** *Curicó, Chile* Part of the Mitjans group and recipient of huge investment both in their Lontué winery and Curicó Valley vineyards. Best known for smooth, oaky Pinot Noir★★ and finely textured, buttery Chardonnay★★. Multi-varietal blend Cavallo Loco is good but a long way from being a Chilean Grange (see PENFOLDS). Watch out for the new premium Stonelake series and a fizz should arrive soon.

**VALENCIA** *Spain*   The best wines from Valencia DO in the south-east of Spain are the inexpensive, sweet, grapy Moscatels. Simple, fruity whites, reds and rosés are also good. Alicante DO to the south produces a little-known treasure, the Fondillón dry or semi-dry fortified wine, as well as a cluster of wines from native and foreign varieties made by a few quality-conscious modern wineries. Monastrell is the main red grape variety. UTIEL-REQUENA DO specializes in rosés and light reds from the Bobal grape. Best producers: (Valencia DO) Cherubino Valsangiacomo (Marqués de Caro), Schenk (Los Monteros), Vincente Gandía Pla; (Alicante DO) Gutiérrez de la Vega, Enrique Mendoza, Salvador Poveda, Primitivo Quiles.

**VALLE D'AOSTA** *Italy*   Tiny Alpine valley sandwiched between PIEDMONT and the French Alps in northern Italy. The regional DOC covers 17 wine styles, referring either to a specific grape variety (like Gamay or Pinot Nero) or to a delimited region like Donnaz, a northern extension of Piedmont's CAREMA, producing a light red from the Nebbiolo grape. Perhaps the finest wine from these steep slopes is the sweet Chambave Moscato. Best producers: Bonin, Charrère, La Crotta di Vegneron★, Grosjean, Ezio Voyat.

**VALLÉE DU PARADIS, VIN DE PAYS DE LA** *Languedoc, France*   With a name like the valley of paradise, the wines from this area to the south-west of Narbonne ought to be heavenly. In fact, they're good, basic quaffers made principally from Carignan, Cinsaut and Grenache.

**VALLET FRÈRES** *Gevrey-Chambertin, Burgundy, France*   Merchant making small amounts of Burgundy in a highly traditional manner. The wines can seem tough and dense when young, but the best – especially the Premier Cru★★ and Grand Cru★★ wines from GEVREY-CHAMBERTIN★★ – can age to a sultry but satisfying maturity over many years. Also good VOSNE-ROMANÉE★ and MOREY-ST-DENIS★. The wines may be labelled Pierre Bourée.

**VALPOLICELLA DOC** *Veneto, Italy*   This Veronese wine can range in style from a light, cherryish red to the rich, port-like RECIOTO and AMARONE Valpolicellas. Most Valpolicella from the plains is pale and insipid, and bears little comparison to Valpolicella Classico from the hills. Made from Corvina (the best grape), Rondinella and Molinara (eliminated from the blend when a more structured wine is required), Valpolicella Classico can be a light, cherryish red of great appeal, for drinking within 18 months of the vintage. A fuller wine of bitter-sweet complexity is made either from a particular vineyard (like ALLEGRINI's La Grola), or by refermenting the wine on the skins and lees of the Amarone, a style called Ripasso, which adds an exciting sweet-sour dimension to the wine. Best producers: Corte Aleardi★, ALLEGRINI★★, Bertani★, BOLLA★, Brigaldara★, Brunelli★, Cecilia Beretta★, Dal Forno★★, Guerrieri-Rizzardi★, MASI★, Mazzi★, QUINTARELLI★★, Le Ragose★, Le Salette★, Speri★, Tedeschi★, Villa Spinosa★, Fratelli Zeni★. Best recent years: **1995 94 93 91 90 88**.

**VALTELLINA DOC** *Lombardy, Italy*   Red wine produced on the precipitous slopes of northern Lombardy. There is a basic, light red, made from at least 70% Nebbiolo (here called Chiavennasca), but the best wines are made under the Valtellina Superiore DOC as Grumello, Inferno, Sassella and Valgella. From top vintages the wines are attractively perfumed and approachable. Sfursat is a dense, high-alcohol red (up to 14.5%) made from semi-dried grapes. Best producers: La Castellina★, Conti Sertoli Salis★, Enologica Valtellinese★, Fay★, Nino Negri★, Rainoldi★, Triacca★. Best years: 1995 **93 90 89 88 85**.

**VASSE FELIX** *Margaret River, Western Australia* One of the originals responsible for MARGARET RIVER rocketing to fame, with decadently rich, profound Cabernet Sauvignon★★ and rare but very special Shiraz★★. Best years: (reds) **1995 94 93 91 90 88 86 84 83 79**.

**VAUD** *Switzerland* With the exception of the canton of Geneva, the Vaud accounts for the vineyards bordering Lake Geneva, forming a seemingly unbroken line from Nyon to Montreux. There are 5 regions: la Côte, Lavaux, CHABLAIS, Côtes de l'Orbe-Bonvillars and Vully. Most of the production is Dorin (Chasselas) and it can be a delightful light white. Reds are from Gamay and Pinot Noir. Best producers: Badoux, Conne, Delarze, Grognuz, Massy, Obrist, Pinget, J & P Testuz.

**VAVASOUR** *Marlborough, South Island, New Zealand* Exciting new winery in the Awatere Valley near MARLBOROUGH's main wine area, enjoying spectacular success since the first release of the 1989 wines. One of New Zealand's best Chardonnays★★, a superb Cabernet Sauvignon-Franc Reserve★★ and fabulous Sauvignon Blanc★★★, already the envy of other Marlborough winemakers. Best years: **1996 94 91 90**.

**VDP** German organization recognizable on the label by a Prussian eagle bearing grapes. Membership is dependent on examination and is only granted to consistently good estates.

**VDQS (VIN DÉLIMITÉ DE QUALITÉ SUPÉRIEURE)** The second-highest classification for French wines, behind AC. Indications are that the authorities would like to phase it out.

**VECCHIO SAMPERI** *Sicily, Italy* A dry but unfortified MARSALA-style wine produced by Marco De Bartoli, being his version of what he believes Marsala was before the first English merchant, John Woodhouse, fortified it for export. Released as 10★-, 20★★- and 30-year-old★★ wines, these are dry, intense and redolent of candied peel, dates and old, old raisins. Some of the finest wines of this style in the world.

**VEGA SICILIA** *Ribera del Duero DO, Castilla y León, Spain* Spain's most expensive red wines, rich, fragrant, complex and very slow to mature, and by no means always easy to appreciate. This estate was the first in Spain to introduce French varieties, and over a quarter of the vines are now Cabernet Sauvignon, two-thirds are Tempranillo and the rest Malbec and Merlot. Vega Sicilia Unico★★★ – the top wine – has traditionally been given about 10 years' wood aging, but this is now being reduced and volatility evident in some vintages should now no longer occur. Vega Sicilia's second wine is called Valbuena★. A subsidiary winery producing the more modern-style Alion, from different vineyards, was launched in 1995. Best years: 1991 85 **82** 80 **79** 76 75 74 **70**.

**VENEGAZZÙ** *Veneto, Italy* The Loredan Gasparini wine estate is known primarily for its red Vino da Tavola, Venegazzù della Casa, based on red Bordeaux varieties. Though a pacesetter in the field, it has faded somewhat as more convincing versions have come on the scene. The black label version★ – equivalent to a Riserva – can still pack a smoky, aggressive black-fruited punch. Best years: 1993 **90 89 88 85**.

**VENETO** *Italy* The Veneto region takes in the wine zones of SOAVE, VALPO-LICELLA, BARDOLINO and PIAVE in north-east Italy. Its huge production makes it the source of a great deal of inexpensive wine, but the Soave and Valpolicella hills are also capable of producing small quantities of high-quality wine. Other hilly areas like Colli Berici and COLLI EUGANEI produce mainly large quantities of dull staple varietal wines, but can offer a few interesting things. PROSECCO DI CONEGLIANO-VALDOBBIADENE is Venice's preferred bubbly. See also Bianco di Custoza, Breganze, Recioto della Valpolicella.

**VERDICCHIO DEI CASTELLI DI JESI DOC** *Marche, Italy* Verdicchio, grown in the hills near the Adriatic around Jesi and in the Apennine enclave of Matelica, became known for making easy-going wine in an amphora-shaped bottle. But over the last decade, as producers began to take it seriously, it has blossomed into central Italy's most promising white variety. When fresh and fruity it is the ideal wine with fish, but some Verdicchio has the size and strength to age into a white of surprising depth of flavours. A few producers, notably Garofoli with Serra Fiorese★★, age it in oak, but even without wood it can develop an almost Burgundy-like complexity. Jesi is the classical zone, but the rarer Verdicchio di Matelica can be as impressive. Best producers: (Jesi) Brunori★, Bucci★, Colonnara, Fazi-Battaglia★, Garofoli★★, Mancinelli, Moncaro★, Santa Barbara★, Tralivio-Sartarelli★★, Umani Ronchi★, Zaccagni; (Matelica) Belisario★, Bisci-Castiglioni★, Mecella★, La Monacesca★★.

**VERMENTINO** The best dry white wines of SARDINIA generally come from the Vermentino grape. Light, dry, perfumed and nutty, the best wines tend to be from the north of the island, where it is DOC in Gallura. Vermentino is also grown in LIGURIA and TUSCANY, though its character is quite different. Best producers: (Sardinia) Argiolas★★, Capichera★, Cherchi★★, Santadi co-op, SELLA & MOSCA★, Vermentino co-op.

**VERNACCIA DI ORISTANO DOC** *Sardinia, Italy* Outstanding oxidized, almost sherry-like wines from the west of the island, which acquire complexity and colour through long aging in wood. Amber-coloured and dry, nutty and long on the finish. Best producer: Contini★.

**VERNACCIA DI SAN GIMIGNANO DOCG** *Tuscany, Italy* The dry white wine made from the Vernaccia grape grown in the hills around San Gimignano gained fame as Italy's first DOC in 1966. It has recently been promoted to DOCG, which hopefully will improve the quality of the wines, generally light quaffers. However, whether the allowance of up to 10% Chardonnay in the blend is a forward step is debatable. There is now a San Gimignano DOC for the zone's up-and-coming red wines. Best producers: Ambra delle Torri★, Baroncini★, Casale-Falchini★★, Montenidoli★, Panizzi★, Pietrafitta★, Pietraserena★, San Quirico, Guicciardini Strozzi, Teruzzi & Puthod★★, Vagnoni★.

**NOËL VERSET** *Cornas AC, Rhône Valley, France* Massive, concentrated rustic reds★★ from some of the oldest and best-sited vines in CORNAS. Yields are tiny here and it shows in the depth and power that Verset achieves in his wine. Worth aging for 10 years or more. Best years: (1996) 95 94 91 90 89 **88 85**.

**VEUVE CLICQUOT** *Champagne AC, Champagne, France* These Champagnes can still live up to the high standards set by the original Widow Clicquot at the beginning of the 19th century, although many are released too young. The non-vintage★ is full, toasty and satisfyingly weighty or lean and raw, depending on your luck: the vintage★★ is that bit fuller and the de luxe, called Grande Dame★★ after the original widow, is hefty but impressive stuff. Best years: 1989 88 85 82 79.

**VICTORIA** *Australia* Despite its small area, Victoria has arguably more land suited to quality grape-growing than any other state in Australia, with climates ranging from hot Sunraysia and RUTHERGLEN on the Murray River to cool MORNINGTON PENINSULA and GIPPSLAND in the south. The range of flavours is similarly wide. Victoria, with more than 170 wineries, leads the boutique winery boom today. See also Bendigo, Geelong, Goulburn Valley, Grampians, Pyrenees, Yarra Valley.

**LA VIEILLE FERME★** *Côtes du Ventoux AC, Rhône Valley, France* A brilliantly spicy, concentrated red produced in a lesser AC by the owners of the world-famous Ch. de BEAUCASTEL in CHÂTEAUNEUF-DU-PAPE. If only all COTES DU VENTOUX were as exciting. Best years: 1995 94 93 90 89 88.

**VIEILLES VIGNES** French term for a wine made from vines at least 20 years old, if not twice that. Old vines give more concentrated wine.

**VIEUX-CHÂTEAU-CERTAN★★★** *Pomerol AC, Bordeaux, France* Slow-developing and tannic red (because of the use of 45% Cabernet), which after 15–20 years finally resembles more a fragrant refined Médoc than a gushing, hedonistic POMEROL. Best years: (1996) (95) 94 93 90 89 88 86 85 83 82 81 79 78 70 64.

**VIEUX TÉLÉGRAPHE** *Châteauneuf-du-Pape AC, Rhône Valley, France* One of the top names in the AC, less tannic than BEAUCASTEL perhaps but with just as much aging potential. The vines are some of the oldest in Châteauneuf and this Grenache-based red★★ is among the best modern-style wines produced in the RHONE VALLEY, even if it has lost a little of its magic in recent vintages. There is also a small amount of white★, which is heavenly to drink at the youngest possible stage. Best years: 1995 93 91 90 89 88 85 83.

**VILLA MARIA** *Auckland, North Island, New Zealand* Founder and co-owner George Fistonich also owns Vidal and Esk Valley. Vidal Cabernet-Merlot★★★ and Villa Maria Reserve Cabernet★★★ are superb. Reserve Chardonnay from Vidal★★ and Villa Maria★★ are power-packed wines. Also scores well with extremely focussed dry Sauvignon★★, less dry Riesling★★ and, at the sweeter end, with stunning Late Harvest Riesling★★★, all from MARLBOROUGH. Best years: 1996 94 91 90 89 87.

**VILLA SACHSEN** *Bingen, Rheinhessen, Germany* Renowned estate recently purchased by Prinz Salm of the PRINZ ZU SALM-DALBERG estate in the Nahe. He needs to work harder, however, if the wines are to match the high quality of the 1980s. Best years: 1990 89 88.

**VILLARD** *Casablanca, Chile* Owner Thierry Villard (formerly of ORLANDO in South Australia) produces his own range of wines at the Santa

Emiliana winery. A big, buttery Chardonnay Reserve★ and clean, crisp Sauvignon Blanc★★, both from CASABLANCA, will doubtless improve further once a winery is built closer to the vineyards. Also produces a good Merlot from Cachapoal.

**VILLIERA ESTATE** *Paarl WO, South Africa* The Grier family have made an impact on the quality wine scene since taking over this estate in 1983. Their speciality is Cap Classique sparklers under the Tradition label; the vintage Première Cuvée has distinctive nutty, yeasty overtones. Of the rest of the range Jeff Grier's Sauvignon Blanc★★ shows classic grassy bite; there's also a consistent Riesling★ and a delicious, partly barrel-fermented Chenin Blanc★. Reds are equally good, especially minerally intense Merlot★★ and Bordeaux-blend Cru Monro★★.

**VIN DU BUGEY VDQS** *Savoie, France* An area of scattered vineyards halfway between Lyon and Savoie. The best wines are the whites, from Chardonnay, Pinot Gris, Mondeuse Blanche, Altesse and Jacquère. Roussette du Bugey is usually a blend of Altesse and Chardonnay. **Best producers: Bel-Air, Crussy, Monin★, Peillot.**

**VIN DE CORSE AC** *Corsica, France* The overall AC for Corsica with 5 superior sub-regions (Calvi, Cap Corse, Figari, Porto Vecchio and Sartène). PATRIMONIO and AJACCIO are entitled to their own ACs. Things are improving on this lovely island but slowly. The most distinctive wines, mainly red, come from local grapes (Nielluccio and Sciaccarello for reds and Vermentino for whites). There are some rich sweet Muscats – especially from MUSCAT DE CAP CORSE. **Best producers: Cantone, Clos Landry, Couvent d'Alzipratu, Gentile, Leccia, Péraldi★, SKALLI★, Torraccia, UVAL.**

**VIN DE PAILLE** *Sweet wine* found mainly in the Jura region of eastern France. Traditionally, the grapes are left for 2–3 months on straw (*paille*) mats before fermentation to dehydrate, thus concentrating the sugars. The wines are a cross between SAUTERNES and amontillado sherry – sweet but slightly nutty. Vins de Paille can be found in COTES DU JURA, ARBOIS and L'ETOILE, and occasionally in the Rhône Valley. **Best producers: CHAPOUTIER★★, CHAVE★★, Rolet★, Tissot★.**

**VIN DE PAYS** *France* The phrase suggests a traditional wine from the country districts of France but the reality is a little different as many Vins de Pays are impressively modern and forward-looking and are now the source of some of France's best-value flavours. This category of wine was created in 1968 to give a geographical identity and quality yardstick to wines which had previously been sold off for blending. It is a particularly useful category for adventurous winemakers (such as RYMAN and SKALLI) who want to use good-quality grapes not allowed under the frequently restrictive AC regulations. Many Vin de Pays wines are labelled with the grape variety.

**VIN DE SAVOIE AC** *Savoie, France* The general AC for the Alpine region of Savoie. The 15 best villages, including Abymes, Apremont, Arbin, Chignin, Cruet and Montmélian, can add their own name to the AC name. The best wines are white and to enjoy the thrilling snap of their tangy fruit drink them young. Occasional good Pinot Noir and excellent beefy Mondeuse reds. **Best producers: Blard, Boniface★, Bouvet★, Cavaillé★, Genoux, Gonnet, Monin, Monterminod★, Neyroud, Perret, Jean Perrier, Quénard, de Ripaille★, Rocailles★. Best years: 1995 93 92.**

**VIN DE TABLE** French for table wine, the lowest quality level.

**VIN DOUX NATUREL** French for a fortified wine, where fermentation has been stopped by the addition of alcohol, leaving the wine 'naturally' sweet, although you could argue that stopping fermentation with a slug of powerful spirit is distinctly unnatural, but there you go.

**VIN JAUNE** *Jura, France*  A Jura speciality made from the Savagnin grape. In CHATEAU-CHALON it is the only permitted wine style. Made in a similar way to fino sherry but not fortified. Vin Jaune usually ages well, too. Best producers: Clavelin★, Courbet★, Macle★★, Perron★.

**VIN SANTO** *Trentino, Tuscany and Umbria, Italy*  The 'holy wine' of Tuscany can be one of the world's great sweet wines – just occasionally, that is, for it is also one of the most wantonly abused wine terms in Italy (in particular avoid anything called Liquoroso). Made from grapes laid on mats after harvest to dry, the resulting wines, fermented and aged in barrels for up to 7–8 years, should be nutty, oxidized, full of the flavours of dried apricots and crystallized orange peel, concentrated and long. Also produced in UMBRIA and in TRENTINO. Best producers: AVIGNONESI★★★, Badia a Coltibuono★, Brolio★, Cacchiano★, Capezzana★★, CASTELLO DI AMA★, FELSINA BERARDENGA★★, ISOLE E OLENA★★★, Pieve Santa Restituta★★★, POLIZIANO★★, San Giusto a Rentennano★★★, SELVAPIANA★.

**VIÑA CASABLANCA** *Casablanca, Chile*  King of the Valley Ignacio Recabaren continues to chase CLOUDY BAY dreams with great success. These are high-impact wines, particularly those using CASABLANCA-sourced fruit, while label wines use vineyards in Lontué, MAIPO and San Fernando. Excellent quince-edged Santa Isabel Estate Chardonnay★★, rose- and lychee-filled Gewürztraminer★★ and inky-black Cabernet Sauvignon★★. Successful experiments include fabulous Chardonnay-Sauvignon blend★★ and low-yield Merlot★.

**VINHO VERDE DOC** *Minho and Douro Litoral, Portugal*  'Vinho Verde' is a region, a wine and a style of wine. 'Green' only in the sense of being young, it can be red *or* white, and in a restaurant the term often refers simply to the younger wines on the list. The demarcated Vinhos Verdes, however, come from north-west Portugal. The reds are an acquired taste, and drunk by few outside the region – though I am one. Both red and white are strongly acidic, usually with a prickle of fizz, and best drunk young and chilled with the local cuisine. The whites range from sharply lemony to aromatically flowery (when made from the Loureiro and Trajadura grapes) and extravagantly fruity (the Alvarinho grape). Because the climate is damp and mild, vines have to be trained high to protect them from fungal infections. Best producers: Avelada, Palácio de Brejoeira, Ponte de Lima co-op, Quinta da Franqueira, SOGRAPE (Gazela e Quinta de Azevedo).

**J P VINHOS** *Terras do Sado, Portugal*  The name has changed since the João Pires Muscat brand was sold to IDV, but the wine-making is as forward-looking as ever, using Portuguese and foreign grapes with equal ease. Australian Peter Bright still consults, though he has established his own company, BRIGHT BROTHERS. QUINTA DA BACALHOA★ is an oaky, meaty Cabernet-Merlot blend, Tinto da Anfora★ lean and figgy, white Herdade de Santa Marta★ rich, greengagy and mouthfilling, and Cova da Ursa★ a tasty, toasty rich Chardonnay that walks on the wild side.

**VINO DA TAVOLA** *Italy* The term for 'table wine', officially Italy's lowest
level of production, is a catch-all that has applied to more than 80%
of the nation's wine with virtually no regulations controlling quality.
Yet this category also provided the arena in the 1970s for the biggest
revolution in quality that Italy has ever seen, with the creation of
innovative, DOC-busting 'Super-Tuscans'. Every region of Italy has
special wines that remain outside the control system, but recent legis-
lation is designed to bring most quality wines into the IGT or DOC
categories, leaving Vino da Tavola to represent simple wines that
carry no vintage or place of origin. See also Super-Tuscans.

**VINO NOBILE DI MONTEPULCIANO DOCG** *Tuscany, Italy* The 'noble
wine' from the hills around the town of Montepulciano is made from
the Sangiovese grape, known locally as the Prugnolo, with the help of
a little Canaiolo and Mammolo. At its best, it combines the power and
structure of BRUNELLO DI MONTALCINO with the finesse and complexity
found in top CHIANTI. Unfortunately, the best was a rare beast until
recently, though the rate of improvement has been impressive. Best
producers: AVIGNONESI★★, Bindella★★, BOSCARELLI★★, La Braccesca★,
Le Casalte★★, La Casella★, Del Cerro★, Contucci★, Dei★, Fassati★,
Gracciano★, Innocente★, Il Macchione★, POLIZIANO★★, Trerose★★,
Valdipiatta★. Best years: (1996) (95) 94 **93 91 90** 88 85.

---

**VIOGNIER** A poor yielder, prone to disease and difficult to vinify. The wine
can be delicious: peachy, apricotty with a soft, almost waxy texture, usually a fragrance of spring flowers and sometimes a taste like crème fraîche.
Now found in LANGUEDOC-ROUSSILLON, Ardèche and the southern RHONE as
well as in CALIFORNIA, where it enjoys great popularity, and Australia.

---

**ROBERTO VOERZIO** *Barolo DOCG, Piedmont, Italy* One of the best of the
younger generation of BAROLO producers, emphasizing fruit and mini-
mizing tannin. Dolcetto★★ is particularly successful, as is barrique-
aged Nebbiolo-Barbera blend, Vigna Serra★★. He took time to adapt
Barolo to his philosophy, but it is now very good even in a difficult
year. The excellent vintages of 1990, 89 and 88 have seen fine Barolo
bottled under 3 crus: Brunate★★, Cerequio★★ and La Serra★★. Best
years: (Barolo) (1996) (95) 94 93 90 89 **88** 85.

**VOLLMER** *Pfalz, Germany* Large firm which produced Germany's first
Cabernet Sauvignon wine. Mainly simple country wines, but from the
Kirchenstück and Bubeneck sites come good Weisser Burgunder and
Riesling. Very fine dry Auslese Gewürztraminer★★, a rich Gewürz-
traminer Trockenbeerenauslese★★ and sweet Ruländer★. Also a good
Dornfelder★. Best years: **1993** 92 91 90 89.

**VOLNAY AC** *Côte de Beaune, Burgundy, France* Volnay is home to the
finest red wines of the COTE DE BEAUNE in terms of elegance and class.
The wines are attractive when young but the best examples can age
as well as any Burgundy. The top vineyards, classified as Premier Cru,
are Caillerets, Champans, Clos de la Bousse d'Or, Clos des Chênes and
Santenots (which actually lies in Meursault but is called Volnay by
courtesy title). Best producers: Ampeau★★, d'Angerville★★, J F COCHE-
DURY★★, Lafarge★★★, LAFON★★★, de MONTILLE★★, Pousse d'Or★★,
Voillot★★. Best years: 1995 93 **91 90 89** 88.

**VOLPAIA** *Chianti Classico DOCG, Tuscany, Italy* Produces light, perfumed but refined CHIANTI CLASSICO★★. Two stylish Super-Tuscans, Balifico★★ and Coltassala★★, are both predominantly Sangiovese. Best years: (1996) 95 **94 93 90 88**.

**VOSNE-ROMANÉE AC** *Côte de Nuits, Burgundy, France* The greatest village in the CÔTE DE NUITS with a clutch of 5 Grands Crus and 13 Premiers Crus (the best of these are les Malconsorts and les Suchots) which are often as good as other villages' Grands Crus. The quality of the village wine is also high. In good years the wines should have at least 6 years' aging and 10–15 would be better. Best producers: Arnoux★, Cacheux★, Engel★, GRIVOT★, A & F Gros★★, JADOT, JAYER★★★, Lamarche★★, MEO-CAMUZET★★, Moillard★, Mongeard-Mugneret★★, RION★, Dom. de la ROMANÉE-CONTI★★★. Best years: 1995 93 90 **89** 88 **85**.

**VOUGEOT AC** *Côte de Nuits, Burgundy, France* The 12.5ha (32 acres) of vines outside the walls of CLOS DE VOUGEOT only qualify for Vougeot AC. The wine, mainly red, is not bad and a lot cheaper than any Clos de Vougeot. Best producers: Bertagna★, Chopin-Groffier★. Best years: 1995 93 **90 89 88 85**.

**LA VOULTE-GASPARETS** *Corbières AC, Languedoc, France* One of the MIDI's most exciting properties, producing 3 different styles of Corbières from old hillside vines. Unashamedly Mediterranean in style with flavours of thyme and baked earth. The Cuvée Réservée★★ and Romain Pauc★★ are the most expensive wines, but the basic Voulte-Gasparets★ is almost as good. Drink young or up to 5 years from the vintage. Best years: **1995 94 93**.

**VOUVRAY AC** *Loire Valley, France* Dry, medium-dry, sweet and sparkling wines from Chenin grapes east of Tours. The dry wines acquire beautifully rounded flavours after 10 years or so. Medium-dry wines, when properly made from a single domaine, are worth aging for 20 years or more. Spectacular noble-rot-affected sweet wines were produced in 1990 and 89 with an intense peach and honey soft sweetness but an ever-present acidity. The fizz is some of the Loire's best. Best producers: Dom. Bourillon-Dorléans★★, Brédif★, Brisebarre, Champalou★, P Delaleu★, Foreau★★, Fouquet★★, Freslier, Ch. Gaudrelle★, HUET★★, Mabille. Best years: (1996) 95 93 **90 89 88 85 83 82 78 76 75 70**.

**WACHAU** *Niederösterreich, Austria* Stunning stretch of the Danube between Krems-Stein and the monastery of Melk, this is Austria's top region for dry whites. Riesling is the grape here, followed by Grüner Veltliner. Best producers: FREIE WEINGARTNER WACHAU★, F HIRTZBERGER★★, Emmerich Knoll★★, NIKOLAIHOF★★, F X PICHLER★★★, F PRAGER★★★.

**WACHENHEIM** *Pfalz, Germany* Wine village made famous by the BÜRKLIN-WOLF estate, its best vineyards are capable of producing rich, yet beautifully balanced Rieslings. Best producers: Josef BIFFAR★★, BÜRKLIN-WOLF★★, Karl Schaefer, Wolf.

**WAIHEKE ISLAND** *North Island, New Zealand* Goldwater pioneered winemaking on this small island in Auckland harbour in the early 1980s. Hot, dry ripening conditions have made high-quality Cabernet Sauvignon-based reds that sell for very high prices. A tiny highly fashionable region that will soon be home to 20 winemakers. Best producers: Fenton★★, Goldwater★★, Peninsula★, STONYRIDGE, Te Motu★★.

**WARRE** *Port DOC, Douro, Portugal* Top-quality vintage ports★★, and a good 'off-vintage' port from their Quinta da Cavadinha★. Nimrod★, a 10- to 15-year-old tawny, is also delicious, and their Crusted★★ and LBV★ wines are both very welcome traditional, full-bodied ports. Best years: (vintage ports) 1994 91 85 83 **80 77** 75 **70 66 63**.

**WARWICK ESTATE** *Stellenbosch WO, South Africa* Until recently this estate was best known for its reds made from traditional Bordeaux varieties, in particular, the complex Trilogy★★ blend, Now dynamic Norma Ratcliffe has burst on the scene with a velvety, suave Traditional Bush Vine Pinotage★★, inspired by the farm's old Pinotage vines and by neighbour KANONKOP. Since 1994, Warwick reds have become a notch softer but remain elegantly European in style.

**WASHINGTON STATE** *USA* The second-largest premium wine-producing state in the US. The chief growing areas are in irrigated high desert, east of the Cascade Mountains. Although the heat is not as intense as in California, the long summer days with extra hours of sunshine due to the northern latitude seem to increase the intensity of fruit flavours and result in both red and white wines of great depth. Cabernet, Merlot, Chardonnay, Sauvignon Blanc and Sémillon produce very good wines here. Some believe that the wines of Washington State will come to be regarded as the best in the US. Best producers: ANDREW WILL★, CHATEAU STE MICHELLE★, COLUMBIA CREST★, Columbia Winery, Covey Run★, L'ECOLE NO 41★★, HOGUE CELLARS★★, KIONA★, LEONETTI CELLAR★★★, Preston Wine Cellars, QUILCEDA CREEK★★, Salishan, Snoqualmie, Staton Hills★ (whites), Paul THOMAS★, WOODWARD CANYON.

**WEGELER-DEINHARD** *Bernkastel, Mosel; Oestrich-Winkel, Rheingau; Deidesheim, Pfalz, Germany* Huge estate with vast holdings in Germany's top vineyards. Over the years Deinhard has been looking for ways of marketing the separate strands of German viticulture. In Germany it spins money with Sekt and its still wines are insignificant. Outside Germany it has led the way in introducing new dry styles. One idea was the village series of PIESPORT, BERNKASTEL, Deidesheim, NIERSTEIN, HOCHHEIM and JOHANNISBERG called the Heritage Selection. The best marketing concept to date has been the range of generic MOSEL-SAAR-RUWER, RHEINGAU, PFALZ Kabinetts and Spätlese wines★. Deinhard continue to market a few top village sites such as Forster Ungeheuer, Rüdesheimer Berg Rottland, Winkeler Hasensprung, Wehlener Sonnenuhr, Bernkasteler Doctor and Oestricher Lencher. These are generally of Spätlese quality, sometimes, as in 1990, of Auslese or even Beerenauslese ripeness and most merit ★★ with the best Doctor and Sonnenuhr Rieslings also meriting ★★. Best years: **1995 93 92 90 89 88 86 85 83 79 76**.

**WEHLEN** *Mosel, Germany* Village whose steep Sonnenuhr vineyard produces some of the most powerful Rieslings in Germany. Best producers: Kerpen, LOOSEN★★★, J J PRUM★★★, RICHTER★★, SELBACH-OSTER★★, WEGELER-DEINHARD★, Dr Weins-Prüm.

**ROBERT WEIL** *Kiedrich, Rheingau, Germany* Previously known as Dr Weil, and now owned by Suntory. It is managed by Wilhelm Weil and makes sweet Auslese★★, Beerenauslese and Trockenbeerenauslese Rieslings (both ★★★) and since 1992 also dry Rieslings★★. The wines are crisp, with vivid fruit character. Best years: 1995 94 **93 92 90 89**.

**DOMDECHANT WERNER** *Hochheim, Rheingau, Germany* Classy estate with well-sited bits of the Domdechaney, Hölle and Kirchenstück vineyards in HOCHHEIM that made especially good wines in 1990★ but had a disastrous 93 and a disappointing 95. Best years: 1994 **92 90 89 88**.

**WEISSBURGUNDER** See Pinot Blanc.

**WEISSHERBST** German rosé wine, a speciality of Baden. The wine is usually dry. The label must state the grape variety.

**WELSCHRIESLING** See Riesling Italico.

**WENDOUREE** *Clare Valley, South Australia* Small winery using old-fashioned methods to make enormous, age-worthy reds★★★ from paltry yields off their own very old Shiraz, Cabernet, Malbec and Mataro (Mourvèdre) vines. There are tiny amounts of sweet Muscat★. Best years: 1994 92 91 90 **86 83 82 81 80 78 76 75**.

**WESTERN AUSTRALIA** Only the south-west corner of this vast state is suited to vines: the SWAN VALLEY and Perth environs being the oldest and hottest district, with present attention focussed on Lower Great Southern, MARGARET RIVER, South-West Coastal Plain and, most recently, Pemberton/Manjimup. Quality rivals the best of the eastern states.

**WIEN** *Austria* Region within the city limits of Wien or Vienna. The best vines come from the south-facing sites in Grinzing, Nussdorf and Weiden; and the Bisamberg hill east of the Danube. Best producers: Bernreiter, Kierlinger, Mayer, Schilling, Wieninger★.

**WILLIAMS SELYEM** *Russian River Valley AVA, California, USA* Pinot Noir★★ was the only wine made here until 1990 and much of the time it is very, very good; made in a traditional style, the wine is big, sometimes very fruity and sometimes just a bit off the wall. However, this SONOMA winery has a cult following and all offerings are snapped up – especially single-vineyard examples such as Rochioli★★★. There is now some impressive Chardonnay and Zinfandel★★ as well.

**WINKEL** *Rheingau, Germany* Rheingau village whose best vineyard is the large Hasensprung Einzellage but the most famous one is SCHLOSS VOLLRADS – an ancient estate that does not use the village name on its label. Best producers: August Eser, Johannishof★★, WEGELER-DEINHARD★★.

**WIRRA WIRRA** *Southern Vales, South Australia* Run by celebrated eccentric Greg Trott who consistently makes whites with more finesse than customary in the region. Well-balanced Sauvignon Blanc★, age-worthy Sémillon blend★★, buttery Chardonnay★★ and soft reds led by delicious The Angelus★★. Also a good-value 'W W' label. Best years: (reds) **1994 93 92 91 90 86 82 80**.

**WO (WINE OF ORIGIN)** The South African certification system was introduced in 1973. The laws are broadly based on those of France and Germany, but are not a guarantee of good quality and only 10% of the national harvest is certified. The three main quality-influencing factors claimed by WO are area of origin, vintage and grape variety.

**WOODWARD CANYON** *Walla Walla AVA, Washington State, USA* Big barrel-fermented oaky Chardonnay★★ is the trademark wine, but there's also good Charbonneau Red (Cabernet Sauvignon-Merlot) and Charbonneau White (Sémillon-Sauvignon Blanc).

**WÜRTTEMBERG** *Germany* Underperforming wine region centred on the river Neckar. More than half the wine made is red and the best comes from the Lemberger, Dornfelder or Spätburgunder grapes, the rest mostly from the awful Trollinger. These reds can be very light due to massive yields. Isolated steep sites sometimes produce fine Riesling.

**WÜRZBURG** *Franken, Germany* The centre of FRANKEN wines. Müller-Thurgau is the bread-and-butter grape, some Rieslings can be great, but the real star is Sylvaner. Best producers: Bürgerspital, JULIUSSPITAL★, Staatlicher Hofkeller.

**WYNDHAM ESTATE** *Hunter Valley, New South Wales, Australia* This brand, ingeniously marketed in the 1980s by Brian McGuigan, is now part of Pernod-Ricard's ORLANDO group. It was the HUNTER's biggest winery, but production is being moved to the group's expanding Montrose winery at MUDGEE. An active exporter, there has been a depressing decline in quality in recent years.

**WYNNS** *Coonawarra, South Australia* The name is synonymous with COONAWARRA, owning the oldest cellars and major vineyard holdings. After a low period in the 1970s standard Cabernet★★ and Shiraz★ have improved steadily, to the point where they are among the best value in the land. They also age well: the better vintages from the 1950s and 60s are still alive and kicking. In peak years the cream of the Cabernet is released (since 1982) as John Riddoch★★★ and Shiraz (since 1990) as Michael★★, both powerful reds. There is also Chardonnay★ in an increasingly fruit-driven style and oceans of cheap quaffing Riesling★. Ovens Valley Shiraz, sadly, has been discontinued. Best years: (premium reds) 1994 93 **91 90 88 86 84 82 76 66 62 55**.

**YALUMBA** *Barossa Valley, South Australia* Large, distinguished old firm, owned by the Hill-Smith family, making a wide range of wines including estate wines Heggies★★ (outstanding Riesling, red Bordeaux blend, Viognier and botrytis Riesling), Hill-Smith Estate★ (Sauvignon Blanc, fine Chardonnay and botrytis Sémillon) and Pewsey Vale★ (fine Riesling and Cabernet Sauvignon). The Yalumba range is BAROSSA-based blends: the Signature red★★, Octavius Shiraz★★ and Reserve Cabernet★★ stand out. From these premium reds down to quaffer Galway Shiraz★, Yalumba reds reflect major improvements. Oxford Landing Chardonnay, Sauvignon and Cabernet-Shiraz are highly successful Riverland quaffers. Yalumba is also the pioneer of remarkably good 2-litre casks. Angas Brut is huge-selling, enjoyable fizz for the masses (me included); Yalumba Pinot-Chardonnay★ and Yalumba D★★ have recently leapt to the fore showing a delicious toasty, creamy style and are now among Australia's best premium sparklers. The fortifieds are also excellent, particularly Liqueur Muscat★★.

**YARRA VALLEY** *Victoria, Australia* With its cool maritime climate it is shaping up as Australia's best Pinot Noir region. Exciting also for Chardonnay and Cabernet-Merlot blends and as a supplier of base wine for sparklers. Best producers: COLDSTREAM HILLS★★, DE BORTOLI★★, GREEN POINT★★, MOUNT MARY★★, Oakridge, ST HUBERTS★★, Seville Estate, TARRAWARRA★★, Yarra Ridge, YARRA YERING★★★, Yeringberg★.

**YARRA YERING** *Yarra Valley, Victoria, Australia* Bailey Carrodus uses quaint methods to create extraordinary wines from his exceptional vineyard. The reds, labelled Dry Red No.1★★★ (Cabernet-based) and No.2★★★ (Shiraz-based), are profound, concentrated, structured for aging, packed with unnervingly self-confident fruit and memorable perfume. The Pinot Noir★★★ is expensive but very fine, and getting finer and wilder by the vintage. Chardonnay at its best is ★★. Best years: **1992 91 90 86 82**.

**YELLOWGLEN** *Ballarat, Victoria, Australia* Big Champagne-method fizz producer owned by MILDARA. The quality is good but the premium wines are released too young. Basic, high-volume lines are Brut NV, Brut Crémant and Brut Rosé. Cuvée Victoria is the finest.

**CH. D'YQUEM★★★** *Sauternes AC, 1er Cru Supérieur, Bordeaux, France* Often rated as the most sublime sweet wine in the world, no one can question Yquem's total commitment to quality. Despite the large vineyard (100ha/250 acres), production is tiny. Only fully noble-rotted grapes are picked, often berry by berry, and the low yield means each vine produces only a glass of wine! This precious liquid gold is then fermented in new oak barrels and left to mature for 3½ years before bottling. It is one of the world's most expensive wines but is in constant demand because of its richness and exotic flavours – loony prices or not. There is presently a battle over ownership which, we must hope, does not affect the superlative quality. A dry white, Ygrec, is produced in some years. Best years: 1990 89 88 86 83 **81 80 79 76 75 71 67 62**.

**ZELL** *Mosel, Germany* Most famous for the generic Schwarzer Katz (or black cat) wines which are rarely better than cheap and cheerful. Zell can produce good Rieslings which offer good value for money if you can find them. Best producer: Albert Kallfelz.

**ZILLIKEN** *Saarburg, Saar, Germany* Estate specializing in Rieslings★★ from the Saarburger Rausch vineyard. In 1990 its wines were among the Saar's best. The Auslese and Eiswein often achieve ★★★. Best years: 1995 94 93 **91 90 89 88 85 83 79 76 75 71**.

**ZIND-HUMBRECHT** *Alsace AC, Alsace, France* Olivier Humbrecht is one of France's outstanding young winemakers, producing a brilliantly nuanced range. The family owns vines in 4 Grand Cru sites – Rangen, Goldert, Hengst and Brand – and these wines (Riesling★★, Pinot Gris★★★, Gewürztraminer★★★ and Muscat★★) are excellent, with the ALSACE VENDANGE TARDIVES and SELECTION DES GRAINS NOBLES ★★★. Even basic Sylvaners★ and Pinot Blancs★★ are fine. The 3 splendid vintages of 1990, 89 and 88 produced an array of delights. Best years: 1996 95 **93 92 90 89 88 85 83**.

**ZINFANDEL** California's very versatile red grape can be used to make anything from an insipid blush wine to a big, bruising, late-harvest-style dessert wine with in-between stops at both light and hefty dry styles with fruit always to the fore. Best producers: Cline Cellars★, FETZER★, GRGICH HILLS★, KENWOOD★, NALLE★★★, PRESTON★, QUIVIRA★★, Rafanelle★★★, RAVENSWOOD★★★, RIDGE★★★, Turley★★.

# INDEX OF MAIN PRODUCERS

**PIPER-HEIDSIECK** *Champagne AC, Champagne, France* Traditionally one of Champagne's least distinguished brands, though the owners, Remy, seem to be trying to improve things. The Piper non-vintage is gentler than it used to be, and can develop complexity. The best wines are the de luxe cuvée, Champagne Rare★, and the ultra-dry Sauvage★. Also has a California outpost, Piper-Sonoma. Best years: **1985 82**.

**PIPERS BROOK VINEYARDS** *Northern Tasmania, Australia* Keenly sought wines combining classy design, clever marketing and skilled wine-making by Andrew Pirie. Steely Riesling★★, classically reserved Chardonnay★★, serious Pinot Noir★ and tasty, barrel-fermented Sauvignon Blanc★ are the highlights from this quality pioneer in Tasmania. Cellar for 5 years or more, though they may be ready after just 2. Best years: **1994 92 91 90 88 86 84 82**.

**PLAIMONT, L'UNION DES PRODUCTEURS** *Madiran AC, Côtes de St-Mont VDQS and Vin de Pays des Côtes de Gascogne, South-West France* This grouping of 3 Gascon co-ops is the largest, most reliable and most go-ahead producer of COTES DE GASCOGNE and COTES DE ST-MONT. The whites★, full of crisp fruit, are reasonably priced and are best drunk young. The reds, especially Ch. St-Go★ and de Sabazan★, are very good too. Also good MADIRAN and PACHERENC DU VIC-BILH.

**PLANTAGENET** *Lower Great Southern, Western Australia* An apple-packing shed in chilly Mount Barker seems an unlikely place to make fine table wines, but John Wade and his successor Gavin Berry have achieved great results. Noted for peppery Shiraz★★, melony/nutty Chardonnay★★, limy Riesling★, plump Pinot★★ and elegant Cabernet Sauvignon★. Best years: **1994 93 91 90 88 86 85**.

**POL ROGER** *Champagne AC, Champagne, France* Makers of Winston Churchill's favourite Champagne and challenging for the title of Champagne's leading quality producer. The non-vintage White Foil★★ is a little richer than usual right now. Pol Roger also produces a vintage★★, a rosé★, a vintage Chardonnay★ and a vintage Réserve Spécial★★★. Its top Champagne, called Cuvée Sir Winston Churchill★★, is a deliciously refined drink. All vintage wines are ready on release but will improve with another 5 years' keeping or more. Best years: **1990 89 88 86 85 82 79**.

**POLIZIANO** *Vino Nobile di Montepulciano, Tuscany, Italy* A leading light in Montepulciano. VINO NOBILE★ is far better than average, especially the Riserva Vigna Asinone★★ and Vigneto Caggiole★★, while the Super-Tuscans Elegia★★ (Sangiovese) and Le Stanze★★ (Cabernet Sauvignon) are packed with fruit and sweet oak. VIN SANTO★★ is unctuous.

**POMEROL AC** *Bordeaux, France* Now one of the most famous and expensive of the Bordeaux ACs, Pomerol includes some of the world's most sought-after red wines. The AC's unique quality lies in its deep clay in which the Merlot grape flourishes. The result is seductively rich, almost creamy wine with wonderful mouthfilling fruit flavours. Best producers: Beauregard, Bonalgue★, BON-PASTEUR★★, Certan-de-May★★, Clinet★★, CLOS RENE★, la Conseillante★★, l'Église-Clinet★★, l'Enclos, l'EVANGILE★★, la FLEUR-PETRUS★★, GAZIN★★, LAFLEUR★★★, LATOUR-A-POMEROL★★, PETIT-VILLAGE★★, PETRUS★★★, le PIN★★★, de SALES★, TROTANOY★★, VIEUX-CH.-CERTAN★★★. Best years: (1996) (95) 94 **90 89** 88 86 85 83 82 81 79 78.

# PORT DOC

*Douro, Portugal*

The Douro region in northern Portugal, where the grapes for port are grown, is wild and beautiful. Steep hills covered in vineyard terraces plunge dramatically down to the Douro river. Grapes are one of the only crops that will grow in the inhospitable climate, which gets progressively drier the further inland you travel. But not all the Douro's grapes qualify to be made into port. A quota is established every year, and the rest are made into table wines.

Port grapes (the main variety is Touriga Nacional) are partially fermented, and then *aguardente* (grape spirit) is added – fortifying the wine, stopping the fermentation and leaving sweet, unfermented grape sugar in the finished port.

## PORT STYLES

**Vintage** Finest of the ports matured in bottle, made from grapes from the best vineyards. Vintage port is not 'declared' every year, but during the second year in cask, if the shipper thinks the standard is high enough. It is bottled after 2 years, and should be kept at least 10 years before drinking, to soften its aggressive fiery youth into something cedary and sweet. Young vintage port can be terrifyingly tannic, but softens with age.

**Single quinta** Usually made from grapes grown on a single quinta or estate, and bottled after 2 years in cask. Often released only when ready to drink.

**Aged tawny** Matured in cask for 10, 20 or 30 years before bottling and sale. Older tawnies have delicious nut and fig flavours.

**Colheita** Tawny from a single vintage, matured in cask for at least 7 years – potentially the finest of the aged tawnies.

**Late Bottled Vintage/Late Bottled** Port matured for 4–6 years in cask then usually filtered to avoid sediment forming in the bottle. Traditional unfiltered examples have much more flavour.

**Crusted** A blend of good ports from 2–3 vintages, bottled without filtration after 3–4 years in cask. 'Crusted' (or 'crusting') port forms a deposit ('crust') in the bottle and should be decanted. Now being phased out as a style.

**Vintage Character** Usually little more than expensive ruby, with no vintage character at all, though maybe a bit more age.

**Ruby** The youngest red port. Ruby port should be bursting with young, almost peppery fruit but it often isn't.

**Tawny** Cheap tawny is usually made by blending ruby with white port and is both dilute and raw.

**White** The best taste dry and nutty from wood-aging; most are coarse and alcoholic and best drunk chilled with tonic water.

See also INDIVIDUAL PRODUCERS.

BEST PRODUCERS

**Vintage** COCKBURN, CROFT, DOW, FONSECA, GRAHAM, NIEPOORT, QUINTA DO NOVAL (Nacional), SMITH WOODHOUSE, TAYLOR, WARRE.

**Single quinta** CHURCHILL (Agua Alta), DOW, (Quinta do Bomfim), FONSECA (Quinta do Panascal), GRAHAM (Malvedos), NIEPOORT (Quinta do Passadouro), QUINTA DO CRASTO, QUINTA DE LA ROSA, Symingtons (Quinta de Vesuvio), TAYLOR (Quinta de Vargellas), WARRE (Quinta da Cavadinha).

**Aged tawny/colheita** CALEM, COCKBURN, DOW, FERREIRA, FONSECA, NIEPOORT, RAMOS PINTO, SANDEMAN, TAYLOR.

**Traditional Late Bottled Vintage** CHURCHILL, FERREIRA, NIEPOORT, SMITH WOODHOUSE, WARRE.

**POMINO DOC** *Tuscany, Italy* Small zone, east of Florence in the hills above CHIANTI RUFINA, noted for its historical use of French varieties in both red (Merlot and Cabernet blended with Sangiovese) and white (where, unusually, Trebbiano plays a supporting role to Pinot Bianco and Chardonnay). FRESCOBALDI's Pomino Il Benefizio★ (a barrique-fermented Chardonnay) was a trendsetting Tuscan white. Best producers: FRESCOBALDI★, SELVAPIANA (Petrognano★).

**POMMARD AC** *Côte de Beaune, Burgundy, France* The first village south of Beaune. At their best, the wines should have full, round, beefy flavours. When good they age well, often for 10 years or more. There are no Grands Crus but les Rugiens Bas, les Épenots and les Arvelets (all Premiers Crus) occupy the best sites. Best producers: Clerget★, Comte Armand★★, de Courcel★★, Garaudet★, Gaunoux★, Joillot★, Lejeune★, de MONTILLE★★, A Mussy★, Parent★, Ch. de Pommard★, Pothier-Rieusset★, Pousse d'Or★. Best years: 1995 93 **92 90 89 88 85**.

**CH. PONTET-CANET★★** *Pauillac AC, 5ème Cru Classé, Haut-Médoc Bordeaux, France* Until the mid-1970s this was one of the most popular and widely available HAUT-MÉDOC Classed Growths, but the wine wasn't château-bottled and so you never quite knew what you'd be finding in your bottle. The result was cheap but hardly authentic claret in considerable quantities. Since 1979, when the Tesserons of LAFON-ROCHET bought Pontet-Canet, we are gradually seeing a return to form – big, chewy and oaky claret that develops a beautiful black-currant fruit. Best years: (1996) (95) 94 93 90 89 88 **86 85 83 82**.

**PONZI** *Willamette Valley AVA, Oregon, USA* A minty Pinot Noir★ in both a regular and Reserve bottling gets the attention but Ponzi was also one of the first in OREGON to make Pinot Gris. The Riesling★ is usually successful – and Ponzi also brews great beer★★.

**PORT** See pages 206–7.

**PORTA** *Rapel, Chile* Boutique winery formed in 1993, making small quantities of elegant, oak-aged Cabernet Sauvignon★★ and Chardonnay★★. French winemaker Yves Pouzet is getting the maximum out of the Cachapoal Valley fruit and a new low-yield Merlot★★ hints at even better things to come. Best years: **1996** 94.

**CH. POTENSAC★★** *Médoc AC, Cru Bourgeois, Bordeaux, France* Potensac's fabulous success is based on quality, consistency and value for money. Owned and run by Michel Delon, the genius of LEOVILLE-LAS-CASES, the wine can be drunk at 4–5 years old, but fine vintages will improve for at least 10 years, and the 1982 for up to twice that. Best years: (1996) (95) **94 93 90 89 88 86 85 83 82 81**.

**POUILLY-FUISSÉ AC** *Mâconnais, Burgundy, France* Dry white Chardon-nay from 5 villages surrounding the Solutré rock, including Pouilly and Fuissé. For several years high prices and low quality meant this was a wine to avoid, but now it is beginning to find a sensible price level and there are some committed growers producing buttery, creamy wines that can be delicious at 2 years, but will often develop beautifully for up to 10. Best producers: Corsin★★, Denogent★★, J-M Drouin★, T Drouin★, Ferret★★, Forest★★, Ch. FUISSE★★★, Guffens-Heynen★★, Lassarat★★, Léger-Plumet★, Luquet★, Valette★. Best years: 1996 **95 94 93 92 90 89**.

286

**POULLY-FUMÉ AC** *Loire Valley, France* Fumé means 'smoked' in French and a good Pouilly-Fumé has a strong, pungent smell that is often likened to gunflint. The only grape allowed is the Sauvignon Blanc and what gives these wines their extra smokiness is that many of the vineyards are planted on slopes of flinty soil called silex. This is an AC of great potential but many wines are rather ordinary given their exalted prices. Best producers: Bailly Père et Fils, Didier DAGUENEAU★★, Guyot, de Ladoucette★, Masson-Blondelet★, Pabiot★, Redde★, Saget, Seguin★, Tracy★. Best years: 1996 **95 93 90 89 88**.

**POUILLY-LOCHÉ AC** *Mâconnais, Burgundy, France* Loché is a village to the east of Fuissé which has added the name of Pouilly to its own. The wines are no better than many MACON-VILLAGES and certainly not a patch on POULLY-FUISSE, but the magic name of Pouilly commands higher prices. The wine can be labelled as POULLY-VINZELLES. Best producer: Cave des Grands Crus Blancs. Best years: **1996 95**.

**POUILLY-SUR-LOIRE AC** *Loire Valley, France* Light appley wines from the Chasselas grape from vineyards around Pouilly-sur-Loire, the town which gave its name to POUILLY-FUME. Drink as young as possible.

**POUILLY-VINZELLES AC** *Mâconnais, Burgundy, France* Like POULLY-LOCHE, the village of Vinzelles has added the name of Pouilly to its own. Best producers: Cave des Grands Crus Blancs, Valette, Ch. de Vinzelles. Best years: **1996 95**.

**CH. POUJEAUX★★** *Moulis AC, Cru Bourgeois, Haut-Médoc, Bordeaux, France* Poujeaux is one of the reasons why MOULIS AC is attracting more and more attention: the wines have a delicious chunky fruit and new-oak sweetness. Attractive at only 6–7 years old, good vintages can easily last for 20–30 years. Best years: (1996) (95) **94 93 90 89 88 86 85 83 82 81 79 78**.

**PRÄDIKAT** The grades that define quality wines in Germany and Austria. These are (in ascending order) Kabinett (not considered as Prädikat in Austria), Spätlese, Auslese, Beerenauslese, the Austrian-only category Ausbruch, and Trockenbeerenauslese. Strohwein and Eiswein are also Prädikat wines. The drawback of a system that grades wine according to the amount of sugar in the unfermented grape juice or must is that it implies that the sweeter the wine, the better it is. Some Spätleses and even a few Ausleses are now made as dry wines.

**FRANZ PRAGER** *Wachau, Niederösterreich, Austria* One of the pioneers of the region, who produced the first Riesling Trockenbeerenauslese in the WACHAU in 1993. Also top dry Rieslings from the Achleiten and Klaus vineyards★★★ and good Grüner Veltliners from the Steinriegl vineyard★. Best years: 1995 **93 92 90 86**.

**PREMIER CRU** The quality level below Grand Cru in the French appellation system. Premier Cru vineyards are usually less well-sited than the Grands Crus. But Premier Grand Cru is the very top level in Bordeaux.

**PREMIÈRES CÔTES DE BLAYE AC** *Bordeaux, France* An improving AC mainly for reds on the right bank of the Gironde. The fresh, Merlot-based reds are ready at 2–3 years but will age for more. The whites are usually sold under the COTES DE BLAYE AC. Best producers: Haut-Bertinerie, Haut-Grelot, Haut-Sociondo, Jonqueyres, Loumède, Segonzac, Sociondo. Best years: 1996 **95 94 90 89 88**.

**PREMIÈRES CÔTES DE BORDEAUX AC** *Bordeaux, France* Hilly region with views overlooking GRAVES and SAUTERNES across the Garonne. For a long time the AC was best known for its Sauternes-style sweet wines, particularly from the communes of Cadillac, LOUPIAC and STE-CROIX-DU-MONT, but in recent years the attractive, juicy reds and rosés have forged ahead. These are usually delicious at 2–3 years old but should last for 5–6 years. Dry whites are designated BORDEAUX AC. Best producers: (reds) Brethous★, Carsin★, Chelivette, Clos Ste-Anne, Grand-Mouëys★, de Haux, Jonchet, Lamothe-de-Haux, Langoiran, Melin, Puy-Bardens★, Reynon★, le Sens, Suau, Tanesse. Best years: (reds) 1996 **95 94 90 89 88 86 85**; (whites) **1996** 95 94 90.

**PRESTON VINEYARDS** *Dry Creek Valley AVA, California, USA* A Sauvignon-Sémillon blend called Cuvée de Fumé★★ is the best wine here. The Zinfandel★★ is also a winner. Drink whites young, particularly the Viognier and Marsanne, but reds, which include Barbera and Syrah, can improve for 5 years or more.

**CH. PRIEURÉ-LICHINE★** *Margaux AC, 4ème Cru Classé, Haut-Médoc, Bordeaux, France* Owned by Alexis Lichine, possibly the greatest promoter of high-quality French wines this century, until his death in 1989. The wine has a gentle, perfumed style, though it does not lack tannin and keeps well for 10–15 years. Best years: (1996) (95) 94 **90 89 88 86 85 83 82.**

**PRIMEUR** French term for a young wine, often released for sale within weeks of the harvest. BEAUJOLAIS NOUVEAU is the best-known example.

**PRIMO ESTATE** *Adelaide Plains, South Australia* Innovative Joe Grilli stuck his winery in one of Australia's hottest climates but works miracles with his own grapes and those from outlying areas. The premium label is Joseph: Grilli adapts the AMARONE method for Cabernet-Merlot★★, uncorks aged still reds to throw into the Shiraz blend for Sparkling Red★, and uses a novel pruning technique to achieve 'cooler' flavours in Double Pruned Cabernet★. He also does a juicy Botrytis Riesling★★, surprising dry white Colombard – and superb olive oil★★★.

**PRINZ ZU SALM-DALBERG** *Wallhausen, Nahe, Germany* Germany's oldest estate produces good wines, including Scheurebe and a very pale Spätburgunder. In 1989 the estate made weird and wonderful Spätburgunder Beerenauslese★★. Riesling Beerenauslese★ from the Wallhauser Pfarrgarten shows skill with that grape too. Best years: **1993 92 90 89 88.**

**PRIORATO DO** *Catalonia, Spain* This beautiful hilly, isolated district is characterized by vineyards planted on deep, pure slate, precipitous slopes. Yields of Garnacha and Cariñena are minuscule. Old-style fortified RANCIO wines used to attract little attention. Then in the 1980s a group of young winemakers revolutionized the area, bringing in state-of-the-art wine-making methods and some French grape varieties to back up native varieties. Their rare, expensive wines have taken Spain, and now other parts of the world, by storm. Drink with at least 5 years' age; the best will last much longer. Best producers: René Barbier Fill★★★ (Clos Mogador), Clos i Terrasses★★★, Costers del Siurana★★, Mas Martinet★★★, Alvaro PALACIOS★★★, Scala Dei★.

**PROSECCO DI CONEGLIANO-VALDOBBIADENE DOC** *Veneto, Italy* The all-purpose fizz of Venice, though Prosecco can also be still (tranquillo).

The Prosecco grape gives soft, scented wine made sparkling by a second fermentation in tank. Though not for aging, it can be a delicious sipping spumante or frizzante. Cartizze, from a vineyard area of that name, is the most refined. Best producers: Adami★, Bernardi★, Bisol★, Carpenè Malvolti★, Case Bianche, Le Colture, Nino Franco★, Merotto, Mionetto, Ruggeri★, Zardetto★.

**PROVENCE** *France* Provence is the home of France's oldest vineyards but, with the possible exception of BANDOL, the region is better known for its nudist beaches and arts festivals than for its wines. Things are changing, however, and Provence is caught up in the revolution which is sweeping through the vineyards of southern France. Provence has 4 small, high-quality ACs (BANDOL, BELLET, CASSIS and PALETTE), but the majority of its wines comes from the much larger areas of the COTES DE PROVENCE, COTEAUX VAROIS, Coteaux de Pierrevert, COTEAUX D'AIX-EN-PROVENCE and les BAUX-DE-PROVENCE. Provençal reds and rosés are generally better than its whites.

**PRÜFUNGSNUMMER** In Germany and Austria this means literally the 'test number' or 'official examination', which all quality wines must undergo. In Germany it is also called *Amtliche Prüfung*, and on labels is generally shortened to AP and followed by a number. In reality the test does not appear at all to be strenuous enough.

**J J PRÜM** *Bernkastel, Mosel, Germany* Estate making some of Germany's best Riesling in sites like the Sonnenuhr★★★ in WEHLEN, Himmelreich★★ in GRAACH and Lay★★ and Badstube★★ in BERNKASTEL. Best years: 1995 **93 91 90 89 88 86 85 83 79 76 75 71**.

**S A PRÜM** *Wehlen, Mosel, Germany* There are a confusing number of Prüms in the Mosel – the best known is J J PRÜM, but Raimund Prüm of S A Prüm comes a decent second. The estate's most interesting wine is Riesling from Wehlener Sonnenuhr★★, especially 1983 Auslese★★★, but it also makes good wine from sites in

BERNKASTEL★, GRAACH★ and Zeltingen★. Best years: 1995 94 **93 90 88 86 85 83**.

**PRUNOTTO** *Barolo DOCG, Piedmont, Italy* One of the great BAROLO producers, whose winemaker Giuseppe Colla pioneered the concept of single vineyards in the zone. Bought by ANTINORI in 1989. Since the sale quality has, if anything, improved, as shown by Barbera Pian Romualdo★★, Nebbiolo Occhetti★ and Barolo from the Bussia★★ and Cannubi★★ vineyards. Best years: (Barolo) (1996) (1995) (95) 94 93 90 89 **88 85**.

**PUGLIA** *Italy* This elongated southern region, which forms the heel of the Italian boot, is noted as the nation's most prolific source of blending wines. But quality potential has been shown by recent progress with native varieties: Uva di Troia in CASTEL DEL MONTE; Negroamaro and Malvasia Nera for SALICE SALENTINO, COPERTINO, SQUINZANO and other reds and rosés of the Salento peninsula; the white Greco for GRAVINA; and Verdeca and Bianco d'Alessano for LOCOROTONDO and Martina Franca. Puglia's Primitivo grape is the same as California's Zinfandel.

**PUIATTI** *Collio DOC, Friuli-Venezia Giulia, Italy* Impressive whites, made without any oak. Pinot Grigio★, Pinot Bianco★, Chardonnay★, Sauvignon★ and Tocai★ have a clearly defined varietal character, good concentration, and are good to drink young but better with age. The Archetipi★★ range is the finest selection; the Enofriulia label is for a less expensive but more consistent varietal range.

**PUISSEGUIN-ST-ÉMILION AC** *Bordeaux, France* Small ST-ÉMILION satellite AC. The wines are usually fairly solid but with an attractive chunky fruit and usually make good drinking at 3–5 years. Best producers: Bel-Air, Branda★, Durand-Laplagne, Guibeau, des Laurets, Producteurs Réunis, Soleil. Best years: (1996) 95 **94 90 89 88**.

**PULIGNY-MONTRACHET AC** *Côte de Beaune, Burgundy, France* Puligny is one of the finest white wine villages in the world and long ago added the name of its greatest Grand Cru, le MONTRACHET, to its own. There are 3 other Grands Crus which are almost as good (BÂTARD-MONTRACHET, Bienvenues-Bâtard-Montrachet and Chevalier-Montrachet), and no fewer than 11 Premiers Crus. Wines from the flatter vineyards use the simple Puligny-Montrachet AC. Good vintages really need 5 years' aging, while the Premiers Crus and Grands Crus may need 10 years and can last for 20 years or more. Only about 3% of the AC is red wine. Best producers: J-M Boillot★, CARILLON★★★, Jean Chartron★, Gérard Chavy★, Clerc★, DROUHIN, JADOT, LABOURE-ROI, Laguiche★★, LATOUR, Dom. LEFLAIVE, Olivier LEFLAIVE★, Pernot★, Ch. de Puligny-Montrachet★, RAMONET★★★, RODET, Sauzet★★★, Thénard★★, Thomas★. Best years: 1995 **92** 90 **89 88 86 85**.

**PYRENEES** *Victoria, Australia* Robust, often eucalyptus-scented reds from Shiraz and Cabernet Sauvignon are the trademark of this hilly central Victorian district, but ripe Sauvignon Blanc and Chardonnay can also impress. Champagne-method bubblies from TALTARNI and French-owned Blue Pyrenees Estate are improving. Best producers: Blue Pyrenees, Dalwhinnie★★, Redbank, TALTARNI★.

**QbA (QUALITÄTSWEIN BESTIMMTER ANBAUGEBIETE)** German for 'quality wine from designated regions'. Sugar can be added to the juice when natural ripeness has not produced enough, and permitted yields are high. Usually pretty ordinary, but some estates downgrade good wines when necessary. In Austria *Qualitätswein* is equivalent to the German QbA.

**QmP (QUALITÄTSWEIN MIT PRÄDIKAT)** German for 'quality wine with distinction'. A higher category than QBA: with controlled yields and no sugar addition. QmP covers 6 levels based on the ripeness of the grapes (in ascending order): Kabinett, Spätlese, Auslese, Beerenauslese, Eiswein and Trockenbeerenauslese.

**QUARTS DE CHAUME AC** *Grand Cru, Loire Valley, France* The Chenin grape, the most raspingly acidic of all France's great grape varieties, finds one of its most rewarding mesoclimates here in the Layon Valley. Quarts de Chaume is a 40-ha (100-acre) Cru within the larger COTEAUX DU LAYON AC and, as autumn mists begin to curl off the river Layon, noble rot attacks the grapes. The result is intense, sweet wines which can last for longer than almost any in the world. Best producers: Baumard★★, Bellerive★★, Pierre-Bise★★, Joseph Renou★★, Suronde★★. Best years: 1995 94 93 **90 89 88 85 83 82 81 78 76 70 69 66 64 59 47**.

**QUEENSLAND** *Australia*  Queensland has the smallest production of all Australia's wine-producing states. About 12 wineries perch on rocky hills up to 800m (2600ft) in the main region, the Granite Belt, near the New South Wales border. Best producers: Bald Mountain, Kominos, Robinson's, Stone Ridge.

**QUILCEDA CREEK VINTNERS** *Washington State, USA*  This tiny winery has built a cult following in Washington because of a big, rich Cabernet Sauvignon★★, the only wine made here. The wine can be a bit overpowering and closed, but it does open up after a few minutes in the glass and has good aging potential.

**QUINCY AC** *Loire Valley, France*  Intensely flavoured, dry white wine from Sauvignon Blanc vineyards west of Bourges. You can age the wine for a year or two but it will always keep its rather aggressive gooseberry flavour. Best producers: Jaumier, Mardon, Mellot, Rouze. Best years: **1996 95 93 90 89**.

**QUINTA** Portuguese for 'farm' or 'estate'.

**QUINTA DA BACALHÔA** *Arrábida IPR, Terras do Sado, Portugal*  Estate near Azeitão growing Cabernet Sauvignon and Merlot grapes. These are made into rich, oaky, long-lived wine★ at J P VINHOS. Best years: **1991 90 89 85 82**.

**QUINTA DO CÔTTO** *Douro DOC and Port DOC, Douro, Portugal*  Table wine expert in Lower DOURO. Basic red and white Quinta do Côtto are reasonable, and Grande Escolha★★ is one of Portugal's best reds, oaky and powerful when young, rich and cedary when mature. Best years: (table wines) **1992 90 87 85 82 80**.

**QUINTA DO CRASTO** *Douro DOC and Port DOC, Douro, Portugal*  Well-situated property belonging to the Roquette family. Very good LBV★★ port and even better table wines, especially the Reservas★★. Best years: (table wines) **1995 94**.

**QUINTA DO NOVAL** *Port DOC, Douro, Portugal*  Bought by a French insurance group in 1993, this immaculate property, perched above Pinhão, is the source of an extraordinary port made from ungrafted vines, Quinta do Noval Nacional★★★. This is probably the best vintage port made, but it is virtually unobtainable except at auction. The other Noval ports (including vintage Quinta do Noval★) are acceptable rather than great. Best years: (Nacional) 1994 91 87 85 **70 66 63 31**.

**QUINTA DE LA ROSA** *Douro DOC and Port DOC, Douro, Portugal*  The Bergqvist family have transformed this spectacular property into a small but serious independent producer of both port and DOURO table wines★★. The vintage port★★ is excellent. Best years: (vintage ports) 1994 92 **91**.

**QUINTARELLI** *Valpolicella DOC, Veneto, Italy*  Giuseppe Quintarelli is the great traditional winemaker of VALPOLICELLA, and his distinctive hand-written labels herald some remarkable wines. His philosophy is one of vinifying only the very best grapes and leaving nature to do the rest. His Classico Superiore★★ is left in cask for about 4 years and his famed AMARONE★★★ and RECIOTO★★ for 7 years or more before release. There is also Alzero, a spectacular Amarone-style wine from Cabernet Franc and Cabernet Sauvignon.

**QUIVIRA** *Dry Creek Valley AVA, California, USA* The best of the new wave Zinfandel★★ producers. Under former winemaker Doug Nalle (now at NALLE WINERY) the mid-1980s Zinfandels quickly established the trend for bright, fruity wine made for short-term consumption. The wines are quite delicious and will age well because of their balance, but California Zin purists are offended by their easy drinkability. A new bottling, Dry Creek Cuvée (Grenache, Mourvèdre, Syrah and Zinfandel), is fruity and delightful. Best years: (Zinfandel) **1994 92 91 90**.

**QUPÉ** *Santa Maria Valley AVA, California, USA* Owner Bob Lindquist, an iconoclastic winemaker with a bent for the unusual, makes a gorgeously tasty Reserve Syrah★★★. His Santa Maria Chardonnay★★★, also made from Santa Maria grapes, has sublime appley fruit. Lindquist, a leading exponent of Rhône-based wines, also has plantings of Viognier, Mourvèdre and Marsanne.

**RAÏMAT** *Costers del Segre DO, Catalonia, Spain* Owned by the CAVA company CODORNIU, this large, irrigated estate can make good to excellent fruity wines from Spanish and foreign grapes such as Cabernet Sauvignon★, Merlot★ and Chardonnay. Best years: (reds) **1992 91 90**.

**RAMONET** *Chassagne-Montrachet, Côte de Beaune, Burgundy, France* The Ramonets (father and sons) produce some of the most complex of all white Burgundies from 3 Grands Crus (BATARD-MONTRACHET★★★, Bienvenues-Bâtard-Montrachet★★★ and le MONTRACHET★★★) and 5 Premiers Crus (les Ruchottes★★★, les Caillerets★★, les Vergers★, Morgeot★★ and les Chaumées★★). The wines are very expensive, so if you want to spare your wallet try the ST-AUBIN★★ or the CHASSAGNE-MONTRACHET white★★ or red★. Generally the whites are in a higher league than the reds. Best years: (whites) 1995 94 93 **92 90 89 88 86 85**.

**RAMOS PINTO** *Port DOC, Douro, Portugal* Innovative port company now controlled by ROEDERER making complex, full-bodied Late Bottled Vintage★ and marvellous aged tawnies (Quinta da Ervamoira★ and Quinta do Bom Retiro★★). Best years: (vintage ports) 1994 **85 83 82**.

**RAMPOLLA** *Chianti Classico DOCG, Tuscany, Italy* Located in the 'golden shell' of Panzano, this is one of the outstanding CHIANTI CLASSICO★★ estates. Sammarco, sometimes ★★★, is mostly Cabernet with a little Sangiovese. Best years: (1996) (95) 94 93 **90 88 86**.

**RANCIO** A fortified wine deliberately exposed to the effects of oxidation, found mainly in Languedoc-Roussillon, Catalonia and southern Spain.

**RANDERSACKER** *Franken, Germany* One of the most important wine villages in FRANKEN, producing excellent medium-bodied dry Rieslings, dry Sylvaners, spicy Traminer and piercingly intense Rieslaner.

**KENT RASMUSSEN** *Carneros AVA, California, USA* Tightly structured Burgundian-style Chardonnay★★ capable of considerable bottle age and a fascinating juicy Pinot Noir★★ are made by ultra-traditional methods. Rasmussen makes occasional small batches of odd wines like Pinotage, Alicante and Dolcetto, which he releases under the Ramsay label. Best years: 1994 **92 91 90 88**.

**RASTEAU AC** *Rhône Valley, France* Rasteau is one of the original 16 villages entitled to the COTES DU RHONE-VILLAGES AC. The AC is for a fortified red or white and a Rancio version which is left in barrel for 2 or more years. Best producers: Cave des Vignerons, Roger Meffre, Rabasse-Charavin. Best years: 1995 94 **92 91 90 89**.

## ACKNOWLEDGEMENTS

**Editor** Pauline Savage; **Wine Consultant** Phillip Williamson;
**Editorial Assistant** Emma Richards; **Designer** Christopher Howson;
**Indexer** Naomi Good; **DTP** Jonathan Harley; **Production** Kâren Smith;
**Editorial Director** Claire Harcup; **Associate Art Director** Nigel O'Gorman.
Thanks are also due to Jane Hughes.

# OLDER VINTAGE CHARTS *(top wines only)*

| **FRANCE** | | | | | | | | | |
|---|---|---|---|---|---|---|---|---|---|
| Alsace | 85 | 83 | 81 | 76 | 71 | 69 | 64 | 61 | 59 |
| | 8◆ | 9◆ | 7◆ | 10◆ | 9◆ | 8◆ | 8◆ | 9◇ | 10◇ |
| Champagne (vintage) | 86 | 85 | 83 | 82 | 81 | 79 | 76 | 75 | 71 |
| | 7◆ | 9◆ | 8◇ | 10◆ | 8◇ | 7◇ | 9◇ | 9◆ | 9◇ |
| **Bordeaux** | 86 | 85 | 83 | 82 | 81 | 79 | 78 | 75 | 70 |
| Margaux | 7◆ | 8◆ | 9◇ | 8◆ | 7◆ | 7◆ | 7◆ | 6◆ | 8◆ |
| St.-Jul., Pauillac, St-Est. | 9◆ | 8◆ | 8◇ | 10◇ | 7◆ | 6◆ | 7◆ | 8◇ | 8◆ |
| Graves/Pessac-L. (R) | 6◆ | 8◆ | 9◇ | 9◆ | 7◆ | 7◆ | 8◆ | 6◆ | 8◆ |
| St-Émilion, Pomerol | 7◆ | 9◆ | 7◆ | 10◆ | 7◆ | 7◆ | 7◆ | 8◇ | 8◆ |
| **Bordeaux (cont.)** | 66 | 62 | 61 | 59 | 55 | 52 | 49 | 47 | 45 |
| Margaux (cont.) | 7◇ | 8◇ | 10◆ | 8◇ | 6◇ | 6◇ | 9◆ | 8◇ | 9◇ |
| St.-Jul. etc. (cont.) | 8◆ | 9◇ | 10◆ | 9◇ | 7◇ | 7◇ | 10◆ | 9◇ | 10◆ |
| Graves etc. (R) (cont.) | 8◇ | 8◆ | 10◆ | 9◇ | 8◆ | 7◇ | 10◇ | 9◇ | 10◇ |
| St-Émilion etc. (cont.) | 6◇ | 8◆ | 10◆ | 7◇ | 7◇ | 8◇ | 9◇ | 10◇ | 10◇ |
| Sauternes | 86 | 83 | 82 | 81 | 80 | 76 | 75 | 71 | 67 |
| | 9◇ | 9◇ | 6◆ | 5◇ | 7◆ | 8◆ | 8◆ | 8◆ | 8◇ |
| Sauternes (cont.) | 62 | 59 | 55 | 53 | 50 | 49 | 47 | 45 | 37 |
| | 8◇ | 9◇ | 8◇ | 8◇ | 8◇ | 10◇ | 10◇ | 9◇ | 10◇ |
| **Burgundy** | | | | | | | | | |
| Chablis | 87 | 86 | 85 | 83 | 81 | 78 | 75 | 71 | 69 |
| | 6◇ | 9◆ | 9◆ | 7◇ | 8◇ | 9◆ | 8◇ | 9◇ | 9◇ |
| Côte de Beaune (W) | 86 | 85 | 83 | 81 | 78 | 75 | 71 | 69 | 64 |
| | 9◆ | 9◆ | 8◇ | 9◆ | 8◆ | 7◇ | 9◆ | 8◇ | 9◇ |
| Côte de Nuits (R) | 86 | 85 | 83 | 80 | 78 | 76 | 71 | 69 | 64 |
| | 6◇ | 9◆ | 7◆ | 6◇ | 8◆ | 7◇ | 9◆ | 8◇ | 9◇ |